Spirit Possession in Buddhist Southeast Asia

NIAS–Nordic Institute of Asian Studies
NIAS Studies in Asian Topics

59 Fieldwork in Timor-Leste: Understanding Social Change through Practice • *Maj Nygaard-Christensen and Angie Bexley (eds)*
60 Debating the East Asian Peace: What it is. How it came about. Will it last? • *Elin Bjarnegård and Joakim Kreutz (eds)*
61 Khaki Capital: The Political Economy of the Military in Southeast Asia • *Paul Chambers and Napisa Waitoolkiat (eds)*
62 Warring Societies of Pre-colonial Southeast Asia: Local Cultures of Conflict Within a Regional Context • *Michael W. Charney and Kathryn Wellen (eds)*
63 Breast Cancer Meanings: Journeys Across Asia • *Cynthia Chou and Miriam Koktvedgaard Zeitzen (eds)*
64 Empire and Environment in the Making of Manchuria • *Norman Smith (ed.)*
65 Mythbusting Vietnam: Facts, Fictions, Fantasies • *Catherine Earl (ed.)*
66 Departing from Java: Javanese Labour, Migration and Diaspora • *Rosemarijn Hoefte and Peter Meel (eds)*
67 Engaging Asia: Essays on Laos and Beyond in Honour of Martin Stuart-Fox • *Desley Goldston (ed.)*
68 Performing the Arts of Indonesia: Malay Identity and Politics in the Music, Dance and Theatre of the Riau Islands • *Margaret Kartomi (ed.)*
69 Hearing Southeast Asia: Sounds of Hierarchy and Power in Context • *Nathan Porath (ed.)*
70 Asia Through Nordic Eyes: Fifty Years of Nordic Scholarship on Asia • *Geir Helgesen and Gerald Jackson (eds)*
71 Everyday Justice in Myanmar: Informal Resolutions and State Evasion in a Time of Contested Transition • *Helene Maria Kyed (ed.)*
73 East–West Reflections on Demonization: North Korea Now, China Next? • *Geir Helgesen and Rachel Harrison (eds)*
74 Spirit Possession in Buddhist Southeast Asia: Worlds Ever More Enchanted • *Bénédicte Brac de la Perrière and Peter A. Jackson (eds)*
75 Fragrant Frontier: Global Spice Entanglements from the Sino-Vietnamese Uplands • *Sarah Turner, Annuska Derks and Jean-François Rousseau (eds)*

NIAS Press is the autonomous publishing arm of NIAS – Nordic Institute of Asian Studies, a research institute located at the University of Copenhagen. NIAS is partially funded by the governments of Denmark, Finland, Iceland, Norway and Sweden via the Nordic Council of Ministers, and works to encourage and support Asian studies in the Nordic countries. In so doing, NIAS has been publishing books since 1969, with more than two hundred titles produced in the past few years.

University of Copenhagen

Nordic Council of Ministers

SPIRIT POSSESSION IN BUDDHIST SOUTHEAST ASIA

Worlds Ever More Enchanted

Edited by
Bénédicte Brac de la Perrière
and
Peter A. Jackson

Spirit Possession in Buddhist Southeast Asia
Worlds Ever More Enchanted
Edited by Bénédicte Brac de la Perrière and Peter A. Jackson

Nordic Institute of Asian Studies
NIAS Topics in Asian Studies, no. 74

First published in 2022 by NIAS Press
NIAS – Nordic Institute of Asan Studies
Øster Farimagsgade 5, 1353 Copenhagen K, Denmark
Tel: +45 3532 9503 • Fax: +45 3532 9549
E-mail: books@nias.ku.dk • Online: www.niaspress.dk

© Bénédicte Brac de la Perrière and Peter A. Jackson 2022

A CIP catalogue record for this book is available from the British Library

ISBN 978-87-7694-309-7 Hbk
ISBN 978-87-7694-310-3 Pbk
ISBN 978-87-7694-726-2 Ebk

Typeset in 11.5 pt Arno Pro by Don Wagner
Printed and bound in the United States by Maple Press, York, PA
Cover design: NIAS Press

Publication of this work was assisted by financial support from the Centre Asie du Sud-Est—Center for Southeast Asian Studies (CASE/UMR 8170 CNRS) in Paris.

Cover illustration: Bangkok shrine displaying images of a Thai spirit medium's personal pantheon of Indian and Chinese deities.

Contents

Contributors ... ix
Notes on Transliteration and Citation ... xii

Introduction – Worlds Ever More Enchanted: Reformulations of Spirit Mediumship and Divination in Mainland Southeast Asia   *Bénédicte Brac de la Perrière & Peter A. Jackson* ... 1

1. Whose Religion is the Cult of the Four Palaces? Genealogies of a Vietnamese Pantheon   *Paul Sorrentino* ... 42

2. Mya Nan Nwe's Birthday: A Forum-like Ritual Event at Botataung Pagoda (Yangon)   *Bénédicte Brac de la Perrière* ... 69

3. The Buddhist-Mediumistic Pantheon in Northeast Thailand (Isan): A Symbiotic Relationship   *Visisya Pinthongvijayakul* ... 98

4. Reorganisation and Realignment of Spirit Mediumship and Spirit Possession in Chiang Mai, Northern Thailand   *Kazuo Fukuura* ... 119

5. 'We Will Never Get Rich if We Follow Buddhism' – The Rise of Brahmanism in Cambodia from 1979 Until Today   *Paul Christensen* ... 144

6. Lottery Mania in Burma/Myanmar: Prosperity Buddhism and Promoting the Buddha's Dispensation   *Niklas Foxeus* ... 164

7. Looking for Fortune in the City: The Enchantment of Divination, Magic and Spirit Rituals in a Cambodian Urban Culture   *Poonnatree Jiaviriyaboonya* ... 188

8. Spirit Bodies, Angel Dolls and Baby Corpses: Transformations of Child Spirit Practices in Thailand   *Megan Sinnott* ... 211

9. Oneiric Encounters: Materialisations of the Invisible Present in Northern Thailand   *Irene Stengs* ... 232

10. Buriram's Possession Complex and the Growing Professionalisation of Village Mediumship in Thailand's Lower Northeast   *Benjamin Baumann* ... 253

Afterword – Rethinking Vernacular Religion Across Mainland Southeast Asia   *Erick White* ... 292

Colour illustrations ... 311
Index ... 325

Figures

Bold = colour

0.1	A spirit medium's domestic shrine in Yangon picturing part of the Burmese spirit possession pantheon	29, **311**
0.2	Bangkok shrine displaying images of a Thai spirit medium's personal pantheon of Indian and Chinese deities	29, **311**
1.1	A spirit medium embodying the Third Great Mandarin of the Palace of Water	49, **312**
1.2	Video-screenshot of a spirit medium embodying the Third Prince of the Palace of Water	50, **312**
1.3	Woodprint featuring spirits of the Four Palaces	54, **313**
1.4	The Seventh Prince represented on a calendar for 2013	55, **313**
2.1	Devotees presenting a glass of milk to Mya Nan Nwe in her green attire	72, **314**
2.2	The original tiny image of Mya Nan Nwe holding *naga* heads and with a *naga* headdress	77, **314**
2.3	Mya Nan Nwe palanquins departing on the Yangon River	87, **315**
2.4	Performing the arch in the *thaik-naga* dance in front of the palanquin, with a *shan Osi* orchestra	89, **315**
3.1	The Third Lunar Month Festival at *Ajan* Tho's monastery	101, **316**
3.2	*Ong* Tue stone Buddha image at Wat Sila-at	109, **316**
4.1	The Three Kings ritual in April 2004	128, **317**
4.2	Participants dancing at the end of the Three Kings ritual in April 2004	129, **318**
4.3	Medium A possessed by Shiva at his annual ritual in March 2018	135, **318**
4.4	Khuang Sing ritual in June 2018	139, **319**
6.1	The seven children from the treasure trove, Nagayon Pagoda	174, **319**
7.1	Cover of the Thai divination book *Patithin Nueng Roi Pi* (100-year calendar)	200, **320**
7.2	Cover of the astrological book *Tamra Phrommachat*	200, **320**
7.3	Numerological tables and chart calculated from the author's day, month and year of birth	201

8.1	*Kuman thorng* Shrine at Wat Pradu, Samut Songkhram Province	220, **321**
8.2	Sign advertising special *kuman thorng* figurines available for adoption at Wat Phai Ngoen, Bangkok	226, **321**
10.1	Villagers sharing mystic potency during a *sador khror* ritual performed by Buddhist monks	269, **322**
10.2	Graphic reconceptualisation of the Southeast Asian 'possession complex'	273
10.3	Types of medium-like ritual specialists active in Buriram's possession complex	275
10.4	Village medium presiding over a *len mae mot* ritual	279, **322**
10.5	Collective possession dance of active devotees of the Hindu goddess Mahakali	280, **323**
10.6	An older female and a younger male medium, both channelling the spirit of a 19th-century heroine	283, **323**

Contributors

Benjamin Baumann is an assistant professor at Heidelberg University's Institute of Anthropology. A graduate in Southeast Asian Studies from Humboldt-Universität zu Berlin, his ethnographic work examines rural lifeworlds, socio-cultural identities and local language games in Thailand's lower Northeast, focusing on how the ghostly structures the imagination and reproduction of social collectives and communal sentiments of belonging.

Bénédicte Brac de la Perrière is an anthropologist at CNRS (CASE) in Paris specialising on Burma, where she has conducted regular field research since the 1980s. She has authored *Les rituels de possession en Birmanie: du culte d'Etat aux cérémonies privées* (1989), and together with Guillaume Rozenberg and Alicia Turner, she co-edited *Champions of Buddhism: Weikza Cults in Contemporary Burma* (2014).

Paul Christensen is a research and teaching staff member at the Institute of Social and Cultural Anthropology at Goettingen University, Germany. He completed his dissertation project 'Spirits in Cambodia – Existence, Power and Ritual Practice' in 2019. Paul is currently working on the research project 'Sandscapes in Southeast Asia', which examines the social consequences of sand mining in Southeast Asia, particularly in the Mekong region.

Niklas Foxeus, Associate Professor (Docent), is currently a research fellow in the Department of History of Religions, ERG, Stockholm University. He received his PhD from that department with a dissertation about Burmese Buddhist esoteric congregations (2011). He has conducted research about the encounter between Buddhism and capitalism (2013–2015), Buddhist nationalism, and tensions between Buddhists and Muslims (2015–2020), and is currently studying doctrinal forms of Burmese Buddhism (2020–).

Kazuo Fukuura received his PhD from Kyoto University and is currently Associate Professor at Toin University of Yokohama. He has conducted cultural anthropological fieldwork on spirit worship, spirit mediumship and Theravada Buddhism in Northern Thailand, focusing on how religious practices and their performative power create communalities and communities in the region.

Peter A. Jackson is Emeritus Professor in Thai cultural history in the Australian National University's College of Asia and the Pacific. He has written extensively on religion, gender and sexuality in Thailand, as well as critical approaches to Asian area studies. His most recent books are *Capitalism Magic Thailand: Modernity with Enchantment* (2022) and *Deities and Divas: Queer Ritual Specialists in Myanmar, Thailand and Beyond* (2022), with Benjamin Baumann. He is currently collaborating with Narupon Duangwises on a study of capitalism, media and masculinity in Thai gay cultures.

Poonnatree (a.k.a. 'Golf') Jiaviriyaboonya is a Thai-Chinese anthropologist at Nakhon Phanom University in the Isan (Northeastern) region of Thailand. Golf completed an M.A. thesis on spiritual healing among ethnic Thai-Khmer communities in Surin and Srisaket provinces while also following her dream to develop her passionate interest in fortune-telling into an academic study. Her Ph.D. dissertation offers alternative perspectives upon the Post-Khmer Rouge revival of astrological and divinatory practices in Cambodia, previously marginalised topics in Khmer Studies.

Megan Sinnott is Associate Professor of Women's, Gender and Sexuality Studies at Georgia State University in Atlanta. She has worked on sexuality and gender identity in Thailand and is now completing a manuscript on spirit practices and capitalism in Thailand. She is the author of *Toms and Dees: Transgender Identity and Female Same-sex Relationships in Thailand* (2004, University of Hawai'i Press).

Paul Sorrentino is an associate professor of anthropology at École des Hautes Études en Sciences Sociales (Paris, France). He studies the articulations between religious, scientific and bureaucratic authority in Vietnam. His ethnography navigates between spirit possession rituals, administrative documents and scientific laboratories or associations. His first monograph, *À l'épreuve de la possession: Chronique d'une innovation rituelle dans le Vietnam contemporain* (Société d'ethnologie 2018), describes the invention of new communication practices between the living and the dead in post-war and late-socialist Vietnam.

CONTRIBUTORS

Irene Stengs is Senior Researcher at the Meertens Instituut (Amsterdam) and Professor by Special Appointment of 'Anthropology of Ritual and Popular Culture' at the Vrije Universiteit (Amsterdam). Her research in the Netherlands and Thailand focuses on popular religiosity, material culture, commemorative ritual and processes of heritage formation. She is the author of *Worshipping the Great Moderniser: King Chulalongkorn, Patron Saint of the Thai Middle Class* (2009 NUS Press, Singapore).

Visisya Pinthongvijayakul is an assistant professor in the Faculty of Humanities and Social Sciences, Chandrakasem Rajabhat University in Bangkok. His research interests cover spirit mediumship, ritual, gender and sexuality. His articles have been published in the *Journal of Southeast Asian Studies* and *American Anthropologist*.

Erick White is an Independent Scholar who has taught at Antioch University, Cornell University and the University of Michigan. His research explores the cultural politics of popular religion in Thailand, the subculture and religious careers of Bangkok professional spirit mediums and the socio-cultural dynamics underlying claims to authority and charisma in Theravada Buddhism.

Notes on Transliteration and Citation

Burmese Transliteration

The rendering of Burmese names and words has varied significantly, both historically and according to individual authors. This book follows this variation in the treatment of personal names, replicating the literature's most common spellings. Regarding place names, however, we defer to advances made by the government of the Union of Myanmar, which since 1989 has revised transcriptions to spellings that sound closer to the way place names are pronounced, such as Yangon now being the name of the city formerly known as Rangoon. Our exception is the best-known name of the country: Burma. Transcriptions of other Burmese-language words are italicised and follow the transcription system recommended by John Okell in *A Guide to the Romanization of Burmese* (1971) without diacritics, with the notable exception of *weikza* (according to Okell), which Niklas Foxeus here prefers to transliterate as *weizzā*.

Cambodian Transliteration

Many scholars have proposed transliteration or transcription systems for Khmer. None of these systems has achieved academic consensus. Khmer words are transliterated according to the system adopted by the US Library of Congress (in short: ALA-LC), which provides the exact transcription of the spelling of the words in Khmer script.[1] Thus, readers with a knowledge of Pali or Sanskrit are quickly led to the original meaning and origin of the word. The problem with this transliteration system is the large difference between spelling and contemporary pronunciation. Therefore, authors here have made a few exceptions in their transcriptions, which they make explicit in their chapters.

Thai Transliteration and Citation

There is no generally agreed system of representing the national language of Thailand in roman script, and all systems have some limitations; the 26

---

1 See www.loc.gov/catdir/cpso/romanization/khmer.pdf

NOTES ON TRANSLITERATION AND CITATION

letters of the Roman alphabet are not sufficient to represent all the consonants, vowels, diphthongs and tones of Thai. In this book we romanise Thai using a modified version of the Thai Royal Institute system. This system makes no distinction between long and short vowel forms, and tones are not represented. We differ slightly from the Royal Institute system in using 'j' and not 'ch' for the Thai 'jor jan', except in accepted spellings of royal titles, where we revert, for example, to the more widely used *chao* rather than *jao* and *racha* as opposed to *raja*. Dashes are used to separate units of compound expressions that are translated as a single term in English, such as *khwam-pen-thai* for 'Thainess'.

Some chapters in this book refer to regional forms of religious and ritual expression that are expressed in Northeastern (Isan or Lao) and Northern (Lan Na) varieties of Tai. These regional forms are marked in parentheses, such as (NT: *yok khu*) for Northern Thai terms and (NE: *khuba*) for Northeastern terms. Where no regional variety is denoted, a term is represented in its form in Central Thai, such as (*yok khru*).

We follow the Thai norm of referring to Thai authors by given names, not surnames, and all citations by Thai authors are alphabetised in the bibliographies by given names. We also follow authors' preferred spelling of their own names in English when known, rather than romanising names in keeping with the system outlined above.

Thai has a large number of honorific titles that are used before the names of respected persons and revered religious personalities, deities and spirits. A person or deity may be honoured with more than one honorific by followers and devotees. To distinguish names from titles, the latter are italicised in this book, such as *Mae* Wan (Mother Wan), *Chao* Dara Rasami (Princess Dara Rasami), *Ajan* Tho (Venerable Tho).

INTRODUCTION

Worlds Ever More Enchanted
Reformulations of Spirit Mediumship and
Divination in Mainland Southeast Asia [1]

Bénédicte Brac de la Perrière and Peter A. Jackson

The failure of Weberian sociology of religion to predict the global rise of diverse and thriving new forms of religious expression has been a major theme in religious studies and the anthropology of religion in recent decades. A notable account of religious 'disenchantment' that builds on Weber's framing of the notion[2] is presented by Marcel Gauchet in *The Disenchantment of the World: A Political History of Religion* (1997). Many critiques of 20th-century sociology of religion target the failure of the secularisation thesis to explain the rise of reformist doctrine-focused and fundamentalist movements within world religions, due to the teleological nature of this thesis.[3] Significantly less attention has been paid to the ways in which diverse new spirit cults challenge Weberian accounts of the soit-disant 'disenchantment' of the world in the face of modern processes of 'rationalisation'.[4] Such cults have effloresced all across mainland Southeast Asia.

This book presents novel perspectives on the growing prominence of spirit mediumship and divination across the predominantly Buddhist societies of mainland Southeast Asia, a regional phenomenon that is one of the more

---

1 The subtitle for this book is borrowed from Bénédicte Brac de la Perrière's 2007 review essay, 'Un Monde Plus Que Jamais Enchanté?'
2 According to Jean Martin Ouédraogo (2010: 241), Max Weber first used the notion of 'disenchantment' in his writing in 1913.
3 Talal Asad and José Casanova, two main critics of the secularisation thesis, presented their works in 2003 and 1994, respectively.
4 Important sources for this introduction are Richard Jenkins' 2000 appraisal of Weber's account of disenchantment and Michael Saler's 2006 historiographic review of modernity and enchantment. Studies that draw on Southeast Asian material to critique Weberian sociology's account of secularisation and disenchantment include: Keyes, Kendall & Hardacre 1994; Pattana 2008; Endres & Lauser 2011; Bubandt & van Beck 2012; and van der Veer 2014.

noteworthy and least anticipated dimensions of religious change, both in the region and internationally. The early 21st century in Burma, Cambodia, Thailand and Vietnam has been marked by an efflorescence of the presence, imagination and agency of diverse forms of spirits among many social strata, including the urban poor, rising middle classes, and economic and political elites. It is especially noteworthy that processes of enchantment are becoming more visible across political divides: in the aborted democracy of military-dominated Burma; in post-Khmer Rouge Cambodia; in military-monarchist-democratic Thailand; and even in ostensibly socialist Vietnam. The parallel rise of ritual practices and institutions linked to the efflorescence of spirit cults across the Southeast Asian mainland raises analytical and theoretical issues that necessitate comparative perspectives. What unites these societies is not their political systems but rather a relaxing of 20th-century political interventions in the religious field, a common commitment to a market economy, growing penetration by new digital communications technologies, and promotion of international policies of 'intangible cultural heritage' as increasingly salient elements of understandings of ethnic, religious and national identity.

In addition to the broad context of globalisation and the marketisation of social life detailed below, these societies also share a deeply embedded model for dealing with the spiritual through rituals of spirit possession in polities that historically have been framed by Indianised ideologies and technologies of power. This commonality may contribute to an explanation of the efflorescence of new devotional figures. While previous scholarship on 'spirited modernities' (Endres & Lauser 2011: 5) has dealt with spirit beliefs and practices re-entering the public field, we suggest that the way these processes are ingrained in a distinctive regional genealogy of spirit possession has in general been under-explored for reasons that are linked to orientalist-derived regimes of knowledge.

Several recent studies have addressed issues of enchantment, magic and modernity in Southeast Asia. Rosalind Morris (2000), Pattana Kitiarsa (2012) and Andrew Johnson (2014) have described the situation in Thailand; Karen Fjelstad and Nguyen Thi Hien (2006), Kirsten Endres (2011) and Philip Taylor (2004) have detailed new spirit cults in Vietnam; and Bénédicte Brac de la Perrière et al. (2014) have documented Buddhist esoterism in Burma. Pattana Kitiarsa (2008), Kirsten Endres and Andrea Lauser (2011) and Volker Gottowik (2014) have also edited comparative studies of related developments throughout the Southeast Asian region.

Gottowik (2014: 22) observes that the aim of his edited collection, *Dynamics of Religion in Southeast Asia: Magic and Modernity*, is to 'undermine the dichotomy by which magic, ritual and religion – that is, the whole sphere of the sacred – is pitted against modernity and to bring religion and modernity into an instructive relationship'. Drawing primarily on research from Indonesia, Gottowik contends that world religions 'are spreading [in Southeast Asia] at the expense of local religious belief systems, which are confronted by demands that they undergo similar processes of rationalization in order to meet the requirements of a modern religion in a modern nation-state' (*ibid.*: 26). This is *not* happening in the predominantly Buddhist societies of mainland Southeast Asia, where, in radical contrast, 'local religious belief systems' are expanding as they modernise *without being rationalised*.

Understanding this phenomenon requires a double intellectual task: firstly, to place spirit possession rituals at the centre of accounts of religious change; and secondly, to understand how modernity produces enchantment. We seek to understand how processes that modernisation theory views as driving forces of rationalisation are instead producing new modalities of enchantment by reinforcing ritual-oriented forms of religiosity across all of mainland Southeast Asia. We place spirit possession at the very centre of our analyses because, as our contributors reveal, the interpenetration of spirit possession rituals with dominant religious traditions is a key aspect of this region-wide efflorescence of new enchantments.

International and multidisciplinary perspectives

Our volume investigates how modernity is inciting an efflorescence of enchantment in which spirit possession rituals are taking increasingly prominent places in the religious fields of Burma, Thailand, Cambodia and Vietnam. This collection does not include a study from Laos, where the emergence of new urban spirit cults awaits further detailed exploration. The studies here reflect the significant recent expansion in international research on spirit possession practices and divination rituals across much of mainland Southeast Asia, bringing together the perspectives of scholars based at universities in France, Denmark, the Netherlands, Germany, Thailand, Japan and Australia. We include contributions from internationally known leaders in studies of religion in Burma, Thailand and Vietnam, as well as from early career researchers from Europe and Southeast Asia, reflecting the rapid development of this field of research and the emergence of an epistemic community that draws on comparative methods which transcend the limitations of single-country studies. The assembled chapters reflect the emergence of an international cross-disciplinary network of scholars of mainland Southeast Asia who are interested in new forms of ritual practice and belief.

This book brings together studies that show the diverse ways that cults of new spiritual agencies – which have taken form historically as well as within the modern contexts of urbanisation, capitalism and new media – both relate to and are differentiated from Buddhism. In the context of diverse processes of rapid social change, spirit cults have transformed into fully developed spirit possession cultures and communities. In societies where these possession cultures and communities were already extant (such as Vietnam and Burma), they have seen further development and differentiation. This has taken place through multiple, mutually reinforcing processes of ritual specialisation, professionalisation, heritagisation, and delocalisation or relocation. Together, all these processes contribute to instituting spirit possession practice vis-à-vis mainstream discourses of religion and hegemonic power, representing major sites of negotiating and contesting established authority.

The studies collected here demonstrate the productive relations among several dimensions of Southeast Asia's globalising neoliberal modernity – most notably, the marketisation of social life – and new spirit cults. In contemporary communities, the presence and agency of spirits still depends on their materialisation and recognition through specific representational regimes. Early 21st-century urban capitalist cultures of mass-produced commodities and digital communications provide diverse new materialisations and forms of expression that add to the variety of spiritual agencies and traditions that mediate relations between spirits and humans.

The geographically focused concentration of our collection on Buddhist societies of mainland Southeast Asia, including Vietnam, also highlights the continuing importance of spatiality in defining the religious and cultural forms that have emerged within neoliberal globalisation, even as older village locality-based forms of ritual have been increasingly replaced by national-level and urban spirit cults. The studies assembled here thus confirm the critical analyses of New Area Studies (Jackson 2003, 2019; Houben 2013) that globalisation has not erased spatiality but rather has restructured the ways in which locatedness manifests in the contemporary period.

Queer ritual specialists and gender transformations in Southeast Asian spirit cults

A topic not dealt with in this book is the intersection between queer cultures and the proliferation of professional spirit mediumship in mainland Southeast Asia, yet several chapters here allude to dramatic changes in the gendering of spirit mediums that have taken place in parallel with the efflorescence and professionalisation of possession rituals. Women traditionally were at the centre of many spirit possession traditions across Burma, Thailand and Vietnam, but their roles are now increasingly being performed by gay men and trans women. Several scholars, including four contributors to this volume – Peter Jackson, Benjamin Baumann, Bénédicte Brac de la Perrière and Visisya Pinthongvijayakul – trace the rise of queer and transgender professional spirit mediums in a companion NIAS Press volume, *Deities and Divas: Queer Ritual Specialists in Myanmar, Thailand and Beyond* (Jackson & Baumann 2022). The companion volume details how spirit mediumship rituals are domains of diverse feminine and masculine gendering that constitute increasingly queer-friendly dimensions of the religious field across mainland Southeast Asia. That book also explores commonalities in the aesthetic and performative dimensions of ritual in queer and religious cultures in Southeast Asia and the West. A central argument is that contemporary queer and spirit possession cultures emerge within a shared formative matrix of capitalism and new media technologies. As a result, commonalities are found where they might not have been expected. For example, both the deities worshipped in Southeast Asian spirit cults and the female singer and actor divas adored by gay men and transgender people are expressions of popular cultures, and both place performance and aesthetics at the centre of technologies of ecstasy and rituals of self-transformation. Through analyses that transcend the modernist opposition of religion against secularity, the studies in *Deities and Divas* draw on transnational cultural and queer studies to detail how queer ritual specialists mediate the interlocking domains of ritual, aesthetics, capitalism and media across mainland Southeast Asia and beyond.

Enchantment, 'magic' and modernity

The claim that the modern world is increasingly disenchanted is a central tenet of Weberian sociology of religion. As Michael Saler observes, by the disenchantment of the world, Max Weber meant the loss of the overarching meanings, animistic connections, magical expectations, and spiritual explanations that had characterised the traditional world, as results of ongoing "modern" processes of rationalisation, secularisation, and bureaucratisation. (Saler 2006: 695)

Richard Jenkins (2000: 12) describes the Weberian notion of disenchantment as

> the historical process by which the natural world and all areas of human experience become experienced and understood as less mysterious; defined, at least in principle, as knowable, predictable and manipulable by humans; conquered and incorporated into the interpretative schema of science and rational government.[5]

In contrast, the forms of modern enchantment produced in the context of contemporary globalisation detailed in the following chapters challenge the view that modernity is necessarily a condition based on the complete rationalisation of social life. In this setting, Jenkins (*ibid.*: 20) provides the following definition of enchantment in the contemporary period:

> Enchantment conjures up, and is rooted in, understandings and experiences of the world in which there is more to life than the material, the visible or the explainable; in which the philosophies and principles of Reason or rationality cannot by definition dream of the totality of life; in which the quotidian norms and routines of linear time and space are only part of the story; and in which the collective sum of sociability and belonging is elusively greater than its individual parts.

Erick White (2014: 433) argues that the expansion of the market and urbanisation in Thailand have fostered novel religious movements based on new forms of charismatic authority, and he offers what can be regarded as a practical definition of the production of modern enchantment when he states that these new movements reflect 'an efflorescence of diverse and

---

[5] A few pages later (p. 19) Jenkins makes the important point that secularisation and disenchantment are not the same, although they are often confused and conflated. The categorical difference between secularisation and disenchantment is highlighted by the fact that the two poles of the modern, ostensibly secularised world, namely, organised religion and non-religious secularism, are equally critical of 'magical' forms of enchantment. While secularist critics represent magical ritual as a superstitious residue of pre-modernity that holds society back from attaining rational scientific modernity, many modern religious doctrinalists see it as a form of heresy that needs to be expunged in order to attain true, pure religious insight.

innovative models of religious personhood, devotional expression, esoteric mastery, and sacralising technique'.

While the term 'magic' is widely used in both academic studies and popular accounts of ritual across the region, particularly in the case of Thailand, it has proved to be a problematic analytical category. Construed as being in opposition to science, religion and modernity, 'magic' typically refers to a wide variety of practices whose only commonality is a shared focus on acting upon concrete situations in the world rather than aiming for salvation. Because practices labelled as 'magical' or 'apotropaïc', in Spiro's words, are deemed by Buddhists as worldly activities, they can be said to be devalued within Buddhism (Spiro 1970: 159). Practices ranging from the recitation of protective *paritta* chants by Buddhist monks to attacks involving witchcraft have at times been equally decried as 'magical' according to more doctrinal reformist Buddhist points of view. The differentiation of ritual vis-à-vis 'religious' practice has also been at stake in the delineation of the category of 'magic'. As the devalued other of evolving forms of 'religion', 'magic' may have lost its analytic ability to describe the striking emergence of cults of new spiritual agencies in the contemporary Buddhist societies of Southeast Asia. In an effort to avoid problems associated with the term 'magic' as an ethnocentric grand category defined negatively against science and religion, White has coined the phrase 'ritual arts of efficacy' to describe the forms of ritual associated with the types of spirit cults detailed in this book. He argues that these arts display 'creativity, innovation and adaptability' in Asian Buddhist societies (White 2016: 17) and 'have experienced a frequently underappreciated transformation in their social organisation, transmission and consumption' (*ibid.*: 16). Despite its problematic history, it is nonetheless difficult to completely avoid using the term 'magic', if only because of its continued widespread use in several fields of anthropology and religious studies, and we denote the term's provisional and contested character by placing 'magic' in inverted commas.

The studies in this collection confirm Bruce Kapferer's (2002: 16) observation that 'magical' practices are 'thoroughly modern'. Kapferer emphasises that

> The crucial argument regarding modern magical practices concerns their disjunction from pasts (histories and cosmologies prior to modern periods ... before the imperial expansions of the West) and the radical

reconfiguration of ideas and practices of the past in terms of the circumstances of the present.

This position presents a major corrective to accounts that see 'magical' practices as survivals of tradition and overlook their current reformulation in the economic, political and social contexts of their use (*ibid.*: 19). As Kapferer observes, contemporary forms of 'magic' in Asia are significant because they reveal 'the fabulations and transmutations of capital in globalizing circumstances, and the magical character of nationalist discourses of the modern and postcolonial state' (*ibid.*: 2).

In seeking to understand the worldwide popularity of ghost and horror movies, film studies scholars have drawn on psychoanalytic models of the return of a repressed premodernity. These scholars argue that the cultures of modernity are haunted by supernatural phenomena that had been excluded during the formation of the modern as an ostensibly enlightened, rational and scientific stage of social life. However, White (2014: 194) argues that it is mistaken to interpret the efflorescence of popular Buddhism as primarily the resurgence of a previously repressed syncretic heritage or polytropic sensibility.[6] More than simply imagining 'magic' as never having been expelled by Weberian processes of rationalisation and disenchantment, we need to turn the relation of modernity and disenchantment on its head. We need to view the sociological forces of modernity as not merely providing spaces for the survival of residues of 'magic' but also as actively producing enchantment anew. *'Magic' is modern*. In the phenomena detailed in the following chapters, we do not see the return of a repressed pre-modernity. Rather, we find formulations of enchanted ritual that are completely novel, despite taking place within regional religiosity structures that are firmly embedded within the regional Southeast Asian possession complex.

The Southeast Asian 'spirit possession complex'

Reconsidering the religious field from the perspective of spirit possession

We regard the new forms of spirit mediumship and divination in mainland Southeast Asia as more than a resurgence; they also constitute an efflorescence and further transformation of existing forms of possession and ritual. 'Resurgence' connotes a return from a period of decline. However,

---

6   For an account of polytropy in Asian religious cultures, see Carrithers 2000.

spirit cults have long been important dimensions of ritual life, and indeed we contend that a 'spirit possession complex' (so dubbed by Kaj Århem [2016a] and adopted by Benjamin Baumann in his chapter here) lies at the historical foundations of the modern religious fields of all mainland societies. Rather than merely 'returning' in recent decades, spirit cults have migrated, coalesced and acquired new visibility in more developed forms, compared to those that emerged in the centralising polities of 18th-century Vietnam and Burma, and 19th-century Thailand.

Spirit possession refers to a wide range of phenomena that cross analytical and religious boundaries. It can refer to pathogenic forms of spirit attack that are believed to cause illness and affliction and for which the typical response is rituals of exorcism. It can also denote voluntary possession that is viewed positively or adorcistically, in which a possessing spirit is domesticated and the visited person becomes a medium. This form of voluntary possession or mediumship has long been present in various settings across the region, as attested by Georges Condominas' regional synthesis (1976). It is also the foundation on which the new spirit cults dealt with in this book have developed.

A range of phenomena also exists on the edges of both spirit attack and voluntary adorcistic possession. In Thailand, Buddhist monks believed to have the power to sacralise potent objects such as amulets claim relations to what Pattana (2012) terms an empowering 'superagency'. In her chapter here, Irene Stengs uses the term 'oneiric space' to refer to the full spectrum of dreams and visions, as well as classical forms of possession, that exist in the dynamically expanding Southeast Asian possession complex. Certainly, Eric Davis's (2016) remark that we need more accurate characterisations of the various ways to represent and deal with the spiritual in Mainland Southeast Asia remains valid. In a paper rethinking spirit possession in Theravada Buddhism, White argues that the variety of modalities of possession documented in ethnographic literature about Thailand demonstrates the existence of a plural and contested field of spirit possession (2017: 195).

The independent genealogy of a Southeast Asian spirit possession complex

Much previous research on religion in mainland Southeast Asia focused on institutional Buddhist practice and doctrine, and tended to overlook the invocation of spirits and other ostensibly 'unorthodox' forms of Buddhist practice. This tendency in Southeast Asian religious studies may be seen as an enduring reflection of the relegation and dismissal of 'superstition' and 'magic', and even 'ritual', as disparaged others in a process that parallels the Enlightenment elevation of ostensibly 'true Christian belief'. This observation becomes all the more ironic when we note that these 'true' (albeit contested) Christian beliefs came to inform the intellectual settings in the Western universities where the academic study of religion began (Tambiah 1990). Indeed, one reason for the relative lack of studies of spirit cults in Southeast Asia is that they have often been dismissed by religious studies scholars as not constituting real 'religion' (or 'true' Buddhism), as well as by local elites influenced by orientalist forms of knowledge, and the bias against subjecting ritual practices of spirit possession and divination to rigorous analysis remains entrenched in the literature on Southeast Asia.

Also at stake theoretically in studying the further efflorescence of ritual in modern Southeast Asia is the delineation of a genealogy of 'spirit possession' as evolving within the region's cosmologies, independently of possession cults in other parts of the world. The distinctive origins, form and evolution of spirit possession in mainland Southeast Asia contrasts with other, established analyses – such as the 'Atlantic genealogy' of Afro-Caribbean spirit cults detailed by Paul Johnson (2014) – that have shaped accounts of the category of spirit possession. Our collection responds to the double omission of Southeast Asian spirit cults within both religious studies and the international literature on possession around the world. Firstly, the chapters in this book demonstrate that possession and divination rituals are central features of the total religious fields of the Theravada Buddhist communities in Burma, Thailand and Cambodia and the Mahayana Buddhist and other religious communities in Vietnam. Furthermore, we locate spirit possession in mainland Southeast Asia in the broader, comparative field of studies of spirit possession internationally.

A significant contribution to the international field of spirit possession studies has been Johnson's (2014) genealogical account of 'spirit possession' as a founding anthropological category. He argues that the origin of the anthropological category of 'spirit possession' lies in the intersection of post-Reformation Christianity and European contact with the spirit cults of West Africa in the context of the slave trade to the Americas. In an attempt to attend to the material economy of spirit possession, Johnson argues that European ideas of slaves as belongings and bodies without will provide the matrix from which the particular form of a spirit's presence in the human world encountered in possession has been identified in the European gaze. However, similar to most literature on this subject, Johnson and the authors in his 2014 edited collection deal only with the African and Afro-Atlantic genealogy of spirit possession. By contrast, early studies on shamanism, which is grounded on a different phenomenology of the spiritual,[7] were mainly concerned with Siberian and Amerindian worlds. This leads one to think that the major analytical categories of spiritual manifestations, namely, spirit possession and shamanism, which together came to displace the older notion of 'animism', were determined according to their respective regional specificities.

Johnson presents a distinctly European- and American-centred perspective of spirit possession that tends to overlook and obscure the distinctive genealogies of this phenomenon in other world regions, notably Southeast Asia. Nonetheless, further developments of spirit possession studies, such as those in a collection edited by J. Brent Crosson (2019: 546), have made use of the 'curious twin production of possession' revealed by Johnson and have started to transcend the 'typical geopolitical provinces of spirit possession' to investigate modern problems of agency involved in this phenomenon.

While striking features of spirit possession, together with disseminated forms of shamanism, are found in a variety of configurations all over mainland Southeast Asia, one rarely comes across any allusions to this in the general comparative international literature on the topic. Southeast Asia is not alone in this regard. In his 'Prologue' to a volume dedicated to spirit possession in South Asia, Gilles Tarabout (1999) makes a similar observation about the marginalisation of the Indian sub-continent in the thematic anthropological literature. Reasons for this lack of interest in large geographical expanses of the international prevalence of spirit possession rituals in academic studies may well originate in the particularly influential genealogy of the anthropological concept among Euro-Amerocentric scholars. This conceptual and analytical bias may have been reinforced in the case of Southeast Asia by the way in which the production of colonial knowledge on the region – in line with binary oppositions between centre and periphery, lowland and upland, state and village societies – became fragmented between orientalist and anthropological approaches, as well as between diverse academic traditions. Commonalities across the region were often overlooked during the colonial

---

7   For the classical distinction between shamanism and spirit possession, see Luc de Heusch 1971. While debated, this distinction still accounts usefully for major differences between these two forms of spirit manifestation in human worlds.

era because research on the French, English and Dutch colonies in Southeast Asia was fragmented, both linguistically and organisationally, between the different academies of the several colonial powers. To add to this state of affairs, the Cold War period caused dramatic political ruptures in the region and, with the notable exception of Thailand, the closure of a large part of it to field research, leading to around a quarter of a century of disruption in the collection of data. As a result, until very recently, religious studies scholars and anthropologists alike have often been unaware of the pervasiveness of spirit possession across the entire mainland region, not to mention its resilience and dramatic reformulation in the process of modern globalisation. Indeed, even today some sections of the international academic community remain largely oblivious to the pervasive and expanding influence of spirit cults across all the countries of the mainland.

However, since the resumption of research in the region with the opening of Burma, Cambodia and Vietnam to scholarly inquiry after a several-decade hiatus, a number of studies have contributed to the growing body of critiques of religious studies' undue emphasis on Buddhism in this religiously rich landscape. These studies also challenge the Weberian modernisation prediction that capitalism's advance beyond the West would be predicated upon a progressive rationalisation of Asian societies.[8] Our collection of analyses of new forms of ritual in mainland Southeast Asia takes the previous studies of spirit possession cults in the region forward in several ways.

In the past, inquiry on these topics tended to be limited by an emphasis on a single country. Furthermore, previous regionally comparative collections were painted with a broad brush that included, for example, explorations of the predominantly Muslim and Christian societies of island Southeast Asia together with largely Buddhist mainland Southeast Asia. This level of comparison has sometimes undervalued the distinctive processes at work on the mainland. Studies have also often postulated a divide between Buddhism and spirit cults, a separation that Brac de la Perrière has already highlighted (2007) and which Visisya Pinthongvijayakul shows in his chapter here to be highly problematic.

The Southeast Asian possession complex is dynamically related to changing external factors. As new social, economic and political conditions

---

8 Of note in this regard are Morris 2000; Taylor 2004; Fjelstad & Hien 2006; Pattana 2008 and 2012; Endres 2011; Endres & Lauser 2011; Johnson 2014; Brac de la Perrière *et al.* 2014; and Gottowik 2014.

emerge, they interplay with the possession complex. However, in contrast to Buddhism, whose doctrinal and institutional histories are well-documented and extensively studied, the histories of spirit rituals are poorly researched. This is due to an academic orientation that defined spirit cults as lying outside the formal category of 'religion', and hence outside from the field of religious studies, as well as to a paucity of historical sources. Regrettably, we lack archival resources that would enable us to write deep histories of the Southeast Asian possession complex, to map long-term changes in the relations of the elements of the complex or detail transformations in the patterns of their hierarchical relations.[9] Nonetheless, rapid changes in societies across the region appear to have led to the possession complex becoming even more variegated and multiform as the number of deities and spirits has grown. Observations over recent decades from throughout mainland Southeast Asia consistently report an expansion of the number of spirit mediums (see, for example, Morris 2000a) and significant changes in the pantheons and rituals of possession (see particularly Paul Sorrentino's chapter here). However, we also cannot overlook the fact that past research emphasis on 'religion', nearly all of which excluded so-called 'superstitious' ritual, might have led to an underreporting of the actual extent of spirit cults across the region in earlier periods. That is, recent critical perspectives that challenge older and more restrictive understandings of 'religion' might be opening the academic gaze to rituals that were ignored or overlooked in the past.

Comparative regional perspectives on the Southeast Asian spirit possession complex

Georges Condominas (1976) was the first to draw a regional synthesis of the Southeast Asian spirit possession complex; he tested the distinction between shamanism and spirit possession that had then recently been reformulated by Luc de Heusch (1971). Condominas proposed a general characterisation of spirit possession in the region as being based on a conception of the person as formed by a plurality of souls, and a variety of spirits that are manifested successively in a hierarchical order in public possession rituals. He also proposed that institutional spirit possession was

---

9 Drawing on literary sources, an interesting example of an historical study of a spirit possession cult that overcomes the general lack of archival sources on this topic is Dror 2007, on the Vietnamese cult of Lieu Hanh.

present at all levels of social organisation in the region – including lineages, villages and polities – to serve diverse functions, from the therapeutic to promoting general prosperity, as well as maintaining the territorial integrity of political orders. Condominas further argued that spirit possession is most often embedded in complex religious configurations, often dominated by Buddhism. The Southeast Asian possession complex is an open system that is nonetheless ordered in hierarchical terms. While the number and characteristics of the spirits from different Buddhist, Brahmanical, Chinese and ethnic historical ritual systems may increase and change over time, they are nonetheless ordered within a systematic hierarchy that is open to change.

Research on forms of spiritual presence in most mainland Southeast Asian societies was only resumed after the end of the Cold War in the 1990s. A reopening to field research accompanied the opening of regional economies to the global market economy and the relative liberalisation of some authoritarian regimes. While the previous period had been one of disruption of local or supra-local ritual practices in many parts of the region, notably in Cambodia under the repressive Khmer Rouge regime and in Vietnam under the Communist government's edicts against 'superstition', the new context of development and globalisation saw an amazing efflorescence of the spiritual in contemporary and urban contexts, which is dramatically reflected in the diverse studies assembled here.

As noted, this efflorescence refuted the then-dominant narrative of 'world disenchantment' and fostered a new wave of anthropological and cultural studies publications on new prosperity cults in the region. This work followed the important analyses of Jean and John Comaroff (1999, 2000) and further built on Shmuel Eisenstadt's (2000) concept of 'multiple modernities'.[10] Also, a number of edited collections that did not focus on spirit possession *per se* nonetheless reported on the vitality of the spiritual in post-Cold War Southeast Asian modernity.[11] On the whole, these studies show that rather than erasing religion, modernity has changed the nature of religious expression in the region, in some cases towards more systematisa-

---

10 See for instance Pattana Kitiarsa's 2011 edited collection *Religious Commodifications in Asia*, which applies the idea of prosperity cults to Southeast Asia as proposed by Jackson 1999.

11 Some of the main publications in this regard are Keyes, Kendall & Hardacre 1994, Endres & Lauser 2011 and Gottowik 2014. Bubandt & van Beek 2012 and Van der Veer 2014, in their own ways, examine the intricate relations of spiritualism and nationalism in Asia as a result of the encounter with Western modernity. Also significant in this regard is White's 'Contemporary Buddhism and Magic' in the 2016 *Oxford Handbook of Contemporary Buddhism*.

tion of doctrines and organisation. However, these studies have also shown an apparent increase in 'magical' cults, or at the very least a growth in the spirit possession cults that are now embedded within modern social formations.

Besides the fact that many of the new prosperity cults in Southeast Asia were based, either directly or indirectly, on existing forms of spirit possession, they have nonetheless experienced remarkable revivals (Vietnam and Cambodia), reframing (Thailand) and expansion (Burma). New ethnographies of spirit possession have appeared during this period, although very few efforts of synthesis at the regional level have been attempted. Lauren Kendall's characterisation of East Asian spirit mediumship in Karen Fjelstad and Nguyen Thi Hien's *Possessed by the Spirits* (2006) deserves to be mentioned in this regard. As a specialist of Korean shamanism, Kendall draws a profile of Southeast Asian spirit mediumship as being based on asymmetrical relationships between humans and powerful entities.

Recent developments of anthropological theory, particularly what has become known as the 'ontological turn', have introduced still another paradigm into the conversation on the spiritual presence in Southeast Asian worlds. Central in this regard is Kaj Århem and Guido Sprenger's 2016 edited collection, *Animism in Southeast Asia*. In his introductory essay to that volume, Århem draws on Philippe Descola's rehabilitation of the old concept of 'animism' to qualify non-modern Amazonian ontologies in which all beings are credited with subjectivity and agency. He transposes this notion to Southeast Asia with the aim of reframing 'regional discussion on indigenous cosmology and religion' (Århem 2016: 4). In Descola's (2005) work, Amazonian animism mainly concerns horizontal and egalitarian relations between humans and forest animals. In contrast, Southeast Asian cosmologies primarily concern relations between humans and spirits (invisible others) and, as long ago pointed out by Condominas, are vertical and hierarchical.

Some contributors to Århem and Sprenger's volume adopt the notion of 'hierarchical animism' to accommodate this situation more readily. However, the use of the label 'animism' in its 'new' framing within Descola's four main ontologies – which he labels as animism, totemism, analogism and naturalism – would appear to require further debate and elaboration if it is to be analytically productive in the mainland Southeast Asian context. This is especially the case when dealing with larger societies rather than the small-scale indigenous groups on which Århem, Sprenger and their contributors focus. In particular, with reference to Descola's (2005) framing of four ontologies, the configuration of dividual personhood and hierarchical relationality that is constitutive of the Southeast Asian spirit possession complex would appear to be closer to analogism than to animism. Benjamin Baumann's chapter here on the regional Southeast Asian spirit possession complex contributes to this further elaboration of 'hierarchical animism', and following his interpretation of 'new animism' he proposes to encompass analogism, totemism and animism *per se* within a broader category of 'animism'.

Why is spirit possession efflorescing in Buddhist Southeast Asia?

This book advances beyond critiques of the 'secularisation' and 'disenchantment' theses to explore the processes of globalising neoliberal modernity that are actively producing enchanted social, cultural and political worldviews. The studies collected here demonstrate that the cults in question are religious forms that emerged out of the productivity of ritual in the inherently modern conditions of capitalism, visual and digital media, cultural heritage industries, and the politics of national and ethnic identity. It is noteworthy that scholars of spirit cults – such as Stanley Tambiah (1985, 1990), Jean Comaroff (1994) and Rosalind Morris (2000) – have been at the forefront of theorising the processes by which modern technologies and forms of life produce new forms of ritual practice and enchanted imaginaries. In accounting for the efflorescence of spirit cults and divination in the context of modern religious change in Asia, scholars have focused variously on the roles of state power, capitalism, media and the power of ritual. However, these accounts of processes of modern enchantment do not yet speak to one another. To date, we have a series of partial perspectives that focus on one or other of the multiple processes at work. These analyses of the multiple impacts of changing forms of modernising state power, the market, new media and ritual need to be brought together if we are to understand the full panoply of processes underpinning the diversification of religious expression across Southeast Asia today.

From state-sponsored to market-based: The retreat of the state and the rise of the market in Southeast Asian religious fields

The new forms of spirit possession and divination across the region could not have become so prominent without a significant shift in the relations between state and religion. Robert Weller regards one of the most important trends related to post-Cold-War market-oriented modernity almost everywhere in Asia as being 'the decline of state-supported religious monopolies', arguing that we 'see the most pluralisation where institutional control over religion is relatively weak' (Weller 2008: 22). Indeed, Tatsuki Kataoka (2012) points out that in Thailand, forms of ritual expression have proliferated and diversified in those fields of religious life that lie beyond the state's supervision and management of institutional Buddhism.

Across the first decades of the 20th century, both absolute monarchs and authoritarian military rulers in Thailand sought to establish legitimacy-enhancing relationships between Buddhism and the state by decree. Buddhism became a state-sponsored and state-controlled religion, and the Department of Religious Affairs was dedicated to monitoring and enforcing state-*sangha* relations, including the organisational structure of the monkhood. However, with the end of the wars in Laos, Cambodia, Vietnam and Thailand in the early 1980s, the Thai state began to follow a less centralist cultural policy; affirmations of local religious and ritual cultures, often expressed in regional languages, were no longer seen as potential threats to national security. Indeed, local cultural differences are now celebrated on domestic and international tourism brochures, and are valued as instances of national cultural heritage.

In British Burma, by contrast, the colonial period was one of benign neglect of Buddhism due to the policy of non-intervention in the religious affairs of the population by the colonial administration. This put an end to the relationships of mutual legitimation between the Buddhist monastic order and Burma's traditional Theravadin kingship (Turner 2014). Upon independence in 1948, the question of the *sangha*'s organisation and control quickly emerged as a contentious issue. A religious administration was formed in 1950 and further developed under Ne Win's *sangha* reform of 1980. Under this reform, all *sangha* branches were unified under the authority of a single religious administration, the *Sangha Maha Nayaka Ahpwe*, which was charged with the purification of the monastic order and placed under the civilian arm of a Department of Religious Affairs. After 1988 events in Burma, a junta (SLORC) implemented a new policy of religious donations to simultaneously enhance its legitimacy and control senior monks. As Juliane Schober observes, '[This] military regime's patronage of Buddhism provided an alternative source of legitimation and transformed a national community into a ritual network' (Schober 2011: 86).

In parallel, the relative market liberalisation that occurred in the 1990s also underpinned a boom of spirit possession rituals as well as an efflorescence of new devotional practices in the field of Buddhist esoterism (Brac de la Perrière *et al.* 2014). After having been under control during Ne Win's era, these phenomena – spirit possession and Buddhist esoterism – re-emerged under the new junta as fluctuating domains and further evolved as dynamically connected fields. In her chapter, Bénédicte Brac de la Perrière observes that the efflorescence of new forms of ritual practice in Burma is partly related to the junta's policies of self-legitimation by sponsoring Buddhist foundations. This subsequently led to the rediscovery of spiritual figures connected to restored Buddhist pagodas, including the *naga*-like female protective spirits of pagoda treasure troves or reliquaries that she considers in detail.

In Cambodia, the dramatic rupture marked by the Khmer Rouge's anti-religion politics (1975–1979) provided for a very different situation. Through the combination of Siamese and French colonial influences, a modernised Buddhism had started to emerge in the early 20th century, with a new focus on canonical scriptures as an element of national culture that fostered a dynamic of 'religionisation' (Guillou 2017: 75). This trend was brutally stopped by the Maoist Khmer Rouge regime. The *sangha* was disbanded, monasteries and pagodas were destroyed and Buddhist practices were forbidden between 1975 and 1979. However, those spirits (*neak ta*) viewed as protecting village establishments had a more resilient destiny. According to Ian Harris (2013), 'animism' and protective ritual practices were performed throughout the Khmer Rouge period, and Matthew O'Lemmon's (2014: 37) informants also reported that the *neak ta* 'remained despite the displacement of individuals'. These authors agree that the dismantling of Buddhism drove people to turn toward the spirits, particularly in rural areas, just after the war. At the same time, the lack of spirit mediums at this time appears to have facilitated the inclusion of the spirits within a Buddhist imaginary and ritual context through the notion of *pāramī* (spiritual power and also virtues of the Buddha) (see Bertrand Didier [2004] and Paul Christensen in this volume).

In Cambodia, John Marston (2014) has documented the reestablishment of the *sangha* by the new state after the fall of the Khmer Rouge regime from 1979 onwards, demonstrating how the state has weighed on the organisational structure and bureaucratisation of religion. However, since the 1990s, political and economic liberalisation has reignited pre-war debates about the delineation of Buddhism against 'tradition' or 'Brahmanism' (see

Christensen here) that thus appear as having been produced by this process (Davis 2016, Ch.8).

In Vietnam, the state had long been a central agent of the religious sphere, particularly through the Confucianisation of the society that started with the Lê dynasty (1428–1788) and contributed to the control of Buddhism and village ritual life. In contrast to Theravada Buddhism in the other societies of mainland Southeast Asia, Mahayana Buddhism in Vietnam never attained the position of a hegemonic religion, where instead the notion of the 'Three Teachings', namely, Buddhism, Confucianism and Taoism, prevailed. Buddhism was positioned as an indigenous religion whose complexity allowed for significant spirit possession figures, such as Lieu Hanh, to find places in its temples (Dror 2007).

During the socialist period (1945–1985), religious affairs were administered by a government office that regulated expressions of popular religion and discriminated against forms of 'superstition'. As a result, festivals and public ceremonies pertaining to the spirit possession cult receded into the private sphere. However, as Robert Hefner (2010: 1032) and other observers note, since the introduction of the *Doi Moi* economic reforms in the late 1980s, a profound reorientation of the Vietnamese state's role has been accompanied by a significant expansion of ritual practices, including support for festivals as nationalist expressions of popular Vietnamese culture (Dror 2007; Sorrentino 2018 and in this volume). In his chapter, Paul Sorrentino reports that Vietnamese authorities actively supported the December 2016 inscription of rituals of the Mother Goddess religion on UNESCO's international register of Intangible Cultural Heritage as part of efforts to promote a distinctly Vietnamese religious and cultural identity.

It is indeed significant that the post-Cold War efflorescence of devotional cults and spirit possession in mainland Southeast Asia occurred with equal intensity in West-aligned capitalist societies such as Thailand and ostensibly socialist countries such as Vietnam. In the post-World War II period, political discourses of rational modernity in both countries critiqued spirit mediumship as a superstitious residue of pre-modern tradition that held each country back from achieving the desired transition to scientific (socialist or capitalist) modernity. Both countries' governments instituted remarkably similar policies against 'superstitions' across the middle decades of the 20th century. However, despite continuing political differences, spirit possession cults have been reformed and expanded in both Thailand and

Vietnam, as well as in neighbouring Burma and Cambodia, in parallel over the period of neoliberal globalisation. The differing political complexions of post-Cold War mainland Southeast Asian societies have proven to be irrelevant to the growth of spirit presence and ritual practices, with spirit mediumship flourishing under 21st-century versions of market-oriented socialism and neoliberal capitalism, all in parallel with continuing processes of 'religionification'[12] and Buddhist reform. In summary, the growth of new spirit cults has taken place in contexts where state power over ritual and religion has been radically transformed, with state policies regarding spirit cults in some mainland Southeast Asian countries, such as Vietnam, now effectively supporting rather than inhibiting or restricting forms of spirit possession ritual.

Marketisation and the cultural logic of neoliberalism

In Southeast Asia, the decline of political control over religion occurred at the same time that economic growth gathered pace, with economic forces rising at the historical moment that political influences over religion and other aspects of cultural production waned. The rise of the economy then created an expanded space for ritual innovation that went beyond the historical scope of state-based authority, with the differentiation of state power and the emergence of a significantly expanded market together creating a domain within which economic forces became more important determinants of religious expression.

Two sets of arguments seek to explain the productive roles of the market, as well as new media, in the emergence of new forms of ritual practice. One argues that capitalism and new media promote the dissemination of information about novel religious movements and make them widely accessible through efficient marketing and communications. Raymond Lee (1993) proposed that religious diversification occurs in capitalist Asian societies because no single organisation can offer all the religious services for which there is a demand in the spiritual marketplace. As a consequence, there will be many faiths, each specialising in meeting the requirements of a segment of

---

12 By 'religionification', Picard 2017 refers to the formation of a distinctive domain of religion, in opposition to 'magic' and so on, on the model of the Western world religions including the borrowing of the word 'religion' or the formation of a new term in local languages to translate this word.

the market. In Thailand, White argues, the expansion of new wealth beyond traditional elites has also been a factor in religious diversification, with the increased wealth now circulating outside the direct control of the state and bureaucratic and economic elites enabling those outside or on the periphery of the Thai state's religious bureaucracy to have a greater degree of religious autonomy than had been the case (White 2014: 236). These accounts detail the processes behind the proliferation of already existing movements and, while helping us understand how new religious practices may be communicated and expand their influence, they do not describe how new movements may emerge. A second set of analyses makes a stronger case, arguing that capitalism and new media are themselves productive sources of novel forms of ritual, in radical contrast to theories of modernity as a process of disenchantment, and contending that mediatised neoliberalism constitutes a set of productive forces that contribute to bringing new devotional cults into being.

Jean and John Comaroff argue that religions in which a 'messianic, millennial capitalism ... presents itself as a gospel of salvation' (2000: 292) are a worldwide phenomenon linked with the global triumph of neoliberal capitalism since the end of the Cold War. Comaroff and Comaroff argue that new forms of market-based enchantment, which they call 'occult economies' (Comaroff & Comaroff 1999), emerged under neoliberalism because, 'Once legible processes – the workings of power, the distribution of wealth, the meaning of politics and national belonging – have become opaque, even spectral' (Comaroff & Comaroff 2000: 305). In this context, 'the occult becomes an ever more appropriate, semantically saturated metaphor for our times' (*ibid.*: 318). Indeed, the popular religiosity that emerged in tandem with 1990s neoliberalism was paralleled by a religion-like faith in the market amongst the ideologues of finance capital. 'Magical' capitalism is not a mere persistence of pre-modern 'superstition', but rather is a refraction through local cultural metaphors of the beliefs of capitalism's ruling elites, for whom neoliberalism is 'a gospel of salvation' (*ibid.*: 291).

While Weber may have described industrial capitalism as presenting an iron cage of bureaucratic reason, the complexity of postindustrial capitalist social orders has outstripped the predictive capacity of many established forms of rational analysis. White (2014: 232) argues that because Buddhism has functioned as a repository of beliefs and practices designed to provide control over insecurity and uncertainty, it is not surprising that popular Thai religiosity has flourished within a social environment characterised by capitalist development. Charles Keyes *et al.* (1994: 15) note that the continuing relevance of religiosity may emerge from the limits of reason that are revealed in marketised neoliberal societies: '[T]he gap between the conclusions reached about the world through recourse to rational decision making and the practical reality of the world generates uncertainty and ambiguity that many seek to resolve through turning to religion.'

This is where ritual and devotional religiosity return, albeit in highly modified, mediatised and commodified forms. Ritual practice is a practical response to living in a decentralised, marketised and increasingly complex world that often defies predictability. This is not a pre-modern survival or an atavistic return to the past. Rather, it is the emergence of ritual and devotion within the conditions of late modern hypercomplexity.

Mass media and technologies of enchantment

Morris (2000: 245) argues that new mass media have also contributed to the expanding popularity of novel spirit cults by delocalising cultic figures and making information about local deities and spirits available to national and indeed international audiences. In this context, many in Southeast Asia now pay respect to figures linked to the common enveloping commercial space of the market. Today's most popular new spirits, which are at the centre of national level cults of wealth (Jackson 1999b), are those which sacralise the national scale economic space. This is especially the case when the space of commercial enterprise is linked to figures regarded as symbols of national protection, such as King Chulalongkorn in Thailand, the cult of the Mother Goddess in Vietnam (Taylor 2004) or the Botataung Lady in Burma (Brac de la Perrière, this volume).

Contemporary media not only contribute to the popularity of one or another devotional movement by disseminating information about them. New media also create magic-like effects that can auraticise cult figures or objects, contributing to the production of new forms of religiosity and practice. In analysing popular culture in contemporary India, Bhaskar Mukhophadhyay argues that the mediatisation of myth now constitutes a political force in that country, 'Mass media have made the gods more real, not less … . It is not a matter of virtuality or "spectacle". It is myth sanctified by technology—a techno-mythologisation of the body politics' (2006: 288–289). Jeremy Stolow observes that media have become central to 'the imagined worlds that constitute the sacred in the global present' (2005: 123), and contends that 'the transcendental, enchanting, thaumaturgical, uncanny, haunting – powers of media technologies themselves' (*ibid*.: 124) induce a 'reactivation of aura' (*ibid*.: 127).

Morris describes how the proliferation of new forms of imaging technology has reignited a 'primordial sacrality' rather than contributing to a decay of sacredness in Thailand. Morris links the resurgence of spirit mediumship in Thailand with the rise of capitalism and marketised lifestyles, on the one hand, and the explosive growth of technologies of image reproduction and mass communications, on the other. She argues that the efflorescence of mediumship in recent decades has its roots in the mass media (Morris 2000: 53) and mediumship's growing popularity is linked to a radically new attitude to imaging technologies. Until the 1970s, it was uncommon for spirit mediums to permit themselves to be represented via photography or the mass media. 'Now', in contrast, 'all mediums display photographs of themselves, and even media personalities have joined the ranks of the possessed' (Morris 2000b: 460). Morris argues that the massive scale of imaging technologies produced within a market-centred consumerist culture distorts established patterns of representation and creates magic-like effects as rational modes of analysis are swamped by waves of promiscuously circulating images. It is here, Morris argues, that we find 'a reinvestment in the power of appearances. This is where the magic returns… . The logic of appearances has changed' (Morris 2000: 238–239).

In considering new professional spirit possession cults, Pattana plays upon the double sense of the term 'medium' as denoting both a technological means of communication and the human vehicle of spirit possession rituals. To emphasise the point that new forms of ritual in Thailand have emerged from contemporary social conditions, he describes both 'magic' monks who sacralise amulets and spirit mediums as 'postmodern mediums' (Pattana 2012: 104).

Ritual and the performative generation of enchantment

In addition to the contemporary forms of neoliberal capitalism and new print and digital media in societies in which the state largely has retreated from managing religion, the very character of ritual action is a force that produces an efflorescence of spirit cults. This is especially the case in settings like popular Buddhism, in which ritual practice is a more important dimension of religiosity than doctrine or stated expressions of faith. In 'The Relevance of Ritual', the conclusion to her 1994 study titled 'Defying Disenchantment', which in significant measure draws on sources from Thailand, Jean Comaroff (1994: 311) argues that ritual 'generates the very force it presupposes' and understanding this process must be central to our 'assessment of religion in the modern world'. Drawing on Tambiah and his comparative studies of the Theravada cultures of Sri Lanka and Thailand,[13] Comaroff presents a performative theory of popular religion as emerging within settings of ritualised action. Comaroff describes ritual as being 'positively productive' in all societies:

> Its productivity lies in its capacity to create morally charged experience, to speak with and without words, in diverse sensory registers and through "multiple channels" (Tambiah 1985: 60ff) … . [Ritual] is intensely pragmatic. It not only makes and remakes its actors, but can also call on them to make and remake worlds. Its modes are indispensable to the forging of "culture" and "society", in the modern world as in any other. Ritual, in the end, defies disenchantment. (Comaroff 1994: 314)

In bringing into being 'collective values' beyond the mundane, Comaroff argues that the performative productivity of ritual is a powerful force that counters the presumed bureaucratic rationalist iron cage of modernity.

Capitalism, media and the enchanting intensities of embodied ritual

When we combine the empirical finding, detailed in the chapters of this study, that the new forms of spirit possession and divination focus more on ritual practice than on belief or faith, with the understanding that ritual is performatively productive in bringing into being that which it invokes, then we begin to understand why the emergence of new forms of enchantment has been such a distinctive feature of modern religious life in Buddhist Southeast Asia. In synthesising the several accounts of modern 'magic' summarised above, we can propose that the enchanting effects of capitalism and new media will be most intense in those societies in which the performative influence

---

13 Tambiah was a major figure in the development of a performative approach to understanding ritual as well as the transcultural, and indeed transhistorical, importance of enchantment in human life. Tambiah, 1977 and 1985, was among the first to draw on the linguistic philosophy of J.L. Austin, who argued that some uses of language effect changes in the world and function as forms of social action, in order to explore the performative features of ritual acts.

of religious ritual is prioritised over belief and doctrine. This finding is also relevant to other mediatised consumer societies in which embodied ritual action is emphasised over belief, faith and reason. Indeed, new enchanted cosmologies have also emerged in modern Japan. In their account of James Foard's (n.d.) description of what he calls Japanese 'endemic religion', Keyes *et al.* (1994: 10) identify the synergistic operation of the same range of forces to those detailed above as inciting the development of new spirit cults and divinatory rituals in Japan. They describe Japanese endemic religion as being 'nurtured by mass media and an elaborate commercialisation of ritual goods and services.' And drawing implicitly on a notion of the performative productivity of ritual, Keyes *et al.* conclude that '[e]ndemic religion derives its authority from its practice, which generates "tradition" as an ongoing process' (*ibid.*). In an observation that is as relevant today as when first published three decades ago, Tambiah concludes his account of the performative force of ritual by stating that the puzzling character of enchantment for moderns, whether in Asia or the West,

> will only disappear when we succeed in embedding magic in a more ample theory of human life in which the path of ritual action is seen as an indispensable mode for man anywhere and everywhere of relating to and participating in the life of the world. (Tambiah 1990: 83)

Significant contributions of the chapters

Professionalisation of ritual specialists

An especially significant development in recent decades that is reported in many of our chapters, and which marks a major transformation, is the professionalisation of divination and spirit mediumship across the region. By selling ritual services, spirit mediums and diviners have increasingly become full-time professionals and formed autonomous subcultures. In his chapter, Benjamin Baumann recognises professionalisation as a core process undergone by lay ritual experts who act as lineage mediums of localised matrilineal spirits in a process involving distancing from locality, rurality and tradition. Through his ethnography, we see how professional mediums based in towns and who organise rituals for their entourage to pay homage to spiritual teachers (Central Thai: *wai khru*) are on the point of replacing village mediums in this region. Baumann's account fills a gap in the ethnography by enabling us to understand the pivotal role of professionalisation in the transformations of ritual from rural forms of life to new urban configurations in Thailand (see also Pattana 2012 in this regard). In his doctoral thesis, White (2014) insists on the relative novelty of professional spirit mediums as religious actors in Bangkok, where, starting in the 1970s, they formed a partially autonomous, networked subculture. In their studies in this volume of different regional possession cults in Northeast and Northern Thailand, Baumann, Irene Stengs, Visisya Pinthongvijayakul, and Kazuo Fukuura all report that within the new cultures of professional spirit mediums, rituals of paying homage to the master (*wai khru* or *yok khu*) now form a significant mechanism of transmission of authority within their distinctive subcultures. This urban model of professional mediumship has proliferated and increasingly replaced older rural forms, thereby complicating local ritual configurations, as evidenced by the material about Thailand and Cambodia that is presented in the following chapters.[14]

In Vietnam and Burma, however, professional spirit mediumship evolved earlier, in the 18th century, as rituals to tutelary spirits were centralised and enrolled in polity-bounded 'pantheons'. In Yangon, Mandalay, Hanoi and Hue, professional spirit mediums have maintained autonomous networks for considerable periods. In his chapter on the Four Palaces Religion, Paul Sorrentino deals with the difficulty of researching the ambiguous histories of the pantheons of Vietnamese spirit mediums because of their open-ended natures. In these cases, professional spirit mediums respond to a vocational calling from entities belonging to an identified institution of spirit possession and channel the collective number of tutelary spirits in spirit possession séances. In both Burma and Vietnam, professional spirit mediums form well-identified subcultures whose positioning in the overall religious field follows defined if fluctuating destinies.

In between traditional mediums bounded to local ritual life and urban professional ritual specialists whose pantheons comprise deities worshipped across the country, Stengs, Visisya and Baumann also report a category of ritual participants in Thailand who Baumann describes as 'active devotees' (referring to the Thai expression *mi ong* 'having a spirit'), who are in the process of developing ritual relations to a possessing entity but have not yet

---

[14] Some of the earlier studies that dealt with village-based forms of spirit possession were those by Tambiah 1970, Kirsch 1977, Irvine 1982 and Tanabe 1991.

attained the status of full possession or mediumship.[15] In Burma, besides the category of 'active devotees'– also being preliminary to mediumship careers and evoked as 'having a spirit' (Burmese *nat shi*) – in their respective chapters Niklas Foxeus and Bénédicte Brac de la Perrière report non-clientelistic modes of possession in the rituals associated with new cults of pagoda guardian spirits. Degrees of professionalisation of spirit mediumship are revealed to be at different stages and levels across mainland Southeast Asia, with the relative incidence of spiritual authority and socio-religious respectability depending on specific historical contexts.

Dynamic and expanding pantheons

The contributors to this volume support Condominas' (1976) proposal that spirit possession in mainland Southeast Asia is characterised by a plurality of beings arrayed in hierarchical order. In his chapter, Paul Sorrentino discusses the qualification of the term 'pantheon' as often applied to the hierarchical assembly of spirit beings in the Vietnamese Cult of the Four Palaces; in his, Visisya Pinthongvijayakul proposes that the spirits in Northeastern Thai cults form a 'Buddhist-mediumistic pantheon'. Following Århem (2016a, 2016b), Baumann describes the diverse spirits invoked by mediums in Thailand's lower northeast as forming part of a 'possession complex'. Burma's cult of the Thirty-seven Lords has long ago been recognised by kings as a hierarchy of spirits. However, Sorrentino notes that there is no vernacular concept of 'pantheon' in Vietnam. The same is true in Thailand and Burma, apart from expressions denoting spiritual collectives such as the 'Thirty-seven Lords' in Burma. Nonetheless, there is a widespread implicit appreciation of an ordered ensemble of spirits in possession cults. This is represented both materially and visually by printed pictures of the ordered inhabitants of the 'Four Palaces' in Vietnam (see Figure 1.3), by statues aligned on the shelves of possession pavilions for Burma's Thirty-seven Lords (see Figure 0.1) and by the multiple images of deities that many Thai spirit mediums arrange on their personal shrines (see Figure 0.2).

---

15 In a study of divination in Bangkok, Siani 2018 notes that while many Thai fortune-tellers (Thai: *mor du*) distinguish themselves categorically from spirit mediums (Thai: *khon song*, *rang song*), they nonetheless claim that their prognosticatory skills derive from an intimate association with a spiritual entity (*ong*).

What distinguishes the possession complexes studied here from older ritual forms is the expansion of local pantheons to include a proliferating array of beings whose guidance and support are sought in various rituals that often induce spirit possession. In Burma, these new beings include many figures in charge of watching over pagoda treasure-troves (See Figure 6.1) and which since the 1990s have found new representations distinct from those of the Thirty-seven Lords, as well as those produced as part of the renewed practice of Buddhist esoterism known as the *weikza* path. Baumann lists Thailand's expanding ritual pantheon as including Hindu deities, Brahmanical hermits, honoured historical figures, child spirits and spiritually empowered Buddhist monks. Visisya includes the Buddha among the pantheon of spirits in Northeast Thailand, while Jackson (1999b) also adds Chinese spirits to the mix, describing this still emerging Thai pantheon as a 'symbolic complex'. Rather than forming a fixed or static hierarchy, Sorrentino describes the expanding number of spirits in the region's cults as reflecting processes of 'pantheonisation', constituting pantheons in the making. The dynamic nature of these processes is reflected by the fact that relations among new spirits, and their links to deities in established cults, are subject to ongoing change that is often marked by incoherencies and contradictions. Visisya describes the evolving affiliation of beings in the Thai pantheon of spirits as a hierarchical topography that is characterised by blurry distinctions, porous boundaries and flows of exchange.

Changing relations of possession rituals to institutional Buddhism

Earlier accounts of Southeast Asian Buddhism often posited a mutually exclusive separation between possession rituals and Buddhist practices – as exemplified in Melford Spiro's 'two religions' theory,[16] and also between the religious roles of spirit medium and ordained Buddhist monk. In contrast, Visisya and Fukuura here report the participation of a growing number of monks in possession rituals in both Northeast and Northern Thailand, although not as professional spirit mediums. This appears to confirm Marjorie Muecke's observations from Chiang Mai reported almost three decades ago (1992) as well as Pattana's (2012) inclusion of 'magic monks' in his category of 'postmodern mediums'.

---

16 See, for example, Melford Spiro's position in the Preface to the second edition of his *Burmese Supernaturalism* (Spiro [1967] 1978).

Figure 0.1. A spirit medium's domestic shrine in Yangon picturing part of the Burmese spirit possession pantheon. **Colour** p. 311.

Figure 0.2. Bangkok shrine displaying images of a Thai spirit medium's personal pantheon of Indian and Chinese deities. **Colour** p. 311.

In his chapter, Paul Christensen argues that the relation between possession rituals and mainstream Buddhism should be depicted as one of mutual construction rather than of mutual exclusion. His account of the contemporary reconfiguration of spirit worship practice as 'Brahmanism' in Cambodia evokes a form of 'prosperity religion' aimed at accruing spiritual power (*pāramī*) for immediate benefit in this life, in contrast with 'modern' Buddhist rituals' focus on acquiring merit. The spirit-related 'ancient' religion that has evolved into 'Brahmanism' also represents an enhancement of pre-Khmer Rouge rural practice dedicated to tutelary spirits (*neak ta*).

Indeed, what further characterises the contemporary evolution of spirit cults across the whole region through their expansion from rural settings to a more 'national' and urban scale is a tendency to status enhancement when considered in relation to the whole religious field. White (2014) contrasts professional urban spirit mediumship in contemporary Thailand with other forms of traditional spirit possession by entities labelled as *phi*, which are characteristically ludic, at times nefarious and usually emplaced within a specific territorial domain. In contrast, professional spirit mediums respond to a vocational calling from higher-status possessing entities that are labelled as *thep* (Pali *deva*, 'deities') or *jao* (lords) and which are viewed as benevolent and more Buddhist (White 2014). In her chapter here, Megan Sinnott also reports that the replacement of older forms of preserved-fetus spirits by angel-child dolls 'rented' from Buddhist monasteries reflects the growing differentiation between malevolent and good spirits prevailing today in Thailand.

This enhancement of the spiritual status of entities involved in contemporary spirit possession or spirit cults in Thailand also corresponds to what Bénédicte Brac de la Perrière and Niklas Foxeus observe in Burma, with the worship of pagoda treasure-trove guardians (*thaik nan shin* and *bobogyi*) growing in the interstitial spaces of esoteric Buddhism and borrowing practices of spirit possession from the contiguous *nat* cult to the Thirty-seven Lords. Foxeus details these practices as Buddhist 'prosperity' cults that provide devotees with a Buddhist means to acquire immediate wealth and prosperity. These cults use spirit possession as a ritual tool for manifesting spiritual potency, which demonstrates the complex relationships that link Buddhism with spirit worship. In Vietnam, Sorrentino's relation of heritagisation and patrimonialisation of the Mother Goddess religion also speaks of an enhancement of the Four Palaces spirit possession pantheon that allows spirit mediumship to avoid its former predicament of being labelled as 'superstition' by gaining recognition as a part of indigenous Vietnamese culture.

Furthermore, our authors show that the professionalisation and autonomisation of spirit medium circles as religious subcultures, together with the enhancement of the spiritual status of the entities at the centre of these cults, have been central dimensions of the reconfiguration of spirit possession within the whole religious sphere, both historically and in the contemporary era. These processes of differentiation have occurred across mainland Southeast Asia in the course of spirit possession's shift and subsequent expansion from the worship of local tutelary or lineage spirits to larger collectivities of divinities or pantheons of deities that have a national import. Rather than speaking of two separate religions, as Spiro (1967) viewed it, these processes reveal intricate and evolving relationships between spirit worship and mainstream Buddhism, providing spaces for efflorescing domains that can be framed as prosperity cults, whether they be Cambodian 'Brahmanism', Burmese pagoda treasure-trove guardian cults or various polyphonic public rituals.

The oneiric space of possession, divination, dreams and visions

In her chapter, Irene Stengs posits a continuity between the importance attached to dreams and meditation-inspired visions (Pali: *nimitta*) by many Buddhist monks and the trance states of mediums in possession. She describes all these phenomena as instances of a common oneiric space, a notion that provides an important analytical foundation for future inquiries that explore spirit mediumship, divination and Buddhism as all being dimensions of an overarching religious field rather than as distinct or mutually exclusive ritual forms.

Cross-border regional influences

Another significant development revealed in several chapters is the growth of cross-border borrowing and influences among the ritual cultures of Burma, Thailand and Cambodia. Foxeus notes the importance of the Thai lottery to the rituals associated with Burmese lottery mania and Brac de la Perrière reports that increasing numbers of Thai tourists are among the faithful who flock to the shrine of the Botataung Lady in Yangon. The Thai cult of amulets, never a significant phenomenon in the Burmese religious field, is now influencing the material dimension of Burmese cults, with amulets of the grandfatherly spiritual figure of the Botataung Bobogyi (see Brac de la Perrière 2019) now being produced for sale to Thai tourist-devotees. Over the past decade, the Burmese *bobogyi* has been included within the expanding pantheon of Thai deities of wealth, where this figure has been renamed in Thai as *Thep Than-jai*, literally, 'The deity who grants wishes expeditiously'. In her chapter here, Poonnatree Jiaviriyaboonya observes that in the aftermath of the destruction of significant parts of the Cambodian ritual tradition under the Khmer Rouge regime, divinatory practices are being reconstituted in the country by borrowing from Thai astrological and other texts, and a number of Cambodian ritual specialists are visiting Thailand to develop skills and proficiency in both Buddhist and divinatory practices.

The chapters in this book

Paul Sorrentino examines processes of heritagisation and autochthonisation that in 2016 led to the registration of the Mother Goddess Religion on UNESCO's list of intangible cultural heritage as a Vietnamese 'indigenous' religion, even though the cult of the Four Palaces from which it evolved had previously been forbidden by the socialist state. He shows that these processes are grounded in the dynamics of 'pantheon' formation, a notion widely used by Western scholars although not easily translated into Vietnamese. Worship practices linked to this 'pantheon' are characterised by spirit possession séances addressed to an ensemble of spirits organised according to two main principles: a hierarchy of ranks and the attribution of an ordinal number within each rank. These practices display a complementarity between male, mandarin forms of legitimacy and a more embodied, female form of indigenous authority, analogous with the dialectics of administrative rule and regional autochthony. Sorrentino argues that the contradiction between the systematic, combined structure of the pantheon and the rich collection of individual beings belonging to it has worked as a device for the integration of local deities into a dynamic aggregate at the national scale.

Bénédicte Brac de la Perrière relates the remarkable formation, since the beginning of the new century, of the annual celebration of Mya Nan Nwe (also known as the Botataung Lady), the *naga*-like guardian spirit of Botataung Pagoda in Yangon, who dwells in her own separate temple. The celebration of the Botataung Lady's birthday has become one of Yangon's important new festive events, whose polymorphous dimensions combine various ritual formats in a novel fashion and give the gathering a striking *forum-like* aspect. While manifestations of spirit possession are banned inside her temple, nearby outdoor ritual pageants prompting specific *thaik-naga* possession dances by female devotees are nonetheless *de rigueur*. These dances are particularly innovative examples of the processes of identification and differentiation enabled by this *forum-like* setting. Mya Nan Nwe's ritual destiny has proved to be an interesting instance of the distinctive value of spirit possession as epitomised in the context of the Burmese Thirty-seven Lords cult, being able to display either positive or negative values in the newly emerging field of pagoda guardian worship, according to positions in the overall religious field.

In contrast to the presumed separation of Buddhism and spirit cults that dominated accounts in earlier literatures, Visisya Pinthongvijayakul examines the participation of the Northeastern Thai monk *Ajan* Tho in possession ritual through his 'having a spirit' (*mi ong*). Based on his observation of mediumistic activity in *Ajan* Tho's monastery – and contextually refuting accounts of the spatial separation of both domains of religiosity – Visisya forcefully advocates for the reciprocal and mutual constitution of Buddhism and spirit cult practices. Although as a Buddhist monk *Ajan* Tho is limited in the full expression of mediumistic ritual practice, he nonetheless depends on networks of spirit mediums' clients to sustain his religious establishment in a context of rural deprivation.

Kazuo Fukuura analyses the reorganisation and realignment of Chiang Mai spirit mediums that occurred in 1996 with the invention of a ritual to commemorate the 700th anniversary of the city's founding by three legendary kings. This novel polyphonic ritual emerged independently from the historical annual ceremony at Chiang Mai's city pillar shrine (Sao Inthakhin) and the possession ritual at the shrine of the pillar spirit, Chaeng Si Phum. Fukuura locates this emergence of new rituals within the vivid landscape of Chiang Mai spirit possession, where collective rituals of professional mediums to honour their transcendental teachers (Northern Thai: *yok khu*), or at historical sites, combine with community-based matrilineal descent cults, whose mediums are also becoming increasingly professionalised. The annual celebration of the Three Kings (1996–2014) was Chiang Mai's biggest-ever collective ritual of mediumship, consisting of dance offerings by three groups of mediums: one for the Three Kings and the two others for descent-group spirits. Examining the careers of two mediums who managed this cultural innovation, Fukuura delineates two conflicting realignments among contemporary mediums in Chiang Mai, one emphasising translocal connections with Hindu deities and the other being more purely local. Finally, he shows that this polyphonic set of rituals has been a tool for local identity politics and for an affirmation of spirit possession as a recognised form of Northern Thai cultural heritage.

Through an ethnographic account of a contemporary medium's ceremony, Paul Christensen illustrates how Buddhism and 'Brahmanism' work together in Cambodia today. In Cambodia, 'Brahmanism' now refers to a contemporary reformulation of religious practice involving spirits. After the radical disruption of the Khmer Rouge period, the rapid revitalisation of Buddhism has paralleled that of Brahmanism, a phenomenon that has not previously been analysed in the scholarly literature. While Buddhist rituals focus on merit-making, 'Brahmanist' ones aim at accruing spiritual power (*pāramī*) with immediate benefits in this life. Christensen argues that, as a contemporary phenomenon and unlike text-based reformist Buddhism, 'Brahmanism' can be understood as a 'prosperity religion' that is more relevant to a period of economic liberalisation and other 'modern' concerns.

Niklas Foxeus also examines Buddhist 'prosperity cults' to pagoda treasure-trove guardians around Mandalay, Burma. Significantly, some of these novel cults are linked to the boom of illegal lotteries in Burma. Foxeus argues that compared to *kammatic* Buddhism (Spiro 1970) and the possession cult of the Thirty-seven Lords, 'prosperity Buddhism' provides an immediate Buddhist means to acquire wealth and prosperity. In the two pagoda clusters that he investigates, devotees and non-clientelistic mediums acting as ritual specialists give uncoded lottery numbers when they are possessed by treasure trove guardians, mainly child spirits who are a new addition to the local spiritual configurations. However, devotees are linked to the spirits through a conditional relationship, being helped to 'hit the jackpot' only if they engage in promoting and practising Buddhism in return. According to Foxeus, this in-built reciprocating mechanism is a recent and specific transformation of merit-making in Burma that helps to enhance Buddhism's contemporary relevance.

Poonnatree Jiaviriyaboonya follows the search of a rural–urban Khmer migrant student for a fortune-teller in Phnom Penh who can help alleviate her painful indecisiveness regarding conflicting life options. Because of the rupture of cultural traditions during the Khmer Rouge period, and also because authentic divinatory knowledge had been considered a preserve of the royal family and only transmitted orally, contemporary fortune-tellers have encountered many obstacles in their attempts to establish their authority. *Grū* Bun, the diviner who finally heals the student, developed his numerological skills through self-study of the many Khmer, Burmese and Thai books he has collected, most particularly the Thai astrological and numerological text, the *Tamra Phrommachat*, that he came to worship as his 'teacher'. Through her analysis of the consultation, Poonnatree shows that *Grū* Bun used numerological techniques to help him visualise the student's life journey in relation to morality, auspiciousness, spiritual power and obligation, rather than to predetermination. She also reveals that Thai astrology has been an important source of knowledge for those who seek to reestablish divinatory authority in contemporary Cambodian urban culture.

Megan Sinnott's chapter focuses on the long tradition of child spirit worship in Thailand. She observes a shift from trafficking in preserved fetus entities that were historically associated with dark magical powers to the adoption of angel-child dolls (*luk thep*), which only emerged in the past decade. This shift from necromancy to family care and love in the worship of child spirits reflects the larger phenomenon of a growing differentiation between malevolent and good spirits. This further illustrates the fluidity of a deeply historical yet also highly contemporary belief system: because communication with the spirit world depends on the presence of a material form of spirits, angel-child dolls 'rented' from monasteries have been substituted for the physical remains of fetuses that were at the centre of older child spirit cults.

In her study of spirit mediumship in Chiang Mai, Irene Stengs posits a continuity between the importance attached to dreams and meditation-inspired visions (Pali: *nimitta*) of many Buddhist monks and the trance states of mediums in possession in Northern Thailand. She describes all these phenomena as instances of a common oneiric space, a notion that provides an analytical foundation for future explorations of spirit mediumship, divination and Buddhism as dimensions of an overarching religious field rather than as being distinct or mutually exclusive. She notes that cults associated with historical figures such as King Chulalongkorn and other Thai royal figures reflect strong nationalistic sentiments linked to contemporary events and settings.

In his chapter, Benjamin Baumann places the manifold forms of mediumship in Thailand's Buriram province squarely within the Southeast Asian possession complex, and locates his study within the theoretical perspective of the 'new animism'. Baumann argues that professional mediums based in towns and who organise rituals for their entourage to 'pay homage to the teacher' (*wai khru*) are on the point of replacing lineage mediums of localised matrilineal spirits in this region. Through professionalisation, these new mediums participate in a mystic field that enables them to establish lasting relations of mutuality with a variety of potent nonhuman beings. In an account that accords with Picard's (2017) description of 'religionification' as the formation of a distinct domain of religion, Baumann argues that in Thailand the religious field has only been separated from this mystic field since the middle of the 20th century.

Further study of the Southeast Asian spirit possession complex

The studies collected here more precisely situate and qualify the rapidly expanding field of spirit possession studies across mainland Southeast Asia. In his Afterword Erick White summarises key findings from the chapters and details important outstanding issues that future research will need to address in taking this field of study forward. For example, there is still a need to specify analytical categories that are both adequate to describe the distinctive forms of spirit possession found in mainland Southeast Asia and also permit productive comparisons to be made across the region's several countries. The shifting place of spirit possession in 'mainstream' Theravada Buddhist ritual as well as in diverse forms of divination, including astrology, also should be addressed. Furthermore, while the existence of a hierarchy of plural cosmologies is common across the Buddhist societies of the region, the ideologies of these multiplicities are not the same in each society. There are distinctive local ways of describing and negotiating the intersection of the plural Buddhist and other cosmologies that have emerged from the different histories and patterns of intersecting trends in each mainland society. An important task of future research will be to develop more nuanced analyses of the diversity of local processes and discourses of negotiating the cosmological plurality that is such a distinctive and fascinating characteristic of what is without doubt one of the most culturally and religiously diverse regions in the world.

References

Århem, Kaj. 2016a. 'Southeast Asian Animism in Context', in Kaj Århem and Guido Sprenger (eds), *Animism in Southeast Asia*. New York: Routledge: 3–30.

———. 2016b. 'Southeast Asian Animism: A Dialogue with Amerindian Perspectivism', in Kaj Århem and Guido Sprenger (eds), *Animism in Southeast Asia*. New York: Routledge: 279–301.

Asad, Talal. 2003. *Formations of the Secular: Christianity, Islam, Modernity*. Stanford, CA: Stanford University Press.

Bertrand, Didier. 2004. 'A Medium's Possession Practice and its Relationship with Cambodian Buddhism: The Grū Pāramī', in John Marston and Elizabeth Guthrie (eds), *History, Buddhism, and New Religious Movements in Cambodia*. Honolulu: University of Hawai'i Press: 150–169.

Brac de la Perrière, Bénédicte. 2007. 'Un monde plus que jamais enchanté? Note de lecture sur la résurgence contemporaine des cultes aux esprits en Thaïlande et au Viêt-nam', *Aséanie* 20 (décembre): 17–25.

———. 2017. 'About Buddhist Burma: Thathana, of Religion as Social Space'. Michel Picard (ed.), *The Appropriation of Religion in Southeast Asia and Beyond*. Palgrave Macmillan: 39–66.

Brac de la Perrière, Bénédicte, Guillaume Rozenberg and Alicia Turner (eds). 2014. *Champions of Buddhism: Weikza Cults in Contemporary Burma*. Singapore: NUS Press.

Bubandt, Niels and Martjin van Beck. 2012. *Varieties of Secularism in Asia: Anthropological Explorations of Religion, Politics and the Spiritual*. London and New York: Routledge.

Carrithers, Michael. 2000. 'On Polytropy: Or the Natural Condition of Spiritual Cosmopolitanism in India, The Digambir Jain Case', *Modern Asian Studies*, 34(4): 831–861.

Casanova, José. 1994. *Public Religions in the Modern World*. Chicago: University of Chicago Press.

Comaroff, Jean. 1994. 'Epilogue: Defying Disenchantment: Reflections on Ritual, Power and History', in Charles F. Keyes, Lauren Kendall and Helen Hardacre (eds), *Asian Visions of Authority: Religion and the Modern States of East and Southeast Asia*. Honolulu: University of Hawai'i Press: 301–314.

Comaroff, Jean and John L. Comaroff. 1999. 'Occult Economies and the Violence of Abstraction: Notes from the South African Postcolony', *American Ethnologist*, 26: 279–301.

———. 2000. 'Millennial Capitalism: First Thoughts on a Second Coming', *Public Culture*, 12(2): 291–343.

Condominas, Georges. 1976. 'Quelques aspects du chamanisme et des cultes de possession en Asie du Sud-Est et dans le monde insulindien', in J. Poirier and F. Raveau (eds), *L'autre et l'ailleurs: Mélanges offerts à Roger Bastide*. Paris: Berger Levrault: 215–232.

Crosson, J. Brent. 2019. 'What Possessed You? Spirits, Property, and Political Sovereignty at the Limits of "Possession"', *Ethnos*, 84(4): 546–556.

Davis, Eric. 2016. *Deathpower: Buddhism's Ritual Imagination in Cambodia*. NY: Columbia University Press.

de Heusch, Luc. 1971. 'Possession et chamanisme', in Luc de Heusch, *Pourquoi l'épouser?* Paris: Gallimard: 226–244.

Descola, Philippe. 2005. *Par delà nature et culture*. Paris: Gallimard.

Dror, Olga. 2007. *Cult, Culture and Authority: Princess Lieu Hanh in Vietnamese History*. Honolulu: University of Hawai'i Press.

Eisenstadt, Shmuel Noah. 2000. 'Multiple Modernities', *Daedalus*, 129(1): 1–29.

Endres, Kirsten W. 2011. *Performing the Divine: Mediums, Markets and Modernity in Urban Vietnam*. Copenhagen: NIAS Press.

Endres, Kirsten W. and Andrea Lauser (eds). 2011. *Engaging the Spirit World: Popular Beliefs and Practices in Modern Southeast Asia*. New York: Berghahn Books.

Fjelstad, Karen and Nguyen Thi Hien. 2006. *Possessed by the Spirits: Mediumship in Contemporary Vietnamese Communities*. Ithaca: Cornell Southeast Asia Program.

Gauchet, Marcel. 1997. *The Disenchantment of the World: A Political History of Religion*, trans. Oscar Burge. Princeton: Princeton University Press.

Gottowik, Volker (ed.). 2014. *Dynamics of Religion in Southeast Asia: Magic and Modernity*. Amsterdam: Amsterdam University Press.

Guillou, Anne Y. 2017. 'The (Re)configuration of the Buddhist Field in Post-Communist Cambodia'. In M. Picard (ed.), *The Appropriation of Religion in Southeast Asia and Beyond*. Palgrave Macmillan: 67–93.

Harris, Ian. 2013. *Buddhism in a Dark Age: Cambodian Monks under Pol Pot*. Honolulu: University of Hawai'i Press.

Hefner, Robert F. 2010. 'Religious Resurgence in Contemporary Asia: Southeast Asian Perspectives on Capitalism, the State, and the New Piety', *Journal of Asian Studies*, 69(4): 1031–1047.

Houben, Vincent. 2013. 'The New Area Studies and Southeast Asian History'. Göttingen: DORISEA Working Paper No. 4.

Irvine, Walter. 1982. 'The Thai-Yuan "Madman" and the "Modernising, Developing Thai Nation" as Bounded Entities Under Threat: A Study in the Replication of a Single Image', PhD dissertation, School of Oriental and African Studies, University of London.

Jackson, Peter A. 1999a. 'The Enchanting Spirit of Thai Capitalism: The Cult of Luang Phor Khoon and the Postmodernization of Thai Buddhism', *South East Asia Research*, 7(1): 5–60.

———. 1999b. 'Royal Spirits, Chinese Gods and Magic Monks: Thailand's Boom-Time Religions of Prosperity', *South East Asia Research*, 7(3): 245–320.

———. 2003. 'Space, Theory and Hegemony: The Dual Crises of Asian Area Studies and Cultural Studies', *Sojourn: Social Issues in Southeast Asia*, 18(1): 1–41.

———. 2019. 'South East Asian Area Studies beyond Anglo-America: Geopolitical Transitions, the Neoliberal Academy and Spatialized Regimes of Knowledge', *South East Asia Research*, 27(1): 49–73.

Jackson, Peter A. and Benjamin Baumann (eds). 2022. *Deities and Divas: Queer Ritual Specialists in Myanmar, Thailand and Beyond*. Copenhagen: NIAS Press.

Jenkins, Richard. 2000. 'Disenchantment, Enchantment and Re-Enchantment: Max Weber at the Millennium', *Max Weber Studies*, 1: 11–32.

Johnson, Andrew. 2014. *Ghosts of the New City: Spirits, Urbanity and the Ruins of Progress in Chiang Mai*. Honolulu: University of Hawai'i Press.

Johnson, Paul C. (ed.). 2014. *Spirited Things: The Work of 'Possession' in Afro-Atlantic Religions*. Chicago: University of Chicago Press.

Kapferer, Bruce. 2002. 'Outside all Reason: Magic, Sorcery and Epistemology in Anthropology', *Social Analysis: The International Journal of Social and Cultural Practice*, 46(3): 1–30.

Kataoka, Tatsuki. 2012. 'Religion as Non-Religion: The Place of Chinese Temples in Phuket, Southern Thailand', *Southeast Asian Studies* (Center for Southeast Asian Studies, Kyoto University), 1(3): 461–485.

Keyes, Charles F., Lauren Kendall and Helen Hardacre. 1994. 'Introduction: Contested Visions of Community in East and Southeast Asia', in Keyes, Kendall and Hardacre (eds), *Asian Visions of Authority: Religion and the Modern States of East and Southeast Asia*. Honolulu: University of Hawai'i Press: 1–16.

Kirsch, A. Thomas. 1977. 'Complexity in the Thai Religious System: An Interpretation', *Journal of Asian Studies*, 36(2): 241–266.

Lee, Raymond L.M. 1993. 'The Globalisation of Religious Markets: International Innovations, Malaysian Consumption', *Sojourn*, 8(1): 35–61.

Marston, John A. 2014. 'Reestablishing the Cambodian Monkhood' in Marston J.A. (ed.) *Ethnicity, Borders and the Grassroots Interface with the State*. Bangkok, Silkworm: 65–99.

Morris, Rosalind C. 2000a. *In the Place of Origins: Modernity and its Mediums in Northern Thailand*. Durham and London: Duke University Press.

———. 2000b. 'Modernity's Media and the End of Mediumship? On the Aesthetic Economy of Transparency in Thailand', *Public Culture*, 12(2): 457–475.

Muecke, Marjorie A. 1992. 'Monks and Mediums: Religious Syncretism in Northern Thailand', *Journal of the Siam Society*, 80(2): 97–104.

Mukhopadhyay, Bhaskar. 2006. 'Cultural Studies and Politics in India Today'. *Theory, Culture and Society*, 23(7–8): 279–292.

O'Lemmon, Matthew. 2014. 'Spirit Cults and Buddhist Practice in Kep Province, Cambodia'. *Journal of Southeast Asian Studies*, 43(1): 23–49.

Okell, John. 1971. *A Guide to the Romanization of Burmese*, London: Luzac and the Royal Asiatic Society of Great Britain and Ireland.

Ouédraogo, Jean Martin. 2010. 'Désenchantement', in R. Azria and D. Hervieu-Léger (eds), *Dictionnaire des faits religieux*. Paris, Presses universitaires de France: 241–246.

Pattana Kitiarsa (ed.). 2008. *Religious Commodifications in Asia: Marketing Gods*. London and New York: Routledge.

———. 2012. *Mediums, Monks and Amulets: Thai Popular Buddhism Today*. Chiang Mai: Silkworm Books.

Picard, Michel (ed.). 2017. *The Appropriation of Religion in Southeast Asia and Beyond*. New York: Palgrave.

Saler, Michael. 2006. 'Modernity and Enchantment: A Historiographic Review', *American Historical Review*, (June): 692–716.

Schober, Juliane. 2011. *Modern Buddhist Conjunctures in Myanmar: Cultural Narratives, Colonial Legacies and Civil Society*. Honolulu: University of Hawai'i Press.

Siani, Edoardo. 2018. 'Stranger Diviners and their Stranger Clients: Popular Cosmology-Making and its Kingly Power in Buddhist Thailand', *South East Asia Research*, 26(4): 416–431.

Sorrentino, Paul. 2018. 'Question religieuse et sécularisation', in Benoît Tréglodé (dir.), *Histoire du Viêt Nam de la colonisation à nos jours*. Paris: Editions de la Sorbonne: 219–238.

Spiro, Melford. 1970. *Buddhism and Society: A Great Tradition and its Burmese Vicissitudes*. Berkeley: University of California Press.

———. 1978 [1967]. *Burmese Supernaturalism: A Study in the Explanation and Reduction of Suffering*. Philadelphia: Institute for the Study of Human Issues.

Stolow, Jeremy. 2005. 'Religion and/as Media', *Theory, Culture and Society*, 22(4): 119–145.

Tambiah, Stanley J. 1970. *Buddhism and the Spirit Cults in North-east Thailand*, Cambridge: Cambridge University Press.

———. 1977. 'The Cosmological and Performative Significance of a Thai Cult of Healing Through Meditation', *Culture, Medicine and Psychiatry*, 1: 97–132.

———. 1984. *The Buddhist Saints of the Forest and the Cult of Amulets: A Study in Charisma, Hagiography, Sectarianism, and Millennial Buddhism*. Cambridge: Cambridge University Press.

———. 1985. *Culture, Thought and Social Action: An Anthropological Perspective*. Cambridge, Mass: Harvard University Press.

———. 1990. *Magic, Science, Religion and the Scope of Rationality*. Cambridge: Cambridge University Press.

Tanabe, Shigeharu. 1991. 'Spirits, Power and the Discourse of Female Gender: The Phi Meng Cult of Northern Thailand', in Manas Chitakasem and Andrew Turton (eds), *Thai Constructions of Knowledge*. London: School of Oriental and African Studies: 183–207.

Tarabout, Gilles. 1999. 'Prologue' in J. Assayag and G. Tarabout (eds), *La possession en Asie du Sud: Paroles, corps, territoire*. Paris: Purushartha, MSH.

Taylor, Philip. 2004. *The Goddess on the Rise: Pilgrimage and Popular Religion in Vietnam*. Honolulu: University of Hawai'i Press.

Turner, Alicia. 2014. *Saving Buddhism: The Impermanence of Religion in Colonial Burma*. Honolulu: University of Hawai'i Press.

van der Veer, Peter. 2014. *The Modern Spirit of Asia: The Spiritual and the Secular in China and India*. Princeton University Press.

Weber, Max. 1958 [1905]. *The Protestant Ethic and the Spirit of Capitalism*, trans. Talcott Parsons. New York: Scribner.

Weller, Robert P. 2008. 'Asia and the Global Economies of Charisma', in Pattana Kitiarsa (ed.), *Religious Commodifications in Asia: Marketing Gods*. London and New York: Routledge: 15–30.

White, Erick. 2014. 'Possession, Professional Spirit Mediums, and the Religious Fields of Late-Twentieth Century Thailand', PhD dissertation, Cornell University.

———. 'Contemporary Buddhism and Magic', in Michael Jerryson (ed.), *The Oxford Handbook of Contemporary Buddhism*. Oxford Handbooks Online. DOI: 10.1093/oxfordhb/9780199362387.013.34.

———. 2017. 'Rethinking Anthropological Models of Spirit Possession and Theravada Buddhism', *Religion and Society*, 8, special section: *Toward a Comparative Anthropology of Buddhism*, Patrice Ladwig and Nicolas Sihlé (eds): 189–202.

CHAPTER 1

Whose Religion is the Cult of the Four Palaces?
Genealogies of a Vietnamese Pantheon

Paul Sorrentino

Introduction

*I*n December 2016, 'Practices related to the Viet beliefs in the Mother Goddesses of Three Realms' were inscribed on UNESCO's Representative List of the Intangible Cultural Heritage of Humanity.[1] This inscription, which took place at the initiative of Vietnamese authorities, can be seen as rather surprising when one knows that no more than three decades ago, those practices, centred on spirit possession séances, were still considered illegal by the Communist state. Seen as a backward superstition that should be cleared from the path to modernity, they had been forbidden following the 1945 revolution and had survived in a state of relative concealment. This worship of an ensemble of deities belonging to three or four 'Realms' or 'Palaces' (*Phủ*), referred to by its practitioners with a variety of names such as 'cult of the Four Palaces' (*thờ Tứ Phủ*), 'cult of the Many Honourable Beings' (*thờ Chư Vị*), or the 'spirits' side' (*bên thánh* – as opposed to the Buddha's side, *bên Phật*), has recently become widely known as the 'Mother Goddess Religion' (*Đạo Mẫu*), one of the official names included in the inventory documents sent to UNESCO by the Vietnamese authorities.

Spreading along with this new name, the idea that these practices pertain to a Vietnamese 'indigenous' (*bản địa*) religion has become commonly accepted within the country. Such autochthony has been invoked in contrast to all the major religious traditions that have currency in Vietnam, such as

---

1 See online: ich.unesco.org/en/RL/practices-related-to-the-viet-beliefs-in-the-mother-goddesses-of-three-realms-01064 (accessed 7 August 2021).

Buddhism, Taoism or Christianity, which are considered as having originated from foreign cultures. Thus, the Mother Goddess Religion would be a properly Vietnamese heritage, as opposed to Indian, European and, particularly, Chinese cultural influences, since the current Vietnamese political context is characterised by growing tensions surrounding relations with China, which the Vietnamese nationalist narrative depicts as the invader *par excellence*.

However, one can only be struck by the overwhelming presence of Sinicised elements in the aesthetics and practices of this cult: heavenly bureaucracy, mandarins in the Jade Emperor's court, Sinographic writings, and so on. This is fundamentally unsurprising, as Vietnamese culture is generally strongly influenced by centuries of belonging to the margins of China – and my point is in no way to attest to either the actual 'Vietnamese' or 'Chinese' character of these practices. But how, then, should one interpret this heritagisation and autochthonisation of a so-called Vietnamese Mother Goddess Religion? This essay aims at questioning the apparent paradox entailed by the promotion of a local Vietnamese identity and the omnipresence of a Sinitic bureaucratic reference.

A few cautionary remarks are necessary. First, much of my understanding of the cult of the Four Palaces is based on my first-hand experience of ethnographic fieldwork as the disciple of a master of ritual (*thầy cúng*) who, among many other tasks, regularly performed the complex invocations preceding the cult's spirit possession séances in various regions of Northern Vietnam. Over this period – mainly between the years 2007 and 2010, and more sporadically since then – I spent long hours sitting with spirit mediums and shared countless 'spirit blessing' meals with them. However, the cult never became a central topic of my research, which soon focused on possession by ancestors and other dead relatives rather than by deified beings. Thus, this chapter is a late, and somehow distant, tribute to the many practitioners who have shared their time and knowledge with me. Secondly, as I have done most of my fieldwork in Hanoi and the Red River delta, my perspective on the Four Palaces is very much a Northern one.[2] However, one of the points of this chapter is precisely to decentre this perspective by questioning centre–periphery relations. Finally, although I am not a historian, this chapter's central argument is somewhat historical. One could say I am trying to make

---

2 As is the case of most publications on Vietnamese Mother Goddess Religion, with the notable exception of Taylor 2004.

sense of traces of historical processes crystalised in the cult's contemporary practices. Without further research in collaboration with historians, it remains speculative in nature. But I believe the arguments formulated here are solid enough to be worthy of scholarly discussion.

After a quick description of the cult's ritual forms, I will recall the way it was constructed as an indigenous religion. From there, I will discuss the kind of imaginary its aesthetics, imagery and poetics construct, suggesting it is less a cosmological than political one. This will lead me to question the notion of 'pantheon,' a central feature in recent literature on the cult, in order to trace its colonial and post-colonial genealogy. Finally, I will show how the cult's practices and forms can be seen as a typically analogist way to articulate autochthony and centralised authority, even in its most recent manifestations, including the scholarship it has given birth to.

Spirit possession and the Four Palaces

The highlight of the cult's worship practices is a ritual called *lên đồng* (literally 'riding the medium') or *hầu bóng* (serving the shadows). It consists in spirit possession séances, which take place in front of an altar dedicated to the deities of the Four Palaces, in a public temple or in a private sanctuary. A *lên đồng* ritual generally involves one spirit medium[3] (*đồng*), who successively embodies several spirits of the Four Palaces, some of whom may be represented on the altar by statues, paintings, or worshipping tablets. The spirit medium is supported by their assistants (*hầu dâng*) who serve the embodied deities, and musicians (*cung văn*) who sing hymns (*văn chầu*) dedicated to the deities of the Four Palaces.

After a preliminary petition ceremony during which the spirits are invited by masters of ritual, the spirit medium sits in front of the altar and the séance begins. Several spirits will then manifest themselves through the medium's body successively, following a given order. For each spirit embodied, the ritual unfolds following a similar sequence of actions, called *giá*, a word that literally refers to the celestial chariot/carriage on which the deity descends to the ritual space, but is commonly used by practitioners to refer to the manifestation of each particular spirit.

---

3 In the Hue area, séances usually entail the simultaneous embodiment of several spirits by several spirit mediums. See Tran Van Toan 1966b; Bertrand 1996; Salemink 2008.

Each *giá* starts with the medium sitting with their head and bust covered by a long red veil, swinging in a slow and circular movement amplified by the soft fabric. After a few seconds, a tremor and a codified hand gesture indicate the arrival of a given spirit. The medium then removes the red veil and, as the musicians start playing the spirit's specific hymn, the assistants dress the medium according to the embodied spirit's identity. Once dressed as the deity, the medium stands up and makes an incense offering, bowing in front of the altar where the deities of the Four Palaces are represented. The medium will then perform a dance, which will vary depending on the spirit's identity: sword or halberd dance for Great Mandarins; candle dance for the Little Lady of the High Regions; rowing dance for the Third Damsel of the Palace of Water; and so on. After the dance, the medium sits back while petitions and offerings are presented to the spirit by the assistants or audience members. Once these offerings are accepted, the embodied deity distributes them back to all the participants as spirit blessings (*lộc*). A few words may be shared with the spirit at this moment, usually limited to stereotypical formulas. After listening to more praising from the musicians, the spirit announces their departure. While the assistants are covering the medium's body with the red veil, the musicians describe the spirit's chariot flying back to the sky. The medium will then announce either the arrival of another deity or the end of the séance.

The ensemble of spirits embodied during *lên đồng* rituals is organised according to two main principles. The first of these two principles is a hierarchy of ranks, alternatively female and male, successively embodied by the spirit medium in decreasing hierarchical order: the three Mother Goddesses will appear first, followed by the Great Mandarins, the Ladies, the Princes, the Damsels and the Young Princes. Spirits of a given rank wear a similar type of clothing and their *giá* tend to share the same kind of atmosphere: mysterious for the Mother Goddesses, who remain hidden under the red veil and only perform an incense offering; solemn for the Great Mandarins; lively or sentimental for the Damsels; playful for the Young Princes; and so on.

The second principle is the attribution, within each rank, of an ordinal number to each spirit, which also indicates which one of the four 'Palaces' they belong to: Heaven, Mountains, Water or Earth. Thus, the First Prince belongs to the Palace of Heaven, the Second Lady to the Palace of Mountains, the Third Great Mandarin to the Palace of Water, and the Fourth Damsel to the Palace of Earth. There are only three Mother Goddesses (of Heaven,

Mountains, and Water), but all the other ranks have more than four known spirits. As a consequence, the ordinal number of each spirit determines a series of details, such as the dominant colour of their clothes and of the offerings dedicated to them (red, green, white and yellow for the Palaces of Heaven, Mountains, Water and Earth, respectively), or the kind of landscapes that are described in their hymns (forests for the Palace of Mountains, rivers and lakes for the Palace of Water).

People get involved in this cult for various reasons, usually converging toward the notion of *căn* (spirit root), that is the idea that one's destiny is troubled because of a particular connection with one or several spirits. As in most spirit possession cults, finding out that one has such a connection very often has to do with a sense of being out of place, misfortune, and subaltern positions. These aspects of the cult have been widely and repeatedly described and commented upon in international scholarship (see Chauvet 2004; Fjelstad and Nguyen 2006; Endres 2011). In this chapter, however, I would like to focus on the fact that, despite being deeply intertwined with individual fates, *lên đồng* rituals are extremely liturgical in nature. In other words, while the cult thrives on individual relations between the practitioners and their spirits of election, its rituals take none of these narratives into account: action in a spirit possession séance for the Four Palaces is basically always the same, and it is very much about displaying the presence of this ensemble of spirits.

The invention of an indigenous religion

The recognition of these practices as a Vietnamese indigenous heritage is the outcome of a long process, not limited to a mere political 'opening' triggered by the implementation of the Communist Party of Vietnam's Renovation policy (*Đổi mới*) from the late 1980s. It rather results from a negotiated rehabilitation entailing the active contribution of Vietnamese scholars. Among them, Professor Ngô Đức Thịnh, a folklorist and anthropologist working at the Institute for Cultural Research of the Vietnam Academy of Social Sciences, played a central role. After organising several academic events and publications on the literary and musical aspects of the cult in the early 1990s – as its more religious aspects were too sensitive to be addressed as such – Ngô Đức Thịnh coined the term *Đạo Mẫu* (Mother Goddess Religion) in a book first published in 1996. Since then, the book has been reprinted and even republished in new versions, and the notion of a 'Mother Goddess Religion' has flourished in parallel with the cult's gradual reappearance in the Vietnamese public sphere.

There were many steps on the path that led to the 2016 UNESCO recognition. These included a special issue of the multilingual journal *Vietnamese Studies* in 1999 and an international conference in 2001 that brought the cult into the paradigm of shamanic studies and attracted the attention of foreign scholars, whose subsequent field research and publications during the following decade benefitted directly from Ngô Đức Thịnh and his colleagues' earlier efforts. The last steps before the Vietnamese government applied for the inscription of the cult's practices on UNESCO's list were the organisation – by a group of Vietnamese intellectuals and spirit mediums – of a public possession ceremony in the French Cultural Centre in Hanoi in 2011 and their recognition by the National Cultural Heritage Committee in 2012.

Although this process has already been commented upon (see Dror 2007; Salemink 2008; Phạm Quỳnh Phương 2009; Endres 2011), I would like to emphasise the specific stakes of the construction of the cult of the Four Palaces as a Vietnamese indigenous Mother Goddess Religion *as opposed to* foreign, and especially Chinese, religious traditions. While Vietnam is still recovering from the wounds left by the border war with China that broke out in 1979 (Goscha 2015), the recent increase in geopolitical tensions surrounding the various territorial claims on islands in the South China Sea (called Eastern Sea in Vietnam) has turned the bilateral relationship into one of the major points of contestation of the Communist Party of Vietnam's legitimacy (Tréglodé 2019). Religion and heritage matters are no exception, as is well illustrated by recent official regulations that repeatedly required that places of worship recognised as sites of historical value be stripped off all ornamental elements of foreign origin, such as the 8 June 2014 circular 2662/BVHTTDL of the Ministry of Culture, Sports and Tourism. These regulations aimed at responding to controversies surrounding images of 'Chinese lions' that were supposedly proliferating at the gates of temples throughout the country. The problem with such a project of purification of Vietnamese spiritual culture is that its limit may be hard to identify: among all the areas of Vietnamese social life, religious practices are probably one among those in which references to Sinitic culture are the most ubiquitous and explicit – through the massive presence of Sino-Vietnamese characters, to begin with.

For that matter, one could raise the same kind of issue about the so-called indigenous Mother Goddess Religion, as its mythology and imagery are imbued with Sinitic culture. Several of the spirits of the Four Palaces are related to Chinese mythology – starting with Princess Liễu Hạnh, the Mother Goddess of the Palace of Heaven and main deity of the cult, who is said to be the Jade Emperor's daughter – or geography, such as Dongting Lake, located in China's Hunan Province, where several spirits are said to have their origins or previous incarnations. Of course, my point here is not to draw a line between what is Vietnamese and what is Chinese – a likely anthropological dead end – but rather to stress the fact that the cult of the Four Palaces has been constructed as an indigenous religion *despite* its Sinicised aspects. Many of the spirits of the Four Palaces, while being avatars or descendants of Chinese mythological characters, are simultaneously identified as historical characters who defended the nation against Chinese invaders during the many conflicts that opposed the early Vietnamese nation and the neighbouring empire.

After all, spirit possession is a common feature of 'peripheral cults' where subaltern views and concerns can be voiced (Lewis 1971). From such a perspective, one could look at the exaggeratedly stiff posture and gait of a Vietnamese spirit medium enacting a Great Mandarin's offering of incense the same way Jean Rouch famously depicted, in 1950s Ghana, Hauka *maîtres fous* who extravagantly embodied British colonial figures such as the 'Lieutenant', the 'General' or the 'Locomotive' in their possession rituals (Rouch 1955; see also Stoller 1995). Of course, such comparisons must take into account very different contexts: while the Hauka spirit possession séances undoubtedly took place in a colonial situation, the cult of the Four Palaces seems to have thrived around the 17th and 18th centuries, when the Vietnamese realm's independence had been secured, and internal fractures and rivalries were much more of a concern than external threats. At that time, the mandarinal administration system had been appropriated by the Đại Việt state. However, this parallel invites us to look at the way Sinitic bureaucracy is depicted in *lên đồng* rituals as a potentially distantiated – if not critical – point of view on a certain form of government, rather than a mere representation of a celestial administration.[4]

4　On the Chinese model of heavenly bureaucracy, see Feuchtwang 2001.

Figure 1.1. A spirit medium embodying the Third Great Mandarin of the Palace of Water. **Colour** p. 312.

The imaginary of the Four Palaces

In order to understand what kind of point of view is suggested in the rituals of the Four Palaces, let us have a look at the kind of imaginary it constructs through its aesthetics, imagery, and poetics. Much of the Vietnamese scholarship and public discourse on the Mother Goddess Religion tends to describe it as a remnant of an ancient agrarian matriarchal indigenous religion (see for instance Le-Van Hao 1963; Nguyễn Đăng Thục 1982 [1967]; Ngô Đức Thịnh 1992; Kiều Thu Hoạch 2019). These writings emphasise the worship of nature (*thờ thiên nhiên*), cosmological aspects (*vũ trụ luận*), and agrarian dimensions (*nền văn minh nông nghiệp*) of the cult, speculating on the notion that the Palaces of Heaven, Mountains, Water and Earth are depictions of the natural world, and that the Mother Goddesses embody fertility and the power of creation.

However, it seems to me that the imaginary of the Four Palaces is less about 'nature' than about politics. Although the structure of the Four Palaces suggests some kind of cosmological organisation, this aspect is not developed in the cult's mythology, hymns and imagery, which do not include theories about the way the universe was created or the systematic relations between Heaven, Mountains, Water and Earth. Similarly, agricultural labour barely appears in the cult, and its practices, including periodical festivals, are rarely connected to agrarian rituals.

Rather, what is made most explicit in the cult's imaginary is its hierarchical bureaucratic system: spirits are organised in ranks, and the attributes of many of them evoke imperial court life. This is particularly obvious when the Great Mandarins are embodied: dressed for solemn audiences with the emperor and displaying their identification plate (*hốt*), they pay their respects against a background of court music (the *lưu thủy* theme). In the *văn châu* hymns, most deities of the Four Palaces are described as aristocratic

Figure 1.2. Video-screenshot of a spirit medium embodying the Third Prince of the Palace of Water. **Colour** p. 312.

figures or as administrators who have been invested with sovereign authority. In videos of spirit possession séances widely shared on digital platforms by spirit mediums, special effects are sometimes added when the embodied spirit 'signs' (using an incandescent incense stick) the petitions which are presented to them, thus suggesting that their spiritual responsiveness lies, at least in part, in their bureaucratic efficacy.

Natural landscapes do appear as a significant aspect of the cult's imaginary. They are a recurrent element in the hymns dedicated to the spirits, and the videos shared by contemporary mediums almost always include slow panoramic shots of lakes, rivers, hills, passes or valleys related to the hagiography of the spirits summoned during the séances (see figure 1.2). However, these landscapes are described less as traces of a process of creation or the universe's complex balance than as spaces and places that need to be watched, protected and managed. This is particularly prominent in the vocabulary of the *văn chầu* hymns. Thus, in the Second Lady's hymn, the deity – who is supposed to have assisted King Lê Lợi in his struggle against the Ming – is said to 'wield power on the mountains and hills' (*quyền hành núi non*) and to have been 'sent down to this world in order to administer the high regions, to administer the valleys and the hamlets' (*giáng sinh hạ giới quản cai thượng ngàn/quản cai các lũng các làng*). Similarly, the Third Great Mandarin of the Palace of Water, 'governs in the name of the sovereign' (*cầm quyền thay chúa*) and is sent on an 'inspection tour on Thương River' (*có phen tuần thú sông Thương*). This vocabulary is not limited to hymns. For example, among practitioners of the cult, the Fifth Great Mandarin is also known as the Great Mandarin Warden of Tranh (*Quan Lớn Tuần Tranh*), in reference to the river where, during his this-worldly lifetime, he would have defeated Chinese armies.

Such a lexical field of political power and administration combined with actual toponyms suggests that, in the imaginary of the Four Palaces, geography is essentially a matter of sovereignty. It is less about landscape as an index of 'nature' than landscape as territory. Myths about the spirits are filled with stories of administrators sent to establish imperial rule in remote regions, away from their lonely spouses. The map drawn by the hagiographies and main sanctuaries of the Four Palace deities spreads between the Lào Cai mountainous border region and the Ngang pass in Hà Tĩnh province, characteristic of the later and restored Lê dynasty era (1533–1788), during which the cult's first expansion probably occurred (Dror 2007). This historicised geography continues to evolve: in most *văn chầu* collections available today, the hymn of the Tenth Lady of the Palace of Earth lists, among the many places where she likes to wander throughout the country, the hill station of Đà Lạt, which was founded in the early 20th century by the French.

The political imaginary of the cult is manifest in one of its most common designations. The notion of *phủ*, translated as 'palace' in most scholarship on the cult while the translators of the UNESCO application survey opted for the more abstract idea of 'realm', can refer to the building where a politically important character resides – and, metaphorically, to a government – as well as to an administrative unit of imperial Vietnam's mountainous areas. Thus, the Four Palaces could as well be called the Four Prefectures. More generally, landscapes described in *văn chầu* hymns are not restricted to so-called 'natural' features, and the latter generally tend to have strategic value for warfare or civil administration (Nguyễn Hùng Vĩ 2018; see also Phạm and Eipper 2009: 61). Thus, the geographic imaginary of the Four Palaces is less evocative of an archaic agrarian society than of an imperial polity's expanding state, with its markets and urban centres, piers and passes, roads and toll gates.

Nonetheless, a certain idea of nourishing wilderness is present in the cult's imaginary, under the traits of the Palace of Mountains, *Nhạc Phủ*, which could as well be translated as Palace of Forests. This realm is somehow duplicated as most sanctuaries include, next to the main Four Palaces altar, an altar dedicated to the 'Mountain Estates' (*Sơn Trang*), which usually features a statue of the Princess of the Mountain Estates (*Chúa Sơn Trang*), also known as the Mother of the High Regions (*Mẫu Thượng Ngàn*), and as the Second Lady of the Palace of Mountains. In their hymns, female spirits of the High Regions – who all belong to the Palace of Mountains – are described strolling in lush forests inhabited by wild animals, where they pick flowers and harvest fruits. The specific offerings presented to them are considered particularly 'natural': betel leaves and areca nuts, boiled river crabs and shrimps, fresh chili pepper and ginger roots.

Female deities of the Palace of Mountains are attributed upland ethnic identities. The Second Lady, for example, is said to have been born into a Mán (or Dao) family in today's Yên Bái province, and the clothes and jewellry she wears are seen as typical of highland women. Although they might be seen as figures of otherness, their hagiographies and hymns suggest that they contribute – or have submitted – to imperial rule by looking after the remote regions they inhabit. The Second Lady, for instance, is known for having helped Lê Lợi, the founder of Lê dynasty, in his struggle against the Ming armies. This suggests that these female deities of the High Regions are less symbols of otherness than expressions of a notion of being indigenous.[5] They are figures of autochthony.

This duplication of the Palace of Mountains and Mountain Estates is manifest in one of the cult's major rituals, the 'opening of the palaces' (*mở phủ*), which finalises the initiation process of a new spirit medium. *Mở phủ* is a spirit possession séance where spirits of the Four Palaces are embodied first by the master medium and then by a newly tenured disciple. The master's intervention is more elaborate, but shorter than a standard *lên đồng* séance, as only a few spirits appear on stage. Besides the five Great Mandarins, who perform a complex set of operations aiming at 'opening the palaces', that is, allowing the new medium to serve the spirits, the master medium embodies only the Second Lady of the Palace of Mountains. This detail – which has been overlooked in scholarship – is of great importance: while the male spirits exert bureaucratic efficacy in order to grant the new medium an administrative mandate, the Second Lady's intervention is meant to prepare the novice, as a person, for mediumship. In order to do so, she performs direct actions on their body (such as purifying it by exposing it to lit candles or spraying perfume on them) and 'transmits the [red] veil' (*sang khăn*), the most precious object in a medium's equipment, quintessential to the practice of spirit possession.

Thus, the Palace of Mountains seems to have a particular status. Like the four other realms, it is administered by a Great Mandarin, but another figure, the Second Lady or Princess of the Mountain Estates, also reigns on the High

---

5   Until the implementation of colonial ethnic categories at the turn of the 20th century, uplanders were not necessarily seen as essential others, but rather as potential kin and inhabitants of the same polity living in physical margins: lowlanders could decide to become uplanders and *vice versa* (Taylor 2001: 29), following a 'view of difference that was mainly political and held possibilities for political action that we cannot imagine for an "ethnic minority" in a modern state' (*ibid*: 33).

Regions, and she makes a decisive contribution to the transformation of a follower of the spirits into a spirit medium. What I would like to emphasise here is a suggested complementarity between a male, mandarinal kind of legitimacy, and a more embodied, female form of indigenous authority.

Through his analysis of the cult's musical and lyrical repertoire, Barley Norton has implied that the main internal opposition within the ensemble of deities of the Four Palaces is the opposition between male and female spirits, which somehow parallels the opposition between lowland/delta and mountain/forest spirits (2009: 62–65). Taking into account the political implications of the Four Palaces' imaginary, I would add that this opposition is analogous with a dialectics of administrative rule and regional autochthony. There is, in the imaginary world of the Four Palaces, something of a narrative tension between managing landscapes and belonging to them.

The Four Palaces as a 'pantheon'

Let us now turn to the way the beings that populate the Four Palaces are organised, as this has become a central aspect in contemporary discourses on the cult. Indeed, foreign scholarship has dedicated many pages to what it refers to as the 'pantheon' of the Four Palaces, but these pages barely touch upon what I have always seen as a puzzling contradiction regarding this so-called pantheon.

On the one hand, the ensemble of spirits worshipped by the mediums seems to be organised in a very systematic way and appears, so to speak, as a combinatory structure, where each spirit is defined by a hierarchical rank and a number indicating their position. As a consequence, the most common way to refer to individual spirits is by assembling a set of two coordinates, such as: the Fifth Great Mandarin, the Second Lady, or the Seventh Prince. This aspect of spirits as generic entities is dominant in the material and visual culture of the cult. The statuary is eloquent: statues displayed on a Four Palace altar have, for a given rank, strictly similar shape and traits. They only differ by the colour of their clothes, indicative of the Palace to which they belong. The same generic aesthetics prevails in the woodprints hung in the sanctuaries (see figure 1.3). They usually feature several spirits, represented sitting in hierarchical ranks, within which individual spirits only differ in colour. Similarly, portraits of deities of the same rank tend to use the same woodblock, with only variations in the colour filling. In the *văn chầu*, this

Figure 1.3. Woodprint featuring spirits of the Four Palaces. **Colour** p. 313.

results in verses or formal elements (melodic patterns, rhythms) shared between spirits belonging to the same rank or Palace.

On the other hand, however, the pantheon of the Four Palaces simultaneously appears as an incredibly rich and complex set of individual deities, with their own stories, geographies and personalities. Although this is far from being the case for all of them, some are endowed with lush and detailed hagiographies. Olga Dror (2007) dedicated a whole monograph to Princess Liễu Hạnh, the Mother Goddess of the Palace of Heaven, comparing and contextualising the numerous versions of her hagiography. Some of the most popular spirits of the pantheon have several names, which sometimes reflect complex, if not contradictory, identities. How could the Fifth Mandarin be the son of the legendary Dragon King of (China's) Dongting Lake, as mentioned in his *văn chầu* hymn, *and* have defeated Qin Chinese invaders near Tranh River, to which he owes his title? The Tenth Prince, whose famous main sanctuary is located at the border of Nghệ An and Hà Tĩnh provinces, is assimilated to at least three different historical characters: Nguyễn Xí and Lê Khôi, two 15th century Lê dynasty war heroes, and Nguyễn Duy Lạc, who fought against the Nguyễn lords under the restored Lê dynasty in the 18th century (Nguyễn Thị Hiệp 2007: 36–37).

Moreover, there are overlaps and resonances among the pantheon's spirits. Versions of myths associated with the Third Mother Goddess and the Third Lady tell the same story of a daughter of the Dragon King incarnated as a human, married to a scholar named Kinh Xuyên, who later sent them into exile because of a jealous second wife's plot. Similarly, several temples

Figure 1.4. The Seventh Prince represented on a calendar for 2013. **Colour** p. 313.

are sometimes described as a given deity's main sanctuary, and several deities can share the same main temple. Some spirits are very clearly identified, like the Seventh Prince, a notorious gambler, womaniser and opium smoker whose sanctuary is located in Lào Cai province. Others are much more weakly defined, such as the Fifth Lady or the Fourth Prince.

This contradiction between an apparent systematicity yet an actual variability and idiosyncratic diversity is also expressed in some recent imagery of the cult, such as painter Trịnh Yên's series of portraits of the pantheon's characters, combining oil painting and electronically edited collage (see figure 1.4). They all feature a realistic full-length representation of the spirit's human incarnation with a highly detailed outfit, surrounded by digitally inserted elements of scenery, paraphernalia or additional characters, referring to the portrayed spirit's hagiography or worship geography. The Seventh Prince is thus represented with his long pipe, surrounded by groups of fairy-like young women. Many of these visual elements are literally copy-pasted and appear on several paintings in the series, very much like musical or narrative motifs distributed in the *văn chầu* repertoire, forming what, in our conversations, the painter referred to as a 'mandala'.

Numerous websites dedicated to the 'Mother Goddess Religion' also produce a new imagery inspired by woodblock images of the pantheon. Interestingly, they accommodate their serial aspects by representing in a single picture the totality of the pantheon's ranks and, within each rank, the twenty or so most commonly embodied spirits. In line with the textual contents of these websites, these images lean towards a more systematic representation of the pantheon combined with a more faithful display of the deities that actually manifest themselves during *lên đồng* séances.[6] Nonetheless, exhaustivity seems unattainable and the choices made in terms of which spirits should appear, what level of detail should be used to distinguish them from each other (colour, clothing, etc.) vary from one image to the other.

In short, the pantheon is characterised by a tension between, on the one hand, a strongly generic and combinatory classification system, in which each deity's identity can be boiled down to a set of two coordinates and, on the other, a rich collection of individual beings with their own hagiographies and geographies, who never seem to perfectly fit the position they were assigned within the classification.

This tension remains unaddressed in scholarship, despite brief comments on 'the pantheon's actual messiness' (Endres 2011:16; see also Norton 2009: 57). Even Pierre-Jean Simon and Ida Simon-Barouh, in their tentative structural analysis of the pantheon's organisation, emphasising its systematic nature, were forced to note that 'a whole portion of the pantheon remains in the dark' (Simon and Simon-Barouh 1973: 79). The problem became particularly acute to me when a Vietnamese colleague sought my advice for the translation of Maurice Durand's seminal study *Technique et panthéon des médiums vietnamiens* (1959) she was working on. Although the word appeared repeatedly throughout the book and in its title, this Vietnamese scholar with a literary background and a solid experience in translation was nonetheless meeting great difficulty in deciding for an accurate translation of this notion of 'pantheon'. Thus, the most influential work on the cult of the Four Palaces and, in its wake, much of the subsequent foreign scholarship, appears to be centered on a notion which does not echo with a vernacular concept.

Durand, a Hanoi-born French-Vietnamese literary scholar who conducted research for École Française d'Extrême-Orient during the 1950s, was the first author to dedicate a whole ethnographic monograph to the cult of the Four Palaces, based on his attendance at séances held by Hanoian mediums. None of the earlier French scholars who had mentioned the cult (Giran 1912 for example) described it in terms of a pantheon. *Technique et panthéon* was published two years after he relocated to Paris and began teaching at École Pratique des Hautes Études.

---

6   For an example, see : phuday.com/he-thong-than-linh-tu-phu.html (accessed 13 December 2021).

The book's title is an explicit reference to Mircea Eliade's *Le chamanisme et les techniques archaïques de l'extase* (1950), which appears in Durand's bibliography as well as in his hypotheses on an 'ancient [Vietnamese] shamanism' (1959: 7). More generally, Durand's search for an archaic shamanic tradition that may transpire through the cult (*ibid*: 7, 45–47) and his rather loose practice of cross-cultural comparison (*ibid*: 7, 16, 21, 28, 29) suggest that his book was written with the readership of 1950s French history of religions in mind. A central figure in this intellectual environment was Georges Dumézil, who was also teaching at École Pratique des Hautes Études, and happened to be Eliade's mentor. Although he is not explicitly cited in Durand's book, Dumézil's approach to the notion of *panthéon* as a structured system for classification of the world (1952) is definitely the one that Durand has adopted in his description of the pantheon of the Four Palaces.

Durand's approach met the agenda of Vietnamese (late-)socialist scholarship in search for the deep roots of a national identity, in line with another recurrent reference in Vietnamese writings on the cult of the Four Palaces, namely, Soviet anthropologist Sergei Tokarev and his evolutionist hypotheses on shamanism (see Ngô Đức Thịnh 1992; Nguyễn Ngọc Mai 2013; Kiều Thu Hoạch 2019). But this appropriation took place without much interest in the French notion of *panthéon* itself, which was incidentally translated in various – and often very literal – ways.

These issues of translation and appropriation of Durand's approach further encourage the examination of what this so-called pantheon is about. Is it a mere scholarly artefact or does it reveal, with its very contradictions, something about what is at stake in the seemingly unfinished construction of an ensemble of spirits under the aegis of the Four Palaces?

An articulation of autochthony and state

Although they haven't been used by Vietnamese scholars as translations of the word 'pantheon', there actually are notions in the lexicon of the worshippers of the Four Palaces that express the kindred idea of a coherent ensemble of spirits. The hymn that opens most *văn chầu* collections is entitled *Tứ Phủ Công Đồng văn*, which literally means the 'hymn for the Community of the Four Palaces.' Its text lists a great number of characters, most of whom are not embodied during spirit possession séances, such as the Jade Emperor and his entourage. In daily conversations, worshippers also refer to the general ensemble of spirits as the 'Many Honorable Beings' (*Chư Vị*), which is also commonly used as a way to name the cult. They also often mention the 'Thirty-Six Chariots' (*Ba Mươi Sáu Giá*), echoing the manifestation of each individual spirit during a possession séance (*cf. supra*). This notion is particularly interesting in the sense that I never met a practitioner who was able or – more importantly – had any interest in listing the detail of the thirty-six spirits referred to by the expression. This number rather indicates an idea of diversity and totality, like the common expression 'thirty-six streets' (*ba mươi sáu phố phường*) referring to Hanoi's old market quarter, which has never had exactly thirty-six streets.

What these notions indicate is that the ensemble of spirits need not be mathematically coherent. This principle of abstract totality actually applies to other series within the Four Palaces, such as the damsels who form the Princess of the High Regions' entourage, whose number varies between 12, 36, and even 120. The very number of domains in the system is subject to variation, as the cult is sometimes said to be dedicated to the Three Palaces (*Tam Phủ*). While this point stirs heated debates among Vietnamese scholars (see Nguyễn Đăng Thục 1992 [1967]: 318; Ngô Đức Thịnh 1992: 16; Kiều Thu Hoạch 2019: 54–55) and my more 'modernist' interlocutors – intellectuals with an interest in spirituality – it does not seem to pose any problem to most worshippers who use the two numbers alternatively.[7] French colonial scholars also tended to approach these variations with unease. Paul Giran, who dedicated a chapter of his *Magie et religion annamites* to the 'cult of the Three Realms', speculated on the late addition of a fourth Palace to the system (1912: 267–294). His evolutionist interpretations of what he saw as a 'lack of detail accuracy and the contradictions' indicative of 'a weakly established and inopportune piece of doctrine'[8] (*ibid.*: 271) stemmed from a mistaken search for an arithmetic coherence within the system of the Four Palaces, missing the point of an abstract idea of totality.

---

7 'Three Palaces' (*Tam Phủ*) are mentioned in a number of ritual texts and procedures, but they are not directly connected to the worship of the ensemble of spirits embodied by spirit mediums, such as the 'Offering to the Three Palaces for the redeeming of destiny' (*cúng Tam Phủ thục mệnh*). The Three Palaces (of Heaven, Water and Earth) summoned in this ritual have little to do with the pantheon of the Four Palaces. The two systems just share very common notions of Sino-Vietnamese cosmology, such as elemental classifications and the overarching authority of the Jade Emperor.

8 As a reminder of the intellectual context, the preface of Paul Giran's monograph was written by Gustave Le Bon, the reactionary inventor of 'psychology of crowds.'

Later scholarship has become familiar with the more wobbly aspects of pantheons. In his appropriation of Dumézil's approach to studying the ancient Greek pantheon, Jean-Pierre Vernant described gods as powers linked by multiple networks of relations, emphasising the importance of so-called incoherencies and contradictions within such structures (Vernant 1963, 1965). In his wake, scholars of South Asia have shed new light on the notion of pantheon from the perspective of Hindu and Himalayan religious traditions, stressing features such as partial correspondences, variable numbers, names and genealogies of deities, and relations of encompassing rather than structural oppositions, allowing the coexistence of multiple viewpoints within a single cult or ritual (Malamoud 1989; Tarabout 1993; Schlemmer 2017).

These properties are typical of what Philippe Descola has coined as 'analogism' (2005: 280–281, 409–412), a predominant concern for coherence in a universe whose diversity is seen as being potentially infinite, textured by relations of correspondence between elements of various natures, such as colours, chemical elements, parts of the human body or of the cosmos, deities, stars or hours of the day. This coherence need not be permanent. On the contrary, societies with a strong analogic tendency are endowed with numerous practices aimed at finding ad-hoc coherence in complexity, such as astrology, physiognomy or numerology. The Chinese (and Sino-Vietnamese) 'penchant for correlative cosmology' (Verellen 2003: 26; see also Granet 1934) is archetypical of such concerns.

Stephen Bokenkamp's assessment of the notion of pantheon in the study of Chinese Daoism (2010) shows that lists of spirits that scholars have tended to essentialise were the outcome of regularisation processes following the agendas of various Daoist schools, sometimes in interaction with the imperial court's normalising efforts. Bokenkamp thus suggests scholarship should 'account for the rhetorical uses to which these lists of deities [were] put' (*ibid.*: 1181–1185) and seek what is accomplished through the mobilisation of this cultural resource.

What, then, is likely to be gained by constructing an ensemble of spirits worshipped within the system of the Four Palaces? My hypothesis is that this ensemble, characterised by one tension between systematicity and individuality and another between territorial administration and autochthony, can be understood as a device for the integration of local deities into an ensemble of national scale. Jack Goody's statement that 'the formalisation of a pantheon is often connected with the formation of the state, with the incorporation or identification of local gods within a wider national framework' (1986: 31–32) should thus be understood as the description of a continuing historical process. What first appeared as an unsolvable riddle then becomes a central feature of the cult: it may be the very fact that the structure of the Four Palaces is apprehended with much flexibility that makes it a powerful integrative tool. The Four Palaces and their Thirty-Six Chariots articulate totality and openness within a political imaginary of territorial administration. They are, so to speak, a tentative national pantheon. The ensemble of spirits worshipped and embodied by Vietnamese spirit mediums in *lên đồng* rituals is in constant evolution and transformation, involving spirits that are or were, in varying degrees, the object of local practices of worship.[9]

In support of this hypothesis, I would like to recount the story of Mother Goddess Cao Tiên (*Mẫu Cao Tiên*), featured in Édouard Diguet's (1895) *Les Annamites: Société, coutumes, religions*. Diguet, a colonial administrator stationed in upland Tonkin from 1893 to 1895, published several book-length studies on Northern highland populations and languages. In his last monograph, Diguet guides the reader through a detailed visit of several temples in the town of Cao Bằng, dedicating a few pages to what he calls the temple of 'Mother Goddess Cao Tiên' (1906: 319–324). According to the legendary account collected by Diguet, Cao Tiên was the daughter of Mạc Kính Vụ, supposedly the last descendant of the Mạc dynasty, known in Vietnamese historiography as usurpers of the Lê (16th century). Entrenched in Cao Bằng province, the Mạc's stronghold situated in the mountain range bordering China, Mạc Kính Vụ was defeated by Lê armies and sought refuge with his Ming protectors. During the battle, his daughter Cao Tiên fled on the back of an elephant, but she drowned in an attempt to cross the nearby Bằng Giang River. Her father's victorious enemies buried her and, following a very widespread pattern in Vietnamese local forms of worship of victims of bad death, the local population benefited from her protection and magical responsiveness, leading to the erection of a temple dedicated to her, which was later granted imperial recognition. According to Diguet's account, however, and despite her popularity among the local dwellers, Cao Tiên seems to have lost pre-eminence in her own home:

---

9   Dror (2007: 75) and Phạm and Eipper (2009: 70) hint towards this direction when they ask whether it was Liễu Hạnh who was added to a broader pantheon or the pantheon that was added to her cult.

At the back of the sanctuary, against the wall, are situated three altars. On the central one [is displayed] a tabernacle containing the statue of 'Liêu Hanh', also called 'Duc Thanh Mâu', the Great Mother Goddess. [...] Here, she takes a place of honour that should belong to 'Cao Tien', the Chapel's Patron. Her cult was brought to Cao Bang from the [Red River] Delta, long after the foundation of the pagoda and this Goddess, whose rank was much higher than that of Mother Goddess Cao Tiên, has, so to speak, usurped her place. [Cao Tien] has her statue [...] in front of the tabernacle. (Diguet 1906: 319)

Diguet's description proceeds by listing the other statues displayed in the temple. Any contemporary reader familiar with the cult would recognise what is now seen as the pantheon of the Four Palaces, somehow wrapped around the local deity.[10] Beyond Diguet's somewhat judgemental interpretation, his description actually illustrates how a particular local deity was materially included into this hierarchical assembly of spirits, even if her hagiography – at least in its then-current state – drew no direct connection to them.[11]

This local addition of the pantheon of the Four Palaces to Mạc Thị Cao Tiên's cult, in her own temple at the end of the 19th century, may well have occurred for very practical reasons, such as harnessing Liễu Hạnh's then well-established popularity in order to attract more worshippers. However, it did not lead to the integration of Cao Tiên into the pantheon of spirits widely worshipped by spirits mediums across Northern Vietnam. Indeed, Cao Tiên is not mentioned in monographs or edited *văn chầu* hymn collections dedicated to the Four Palaces or the Mother Goddess Religion, nor on any of the numerous websites listing their deities. None of the practitioners and specialists I have worked with in Hanoi and the Red River delta has ever mentioned her. Those I could ask while writing this chapter confirmed they had never heard about this deity. It seems, therefore, that to this day Mother Goddess Cao Tiên has not been assigned a position within the pantheon of the Four Palaces, nor has she been assimilated to any of its other members. Thus, what Diguet may have been witnessing is less Liễu Hạnh's usurpation of Cao Tiên than a failed attempt to integrate Cao Tiên into the unfinished pantheon of the Four Palaces.

---

10   Interestingly, the pantheon as it appears through the statuary described by Diguet does not fit exactly its current state, which further supports the idea of a historically flexible, integrative device.

11   For another example of a temple's 'usurpation' by Liễu Hạnh, see Nguyen The Anh 1995:62.

Other local spirits with similar profiles have known a brighter fate, as they have been fully integrated into the Four Palaces. Such is the case of the Mother Goddess of Tiên La (*Mẫu Tiên La*), known during her earthly lifetime as Vũ Thị Thục Nương, a female general of the Trưng Sisters' army (1st century). Many temples are dedicated to her in Thái Bình province, where her cult seems to have originated, as well as in Lạng Sơn, Hưng Yên, Phú Thọ and Vĩnh Phúc provinces. The contemporary figure of the Mother Goddess of Tiên La may well result from the fusion of several characters worshipped in those different locales; in any case, among practitioners of the cult of the Four Palaces, there is a broad consensus about her being the Eighth Lady (*Chầu Bát*) of the Palace of the Earth.

Thus, one could see the pantheon's systematic aspect, the ensemble of positions located by a set of two coordinates (rank and number), like a series of slots, shelves or boxes, where a given spirit or local deity may be installed. Some of these slots, like that of the Seventh Prince, have been filled by a single, well-identified character. In some instances, several spirits may cohabit in one of these boxes, sharing their coordinates, like the several historical characters originating from Nghệ An to whom the Tenth Prince is assimilated. Other slots remain available, corresponding to spirits of the Four Palaces whose identity lacks thickness and who are rarely – if ever – embodied by spirit mediums. The Fifth Lady and the Fourth Prince fall into this category.

In turn, certain local spirits appear to be on their way to the Four Palaces, although they have not definitively been assigned a place in the system. This is the case of Princess Vũ Nương (*Vũ Nương Công Chúa*), also known as Lady Vũ (*Bà Vũ*). A victim of drowning, she became, much like Cao Tiên, a responsive spirit whose temple is located on the banks of the Red River in today's Hà Nam Province. According to some of her worshippers, she appeared in Emperor Lê Thánh Tông's dream on his return from a campaign in Champa. An altar dedicated to the Mother Goddesses and the Four Palaces was installed in her temple, and spirit mediums regularly hold *lên đồng* séances there, assimilating Princess Vũ Nương to the Mother Goddess of the Palace of Water. Although her followers remain limited in number, her case illustrates the fertility of the notion of reincarnation in this system.

Indeed, it is common among worshippers to describe spirits sharing a number of traits as reincarnations or avatars (*hóa thân*) of a similar figure, as is the case for the Mother Goddess of the High Regions (*Mẫu Thượng Ngàn*), the Second Lady (*Chầu đệ Nhị*), the Sixth Lady (*Chầu Lục*), the Small Lady

(*Chầu Bé*), and the Small Damsel (*Cô Bé*). With this idea of reincarnation, the tension between systematic and individual aspects of the pantheon plays full swing and provides a good illustration of this process of pantheonisation: the existence of a few similar traits – which need not cover the whole extent of their particular identities – allows the gradual assimilation of local deities into a common system, and sometimes into a single entity.

Spirits as worshippers and scholars as promoters

If there is a pantheon of the Four Palaces, it is definitely one in the making. The differences of detail between the ensembles of spirits worshipped by spirit mediums in different locales are not variations of an original or national model. Rather, the national pantheon is a dynamic aggregate of local cults, which are assimilated with good or not-so-good fortune within this broader, abstract ensemble. The Four Palaces somehow function like a spiritual – and slightly more flexible – Mendeleev's periodic table of elements: a limited number of coordinates determine theoretical positions ready to be filled by an actual entity whose characteristics match those coordinates. But in the case of the pantheon of Vietnamese spirits, the rules can be bent in order to serve particular agendas in a game that constantly gravitates around the idea of a national ensemble of spirits into which local figures may or may not be considered fitting.

An intriguing detail in the spirit possession rituals described in the first section of this chapter can finally be interpreted. As we have seen, one of the first actions performed by each spirit embodied by a spirit medium during a séance is an offering of incense to the Four Palaces. This puzzling recursive aspect of the ritual – a spirit performing an act of devotion to the spirits – is now easier to understand: this action portrays the embodied spirits themselves as worshippers, just like some details in *văn chầu* hymns portray them as pilgrims. Thus, every time they get on the ceremonial stage, spirit mediums enact each deity's acknowledgement of, and participation in, a superior unity, that of the Four Palaces, which transcends and connects local cults at the national level. In a sense, from the perspective of the spirits, *lên đồng* séances are rituals of devotion – or, to put it in more political terms, rituals of submission.

These *longue durée* dynamics, embedded within the contemporary ritual and visual culture of the Four Palaces, shed new light on the cult's recent history. What can be observed through the cult's documentation since the colonial era is that, having reached a certain degree of systematicity, most attempts to describe the cult somehow tended to reinforce this aspect. This tendency towards systematisation was supported by the very material media of the cult's perpetuation, such as statues and woodprints. Because of their formal properties, these lean strongly towards downplaying the characteristics of the individual spirits in favour of their structural assimilation. A similar dynamic may be at play nowadays, with many websites dedicated to the Four Palaces attempting to systematise the pantheon. This encyclopedic leaning may well inherit from another kind of contribution to what one could call the cult's irresistible systematisation.

Indeed, Vietnam scholars, local and foreign alike, from the colonial times until now, have gradually intensified this reification of the cult of the Four Palaces and its so-called pantheon. Ngô Đức Thịnh's seminal publication on the 'Mother Goddess Religion' (1994), reprinted numerous times and often found in spirit mediums' sanctuaries, is archetypal of this trend. Gathering into a single account a variety of cults to female deities, including figures with a long influence on the Four Palaces, like the Cham-influenced Thiên Y A Na, as well as characters not yet included in the common pantheon, like the Southern Lady of the Realm (Bà Chúa Xứ), this book contributes to the very process that is at the core of the Four Palaces. It does so following its own modalities, pertaining to heritage-leaning academic discourse, which later enabled tapping into international sources of legitimacy, thus involving UNESCO in this irresistible systematisation of the Four Palaces or Realms.[12]

In turn, these practices become an element of the nation-building discourse they had to accommodate to. Historical circulation of deities between centres and peripheries, their harnessing by states and their astute mobilisation by local populations have been thoroughly documented in Vietnam (Taylor 1986; Womack 1995; Dror 2007; Kelley 2015) and in the Sinitic world (Watson 1985; Hansen 1993; Dean 2003). Among other cases in Southeast Asia, Bénédicte Brac de la Perrière has shown that the Burmese 'national pantheon' of the Thirty-seven Lords is the 'product of the unification

---

12 For another incidental example of scholarly contribution to the pantheon's internal systematising dynamics, see the recent republication of Durand's *Imagerie populaire vietnamienne* by École Française d'Extrême-Orient (2011 [1960]), where minor corrections by the editors – whose work is of astounding scholarly quality – tend to homogenise the names of featured deities (see image 149 in the original and reprint).

and Burmisation' of local cults, carried out through the territorialisation of historical dynastic figures by projecting them onto local worship figures, and through their ritual submission to Buddhism (Brac de la Perrière 2005: 287). Spirit mediums were deeply involved in this process as, in 18th century Burma, they were professionalised as servants for the royal court, which created a collation between official lists of worshipped spirits and the ensembles of spirits embodied in possession séances (Brac de la Perrière 2007).

In Vietnam, however, such a close collaboration between spirit mediumship and the royal court never existed and, to my knowledge, stories and certificates issued by the Vietnamese dynasties never mentioned or appropriated the systematic aspects of the Four Palaces. Who, then, is the author of this pantheon? Whose agency is at play in this ongoing centralisation of spirit cults? In her powerful analysis of the cult of Mother Goddess Liễu Hạnh, Olga Dror (2007) demonstrates that rather than folk stories, many established narratives about the deity pertain to anti-folk politics, that is, the appropriation and reinterpretation of popular spiritual figures in order to give them new meanings more in line with the elites' ideas – Vietnamese monarchs have long harnessed spirit narratives into the service of their political agendas: construction of figures of virtuous kings under the Lý, promotion of a Buddhist dynasty under the Trần, reconstruction of a Confucian state under the Lê, and so on.

In her book, Dror prudently circumscribes her analysis to the 'content' (or 'wine') of the goddess's cult, the ideas conveyed through its narratives, as opposed to its 'form' (or 'bottle'), the practices through which it was perpetuated. My analysis of the contemporary ritual and visual culture of the Four Palaces may displace Dror's question to the terrain of form. What I have attempted to show in these pages is that the practices themselves, as well as the way they have been documented in the 20th century, through the construction of what has been described as a 'pantheon', contribute to centralising endeavours rather in line with the post-Đổi mới Vietnamese state's project of construction of a nation endowed with a strong 'cultural identity' (*bản sắc dân tộc*) united against external threats.

However, rather than approaching Sinicised aspects of Vietnamese culture as exogenous elements in need of purification, the cult of the Four Palaces articulates them into a dialectics of autochthony and state power.[13] Taken into

---

13 Further research is needed to understand where this strongly efficient mechanism of integration of local cults into a pantheon stems from. One could investigate, among other threads, the

the self-perpetuating structure of the pantheon, practitioners and amateur or professional scholars alike may well be contributing to the construction of a certainly state-like, but nonetheless cosmopolitan, national imaginary.

It is not my place to judge whether the contemporary construction of a so-called 'Mother Goddess Religion' on the basis of the UNESCO sanctioned 'Four Realms' is an accurate historical narrative or merely an invented tradition. However, and somehow wrong-footing the typical heritage studies perspective as well as my own constructivist leaning, I am tempted to conclude by saying that when, in the 1990s, Vietnamese scholars decided to see the cult of the Four Palaces as a Vietnamese indigenous religion, they were right to do so. Not because it would solely emanate from a hypothetical pure Vietnamese culture, but because, with its tension between managing landscapes and belonging to them, this cult approaches national identity not as a final answer but rather as an open question.

References

Bertrand, Didier. 1996. 'Renaissance du *Lên đồng* à Huế (Việt Nam). Premiers éléments d'une recherche', *Bulletin de l'Ecole Française d'Extrême-Orient*, 83.

Bokenkamp, Stephen R. 2010. 'Daoist Pantheons', *in* John Lagerwey and Pengzhi Lü (eds), *Early Chinese Religion: Part Two: The Period of Division*. Leyden: Brill.

Brac de la Perrière, Bénédicte. 2005. 'A Presentation of a Parabaik Written by Kawi Dewa Kyaw Thu, Ritual Officer at King Mindon's Court', *Myanmar Historical Commission Conference Proceedings: Part 2*. Yangon: Myanmar Historical Commission.

———. 2007. 'Le traité des apparences du monde. Analyse des rituels de la royauté birmane d'après un traité du dix-huitième siècle', in Bénédicte Brac de la Perrière and Marie-Louise Reiniche (eds), *Les apparences du monde: Royautés hindoues et bouddhiques de l'Asie du Sud et du Sud-Est*. Paris: Ecole Française d'Extrême-Orient.

Chauvet, Claire. 2012. *Sous le voile rouge: Rituels de possession et réseaux culturels à Hà Nôi (Việt Nam)*. Paris: Les Indes Savantes.

Dean, Kenneth. 2003. 'Local Communal Religion in Contemporary South-east China', *The China Quarterly*, 174.

---

role of local scholars, in imperial as well as contemporary Vietnam, through the composition or collection of *văn chầu* hymns and hagiographies, and the contribution of practices of pilgrimage (*hương hành*) and 'spiritual tourism' (*du lịch tâm linh*) to the connecting of distant local cults together within a broader system, constructing what has been described, in other contexts, as a 'circulatory territory' (Delage 2016).

Delage, Rémy. 2016. 'L'espace du pèlerinage comme 'territoire circulatoire': Sehwan Sharif sur les rives de l'Indus', *Les Cahiers d'Outre-Mer*, 274(2).

Descola, Philippe. 2005 *Par-delà nature et culture*. Paris: Gallimard.

Dror, Olga. 2007. *Cult, Culture, and Authority: Princess Liễu Hạnh in Vietnamese History*. Honolulu: University of Hawai'i Press.

Dumézil, Georges. 1952. *Les Dieux indo-européens*. Paris: Presses universitaires de France.

Durand, Maurice. 1959. *Technique et panthéon des médiums vietnamiens 'Đồng'*. Paris: Ecole Française d'Extrême Orient.

———. 2011 [1960]. *Imagerie populaire vietnamienne*. Paris: Ecole Française d'Extrême Orient.

Eliade, Mircea. 1950. *Le chamanisme et les techniques archaïques de l'extase*. Paris: Payot.

Endres, Kirsten. 2011. *Performing the Divine: Mediums, Markets and Modernity in Urban Vietnam*. Copenhagen: NIAS Press.

Feuchtwang, Stephen. 2001. *Popular Religion in China: The Imperial Metaphor*. London: Curzon.

Fjelstad, Karen and Nguyen Thi Hien. 2006. *Possessed by the Spirits: Mediumship in Contemporary Vietnamese Communities*. Ithaca: Cornell University Press.

Goody, Jack. 1986. *The Logic of Writing and the Organisation of Society*. Cambridge: Cambridge University Press.

Goscha, Christopher. 2015. 'La géopolitique vietnamienne vue de l'Eurasie: quelles leçons de la troisième guerre d'Indochine pour aujourd'hui?' *Hérodote*, 157.

Granet, Marcel. 1934. *La pensée chinoise*. Paris: Albin Michel.

Hansen, Valerie. 1993. 'Gods on walls: A Case of Indian Influence on Chinese Lay Religion?' in Patricia Buckley Ebrey and Peter N. Gregory (eds), *Religion and Society in T'ang and Sung China*. Honolulu: University of Hawai'i Press.

Kelley, Liam. 2015. 'Constructing Local Narratives: Spirits, Dreams, and Prophecies in the Medieval Red River Delta', in J. Anderson and J. Whitmore (eds), *China's Encounters on the South and Southwest*. Leiden: Brill.

Malamoud, Charles. 1989. *Cuire le monde: Rite et pensée dans l'Inde ancienne*. Paris: La Découverte.

Ngô Đức Thịnh. 1996. *Đạo Mẫu ở Việt Nam*, 2 vols, Hanoi, Nhà Xuất bản Văn hóa – Thông tin.

——— (ed.). 1999. *Etudes Vietnamiennes*, 131, Special issue on 'Le culte des Saintes-Mères au Vietnam'.

Nguyễn Đăng Thục. 1992 [1967]. *Lịch sử tư tưởng Việt Nam*, vol. 1. Ho Chi Minh City: Nhà Xuất bản Thành phố Hồ Chí Minh.

Nguyễn Ngọc Mai. 2013. *Nghi lễ lên đồng: Lịch sử và giá trị*. Hanoi: Nhà Xuất bản Văn hóa – Thông tin.

Nguyen The Anh. 1995. 'The Vietnamization of the Cham Deity Po Nagar', *Asia Journal*, 2(1).

Nguyễn Thị Hiệp. 2007. 'Génies légendaires au Vietnam: textes littéraires et croyances populaires', *Cahiers d'études vietnamiennes* 19.

Norton, Barley. 2009. *Songs for the Spirits*. Urbana and Chicago: University of Illinois Press.

Phạm Quỳnh Phương. 2009. *Hero and Deity: Tran Hung Dao and the Resurgence of Popular Religion in Vietnam*. Chiang Mai: Mekong Press.

Phạm Quỳnh Phương and Chris Eipper. 2009. 'Mothering and Fathering the Vietnamese: Religion, Gender, and National Identity', *Journal of Vietnamese Studies*, 4(1).

Rouch, Jean. 1955. *Les maîtres fous*. Paris: Les films de la Pléiade.

Simon, Pierre-Jean and Ida Simon-Barouh. 1973. *Hau bong: un culte viêtnamien de possession transplanté en France*. Paris and The Hague: Mouton.

Stoller, Paul. 1995. *Embodying Colonial Memories: Spirit Possession, Power, and the Hauka in West Africa*. New York: Routledge.

Tarabout, Gilles. 1993. 'Quand les dieux s'emmêlent: Point de vue sur les classifications divines au Kérala', in Vérionique Bouillier and Gérard Toffin (eds), *Classer les dieux? Des panthéons en Asie du Sud*. Paris: EHESS.

Taylor, Keith. 1986. 'Authority and Legitimacy in 11th Century Vietnam', in David Marr and Anthony C. Milner (eds), *Southeast Asia in the 9th to 14th Centuries*. Singapore: ISEAS.

———. 2001. 'On being Muonged', *Asian Ethnicity*, 2(1).

Taylor, Philip. 2004. *Goddess on the Rise: Pilgrimage and Popular Religion in Vietnam*. Honolulu: University of Hawai'i Press.

de Tréglodé, Benoît. 2018. *Histoire du Viêt Nam de la colonisation à nos jours*. Paris: Editions de la Sorbonne.

Verellen, Franciscus. 2003. 'The Twenty-four Dioceses and Zhang Daoling: The Spatio-Liturgical Oranization of Early Heavenly Master Taoism', in Shinohara Granoff (ed.), *Pilgrims, Patrons, and Places: Localizing Sanctity in Asian Religions*. Vancouver: University of British Columbia Press: 15–61.

Vernant, Jean-Pierre. 1963. 'Hestia-Hermès. Sur l'expression religieuse de l'espace et du mouvement chez les Grecs', *L'Homme*, 3(3).

———. 1965. *Mythe et pensée chez les Grecs: Etudes de psychologie historique*. Paris: La Découverte.

Watson, James. 1985. 'Standardizing the Gods: The Promotion of T'ien Hou (Empress of Heaven) along the South China Coast', in David Johnson, Andrew Nathan and Evelyn Rawski (eds), *Popular Culture in Late Imperial China*. Berkeley: University of California Press.

CHAPTER 2

Mya Nan Nwe's Birthday
A Forum-like Ritual Event at Botataung Pagoda (Yangon)

Bénédicte Brac de la Perrière

*T*he Botataung Lady, also known as Mya Nan Nwe, belongs to a category of Burmese spiritual beings that are associated with the guardianship of Buddhist pagodas.[1] This chapter relates the remarkable formation of an annual celebration focused on Mya Nan Nwe worship since the beginning of the new century. Among pagoda-guardian spiritual figures, one can include 'respected grandfathers' (*bobogyi*) and voracious ogres (*bilu*) as well as young *naga*-like ladies in charge of pagoda treasure troves or reliquaries – like Mya Nan Nwe, whose generic designation is *thaik nan shin* (lit. 'in charge of the treasure palace'). Cults whose members worship these kinds of figures, linked to the guardianship of pagodas and thus considered to be caretakers of the Buddhist material dispensation (*thathana*, Pali *sāsana*), have grown dramatically since the 1990s. This is partly related to the Burmese junta's policies of self-legitimation through sponsoring religious foundations and the subsequent rediscovery and materialisation of spiritual figures connected to restored pagodas.

At first glance, this transfiguration of Burma's religious landscape may be compared to the efflorescence of 'prosperity' cults in neighbouring Theravadin countries in a context of rapid modernisation and globalisation.[2] In Burma, brand new images that materialise pagoda guardians have appeared in many sanctuaries where they had not previously existed, or

---

1 In literature about Burma and for the Burmese, 'pagoda' (*hpaya*) is used to designate a stupa, the main Buddhist monument generally containing relics, together with its cultic architectural environment dedicated to lay devotion. 'Pagoda' (*hpaya*) is used for both the compound and the reliquary monument. Also, as sanctuaries devoted to the laypeople worship, pagodas (*hpaya*) are clearly distinguished, conceptually and spatially, from monasteries (*hpongyi kyaung*) where monks reside.
2 Peter Jackson was among the first to identify and comment on these developments in Thai religiosity in two seminal contributions (Jackson 1999a and 1999b). On the formulation of 'prosperity' cults, see also Pattana Kitiarsa 2011.

replaced tiny, old-fashioned images. However, this has transpired during an era when the military's grip on power left the country behind the global modernisation trend and seemingly cut it off from foreign influences, yet beginning to experiment with a market economy.[3]

Changes in Burma's economic conditions had a broad range of consequences for religious practices. The junta embellished the Buddhist material dispensation and financed restorations by offering monopolistic positions to tycoons who were willing to provide major religious donations.[4] However, the mushrooming of the iconography of pagoda guardians in many Buddhist sanctuaries since the 1990s cannot be attributed solely to the junta's intervention. This new iconography also reflects the new needs of growing urban populations and their impact on the practices of ritual specialists of various stamps. On the one hand, the growing visibility of pagoda guardians, which are associated with the protection of the Buddhist material dispensation, is interlocked with the expansion of the sphere of esoteric Buddhist practices known as the *weikza* path under the post-1988 juntas. On the other hand, pagoda guardians also entered the spirit mediumship domain through being summoned and embodied by spirit mediums during spirit possession ceremonies – a point of intersection of spirit possession with Buddhism in the field of religion that parallels the cases presented in this book by

---

[3] Prompted by the regime's economic failure, General Ne Win's one-party-led 'Burmese Way to Socialism' ended with the 1988 general insurrection. In September of the same year, a coup restored military rule under the State Law and Order Restoration Council (SLORC), which subsequently mutated into the State Peace and Development Council (SPDC) in 1996. Both these regimes allowed for a market economy that mainly profited military allies. While a 'Roadmap to Democracy' had already been laid out in 2003 it was only implemented in 2008, following the monk-led Saffron Revolution and the Nargis cyclone disaster, when a new constitution was submitted to the people. In 2011, a first semi-civilian government was set up with a mandate to lead the political transition, after the military-linked USDP (Union for Solidarity and Development Party) had won the general elections. The Aung San Suu Kyi led National League for Democracy won the 2015 general elections, enabling the first democratic transfer of power under the new constitution as well as the subsequent elections, in November 2020, by landslides. However, the then-chief of the army, Min Aung Hlaing, contested the result and took over power on 1 February of 2021, thus bringing an abrupt end to the democratic experiment.

[4] Juliane Schober (2011) explains how the Burmese junta's post-1988 systematic policy of funding and supporting Buddhist institutions as an alternative source of legitimation led to the transformation of the whole Buddhist national community into a ritual network. To date, documentation of cases of junta-sponsored foundation or renovation of Buddhist monuments and institutions, which networks were activated, and under which procedures, has not been undertaken systematically.

Visisya Pinthongvijayakul, Kazuo Fukuura and Irene Stengs. The growing visibility of pagoda guardians throughout Burma also corresponds to a new stage in these processes of simultaneous and recurrent identifications and differentiations within the 'religious field' (Bourdieu 1971).

The growing fame achieved by Mya Nan Nwe, the guardian lady of Botataung Pagoda in Yangon, pertains to this broader ritual context. Mya Nan Nwe, the personal name by which she came to be known, could be rendered as the 'Creeper of the Emerald Palace'. Recently, she has gained repute among tourist devotees from Thailand as the 'Whispering Lady'. However, when ritual specialists evoke various *thaik nan shin*, they call her the 'Botataung Lady' (Botataung *medaw*), thus acknowledging the name of the Buddhist sanctuary in Yangon that she presides over.

She gets her own dedicated sanctuary located outside of the Botataung Pagoda enclosed coumpound, which occupies about half of a city block, 100 metres by 150 metres, with gardens and various pavilions around the platform that supports the stupa and its surrounding walkway. Outside of this enclosure and across from its main entrance, a two-storey pavilion hosts a beautiful golden image of Gotama Buddha replete with royal paraphernalia. In the middle of the large room, one's eyes are drawn to the image of Mya Nan Nwe, pictured as a young, kneeling woman. Surrounded by all sorts of offerings, she is dressed alternatively in the pink attire of a Buddhist nun or in the green regal costume of a *naga*-like princess, according to the time of the year and the particular vows of devotees who dress her on a given day. This difference in dress reflects the ambiguity of this figure who is imagined both as a Buddhist devotee and as a *naga* species: *naga* are spiritual ophidian beings living underground or under water. With time, Mya Nan Nwe's public support has grown and devotees now must queue to get closer and address their requests to her; as she is known to whisper messages in reply to her worshippers.

The Lady's pavilion is a unique invention from the late 1990s; before this, as with most pagoda guardians, she occupied a humble shrine on the platform around the stupa. As her cult gained popularity, however, critics of a variety of stripes converged on the idea that her image should be relocated outside of the pagoda enclosure. This speaks of a possible contestation regarding what is 'acceptable' or not in a 'religious' space, according to relative positioning in a given socio-religious context.

Figure 2.1. Devotees presenting a glass of milk to Mya Nan Nwe in her green attire. **Colour** p. 314.

Debates about the delineation of 'religion' are largely informed by the construction of this normative category in the wake of the 19th-century Western imperial encounter with the 'other'.[5] In Burma, the overall relationships between lay and monastic domains were reordered to conform with the construction of Buddhism as a 'religion'.[6] This reordering had multiple implications. Among them was the autonomisation of the pantheon of tutelary spirits (*nat*) known as the Thirty-seven Lords from the overarching sovereignty of Buddhist kingship and the subsequent development of professional spirit mediumship, as I discuss in other works.[7] Another effect

---

5   'Religion' is a Western category initially meant to designate Christianity. The modern understanding of this term emerged both out of the encounters of Christendom with other 'religions' and of the Enlightenment struggles to differentiate rational knowledge from doctrinal precepts. First appropriated by Western scholars to make sense of a wide variety of practices, beliefs and experiences observed among non-Western peoples, 'religion' emerged from this genealogy as a prescriptive and normative category that was then re-appropriated by those non-Western peoples. In other words, as a category, 'religion' is the product of entangled histories between the West and the rest of the world and needs to be analysed as such. For a critique of 'religion' as a category, see, among others, Masuzawa 2005. For its appropriations in Southeast Asian contexts, see Picard's *Introduction* to his edited volume (Picard 2017), and my chapter in the same volume (Brac de la Perrière 2017).

6   On the impact of the Western encounter on the Buddhist religious field in Burma, see Houtman 1990, Alexey Kirichenko 2009, Turner 2014, and Brac de la Perrière 2017. 'Religion' in the Western sense of a faith individually professed appeared for the first time in Anglo–Burmese dictionaries around 1850 as one of the meanings of *batha* (from Pali *bhāsā*, language), in addition to the pervasive notion of *thathana* (Pali *sāsana*) denoting the Burmese Buddhicised social space.

7   For a synthesis of these works, see Brac de la Perrière 2016. For an account of the late 20th-century emergence of professional spirit mediums in urban Thailand inspired by Bourdieu's theory of the dynamics of religious fields, which is akin to my own, see White's thesis, 2014.

was the coalescence of a distinctive esoteric field around the *weikza*. *Weikza* are figures representing lay religious virtuoso experts in various mundane 'knowledges' (*weikza* from the Pali *vijjā*) that gradually had been expelled from the monastic curriculum through various reforms implemented by 19th-century kings Bodawpaya and Mindon (Dhammasami 2004). Through intensive religious practice and expertise, these virtuosi were considered to have gained extraordinary powers that enabled them to escape the cycle of rebirth while remaining available in this world to rescue people and defend the Buddha's teachings and dispensation (*thathana*, from the Pali *sāsana*). A number of these figures are known to have headed the insurrections that followed Upper Burma's annexation by the British in 1885.[8] Today, the most-worshipped figure among *weikza* followers is Bomingaung, a virtuoso who is supposed to have escaped from the cycle of life and rebirth at Mt Popa (Central Burma), in 1952.

Nat and *weikza* domains continued to evolve throughout the 20th-century in Burma through continuous interplay and also with the domain of monasticism. Together, the three domains now bound the entire 'religious field' defined as the Buddhist *thathana*. Insiders on each of these paths assert that their specific beliefs and practices are 'truly' Buddhist and Burmese. *Nat* worshippers also make this claim, but modernist Buddhists dismiss them on the ground that *nat* worship is more 'traditional' than 'pure' Buddhism. Similarly, claims by *weikza* followers are seen as reminiscent of the 'false' medieval *ari* Buddhism, which had been eradicated when new doctrinal trends introduced from Ceylon were institutionalised. In other words, practitioners on these paths evaluate each other in relative terms, according to a Buddhist discursive scale of value in the overall 'religious field' as captured by the term 'Burmese Buddhism'.

Another debate affecting the understanding of the development of new cults, such as that of Mya Nan Nwe, pertains to 'new animism' ontologies, as expounded by Benjamin Baumann in his chapter here, which posit a kind of relationality that crosses human and nonhuman realms. As we shall see, as an object of worship, Mya Nan Nwe displays a marked ambiguity, being both a devotee who works at the pagoda and a female *naga* who emerges from the underground and can assume a womanly form for periods of time. This

---

8   On the *weikza* path as an original aspect of Burmese Buddhism see Mendelson 1961, Spiro 1967 and Brac de la Perrière, Rozenberg & Turner (eds) 2014.

ambiguity, created by the varieties of practice associated with her, makes it difficult to understand this cult as the pure product of an 'animist collective' rationale. It also brings to light the fact that religious change emerges from shifting ground rather than forming a linear continuity: Mya Nan Nwe is not uniquely shaped by analogical 'traditional' worship of tutelary spirits (*nat*) nor by animist logic.

In this chapter, I show how such internal dynamics of the religious field operate today in a specific place, the Botataung religious complex in Yangon, by focusing on the annual celebration of the *thaik* Lady, Mya Nan Nwe. In a previous paper, I argued that by relocating the image and shrine of the Lady outside of the pagoda compound in the late 1990s, her ambiguity as a religious and spiritual figure has been allowed to fully express itself (Brac de la Perrière 2011: 172–173). I now want to show how the Lady's birthday celebration emerged as a complex event that combines features of a religious virtuoso anniversary with those of a spirit festival; of a traditional seasonal ritual to the Buddhist saint Upagot (Upagutta) together with a typical pagoda festival. In other words, this celebration has become a *forum* where actors from various segments of the complex Burmese religious field interact, compete and differentiate themselves.[9]

After locating Botataung Pagoda as a place in Yangon's Buddhist landscape, this chapter proceeds to trace the postwar history of the Lady's place in the religious complex. Competing interpretations of the Lady's relocation out of the Buddhist sanctuary are then analysed before discussing day-to-day and birthday ritual practices. I propose to anlyse the Lady's birthday as a forum-like ritual event, in light of divergent embodiment politics displayed according to multiple, involved segments of the religious field.

Botataung Pagoda as a place in the Buddhist city landscape

As is the case for all pagoda guardians, the *naga*-like Lady known as Mya Nan Nwe is spiritually attached to the Buddhist stupa she is supposed to

---

[9] Materials for this chapter have been gathered during my recurrent visits to the site since the end of the 1990s. I conducted a more systematic observation of rituals and interviewed local personalities in 2010, 2011, 2013, 2015 and 2016, particularly during the Lady's birthday period at the end of December. Finally, I met with the new trustee-board members of the Botataung religious complex in February 2019, for an interview aimed at following up changes since their coming to office in 2016, and I also observed the January 2020 celebration.

serve, even though her own sanctuary has now been relocated outside of the pagoda enclosure. Botataung Pagoda is located at the southeast corner of Yangon's urban grid. The British authorities designed this grid when they choose to make Yangon the capital of their new colony after the Second Anglo–Burmese war in 1853. The grid, positioned with Sule stupa at its centre, stretches from West to East along the Yangon River. It was organised in such a way that all the Buddhist monasteries were relocated to either end, along Phongyi Road to the west, and Botataung Road to the east.[10] Botataung Pagoda sits on a large esplanade along the river leading to the Botataung jetty, where many commuters from the suburbs across the river arrive and depart daily. Dockworker housing is located to the west, on the street behind the pagoda enclosure, and the large grounds devoted to port activities are just beyond the grid, behind the monasteries towards the east. Botataung Pagoda is thus a port landmark, as well.

To the North of the colonial urban grid lies Shwedagon Pagoda, which contains a major historic stupa that served as a pilgrimage centre for Buddhist kings and is still the dominant feature of the Yangon cityscape. All three Buddhist sanctuaries, Shwedagon, Sule and Botataung, are famous for their ancient stupas, which are known to contain hair relics of the Buddha. Together with Kyaikkasan Pagoda and other sanctuaries located in the neighbouring towns of Hmawbi and Twanthe, they contribute to an overarching narrative of the Irrawaddy delta's Buddhicisation, conveyed through evolving pagoda histories and imaginings. This narrative focuses on Shwedagon Pagoda and is the outcome of a progressive elaboration that followed the urban development of Yangon (Brac de la Perrière 1995).

The founding legend of Shwedagon deals with hair relics given by the living Buddha to two merchant brothers who brought them back from India to Okkalapa, a legendary Mon king (Pearn 1939: 9). The hair relics were then enshrined on the top of Shwedagon hill, identified as a site where Buddhist relics from Buddhas of preceding eras had been buried and, thus, was imagined worthy of receiving the new relics. According to this story, King Okkalapa's rediscovery of this Buddhist site during Gotama's time was facilitated by very old Buddhist spirits known as *bobogyi*, who had been granted guardianship of relics by Thidja/Sakka, the head of the abode of divinities and guardian of Buddhism. As the Yangon urban space developed, this story

---

10 On urban planning as a secular colonial pedagogy, see Turner 2021.

evolved as well; the agency of *bobogyi* figures was invoked to describe and explain a single network that came to include several neighbouring ancient hair relic pagodas (Brac de la Perrière 1995, 2019).

According to Donald Stadner (2011: 86), the Botataung Pagoda had not been a part of this narrative until World War II, when bombings destroyed the masonry of the original stupa and disclosed a hair reliquary in the inner chamber. The reconstruction of the sanctuary was one of the collective undertakings that bonded the Burmese Buddhist community together during the early Independence period. A completely new design was envisioned to keep the newly discovered inner reliquary visible for devotees. While the architectural change supported the narrative evolution, it also sustained the imagination of reliquary guardian spirits. At this time, Botataung Pagoda's history was rewritten and included in the Shwedagon founding narrative as follows: King Okkalapa would have insisted that one of the merchant brothers build a stupa for one of the hair relics on the spot where the boats had landed, that is, Botataung.[11] Further, when the newly designed monument was first presented to the public, a *bobogyi* image appeared, on the sanctuary platform (Stadner 2011: 86). In other words, Botataung Pagoda can be seen as one of the places where the Burmese have imagined their collective Buddhist identity as a modern and independent national community after Independence – and also as one of the sites that mark the urban landscape of Yangon as Buddhist.[12]

The research setting

The Botataung Lady made her appearance in parallel with the *bobogyi*'s entry in the pagoda coumpound when the stupa was rebuilt after the war. Nobody remembers who first donated the small statue of the Lady, the one that graced the restored stupa's platform until the 1990s. But the common opinion is that it must have been someone among the volunteers who enthusiastically contributed to the rebuilding of the monument. Because they are believed

---

11 While I was unable to locate Botataung Pagoda's history pre-dating World War II, I recently collected a book on Mya Nan Nwe by the late pagoda trustee, Aung Hsu Shin, in which he refers to three successive versions of the Botataung relic history (2008).

12 Of course, this imagination of the Yangon urban landscape as Buddhist flies in the face of numerous mosques, Hindu temples and churches, particularly inside the colonial urban grid where the colonial authorities had set aside locations for various other religious communities' sanctuaries in addition to Buddhist ones.

Figure 2.2. The original tiny image of Mya Nan Nwe holding *naga* heads and with a naga headdresss. **Colour** p. 314.

to be in charge of protecting the concealed riches of pagodas, most pagoda treasure-guarding Ladies (*thaik medaw*) are imagined as *thaik-naga*, that is, *thaik* of the *naga* species, which take on a human appearance.[13] Like many other *thaik,* the Lady of Botataung was then represented as a young and beautiful standing woman with a *naga* headdress and holding *naga* heads in each of her hands. She stood in a small shrine on the stupa's platform, and devotees would present small offerings, such as flowers, in exchange for her blessings. When the boon requested of the Lady was significant, she was presented with the standard offering of *kadaw bwe*, comprising a coconut, some bananas, some betel and assorted leaves, and which may be offered to any spiritual being in Burma.

This was what I observed when I visited the pagoda in the mid-1990s, before this original image of the Lady was moved to her new location in a pavilion outside of the pagoda coumpound. At that time, Botataung Pagoda was somewhat forgotten, nothing more than a remote and poorly maintained urban pagoda, lying amidst sluggish port activity in a part of the city with many decrepit old buildings, which seemed asleep and flooded badly during the monsoon rains. Nothing is the same today. Since the middle of the first decade of the new century, this part of the city has undergone tremendous change. Large middle-class housing has been systematically developed. Gradually, a more cosmopolitan population has inhabited the area and Botataung open space has become a favourite spot for new open-air

---

13 However, as we shall see, the *naga* nature of *thaik* Ladies may be contested by some informants. The ambiguity of these spiritual beings may be associated with that of *naga* as a species in the Buddhist cosmology.

activities. Port traffic is now vigorous, and piles of containers jut out just beyond the monasteries' luxuriant gardens. Above all, the pagoda has been refurbished again, and is now visited by flocks of Burmese pilgrims and foreign tourists who add vigour to the local economy.

This restored prosperity, although mirroring the renewed affluence of the surroundings, seems to have been first elicited by the increase of worship to the Botataung Lady, which is consistent with the general intensification of *thaik nan shin* worship. During the 1990s, Mya Nan Nwe attracted ever more numerous worshippers beyond the local public, many of whom sought specific boons from her. Because of the growing number of worshippers, the pagoda's trustee board decided to accommodate her devotion in a specific two-storey building that has since served as her sanctuary, opposite the entrance of the pagoda compound. The decision was made partly out of convenience, to rationalise the collection of the growing offerings to the Lady that benefited the whole religious complex. At the same time, it returned the focus within the pagoda to the Buddha's relics inside the stupa; the Lady was relegated outside to a less valued location that was in keeping with the trustees' understanding of her religious status.

In this sense, the Botataung Lady, whose post-Independence representation preceded a wave of pagoda-guardian materialisations of the 1990s, has met with a unique destiny by being ousted from the Buddhist sanctuary. Since that time, Mya Nan Nwe's new shrine has become a major attraction of the Botataung religious complex, which has led to further developments and diversifications of the ritual activities associated with her. Further, in a major policy change following trustee elections in 2016, the new board decided that all contributions collected from the Lady's worship would be devoted to her pavilion maintenance.

The Lady's ability to flourish despite banishment is a significant precedent of the new pervasiveness of pagoda guardians. Local ritual activities have expanded at an incremental pace, and Mya Nan Nwe's influence goes beyond Botataung and into various domains of Burmese religiosity. Together with Saw Mun Hla,[14] she has even become one of the two main *thaik nan shin* figures of possession in spirit possession ceremonies to the Thirty-seven Lords.

---

14 Saw Mun Hla, a Shan spouse of King Anawratha, is the guardian Lady of Shwezayan Pagoda, on the road from Mandalay to the Shan states in Upper Burma. See Foxeus 2017 about her cult's new developments.

A pluralistic history of the Botataung Lady's displacement

While talking with various people linked to Botataung religious complex in the course of my observations, I came across competing versions of the Lady's relocation outside the pagoda enclosure. Her particular destiny is related to the fact that the inner reliquary of the stupa to which she is bound as a spiritual figure was uncovered during World War II. However, stories of the Lady are not willingly revealed by devotees. Only when I discovered her transfer, in 2002, was I told that cultic activities around the Lady had grown to such an extent that it was no longer possible to accommodate them on the walkway around the stupa. The pagoda trustees had decided to expel the Lady from the Buddhist sanctuary because the devotions she received were not compatible with such a place.

However, the story I heard in 2011 from Uncle Hsu, then head of the pagoda's trustee board, was somewhat different.[15] I had been introduced to this official by Daw Saw, a woman professing to be a specialist of the *weikza* path and active in the celebration of the Lady's birthday, performed around the end of December since its inception in 2001. An old man of 86, Uncle Hsu had worked as an architect. Bright and articulate, he was also fluent in English and turned to this language every time he addressed me specifically. Daw Saw, who also understands English, concluded with a disapproving air that the story he had told me was different from the one she had previously heard from him. Here is the version he gave me.

When he became the head of the trustee board in 1988, Uncle Hsu immediately planned to repair an old pavilion that housed a valuable Buddha image opposite the entrance of the pagoda compound. The image probably had been donated long ago by a rich woman who owned a ruby mine in Mogok, Kachin State. He looked for her without success. She was probably already dead. Then he thought about secretly ordering a statue that represented this rich devotee in a unique, kneeling position, and to place it in the pavilion. He tried to convince the trustees to support his project, but they asked him to first gain support from the nearby monasteries. Seven monks

---

15 Uncle Hsu, aka Aung Hsu Shin, was head of the trustee's board from 1988 until his death in 2015. He had already been interviewed by Western scholars on the cultic history of the Lady, as we can learn from Mandy Sadan (2005: 98) and Donald Stadner (2011: 86). He had also authored a book in Burmese on Mya Nan Nwe about which he told me nothing when I met him; I discovered it recently, while conducting background research for this chapter (Aung Hsu Shin 2008).

voiced their strong opposition against this iconographic innovation, even after he pointed out the economic value of his proposal. They finally changed their minds after he took them to the Ananda Pagoda in Pagan and showed them a representation of King Kyanzitha kneeling in front of the Buddha's image that convinced them of the acceptability of this iconography.

The head trustee told me this history without any reference to the *thaik nan shin* Lady, although the image of the Lady that had graced the stupa platform was duly relocated outside the compound, next to the new representation of the kneeling devotee-woman. He presented this new development of the Botataung Buddhist establishment as the result of his negotiation with the monks and of the devotion of the general public. Indeed, devotees come in large numbers to worship Mya Nan Nwe and make ritual offerings to her in her new sanctuary. The tiny golden statue of the standing *thaik-naga* Lady is still visible close to the shiny colourful new one of the kneeling devotee-woman, testifying to their spiritual connection. In Uncle Hsu's narrative, the elision of the previous appearance of the tiny *thaik-naga* Lady statue on the stupa walkway bespeaks of his reluctance to make a place for her in the picture he drew for me. I had received a somewhat rationalised version of the Botataung Lady's worship history, which contrasted with his Burmese-language book's narrative that can be read as seeking to arouse uncanny feelings and a sense of devotion among the Burmese Buddhist public.[16]

The new image is alternately dressed in the flashy green robes of *thaik-naga* Ladies or in the pink ones of nuns, testifying to the caring love of her worshipers as well as of their imagination of her as both a Buddhist devotee and a *thaik-naga* being. The space around the statue is full of coconuts along with glasses of milk, a specific *naga* food. Glass donation boxes are full of banknotes. To everyone in the public, the figure of the kneeling devotee-woman is that of the Botataung Lady. Even the head trustee's plan to rationalise the collection of religious donations was meant to direct the economic elements of this growing devotion toward the religious estate more generally. When I remarked that his actions contributed to her fame, he agreed, somewhat mischievously. Actually, the old man had played on the ambiguity of the kneeling woman, who captures the imagination of Mya

---

16 Uncle Hsu's somewhat flattering declaration during our discussion that I would be an ambassador of Burmese culture in writing about Mya Nan Nwe made it obvious to me that he was fully aware that his statements about the Lady of Botataung could impact Westerners' perceptions of Burmese Buddhism abroad.

Nan Nwe's devotees and can also be interpreted as an ancient representation of 'pure' Buddhist devotion, complete with an incontrovertible historical precedent at Pagan.

The abbot of the Neikban Kyaung, a nearby monastery belonging to the monastic complex opposite to the pagoda, has a somewhat different version of Mya Nan Nwe's story. He was not part of the meetings related by Uncle Hsu. But he had heard the story from one of the monks involved in the decision to develop a new Mya Nan Nwe sanctuary. According to this story, Mya Nan Nwe was a woman who volunteered to rebuild the pagoda after World War II and who later offered the valuable Buddha image before she disappeared. Nobody has ever heard from her since, nor has she ever been seen, of course. Without establishing an explicit causal link, the monk then further explained that she was a *naga*, a being linked to the water realm. *Naga*s are snakes created out of the imagination of craftsmen, he told me, but the way he explained the weird vanishing of the woman fits well with one of the features of *naga* imaginary. *Naga*s can only take on the appearance of human beings for a short time. Quite reluctantly, the monk implicitly revealed the story as it is envisioned by many devotees: the woman who helped restore the pagoda and who offered a Buddha image was actually the *thaik-naga* guardian of the pagoda. In the monk's story, the figure's rationalisation takes a deeper dive: the focus on the pagoda-builder aspect of the Lady nurtures her role as a pagoda guardian.

The old muddy market for ritual offerings (coconuts, bananas, leaves and flowers) was rebuilt to new standards in 2016. Here, a vendor of coconut and banana offerings for the Lady's worship told me yet another tale. In his eyes, to worship Mya Nan Nwe in this way was not 'truly' Buddhist. This was an Indian practice, he explained to me, using the common but derogatory term *kala* for 'Indian'. Indeed, the offerings to the Lady were called *puzaw bwe*, a word that derives from the Sanskrit word, *pūja*.[17] Besides that, among the flock of devotees, 'only 6 out of 10 were Burmese'. Distancing himself from these practices – which in his eyes were not Buddhist enough because they were not Burmese enough – the sceptical merchant nevertheless stated that selling coconut and banana offerings was *ahlu*, a Buddhist meritorious deed.

---

17 However, the devotees would rather use *kadaw bwe*, 'ritual offerings', for the offerings to the Botataung Lady. By using *puzaw bwe*, the merchant clearly located himself in a Buddhist reformist discourse, dismissing devotional offerings to spirits as not 'truly' Buddhist. On the differentiation of religious transactions, see Brac de la Perrière 2015.

Ahlu, Burmese for the Pali *dāna*, means 'religious donation' that forms the heart of the religious practice of lay Buddhists in Burma. While criticising the worship of the Lady with offerings, he nonetheless believed that the devotees' purchases from his business rose to the level of *ahlu* and contributed to his own merit.

Well aware of the developments involved with the place, the seller accurately stated that many devotees were not Burmese. A lot of them are from the newly expanding middle classes of Burma's Theravada Buddhist neighbour, Thailand, who have started to tour the region in imitation of the global touristic leisure culture. The rumour about the 'Whispering' Lady's powers has quickly disseminated among Thai tourists, many of whom request a visit to Botataung Pagoda as a part of their visit to Yangon. This has contributed to reinforcing the transformation of the whole site as a commodified cultic place while also boosting the worship of Botataung *bobogyi*, the male guardian who remained inside the pagoda compound while the Lady's worship was taken out. A special corner of the market is now well stocked with Thai-style glass amulets containing a miniature of the Botataung *bobogyi*, making it a body-portative image, something never heard of in Burma before this market's renovation.[18] Finally, in the pagoda compound, the *bobogyi* pavilion has been renovated by the new trustee-board so as to accommodate the growing flux of tourists and pilgrims coming to pay him their homage.

Commodification of devotional practice is clearly on the rise, facilitated by the development of inter-Asian tourism. However, the Burmese public continue largely to distance themselves from Thai tourists' behaviour at religious sites and they have not adopted Thai-style amulets. Still, unlike the coconut seller above, they do not dismiss Thai tourists' practices as not being truly Buddhist. Some Burmese devotional figures have been introduced into the Thai spiritual landscape and, when tourists visit them at their original sanctuaries in Burma, Thai ways of worship have been accommodated at

---

18 Amulet worship in Thailand dates back to the 1950s and has since developed into a prosperous economy of commodified religious goods. See particularly Tambiah 1984, Jackson 1999a, 1999b and Pattana 2012. Significantly, Burmese *bobogyi* have also found their way to Thailand as explained by Neeranoch Malangoo in her talk at the workshop 'Interrogating Buddhism and Nationalism' (Oxford, 27–28 January 2018). Temples with Burmese *bobogyi* now exist in Thailand, which speaks to the development of transnational ritual exchanges. In the past decade, the cult of Botataung *bobogyi* has been established in Thailand where he is renamed in Thai as *Thep Than-jai*, 'the deity who grants boons expeditiously'.

touristified places such as the Botataung complex, even though they have not entered Burmesse practice. However, the high regard that Thai tourists have for the Botataung Lady and *bobogyi* enables Burmese to grasp something of the potency that their devotional figures may have for Thais.

The Lady's fame not only contributes to making the Botataung site a forum-like place where all kinds of Burmese religious practitioners converge, but also adds a new sense of cosmopolitanism that fits well with the development of the urban surroundings. The large religious estate and the port open space have also became a major recreational spot. Going from one group to another among those making their living out of Mya Nan Nwe's fame, one encounters various impressions of the mysterious Lady. Above all, she is a polyvalent figure that can accommodate various personae: at the very least, a *thaik naga*, a Buddha devotee or a nun, a multiplicity that appeals to growing flocks of devotees from various strands of the complex religious field described above.

Day-to-day devotional rituals: A spiritual presence without embodiment

During everyday rituals performed by devotees and visitors alike at Mya Nan Nwe's temple, people come in small groups to present their requests to her and offer the standard basin with coconuts, bananas and leaves (*kadaw bwe*), together with foods specific to the worship of *naga* beings (fuits and milk), and the green scarves that are given to all *thaik* ladies. Until recently, no ritual specialist had been assigned to the Lady's sanctuary, which instead had been a public worship place open to anyone wishing to experience personally her spiritual presence through her figurative image. It was made for devotees who arrived as individuals, presenting their offerings and their requests to the Lady. However, with the increase in the size of the crowds over time, the new trustee board has allowed registered laymen with a religious inclination to assist the many devotees who do not dare to address the Lady directly, phrasing their requests in an appropriate way.

The main activity in the shrine is the presentation of these offerings to the main image of the Lady. The devotees do not carry these items themselves. Rather, a team of women makes a meagre living from bearing basins filled with newly purchased offerings from the nearby stalls of the sellers into the sanctuary and placing them near the Lady's figure, and replacing them with new ones. In addition, the board of trustees hires custodians who maintain vigil all day long and ensure that everything goes well. The continuous flow of devotees and their offerings speaks to the Lady's popularity.

However, the success of the Lady would not have reached such heights without the mediation of ritual specialists who bring their devotee-clients to the Lady. Most of these specialists, identified as *medaw* or *bodaw* – mostly but not exclusively women (*medaw*) from what I have observed – are followers of the *weikza* path whose mediation with spiritual entities related to the *weikza* sphere – *bobogyi*, *thaik* ladies, *bilu* and other *weikza* figures – is sought after by simple devotees.[19] Guiding their clients to the shrine and presenting their offerings to Mya Nan Nwe, *medaw* sometimes start to speak with the Lady's voice, softly, foretelling the devotees' future.[20] If a custodian takes notice, he swiftly puts an end to the process – unless he is offered a small bribe for his understanding. However, the main activity in the sanctuary remains individual, face-to-face encounters with the Lady, whose numerous devotees whisper their most secret wishes directly into her ears.

Some professional spirit mediums (*nat kadaw*) come to the Lady's shrine as simple devotees, without performing spirit possession in this context. Indeed, at one time, signs written in bold red letters warned the public that any manifestation of the Lady through oracles or any embodiment of the Lady through dances was forbidden inside the building. Her role as a caretaker of the local Buddhist material dispensation has led the pagoda trustees' board to ban any form of spirit mediumship inside her shrine. However, striking features of the place are the multiplication of pictures of the Lady donated by devotees and the mirror reflecting her representation. In these many images, she is dressed in her various religious or regal clothes. These many images create a saturated visual space, producing a deep feeling of Mya Nan Nwe's presence, what Irene Stengs in her chapter here aptly describes as an 'oneiric space'.[21]

This charged atmosphere may compensate for the ban on the Lady's manifestation through possession dances or oracles inside her sanctuary. But it may also induce embodiment among the ritual specialists who practise in the contiguous field of spirit possession. Possession dances are certainly

---

19 *Medaw* may also be addressed as *hasayama*, 'female teacher' (See Foxeus, this volume).
20 I occasionally observed this form of oracular possession in this context some years ago, but not recently: its repression seems to have put an end to these possessions.
21 See Chapter 9 in this volume.

not expected in the Lady's sanctuary, contrary to what happens in temples of the Thirty-seven Lords' pantheon and in Saw Mun Hla's sanctuary at Shwezayan pagoda (Foxeus 2017), the other *thaik* Lady who commonly possesses specialists during spirit possession séances.

Actually, the absence of any dance or music orchestra marks out Mya Nan Nwe's sanctuary as distinct from spirit (*nat*) temples and Saw Mun Hla's shrine. The spatial ordering also contrasts. Offerings and devotion focus on the central kneeling Lady's figure, herself paying homage to the Buddha's image, rather than on the 'sacred' side of the room where the golden statue of Gotama sits. Through this *mise en abyme* of devotion to the devotee, the Lady's worship in her new Botataung sanctuary is distinguished from the worship of other spiritual figures by various specialists, such as the spirit mediums (*nat kadaw*) or *medaw* and *bodaw* who follow the *weikza* path. Paticularly, spirit mediums' practices in their respective ritual contexts focus instead on spirit mediumship, that is, on the re-presentation of the spiritual through its embodiment.

The Lady's annual birthday celebration: A forum-like ritual event

Truly diversified ritual practices come together during Mya Nan Nwe's annual birthday celebration. On this occasion, the ability of the figure to attract a large range of specialists is fully visible. The Lady's birthday has been celebrated around the end of December every year since 2001, two years after she had been relocated to her new pavilion opposite the pagoda compound main entrance. This probably started as a limited celebration by her closest followers.[22] Mya Nan Nwe's birth date was determined by the pagoda trustees' board after the Lady's main *medaw* reported having learnt this date by a direct oracular message from the Lady in her dreams.[23]

---

[22] To note, the anniversary of Bomingaung, the main cultic figure among the *weikza* today, started in the same way as a limited celebration from 1994 onwards to celebrate the *weikza*'s exit from the life cycle (*htwek yap pauk*) on the second waning day of Tawthalin (in September) in 1952 at Mt Popa in Upper Burma. Since 2002, it has become a huge gathering of *weikza* followers and ritual specialists known as the festival of (Bomingaung's) 'way out' (*htwek bwe*) (Brac de la Perrière 2014).

[23] This event reveals the importance of oneiric manifestations in the development of Mya Nan Nwe's cult, which is also consistent with the development of many cults pertaining to the *weikza* field. In his book, Uncle Hsu does not identify who among the main actors of the celebration was his informant, but he does include a photograph of the Buddha image Mya

The event started as a small affair: *medaw* and *bodaw* who claimed to be spiritually linked to the Lady presented religious offerings, shared birthday cakes, and called on their followers to take turns celebrating in the privacy of the shrine's upstairs room.

The celebration of her birthday in 2020 took place from 2–4 January to give devotional space to the three main original groups of devotees, led by *medaw* who took charge, in turn, of each day's celebration.[24] The birthday program started the night before, when the kneeling Lady was given new make-up and clothes, a ritual repeated each evening as the *medaw*s competed to create the most resplendent figure. Each day's program combined birthday celebration with Buddhist prayers and meritorious practices.

On the first day, a marginal group led by two male devotees calling themselves *nagani* (red *naga*) set up luxuriant flower decorations around the kneeling Lady. They also made three impressive flower piles inside the Lady's pavilion for the three main guardian divinities of Botataung Pagoda and at 10:00 a.m. led the collective Buddhist recitation of the 'flower *cetiya*' (*pan zaydi*) prayer in front of the Buddha image, which really started the celebration. The opening ceremony was then performed outdoors, in front of the pavilion's entrance with a release of balloons, group photographs, and music and dances performed exclusively by ordinary devotees; as usual, devotee leaders refrained from dancing in public. Then, a chapter of 11 monks whose day had begun with breakfast served upstairs at 5:30 a.m. came back from their monasteries where they had retired in the time between. The senior monk delivered a Buddhist predication to the collective of devotees, also upstairs, which was followed by a joint merit-sharing ritual, before the monks' principal meal service around 11:30 a.m. This program was replicated on the following day with the addition of spectacular birthday cakes being shared among the leaders' entourages and the singing of *Happy*

Nan Nwe had donated. The photo includes a black signboard that identifies the Lady's birth date as 22 December 1906; this signboard is no longer exhibited publicly (Aung Hsu Shin 2008, picture 5 and pp. 27–28). The date corresponds to the 9th of Pyatho according to the Burmese calendar, which is the reference used to calculate the date every year.

24 The three main devotee leaders are Daw Wa Wa Tan, Shwe Naga Daw Saw and Daw Tin Myint, who set up the birthday celebration together with the trustees around twenty years ago. The two associate devotees in charge of the floral decorations are Hsaya U Nan Way Aung and Naga Ni Ko Nyunt Win. These two devotees claim to have had a long spiritual relationship with Mya Nan Nwe and to have organised the cult to her before her first birthday celebration. They are also critical of the trustees' version of Mya Nan Nwe's emergence story.

Figure 2.3. Mya Nan Nwe palanquins departing on the Yangon River. **Colour** p. 315.

Birthday to You in English, followed by hand clapping. The third and final day concluded with a final predication by monks, upstairs in the pavilion, and sharing of merit. Then, the celebration was declared successful as audience members threw banknotes and proclaimed 'Victory!' (*Aung bi*).

During these upstairs proceedings, ordinary devotees and pilgrims continued to pay their respects to the Lady in the temple's main room, which became overloaded with flower decorations and offerings. A number of food distributions also occurred downstairs, offered by devotee leaders to any visitor, which added to the affluence and the joyful atmosphere. Over the years, this birthday celebration program has progressively expanded outside of the temple and, by 2020, it had become an extraordinarily complex and festive event, a forum-like one in which various actors – other than the three original devotee leaders – come together, each with a discrete agenda associated with their specific religious or ritual strand. Snowballing awareness via word of mouth and reports that appeared in the specialised press explain this success.

Relatively new innovations to the basic celebration include rituals that take place outside of the shrine and involve boatmen who work at the nearby Botataung jetty. Independent groups of devotees buy makeshift palanquins adorned with the Lady's image and loaded with *kadaw bwe*, fruits and milk bought from local vendors.[25] They form pageants that include groups of invited musicians called *shan Osi* – from the Shan drum that every group features – who perform mainly for Buddhist ceremonies but not for spirit possession séances (*nat kana bwe*), which require a classical music orchestra (*hsaing waing*). After having paid their respects to the pagoda and the Lady's

---

25 The image composing the background of the palanquins was first that of the tiny golden *thaik* Lady holding *naga* heads in each hand. The number of palanquins that featured the kneeling devotee-woman was far greater in 2020 than ever before (personal observation).

temple, the pageants head to the jetty where the palanquins are taken by boatmen to be discarded in the middle of the river.

The parade has become an occasion for the Lady's manifestation within the bodies of female devotees. To the sound of the lively *shan Osi* music, devotees perform the same stunning *thaik-naga* dance that one observes in spirit possession ceremonies (*nat kana bwe*) on two occasions: when Amay Shway Nabay, a *naga* lady in the Thirty-seven Lords pantheon, enters her female mediums;[26] and during spontaneous 'wild' (*yaïn*) possession dances by women in the audience, dances that are usually attributed to unidentified *thaik-naga*. The *thaik-naga* dance is performed with both arms stretched upward along each side of the head, with intermingled hands. In the open-air context of the Botataung parades, dancers remain standing while in the indoor context of spirit-possession ceremonies, they end up rolling on the ground (*lu-*), 'as a crawling snake' after having fallen down backwards, forming an arch.[27] Women involved in *thaik-naga* dances during Mya Nan Nwe palanquin pageants look as if their actions are spontaneous, not displaying any particular link to professional mediumship or to a particular *weikza* ritual specialisation. However, a closer look at who participates in these dances soon reveals that a lot of them do in fact belong to these circles. The series of palanquin pageants such as these, accompanied by dancing groups of devotees, make the three-day event a joyful and very entertaining one.[28]

In 2015, one famous spirit medium, U Win Hlaing, started to perform a full spirit possession ceremony on the occasion of the Lady's birthday, using his connections to charter a boat for the elaborate ceremony. He first dedicated his own palanquin to the Lady after having it blessed by a monk and before the boat left the jetty for the one-day performance of Thirty-seven Lords possession dances. Then, he introduced the celebration day by embodying the *naga* king. Indeed, as documented in previous works (Brac

---

26 Amay Shway Nabay is an exception among the spiritual figures fostering dances in spirit possession séances in that she mainly possesses female mediums, which contrasts with all the other possessing figures that can enter men as well as women, regardless of their own gender identity.

27 An outstanding counter-example of *naga* dance ending up with rolling on the ground in an outdoor context is that of the Amay Shway Nabay festival at Myittu, when the spirit medium rolls out of the shrine on the ground all the way to the waters of the canal (Brac de la Perrière 1998a).

28 During the 2016 celebration, according to vendors at the pagoda market who make the palanquins and sell them for 40 to 100 USD, up to 100 palanquins were sold. And according to the boatmen, 11 boats were fully employed during the three days of the festival to dispose of the palanquins in the river.

Figure 2.4. Performing the arch in the *thaik-naga* dance in front of the palanquin, with a *shan Osi* orchestra. **Colour** p. 316.

de la Perrière 2011, 2014), in the wake of growing figurative representation of pagoda guardians during the 1990s, the growth of devotion to these figures has also allowed for their embodiment during spirit possession performances. However, as *thaik nan shin* are considered to be of a higher rank than spirits belonging to the Thirty-seven Lords, their embodiment at the beginning of the séances is characterised by hieratic dances, which contrast with *thaik-naga* dances performed for Amay Shway Nabay incarnation or outbursts of 'wild' possession. U Win Hlaing, one of the most innovative and up-to-date spirit mediums today, has enthusiastically embarked on this path and has sought to enhance his style even more by organising his on-the-water event.

For the past few years, another kind of palanquin has entered Botataung jetty: the Botataung dockyard corporation has set up temporary pavilions that back onto the seafront and are used to celebrate Shin Upagot (Upagutta). During a traditional seasonal Buddhist ritual, rafts loaded with images representing this Buddhist saint are released on waterways. He is pictured as a monk sitting and holding his alms bowl, looking upward, illustrating that he is supposed to dwell in the ocean and wait there for food offerings. Because Shin Upagot is linked to the water realm, seamen and boatmen alike worship him. He is commonly called on at the beginning of any Buddhist event to keep trouble away.

Combining its own specific devotion to the seasonal tradition and taking advantage of the Lady's birthday, the dockyard corporation thus adds its own celebration to those of *weikza* path followers and of spirit mediums. The Shin Upagot pavilion is open to the public throughout the Lady's birthday celebration; donations are expected and these are managed by the dockyard event's leaders. On the second day, monks are invited to recite *aneikaza*, the first verse of the first sermon delivered by the Buddha, in front of Shin Upagot's image. In Burma, this performance in the presence of a representation of the Buddha takes place at the consecration of Buddhist images (Brac de la Perrière 2006). Then, the meritorious offering of a meal to monks (*ahlu*) takes place and members of the corporation and their families also share a festive meal together. On the third day, Shin Upagot is released onto the river, retrieved and then taken to the monastery of another community down the river. The leaders of the dock corporation hold that, although its ritual palanquin processions look similar to those for Mya Nan Nwe, and although the two kinds of rituals are celebrated simultaneously, the two celebrations are entirely separate from one another. According to their stance, the Shin Upagot celebrations are exclusively auspicious (*mingala*) and meritorious in intention, and thus 'truly' Buddhist in nature.

In 2020, the celebration further evolved when cruise boats were rented by affluent donors to devotee groups and, following U Win Hlaing's initiative, accommodated a *shan Osi* orchestra and *thaik-naga* dances on board, after having poured onto the waters a special milky preparation to feed the *naga* supposedly living under water. The number of pageants has also grown. On the last day of the 2020 celebration, the trustees opened the pagoda's gardens to eleven pageants, each complete with palanquins, *shan Osi* musicians, specialists and devotee groups, as they waited for tide time, because the port esplanade was too crowded to accommodate them. All devotees, some hundreds of people, were busy eating snacks, performing various devotions and fidgeting with impatience inside the pagoda precincts before the start of the pageant on the port esplanade. In this febrile atmosphere, some rhythm could not be prevented from being beaten by a drum, which immediately prompted dances by devotee-women. This drew U Ye Myint, the new trustee head, to the spot with two guards who he ordered to suppress the dance upsurge. When I asked him, U Ye Myint repeated that possession dances were strictly forbidden in the pagoda precincts and he revealed to me that for him they were just *meihsa*, 'heresy'. As a trustee, he had to manage the pageants, but next year the board would implement new arrangements to avoid such embarrassment!

Concluding comments

Altogether, the pageants of Mya Nan Nwe devotees, the spirit possession ceremony of a spirit medium, the celebration of Shin Upagot by the dockworkers, plus the commercial fair and the night sermons delivered by famous monks that the pagoda trustees arranged for the same period, contribute to making the Botataung Lady's birthday an important festive event in Yangon. The whole celebration is characterised by its polymorphous dimensions, informed by the polyvalence of its central figure. Inside the Lady's temple, the combination of Buddhist devotion with the birthday celebration is addressed to Mya Nan Nwe as a Buddhist devotee by the main original devotee groups, while on the port esplanade palanquin pageants accompanied with *shan Osi* music prompt *thaik-naga* dances by ordinary women-devotees.

While not commenting on the arguably competitive relationships between local actors involved (the pagoda trustees' board, the local monasteries' abbots and the Botataung dockyard community), their respective roles need to be further explored in this history of ritual development. Paradoxically, this history is linked to the growing importance of both male and female *weikza* path ritual specialists who, with all their rivalries between themselves and with spirit mediums (*nat kadaw*), act in common as devotee-group leaders during Mya Nan Nwe's birthday celebrations. Interestingly, the Lady's banishment from the pagoda facilitated spirit-oriented ritual developments that would not have occurred so readily if she had remained inside that space.

While all these ritual formats are well represented elsewhere in Burma, their combination in the Botataung Lady's celebration gives the gathering a remarkable forum-like aspect. In this regard, it resembles annual festival celebrations of the *nat* in their respective original places in Upper Burma, except that the latter are perceived as 'traditional' (*yoya*). Another instance of forum-like celebration, calling on a range of spiritual beings and practitioners from various strands of religious life, is the *weikza* Bomingaung's wayout anniversary at the Mt Popa religious complex, which took this dimension from the 2002 celebrations onwards (Brac de la Perrière 2014). In the Lady's celebration, this combination has developed across the same period of time, and precisely following the transfer of the Lady's figure to her new pavilion at the end of the 1990s, when a broader efflorescence of devotion to pagoda guardian spirits was also witnessed throughout Burma.

Comparatively, the development of Mya Nan Nwe's birthday in a forum-like ritual event may be seen as paralleling the expansion of the festival to the Lady of the Kingdom at the South Vietnam border, since the Doi Moi opening of the Vietnamese economy (see Philip Taylor 2004). There too, groups of recently urbanised devotees attend the festival led by spirit mediums whose practice of goddess embodiment through dance is severely restricted within the temple by the officials in charge, but is expected on the outside, where no oversight is exercised (*ibid.*: ch. 6).[29] In this case of a newly developed ritual event that reflects the dynamics of rapid social change, the growing fame of a public devotional figure elicits the spontaneous development of celebrations and attracts specialists from various brands of religiosity. At the same time, at least within the temple, divinity's dignity is shielded from practices deemed to devalue it as the embodiment of spiritual beings through possession dances.

Mya Nan Nwe's celebration has produced palpable ritual innovations that draw on many sources. The processional aspect and discarding onto waters of this celebration clearly borrows from the traditional Shin Upagot ritual form. At the same time, the popularity of the Lady's celebration surely figured in the dockyard community's decision to revive the Shin Upagot celebration. Another influence at play is the Myittu festival in Upper Burma, dedicated to Amay Shway Nabay, one of the Thirty-seven Lords. Here, Amay Shway Nabay, a *naga* Lady, is embodied by a female spirit medium who ends her performance by rolling down from the ritual pavilion into the canal waters (Brac de la Perrière 1998). This very specific feature serves as the template for the specific *thaik-naga* dance seen in Botataung, as well as for the discarding of the Lady's palanquins in the river. Further, Botataung pageants have developed in a way that allows independent groups of devotees to conduct *thaik-naga* possession dances outdoors. Thus, the ritual form of sending the Botataung Lady into the river via a palanquin parade is a local innovation that makes use of selected features from various paths of Burmese ritual practices.

Botataung pageants provide ritual space for *thaik-naga* possession dances outside of the institutionalised setting of the Thirty-seven Lords possession séances. In fact, the embodiment of pagoda guardians seems to be a recently developed practice in ritual settings that accommodate spirit mediumship. As guardians of the *thathana*, the relatively high status enjoyed by pagoda guardians forces spirit mediums to give them precedence under their ceremonial pavilions: they are the first invited to 'enter' their mediums through

---

29 It also evokes large-scale Hindu festivals such as Navaratri in Bangkok as analysed by Erick White, in which a diverse collection of Thai Buddhists also participate. He observes that spirit mediums take part in the final procession with all other Thai Buddhist devotees, setting up temporary altars along the route that become focuses of religious devotion. White underscores the 'social possibilities opened up by a large-scale spectacle of Buddhist devotionalism … sanctioned by orthodox Hinduism' (2017: 287).

hieratic dances. Spirit mediums now call upon pagoda guardians to provide new avenues of spiritual embodiment practice, in order to satisfy the needs of a diversifying urban public. For them, embodying pagoda guardians through possession dances is one among several strategies that aim to upgrade their practice in Burma's total Buddhist-dominated religious field.

For *weikza* specialists, the manifestation of spiritual partners relates to the display of an energy (*dat si-*) produced by spiritual perfection and departs significantly from the dances characteristic of spirit possession (*nat win-/nat ka-*).[30] The embodiment of perfect beings such as *weikza* within human specialists tends to be devalued among their followers. If it occurs at all, it is conceived of as *ideally* being a masculine role. It is static and seated manifestations in the context of *medaw* and *bodaw* private shrines or in pagodas known as places where *weikza* have practised religion, and thus where energy (*dat*) has been accumulated. By contrast, the *nat* dances are performed by spirit mediums *ideally* conceived of as women (*nat kadaw*, the 'female spouse of a male spirit') in the context of spirit possession séances. Obviously, this stereotyped contrast needs to be nuanced. Men and transgender women, are also preeminent actors on the mediumship scene. Nevertheless, in spirit possession ceremonies (*nat kana bwe*), the spirit medium's role ideally requires the crossing of gender boundaries.[31] The gender contrast in the manifestation of the spiritual by spirit mediums and *medaw* or *bodaw*, is expressed at a discursive level and takes complex forms in the actual performances.

As for the manifestation of *thaik* ladies in spirit possession séances, they now are performed right from the start by both male and female spirit mediums in hieratic dances which serve to upgrade these events. More traditional *thaik-naga* dances occur later on during the séance, either to embody Amay Shway Nabay or when 'wild', unidentified *thaik-naga* break in with intermingled hands, arch and roll on the ground. By contrast, *thaik* ladies are also embodied by devotee-women in front, for example, Saw Mun Hla's shrine at Shwezayan pagoda, through *thaik-naga* dances similar to those performed during spirit possession *séances*. As for Mya Nan Nwe devotees' outdoor dances along the palanquin parades, they are also of the *thaik-naga* kind, except that most of them stop before rolling on the ground. The case

---

30 Brac de la Perrière 2011.
31 About the gender qualification for spirit medium's role, see Brac de la Perrière 1998b and about the presence of transgenders on the mediumship scene, see Brac de la Perrière 2022.

of Mya Nan Nwe stands out as an exception among pagoda-guardian ladies in two ways; because her shrine has been displaced outside of the pagoda that she guards and because, even so, *thaik-naga* dances of her devotees occur mainly outside her pavilion, on the port esplanade.

Arguably, by making use of selected features of various ritual practices, Botataung's innovative ritual pageants can be seen in light of hybridity theories that Pattana Kitiarsa suggests make sense of the changing landscape of contemporary Thai religion (Pattana 2005: 468). However, considering the processes involved in the cultic history of the Botataung Lady, one realises that rather than 'hybridisation' it is constituted by a series of appearances of her spiritual agency, each time removed from the core of mainstream official religious institutions. After World War II, uncovering of the Buddhist sanctuary relics enabled the efflorescence of the Lady in a material form. In the 1990s, her growing fame surfed on the wave of pagoda guardian appearances and led to her relocation in a separate shrine. Then, the attention received by this newly prominent spiritual figure led spirit possession manifestations to be banned from her sanctuary. These developments occurred as a series of practice purifications whose ultimate target has been spirit possession manifestation. Particularly, *thaik-naga* dances have been discriminated against because they are deemed less 'religious' in some contexts, while indulged in for their evocative power of the Lady's presence in other settings.

Finally, it seems that the displacement of the Lady of Botataung has created a space where her polyvalent nature as a pagoda guardian has been allowed to fully express itself. In this place different lines, more or less 'religious' – which is mutually evaluated according to their respective compliance to mainstream Buddhism – meet around her new material manifestation as a devotee-woman rather than a *thaik-naga* Lady. But rather than a blurring of delineations, this forum-like place produces a reinforcing of boundaries between devotions to the Buddha and his saints, *medaw* and *bodaw* direct communication with the pagoda guardians belonging to the *weikza* field, and spirit mediums' (*nat kadaw*) danced embodiment of spiritual beings.

Lines are manifested side-by-side, but they do not merge. In this sense, the forum-like quality of the event actually expresses and reinforces the process of autonomisation of each field through mutual confrontation. The Lady's birthday celebration may be seen as a perfect site to illuminate processes of identification *and* distinction selectively operating through competition, disregard or contempt between ritual specialists belonging to different mutually determining segments of the religious field. While these dynamics do occur in the contemporary context of urban modernity, they belong to a longer story of 'religious' differentiation.

References

Almond, Philip. 1988. *The British Discovery of Buddhism*. Cambridge: Cambridge University Press.

Aung Hsu Shin (Thakiwin). 2008. *Parami Shin Ma Lay Mya Nan Nwe* (Lord of Virtues, Mya Nan Nwe). Yangon: Shin Shin Sapay Taik.

Bourdieu, Pierre. 1971. 'Genèse et structure du champ religieux', *Revue Française de Sociologie*, 12(3): 295–334.

Brac de la Perrière, Bénédicte. 1995. 'Urbanisation et légendes d'introduction du bouddhisme au Myanmar (Birmanie)', *Journal des anthropologues*, (61–62): 41–66.

———. 1998a. 'Le "roulis de la Dame aux Flancs d'Or". Une fête de *naq* atypique en Birmanie centrale', *L'Homme*, 146: 47–85.

———. 1998b. "Etre épousée par un *naq*. Les implications du mariage avec l'esprit dans le culte de possession birman (Myanmar)', *Anthropologie et Sociétés*, 22(2): 169–182.

———. 2006. 'Les rituels de consécration des statues de Bouddha et de *naq* en Birmanie (Myanmar)' in G. Tarabout and G. Colas (eds), *Purushartha 25, Rites hindous, Transferts et Transformations*. Paris: EHESS: 201–236.

———. 2011. 'Being a Spirit Medium in Contemporary Burma', in Kirsten W. Endres and Andrea Lauser (eds), *Engaging the Spirit World: Popular Beliefs and Practices in Modern Southeast Asia*. New York: Berghahn Books: 163–183.

———. 2014. 'Spirits versus Weikza: Two Competing Ways of Mediation', in Bénédicte Brac de la Perrière, Guillaume Rozenberg, and Alicia Turner (eds), *Champions of Buddhism: Weikza Cults in Contemporary Burma*. Singapore: NUS Press: 54–79.

———. 2015. 'Religious Donations, Ritual Offerings, and Humanitarian Aid: Fields of Practice According to Forms of Giving in Burma', *Religion Compass*, 9(11): 386–403.

———. 2016. 'Spirit Possession: An autonomous Field of Practice in the Burmese Buddhist Culture', *The Journal of Burma Studies*, 20(1): 1–30.

———. 2019. 'From Tree Spirits to Pagoda Guardians: *Bobogyi* as a Burmese Spiritual Figure', in Bénédicte Brac de la Perrière and Christophe Munier-Gaillard (eds), *Bobogyi: A Burmese Spiritual Figure*. Bangkok: River Books: 10–37.

———. 2022. 'Hpyo's Choice: Activism or Mediumship? A Gay Person's Dilemma in Contemporary Myanmar', in Peter A. Jackson and Benjamin Baumann (eds), *Deities and Divas: Queer Ritual Specialists in Myanmar, Thailand and Beyond*, Copenhagen: NIAS, Press.

Brac de la Perrière, B., G. Rozenberg and A. Turner (eds). 2014. *Champions of Buddhism: Weikza Cults in Contemporary Burma*. Singapore: NUS Press.

Dhammasami. 2004. 'Between Idealism and Pragmatism: A Study of Monastic Education in Burma and Thailand from the Seventeenth Century to the Present', PhD dissertation, Oxford University.

Foxeus, Niklas. 2017. 'Possessed for Success: Prosperity Buddhism and the Cult of the Guardians of the Treasure Trove in Upper Burma', *Contemporary Buddhism*, 18(1): 108–139.

Houtman, Gustaaf. 1990. 'How a Foreigner Invented Buddhendom in Burmese: From *Tha-tha-na* to *Bok-da' ba-tha*", *Journal of the Royal Anthropological Society of Oxford*, 21(2): 113–128.

Jackson, Peter. 1999a. 'The Enchanting Spirit of Thai Capitalism: The Cult of Luang Phor Khoon and the Post-modernization of Thai Buddhism', *South East Asia Research*, 7(1): 5–60.

———. 1999b. 'Royal Spirits, Chinese Gods, and Magic Monks: Thailand's Boom Time Religions of Prosperity' *South East Asia Research*, 7(3): 245–320.

Kirichenko, Alexey. 2019. 'From *Thathanadaw* to Theravāda Buddhism: Construction of Religion and Religious Identity in Nineteenth- and Early Twentieth-Century Myanmar', in Thomas D. DuBois (ed.), *Casting Faiths: Imperialism and the Transformation of Religion in East and Southeast Asia*. New York: Palgrave Macmillan: 23–45.

Masuzawa, Tomoko. 2005. *The Invention of World Religions: Or, How European Universalism Was Preserved in the Language of Pluralism*. Chicago: University of Chicago Press.

Mendelson, E. Michael. 1961. 'A Messianic Buddhist Association in Upper Burma', *Bulletin of the School of Oriental and Africa Studies*, 24(3): 560–580.

Pattana Kitiarsa. 2005. 'Beyond Syncretism: Hybridization of Popular Religion in Contemporary Thailand' *Journal of Southeast Asian Studies*, 36(3): 461–487.

———. 2011. '*Buddha Phanit*. Thailand's Prosperity Religion and its Commodifying Tactics', in Pattana (ed.), *Religious Commodifications in Asia. Marketing Gods*. Routledge: 120–143.

———. 2012. *Mediums, Monks and Amulets: Thai Popular Buddhism Today*. Bangkok: Silkworm.

Pearn, B.R. 1939. *A History of Rangoon*. Rangoon: American Baptist Press.

Picard, Michel (ed.). 2017. *The Appropriation of Religion in Southeast Asia and Beyond*. New York: Palgrave Macmillan.

Sadan, Mandy. 2005. 'Respected Grandfather, Bless this Nissan. Benevolent and Politically Neutral Bobogyi', in M. Skidmore (ed.) *Burma at the Turn of the 21st Century*. Honolulu: University of Hawai'i Press: 90–111.

Schober, Juliane. 2011. *Modern Buddhist Conjunctures in Myanmar: Cultural Narratives, Colonial Legacies and Civil Society*. Honolulu: University of Hawai'i Press.

Spiro, Melford E. 1967. *Burmese Supernaturalism: An Explanation on Suffering Reduction*. Philadelphia: Institute for the Study of Human Issues.

Stadner, Donald M. 2011. *Sacred Sites of Burma: Myth and Folklore in an Evolving Spiritual Realm*. Bangkok: River Books.

Tambiah, Stanley B. 1984. *The Buddhist Saints of the Forest and the Cult of Amulets*. Cambridge: Cambridge University Press.

Taylor Philip. 2004. *Goddess on the Rise: Pilgrimage and Popular Religion in Vietnam*. Honolulu: University of Hawai'i Press.

Turner, Alicia M. 2014. *Saving Buddhism: The Impermanence of Religion in Colonial Burma*. Honolulu: University of Hawai'i Press.

———. 2021. 'Secular Colonial Pedagogy in Bricks and Mortar and the Problematic Monks of the Mango Grove', *Journal of Southeast Asian Studies*, 51(2): 26–48.

White, Erick. 2010. 'The Cultural Politics of the Supernatural in Theravada Buddhist Thailand', *Anthropological Forum*, 13(2): 205–212.

———. 2014. 'Possession, Professional Spirit Mediums, and the Religious Fields of Late-twentieth-century Thailand', PhD dissertation, Cornell University.

———. 2017. 'Staging Hinduism in the Bangkok Metropolis: Ritual Spectacle and Religious Pluralism in an Urban Thai Buddhist Milieu', in Pavin Chachavalpongpun (ed.), *The Blooming Years: Kyoto Review of Southeast Asia*. Kyoto: Kyoto University Press: 280–288.

CHAPTER 3

The Buddhist-Mediumistic Pantheon in Northeast Thailand (Isan)
A Symbiotic Relationship

Visisya Pinthongvijayakul

Introduction

*A*t *Ajan*[1] Tho's Thammayut Order monastery or *wat*, located not far away from Chaiyaphum city centre, on the occasion of the Third Lunar Month Festival in February 2013, cars, three-wheeled *tuk tuk* taxis and motorbikes overfilled the parking area in the morning. Crowds of villagers were sitting in the central court and at a nearby pavilion. On an ordinary day, anyone on their first arrival might not recognise the place as a Buddhist *wat*; when one walks through the main entrance, neither a chapel, a pagoda, nor a crematorium can be seen. Instead, the *wat* is encircled by a continuous range of spirit shrines and cement statues of mythical figures hiding the usual Buddhist temple complex and monk dwellings from view. On that day, *Ajan* Tho's disciples, mostly women in their 50s and 60s, were dressed in neat and colourful clothes. Each of them wore a long saffron scarf on their shoulders that crossed their chests to the right side of their waists, sort of a minimalised distant relation to a monk's robe and, clearly, some sort of ritual uniform. They carried *khan ha*[2] bowls, offerings for respected figures, including *Ajan* Tho, as well as their possessing spirits, including his.

---

1   *Ajan* can be equivalent to 'master.' The locals use this title to refer to monks or teachers.
2   The word *khan* means 'bowl,' a metal water container that the people of Northeast Thailand use in their everyday life. *Ha* is the Thai number 'five'. *Khan ha* literally means 'a bowl of five (offerings).' *Khan ha* is the material representation of personhood. It is the salient personal totem whenever a person is present in a ritual domain. For example, a spirit medium will present *khan ha* to her master to allow her to enter and leave ritual trance. Villagers create *khan ha* in various ways. Mediums and their disciples skillfully put a pair of specific flowers and a pair of small candles together in five banana-leaf cones inside the bowl. Laypeople might add five pairs of flowers and five pairs of candles, more or less, to the bowl.

On the far side of the crowd, which was supposed to be the front arena of this gathering, some were preparing trays of food, fruits and gifts on row upon row of long, white tables.

This was not a usual Buddhist festival organised according to the Buddhist calendar. Nor was it a regular feature in other local monasteries. This was not the day that temple affiliates would come to listen to prayers, give alms, or make merit. And it was not a scheduled monastic gathering for meditation or practice of Buddhist precepts. Rather, it was an occasion on which *Ajan Tho* and other monks would make contact with their possessing spirits. It was the stage on which the abbot would sing songs from the mediumistic repertoire, to the accompaniment of a *mor khaen*[3] musician who cast an enchanted overture over the ensemble of his disciples. It was a rendezvous for these disciples who, entranced, would dance unceasingly as the musicians shifted pace and pattern. It was an occasion of communitas in which the disciples would perform a topsy-turvy burlesque in the monastery: they would become possessed, transgress gender categories, drink liquor and signal lucky lottery numbers. It was a venue where all food, fruits and gifts would go through processes of reciprocal exchange to please respected spirits and ensure the worshippers' wellbeing. And it was a time for a renewal of *barami* (charisma or auric power) and a revitalisation of local religiosity.[4]

This chapter seeks to resolve a tension within Thai religiosity: the presence of mediumistic activity in a *wat*. The Buddhist monastery provides space for the shrines of local gods, as well as for the humans who congregate to celebrate these spirits. Mediumistic practice adds vitality to the monastic domain. The ritual sequence was supervised and directed by the medium-abbot. All temple-goers on this occasion were disciples in *Ajan Tho's* mediumistic network. They had been healed and cared for by his Buddhist

---

3   A musician who plays *khaen*, *mor khaen* combines two words. *Mor* in Thai means a specialist in ritual traditions associated with healing and now is the modern Thai word for 'doctor.' *Khaen* is a bamboo mouth organ that is common in Isan. A *mor khaen* is then a musician regarded as a ritual specialist in playing the *khaen* bamboo mouth organ, which is a central element in the performative ritual of spirit possession in Northeast Thailand.

4   What I have described here offers a good illustration of Victor Turner's (1969) classic analysis of liminality. However, my data potentially collapses the rigid boundary of structure and anti-structure since what, in Turner's terms, would seem to be role reversal within the ritual actually extends in a more porous fashion to everyday life practice. For instance, the medium-monk is called by the name of his possessing spirit or female mediums are called *khuba* – a Northeastern Thai term normally reserved for highly respected monks outside ritual domains.

mediumistic power. In their perception, Buddhist altars and spirit shrines are composite images of local religiosity that become meaningful in their everyday life.

This opening vignette raises a number of questions: How can we define the relationship between Buddhism and spirit mediumship? In these mediumistic rites, how can we understand the copresence and interpenetration of elements that commonly are held to belong to distinct religious realms? And how can we make sense of the transgression and inversion of hierarchy in the monastic domain where both Buddhist monks and laypeople are present?

This chapter explores an aspect of religious dynamism and modification in contemporary Northeast Thailand, or Isan, as it is known by locals. It questions the understandings of work that conceptualised the relationship between Buddhism and spirit mediumship as one of segregation: functional, social, spatial. In contrast, I suggest that the relationship should be perceived as reciprocal, involving mutually constitutive and inextricable elements of a composite religious domain. In Chaiyaphum Province, Buddhism and spirit cults enjoy a symmetrical and compatible rapport. I draw upon ethnographic observations from my field site and investigate the existing literature to re-conceptualise the interplay between Buddhism and mediumship as one in which processes of exchange and mutual incorporation are manifest. I argue that the realms of Buddhism and spirit mediumship are not segregated but are interpenetrated and interdependent. By drawing on ecological discourses, I propose to model the relationship as one of 'religious mutualism' whereby both religious constituents partner in service of the villagers' world.

Buddhism and spirit cults are mutually constituted, that is, they are each made up of the other. It should be noted here that my data reflects the local situation in Isan. I suspect that the co-presence of Buddhism and supernaturalism in Bangkok is similar, but perhaps different in degree. In March 2016, I participated in a Brahmanistic teacher worship (*wai khru*) ceremony organised by a group of divination practitioners in a famous *wat* near the Grand Palace in Bangkok's old city. Supernatural ritual processes were performed; stories of magic, dreams, and trance were circulated among the attendants. Additionally, it should be emphasised that a majority of monks in many of Bangkok's important *wat*s come from Isan. I know one, an associate abbot at a well-known monastery on the Chao Phraya riverbank, whose life is guided by a prophecy made by a spirit medium from his village in Chaiyaphum. Official Buddhism and spirit beliefs comingle in complex

Figure 3.1. The Third Lunar Month Festival at *Ajan* Tho's monastery. **Colour** p. 316.

ways that might be defined as dynamic syncretism or, perhaps, Thai ecumenism. In Chaiyaphum, Buddhism cannot be defined in terms of either the absence or presence of spirit mediumship. And spirit cults are not always subordinate to Buddhism. Finally, I argue that processes of exchange and mutual incorporation make tangible the transposable inversion of hierarchy between the two realms.

Re-examining the relatedness of Buddhism and mediumship

One morning, I discussed the relationship between Buddhism and spirit mediumship in Chaiyaphum with *Ajan* Tho, who told me:

> Firstly, villagers believe that the Buddha, his teachings and demerit/merit exist. However, in their consciousness and spiritual world, they believe in local supernaturalism (*sing saksit*): tutelary gods (*phra phum*), guardian spirits (*jao thi*) and those spirits in their fields (*phi rai, phi na*). They don't believe in Buddhism only. Supernaturalism and Buddhism coexist in people's way of life. In their ritual practices and everyday life, they don't neglect any of them. It is impossible to prohibit villagers from worshipping their pre-existing beliefs that have been transferred and passed down from their ancestors. (My fieldnotes, 13 March 2013)

Ajan Tho emphasised that in the villagers' religious life, it was impossible to separate spirit cults and Buddhism. His opinion illuminates his ecumenical ritual practice and depicts the way villagers believe and perform ritual in their everyday life. His explanation brings forward the idea of incorporation between Buddhism and supernaturalism. Existing works compartmentalise Thai religious complexity into components that separate principal Theravada Buddhism from lesser supernaturalism (Kirsch 1977, Wijeyewardene 1986,

Tambiah 1970, Hayashi 2003). These accounts of a hierarchical segregation of Buddhism and local spirit cults may well have been accurate and correct in 1970s Thailand. The incorporation of both realms into the forms of Thai religiosity that I have observed may well be a recent innovation. To re-conceptualise the dynamism in the relationship between Buddhism and spirit mediumship, I will highlight a quality of interpenetration of the two realms and show the processes of exchange and mutual incorporation. While the existing literature contends that the relationship between Buddhism and mediumship is functionally, socially, and spatio-temporally segregated, I argue that it is reciprocal and co-dependent. Buddhism cannot be defined in terms of the absence of spirit mediumship. And spirit mediumship cannot be understood without Buddhism. They comprise each other.

The functional-structural viewpoint yields a model of Thai religion as separated sub-components that serve in the different domains of the monastery and spirit cult. Through this lens, religious practitioners function according to their segregated domains (Hayashi 2003). Monks function as the intermediaries in the monastery while spirit officiants serve local cults. Anthropological studies of Thai religious practices recount the details of practitioners who specialise in particular rituals and purposes (Tambiah 1970, Hayashi 2003). These studies categorise practitioners by reference to authority derived from distinct religious institutions and their respective functions.

However, there is no such functional separation among officiants of specific domains in the Chaiyaphum monasteries and ritual activities that I studied. Spirit mediums are active monastic attendants. Monks become prominent specialists in village spirit cults and sometimes are possessed by spirits. The religious efficacy of Chaiyaphum monks and mediums is comprehensive, correlative and interchangeable. Mediums are usually invited to conduct lifecycle rituals and rites of passage in the same way monks do. *Mae*[5] Mala is famous for her ability at reciting Buddhist Pali mantras with her beautiful voice and incredible memory. Her hobby at home is to read and memorise books of Buddhist mantras. She embodies Buddhist power from her active learning of local Buddhist texts and her active engagement in monastic affairs. Villagers often invited her to perform new house-warming ceremonies, rituals that monks usually perform in the Thai context. *Mor*

---

5   *Mae* means 'mother' and is a kin term of respect that is used to address and refer to honoured senior women.

Num is a young male medium who had been ordained as a monk during the Buddhist Lent. His Buddhist knowledge is incorporated into his mediumistic practice. He has become a famous specialist of both Buddhist and spirit rites. Like *Mae* Mala, he recites Buddhist mantras and sings mediumistic melodies. Whenever someone dies in the village, the relatives invite *Mor* Num to conduct the funerary processes. Additionally, it should be noted here that, in rituals revolving around *Phaya* Lae, the heroic figure and divine governor of Chaiyaphum Province, it is not unusual to see that Buddhist monks and spirit mediums are present and perform rituals at the same time both in Chaiyaphum city and in rural locations. At one ceremony during the construction of a statue of *Phaya* Lae in a monastery, monks were chanting Buddhist sutras in the temporary pavilion while a group of mediums were dancing and leading participants in a parade around the monastery's pagoda.

We have already learned that, in Thailand, the urban middle class has spurred the growth of supernatural ritual (Pattana 1999, Irvine 1984). In contrast to Max Weber's classic speculation in *The Protestant Ethic and the Spirit of Capitalism* (1985) about the disenchantment of religion after the rise of capitalism, both the urban middle class and middle-income peasants are creating religious behaviours that give rise to a re-enchantment of Thai spiritualism. In the past, court support, governmental programs, and the practices of state-sponsored monks contributed to a rationalisation of Buddhism. These elite-driven efforts have been outflanked as the political economy has reshaped power relations. Together with a decline of the nation state's centralised power over religious expression (Jackson 1997, 2012; Pattana 1999, 2005, 2012), the emerging rural middle class and urban middle class are actively inserting their religious culture into the practice, sponsorship, and representation of religion in Thai society.

As noted above, early studies of the relationship between Buddhism and non-Buddhist beliefs tend to segregate and compartmentalise Thai religious complexity (Kirsch 1977, Tambiah 1970, Hayashi 2003). They have omitted the ideas of co-dependency and interpenetration. They also emphasised the primacy of Buddhism over animistic beliefs. Moreover, the relationship between religious practitioners across the religious field was overlooked. Buddhist monks were portrayed as superior to other religious practitioners. However, in Chaiyaphum, I often observed female mediums actively distributing blessings and drawing more audience attention than monks or Brahmanistic priests who performed the same activity. At my field site in

Chaiyaphum, Auntie Pam, a medium who moved from another Isan province and married a local high school teacher, provided a complementary form of religious rapport. She compared the relationship of Buddhism, Brahmanism, and local superstitious belief with the pastoral imagery of 'three supporting poles' and 'a traditional stove formed by three bricks' (NE: *mai kham yan, korn sam sao*) as the indispensable assembly that any kind of religious practitioner is required to draw upon in order to help humankind. None of the poles can be maintained without the continued presence of the others; nor can a two-brick stove be used to cook. Other mediums gave me similar metaphorical explanations for the necessary incorporation of three belief systems into complementary, effective power. Auntie Pam told me that at one household ceremony, monks are invited to have their late morning meal at the house, where they will lead a Buddhist chant session. Then a spirit medium will come and perform a dancing blessing in a celebration session. Both monks and the medium work hand-in-hand to bring the sense of 'auspiciousness' (*sirimongkhon*) and 'celebration' (*chalorng*) to the one ceremony.

Medium-sponsored Buddhism

In Chaiyaphum, Buddhism lacks potentiality and functionality if it is practised without the presence of spirit mediumship. This section explores the reciprocating flow from spirit mediumship to Buddhism: mediums bring both materiality and praxis to the monastic domain. People and money are the prominent elements that mediums draw to temples. But I intend to demonstrate their additions of life and frameworks, namely new ideas, trends, religious formats and excitement, into temple rituals. These subtle sub-components are vital in terms of upgrading temples and practices that make the temples more responsive to contemporary desires.

In Chaiyaphum, spirit mediums play a crucial role as the sponsors of local Buddhism. I suggest that spirit mediumship is like the womb in which local monasteries originate and flourish. Important monasteries are built upon the sites of earlier spirit shrines. Spirit mediums made pilgrimages to these sites prior to the emergence of the *wat*. Even today, throughout the year, spirit mediums' congregations draw crucial public attention, temple goers, activities and financial support to these monasteries.

Many Buddhist monasteries rely on mediumistic practices. *Ajan* Tho's monastery has been nurtured by his mediumistic network for more than ten years. He told me that, in his youth, the spirit of an ancient god in the ruins of a Khmer-era chapel hospital in Chaiyaphum city gave him his vocation as a spirit medium. His disciples also pay respect to the spirit; they are as likely to address him by the spirit's name, *Luang Pu* Thongsamrit, as by his monk name, *Ajan* Tho. He and his network enabled the establishment of the monastery. According to the National Office of Buddhism, the state requires an applicant to demonstrate the availability of communal property and local consent before a monastery can be built and registered. *Ajan* Tho sought assistance from his mediumistic network in the village. These spirit mediums helped him to buy the land and build the monastery. After its establishment, *Ajan* Tho sought to enhance the monastery's reputation by inviting villagers to participate in monastic activities that would inspire them to leave donations needed for the monastery's maintenance. He revealed to me his strategy to enhance the number of temple-goers by using his mediumistic power. As a medium, he went to heal villagers and conduct rituals in everyday environments. Later, these people and their relatives became disciples in his mediumistic network and also acted as supportive attendants at his monastery. It is true that the medium-abbot also had some disciples who were not spirit mediums and who donated to the monastery and helped him in other ways. But these spirit mediums helped intensively, on an everyday basis. They provided the voluntary labour needed to support the monastery's activities, and worked directly under the abbot's supervision. Every time I made a call from Bangkok to *Ajan* Tho's main disciples, they were always at the *wat*. They explained that when the monk called them to help in mediumistic practice and monastic activities, they immediately stopped working in the fields and gardens and made their way to the monastery. They considered it compulsory to help the monk because he was their *khuba*[6] (spiritual master) and, by doing this, they gained merit and prosperity. The notion of 'supporting and maintaining' (NE: *kham khun*) between Buddhism and mediumship is crucial. As monks are not allowed to dance, among other things, *Ajan* Tho could not personally conduct a full mediumistic process, so he was dependent upon his disciples. The medium-abbot usually initially sang during the introduction to a ritual,

---

6 In Chaiyaphum, *khuba* is a title for both monks and mediums. While *khuba* can be used for both male and female master mediums, the title *ajan* is usually used for only male master mediums.

and then three other mediums would take the stage and play the roles of three muses, singing and dancing to heal or conduct other ritual processes.

In Chaiyaphum, villagers frequently request help from divine lords and spirits (*jao phor*) for everyday problems. Mediums are therefore in high demand to perform services beyond the monastery. Housewives, students, policemen, politicians and peasants are customer-devotees who pay money for reciprocal processes mediated by spirit mediums. They give white, money-filled envelopes to mediums, their assistants and *mor khaen* after the requested ritual service has been performed. The amount of money given varies according to the customer-devotee's financial status. Master mediums divide this money into a small part for personal sustenance and the overwhelming majority for charity, most of the latter being given to the monastery, which uses the resources as it sees fit.

With their substantial income from mediumistic missions, individual mediums are often in a position to be strongly supportive of local monasteries. *Mae* Mala was an enthusiastic patroness of local temples and monastic charity. She was a respected master medium in her sub-district. All her four children had good jobs and sent her remittances regularly. Both outmigration from Northeast Thailand and difficult livelihood conditions in the region have resulted in the gradual decline in the number of everyday temple-goers. Each village attempts to arrange a weekly timetable in which a few villagers, mostly female, prepare and bring food for the monks both in the early morning round at 7:30 am (NE: *janghan*) and the late morning round at 11:00 am (NE: *phen*). *Mae* Mala committed to bring food to the monastery for both rounds every day, except for the day she scheduled for her ritual missions. Apart from consistently attending and preparing food, she used personal money to cover various monastery expenses. For example, she paid a monthly remittance for novices who commuted to study at another monastery. *Mae* Mala revealed to me that she had opened a bank account under the name of *Phaya* Lae (*banchi jao phor*) where she deposited what she received from conducting rituals and then spent to support temples and other local charities. Likewise, at the shrine room of another female medium, *Mae* Som, customer-devotees placed white envelopes in the wooden bucket in front of her spirit shrine after the ritual process was complete. She spent most of this money on monastic charity and preparation for every morning's food offering for monks, but sometimes asked permission from the deity of the shrine to split some money for her own use.

Another female medium, *Mae* Sim OK, a strong, confident and talkative woman in her late 70s, could be described as an unfortunate woman but also was a powerful, charismatic *khuba*. She lived in a small, old house with her niece in Kaengkhror District, about 50 kilometres from Chaiyaphum city. She had her own rule about managing the money she earned from mediumistic rituals: she gave *all* away to monasteries and charities. She supported herself by raising pigs and selling them at the local market. Villagers knew her reputation and shared the motto that everything you brought to her would be arranged smoothly and would be OK. That is why people gave her the name *Mae* Sim OK. The lady considered her poverty as a self-aware, moral renunciation of secular greed. She provided all facilities that monks in the village monastery asked for, from refrigerators to TV satellite dishes, by using the money from her mediumistic profession.

Monasteries embrace spirit mediums because they recruit and attract patrons to them. In 2012, when he was 21 years old, *Mor* Num was temporarily ordained and moved his spirit shrine into his temporary dwelling at the local monastery. During the three months of Buddhist Lent that year, *Mor* Num supervised many mediumistic healing rituals there. Like *Ajan* Tho, his direct participation was limited,[7] but his three assistant mediums danced and touched the patients. Mediumistic ritual processes are bodily and intimate activities. While dancing to heal, the embodied spirit touches the skin, grabs the hands, pats the head, and caresses the face of patients. It is also unacceptable for a monk to dance, and since the touching occurs 'while dancing', an assistant – and not the monk – will perform this ritual element. I asked *Mor* Num if the abbot of the local temple was worried about the unorthodox practice. He told me the abbot did not mind. One reason was that there were only a few monks residing there and the abbot might have needed to recruit more male youths to be ordained at the monastery. *Mor* Num told me the abbot often asked him if he could permanently stay in the monastery. But *Mor* Num declined to do so, and resumed lay life after three months as a monk.

---

7   Even though singing and dancing are not allowed for monks, we might find some monks dancing in private areas. When I visited *Mor* Num's house and attended his shrine reconsecration a few years later, I observed a monk and a novice sitting among his disciples. They were friends of *Mor* Num. When the celebratory dance session began, the monk and the novice became possessed and started dancing fanatically in trance.

The abbot saw *Mor* Num's mediumistic rituals while he was an ordained monk as opportunities to draw more people into the temple. According to *Mor* Num's protocol, a patient would be healed in the morning and, as a final procedure of the healing session, the patient's lost soul, or *khwan*, would be called back in the afternoon. Thus, patients and their family members would stay in the monastery and go for the food offering in the late morning round (NE: *phen*), where *Mor* Num also sat at the second place after the abbot. The abbot seemed to be happy with the increasing number of monastery visitors. He communicated to the patients and their family members that the merit they made by offering food to monks would speed up the healing efficacy of *Mor* Num's mediumistic power, and all family members would be blessed from this as well.

Mutual incorporation

Wat Sila-at, one of the most famous pilgrimage sites in Chaiyaphum, about 15 kilometres from the city centre, has flourished and been maintained by spirit mediumship. This monastery was constructed to accommodate *Ong* Tue[8], the name of a stone-carved Buddha image that can be dated back to around the 13th century. Spirit mediums travel from their villages in Chaiyaphum and nearby provinces to Wat Sila-at four times a year: the third lunar month (February); the fifth lunar month (*Songkran* or Thai New Year in mid-April); the eighth lunar month (the beginning of Buddhist Lent in August); and the eleventh lunar month (the end of Buddhist Lent in October). After visiting Wat Sila-at on these auspicious occasions, mediums might also travel to other pilgrimage sites in Chaiyaphum Province.

Wat Sila-at is situated far from local communities on a vast, rocky hill and is somewhat deserted on ordinary days. During these annual gatherings, however, the *wat* is occupied by hundreds of mediums from several networks. Most stay overnight because they have to offer food and gifts to nearby spirit shrines and statues at specific times, mostly in the early morning. They also believe that spending nights with *Ong* Tue will bring more *barami* to them. This tradition is similar to the one practised by villagers who occasionally remain at their local *wat* on nights that precede Buddhist holy days, practising moral precepts and praying.

---

8   *Ong* is a title and classifier for sacred and royal beings.

Figure 3.2. *Ong* Tue stone Buddha image at Wat Sila-at. **Colour** p. 316.

Anyone who walks into Wat Sila-at in these pilgrimage periods will see the festive temple fair at first sight. Behind the gate, dozens of temporary food stalls and shops are lined up along the street that leads up the hill to the temple hall and the *Ong* Tue's pavilion. There is a big stage on the left-hand side of the central ground that will become the site for an ear-splitting concert and entertainment at night. In Northeast Thailand, community monasteries usually provide areas for hosting seasonal caravans of *mor lam*[9] concert troupes, a massive entertainment industry that attracts a great number of viewers from nearby villages, districts, or even distant provinces. On stage, attractive singers perform series of *luk thung* folk and *mor lam* songs. Many rows of pretty women, transgender people, and gay men with thick make-up and spectacular costumes dance behind, moving and gesturing among glittering lights according to each song's lyrics and rhythms. We often see some monks sitting in the front rows. Food stalls and shops encircle the viewers and the central stage.

For Wat Sila-at and other monasteries, the throngs attracted by this kind of event are central to their development and functions, which generate a lot of cash flow and donations. A commodity economy operates through the production of iconography. A person who walks into *Ong* Tue's pavilion will hear a combination of *khaen* music and monk chants, and see spirit mediums dance in front of the Buddha image. Mediums and temple-goers quickly fill and refill transparent donation cabinets with coins and colourful banknotes. At the chamber on the opposite side, a microphone-holding monk's amplified voice directs passers-by toward glass cabinets filled with amulets made in the image of *Ong* Tue and available in all price ranges. Thailand has rarely

---

9   The word *lam* in the Isan dialect means to sing and dance. Here, *mor lam* has two meanings. First, it refers to a spirit medium because she is a religious practitioner who enters a trance state. Second, *mor lam* is a genre of contemporary Isan music characterised by fast-paced, funky songs with a lively beat.

been given to iconoclasm, but image representation and icon fetishism have been persistent and unquestionably popular. Nowadays, the occult market is an important source of income and many local monasteries promote the sale of sacred objects and supernatural shrines in the monastic space. Together with more mainstream daily and seasonal donations, these income streams generally suffice to cover the regular expenses of the monastic facilities.

When I was in Chaiyaphum in 2012 and 2013, I heard many stories of local monasteries where sacred tree trunks (*takhian*) were retrieved from rivers in the villages and exhibited under temporary pavilions close to the main halls or pagodas. Monasteries embraced these occult objects because they drew in people, money, and activities. Villagers went inside the main hall or pagoda to pay respect to the principal Buddha images, and then they went to worship these uncanny yet sacred objects. A few days before the bi-monthly national lottery, groups of villagers came to rub the tree trunk's surface with baby powder and used their mobile phones to take pictures in the hope that the powder would highlight magical indentations in the wood and the image would reveal some lucky lottery numbers.

At Wat Sila-at, we see a popular reclassification of the Buddha as a member of the Northeast spirit pantheon. I observed that it was *Ong* Tue, the spirit of the image of the Buddha, who emerged at will whenever mediumistic rituals took place and possessed spirit mediums in the inaugural stages to grant auspicious blessings. The Khorat Plateau in the region of Isan is full of mythical stories of the flying Buddha, who is said to have come to meet local guardians, deities and spirits, and left his footprints on the rocks as the memorials of his ancient visit to the region. A lot of monasteries have been built to celebrate these traces. Today, when Lao people in Northeast Thailand talk about the Buddha, it is not the same Buddha as the one imagined by the average central Thai *sangha* authority. The Buddha of the Northeast is more akin to the magical, supernatural travelling Buddha of the Lao *That Panom Chronicle*, as documented by Constance M. Wilson (1997), or the 'inspirited' Buddhas of Laos described by John Holt (2009). The Buddha is regarded as one of the members at the pinnacle of the Northeast spirit pantheon.

Transposable inversion of hierarchy

Modern South and Southeast Asian states share an outstanding religious feature in which world religions coexist with autochthonous belief systems.

Similarly, Theravada Buddhism and local animism constitute Thai religious complexity. This complexity has been characterised as 'syncretic' (Kirsch 1977; Terwiel 2012; Muecke 1992) and 'hybrid' (Pattana 1999, 2005, 2012). Even though these characterisations derive from structural-functional and postmodern anthropological frameworks, respectively, they both present the relationship between Buddhism and supernaturalism as separate realms with blurry distinctions in a hierarchical topography in which the former is paramount. Deep and rich ethnographic studies attempt to indicate the contestation of the hierarchy in which mediumship provides a stage for human agency in the regimes of gender and power (Lewis 1971; Irvine 1984; Balzer 1981; Norton 2006; Bacigalupo 2004). However, contestation in the regime of religion is overlooked. Anthropologists of Thailand seem to accede to the notion that spirit mediumship is subordinate to Buddhism (Pattana 2012, 1986; Hayashi 2003).

In this section, I aim to explore the hierarchical disposition of Buddhism and spirit mediumship. I realise that there are some limits to the interpenetration of Buddhism and spirit cults, such as the exclusion of women from the *sangha* and the *vinaya*'s prohibition of monks from dancing and singing, but these distinctions are increasingly in flux. What I am suggesting here is that we might be able to understand the relationship in terms of modes of becoming rather than modes of being, which leaves some room for the dynamic and changeable ontological make-up of religiosity to reveal itself. In the ethnographic accounts presented above, I have laid out the processes of exchange and mutualistic incorporation between the two realms and presented the relationship as one of interpenetrating religious fields. Because of this quality of co-dependency, it is difficult to define Buddhism as being in a higher place and mediumship as in a lower place even though that is what official discourse suggests. Rather, the local experience in Chaiyaphum provides a sense of dynamic and egalitarian pairing. Careful anthropological probing reveals not a perpetually stable hierarchy between the complementary pair, but rather a form of transposable inversion, a condition that makes sense of the transgressive nature of ritual actions in monastic and mediumistic domains. I suggest that the border between the two realms is porous, allowing flows of exchange. In Chaiyaphum the power relationship between Buddhism and spirit mediumship is like tidal amplitude, especially as regards reciprocal moments in ritual space and time. My ethnographic data testifies to the transposable inversion of hierarchy in the spatio-temporal respect of ritual.

In the social context in Chaiyaphum, Buddhist temples disseminate the idea of an ethical life and determine everyday behaviours. But when a ritual takes place there, we can observe the inversion of hierarchy where spirit mediumship regulates villagers' actions according to its divine cosmology. It was 9:20 am on the occasion of the third Lunar Month Festival at *Ajan* Tho's *wat* in the opening vignette of this chapter. When the ceremony began, some devoted disciples moved into his dwelling, far behind the central court. The medium-abbot and other monks were sitting there, packed tightly, hemmed in knee-to-knee. They turned their faces to the left wing of the dwelling and looked into a room filled with variously sized Buddha images. Two *mor khaen* behind the monks started a slow line of harmonic music. *Ajan* Tho closed his eyes, opened his lips and sang a song in the Isan dialect; the others recognised it as coming from the mediumistic repertoire. Many put their palms together at chest level and bent their heads slightly down. The crowd's noise outside stopped. The song lifted up and radiated over the landscape. The temple was being transformed into a stage where an episode of divine communication, human aspiration and idioms of fertility would be enacted.

I was sitting outside *Ajan* Tho's dwelling when the ritual began. What struck me was the composition of the second row behind *Ajan* Tho: two laymen and two monks. Supposedly in temple rituals monks should sit in front of and separately from laymen and in order of seniority. But the first and the second positions were laymen with monastic robes on their left shoulders indicating that their possessing spirits were the spirits of the Buddha images located in the *wat*. The first layman was *Ajan* Tho's chauffeur, who had been in the monkhood but disrobed to have his family. The second layman was a university lecturer who had also been ordained by *Ajan* Tho and had stayed in this monastery for a while. The third position was taken by a young, thin man who remained in the monkhood because *Ajan* Tho prophesied that he was fated to get sick and die if he left the monkhood and resumed life as a layman. The man considered this prophesy to be eminently plausible. When he had been a layman, this monk had encountered life difficulties and accidents. His parents took him to *Ajan* Tho for a soothing ritual. The monk's possessing spirit, later identified as a spirit of a Buddha image at the *wat*, told the parents that their son should be ordained at once. The last in the row was a plump monk who looked more solemn than the others. Participants shared a common recognition that these monks had possessing spirits (*mi ong*) just as as spirit mediums did. This sitting pattern of hierarchical order typically took place on other occasions of mediumistic ritual.

Ajan Tho finished singing, but the *mor khaen* continued their music. All disciples took their own *khan ha* bowls of offerings and arranged themselves, kneeling into a single line in order of seniority. The chauffeur and the lecturer bowed and presented *khan ha* to *Ajan* Tho to touch as an indication of asking permission to enter the ritual realm. What surprised me then was that both of the monks joined in the action, after presenting their *khan ha* to *Ajan* Tho, and showed respect to the two laymen. They bent down their heads and presented their *khan ha* to the chauffeur and the lecturer to touch. Other disciples followed the pattern, on and on. *Ajan* Tho explained to me later that the possessing spirits of the chauffeur and the lecturer were in higher rank, so the monks had to pay homage to them. This experience is not unique. Hierarchical relations of spirits of warriors and heroic figures in Chaiyaphum's cosmology are based on the same principle as the local bureaucracy when the 19th century Mueang Chaiyaphum had formed in the villagers' historical memory. *Phaya* Lae sat on the top as the governor, followed by a descending ladder of official military ranks. Furthermore, spirits of characters from folktales and Buddha images, whose names are recognised by Northeasterners across the region, are categorised according to the principles of precedence and kinship. I found a similar spiritual structure and arrangement as *Ajan* Tho's *wat* in other mediumistic networks. At villages, senior female mediums went down on their knees to present *khan ha* to young male mediums, who were the same age as their sons, before entering into trance, because these young male mediums' possessing spirits were of higher rank in their spirit pantheon. The spirits' power relations and hierarchies in the local religious cosmology would determine human relationships and actions. Also, established hierarchies of laypeople and monks in the human realm can be inverted in ritual contexts.

The dynamic inversion of hierarchy between Buddhism and mediumship happens not only in the monastery but also in the homes of spirit mediums. In Chaiyaphum, it is not unusual that Buddhist monks are among the customers who visit a spirit shrine in hope of suggestions about their everyday lives, luck and fortune. Previous ethnographic research reports the scene of interaction between the two parties of monks and laypeople in a medium's house. Pattana (1999: 153–154) observed an interaction between a female medium and two visiting monks at a deity shrine in Khorat, the biggest province in Isan. He reports that, according to the medium, 'monks and Buddhism have a higher religious and spiritual rank when compared to mediums and deities. Buddhist monks never pay respect to spirit mediums. The mediums, on the other hand, have to pay homage to the monks' (Pattana 1999: 154). However, I found my ethnographic experience to be in opposition to Pattana's findings. In Chaiyaphum, spirit mediums take the dominant role over Buddhist monks. At *Mae* Som's private shrine, monks who sought divine help had to pay respect to the shrine and the medium because her possessing spirit was the spirit of a celebrated Buddha statue in Isan, *Jao Phor* Inpaeng. This Buddha statue is located in Ubon Ratchathani Province. We can see here that women can be mediums for the spirits of Buddha statues. Moreover, such spiritual connection sometimes provides them with confidence and power over Buddhist monks. *Mae* Som often complained to me about some monks who went to beg for her help but showed an arrogant manner in front of her shrine and didn't bow before her.

Pattana depicts elsewhere (2012: 107) spirit mediums with no Buddhist authority and who, therefore, consider themselves inferior to Buddhist monks. In my investigation of monks' contact with spirit shrines in Chaiyaphum, if Buddhist monks wished to be successful in resolving personal matters or recovering from illness, they had to 'surrender' (NE: *orn yorm*) to the spirits. On one occasion at *Mae* Mala's house, an abbot was diagnosed with an illness caused by the attack of the spirit of a late abbot in the monastery who was angry at his offence. The monk's disciples visited *Mae* Mala in two pick-up trucks while the abbot was hospitalised. They gave him a call and exhorted him to surrender to *Mae* Mala's possessing spirits. They turned on the mobile phone's speaker and said, 'Venerable father, just surrender, surrender!' (NE: *luang phor, yorm phoen, yorm!*). The abbot complied with their request. He said, 'Yes, I surrender then!' (NE: *yorm, yorm yu!*). Once the monk expressed his subjectivity as subordinate to the spirit power – and only then – could he be helped in recovering from his illness.

Marjorie Muecke (1992) presents an astonishing account of an interaction between monks and mediums in a Buddhist Lent-entering (*khao phansa*) ritual organised by a master medium at her Chiang Mai house in 1978. The monks kneeled before the female master medium, who sat on an elevated platform before them, and paid respect by *wai*-ing[10] to her three times and 'then received her blessing: "she" cupped the head of each monk

---

10 *Wai* is the action when a person puts their palms together at chest level and bends the head down in order to show respect to another senior person.

in "her" hands as "she" recited khathaa11 and blew on their heads, then "she" did the same over a bucket of water that each monk presented to "her," thereby sacralising into *naam mon*'[12] (Muecke 1992: 101, bold emphasis in original). Muecke also portrays an episode when the monks performed a meditation dance of elaborate choreography. Muecke interprets this fascinating vignette as religious syncretism in which the customary relationship between Buddhism and spirit mediumship is reversed.

However, Muecke sees the situations she describes as a paradox concerning the social and moral supremacy of orthodox Buddhism over folk religion and disregards the transposable reversal in this religious mutualism. She still situates the relationship between Buddhism and spirit cults as separate domains that practitioners cannot cross over. Muecke reports that once possessed, spirit mediums in Chiang Mai did not participate in Buddhist ritual. They recognised functional boundaries between the two forms of religion. She writes, 'Both groups, mediums and monks, aspire to the same end, an end that each group complements the other in achieving. Monks, after all, are not permitted to become mediums, and mediums, usually by virtue of their gender (or if male, by virtue of their homosexuality) … may not become monks' (Muecke 1992: 102).

Likewise, Pattana (2012) studies the life of *Luang Phor*[13] Khun, a famous magical monk in Khorat, Isan. He argues that the monk is a postmodern medium 'whose religious charisma and ascetic practices have had phenomenal implications for contemporary Thai popular religion and public culture' (2012: 85). However, both Pattana and Muecke locate the magical monks in their accounts within the institutional framework of official Buddhism, while situating spirit mediums into separate, inferior positions of authority and power in Thai popular religion. My account shows that monks and mediums in Chaiyaphum operate their function and power correlatively in the same domain of religiosity. Monks can be spirit mediums. Spirit mediums can become monks. Within a single body, the subjectivity is comprised of Buddhist authority and spirit power (see Kazuo Fukuura in this volume for

---

11   *Khathaa*, also written, *khatha*, here denotes magical or Buddhist mantras.
12   *Naammon*, or *nam mon*, in Thai means sacralised water blessed by monks or religious practitioners. It is believed to contain magical power that can protect a person from bad luck and bless him or her with prosperity.
13   *Luang Phor* is a Thai term used to address a senior monk. It can be rendered as 'Father,' 'Reverend Father' or 'Venerable Father.'

comparative accounts from Northern Thailand). The expression of 'having a possessing spirit in the body' (*mi ong*) is the discourse in spirit cults that describes the way in which a person consents to permit a spirit to possess them. *Ajan Tho*, the medium-abbot, is a Buddhist monk who has *mi ong*. He is an exemplary figure who demonstrates the way one body can contain the mutual domains of Buddhist charisma and mediumistic power and perform the transposable inversion of religious hierarchy.

Conclusion

This chapter has examined the relationship between Buddhism and spirit mediumship in contemporary Northeast Thailand. It reviews the understanding from some existing literature, which tends to presume the relationship between Buddhism and spirit mediumship to be thrice-segregated: functionally, socially, and spatially. By drawing upon ethnographic information from Chaiyaphum, I argue that, firstly, the domains of Buddhism and spirit mediumship are not always segregated, but interpenetrate and are dependent on each other. The interplay between Buddhism and spirit mediumship can be understood as being composed of processes of exchange and mutual incorporation, that is, as 'religious mutualism'. Buddhism and spirit cults have a symmetrically compatible rapport. Religious practitioners in each domain cross over the boundaries to cultivate and perform power associated with the other domain. This complexity can be described as Thai religious ecumenism. In Chaiyaphum, Buddhism cannot be defined without reference to spirit mediumship, nor vice versa. And spirit cults are not always subordinate to Buddhism. Finally, I argue that the processes of exchange and mutual incorporation between official Buddhism and supernaturalism makes the transposable reversal of hierarchy between the two realms explicitly tangible.

References

Bacigalupo, Ana Mariella. 2004. 'The Mapuche Man Who Became a Woman Shaman: Selfhood, Gender Transgression, and Competing Cultural Norms', *American Ethnologist*, 31(3): 440–457.

Balzer, Marjorie Mandelstam. 1981. 'Rituals of Gender Identity: Markers of Siberian Khanty Ethnicity, Status, and Belief', *American Anthropologist*, 83(4): 850–867.

Hayashi, Yukio. 2003. *Practical Buddhism among the Thai-Lao: Religion in the Making of a Region*. Volume 5. Kyoto: Trans Pacific Press.

Holt, John. 2009. *Spirits of the Place: Buddhism and Lao Religious Culture*. Honolulu: University of Hawai'i Press.

Irvine, Walter. 1984. 'Decline of Village Spirit Cults and Growth of Urban Spirit Mediumship: The Persistence of Spirit Beliefs, the Position of Women and Modernisation', *Mankind*, 14(4): 315–324.

Jackson, Peter A. 1997. 'Withering Centre, Flourishing Margins: Buddhism's Changing Political Roles', in Kevin Hewison (ed.), *Political Change in Thailand: Democracy and Participation*. London, New York: Routledge: 75–93.

———. 2012. 'The Political Economy of Twenty-first Century Thai Supernaturalism: Comparative Perspectives on Cross-genderism and Limits to Hybridity in Resurgent Thai Spirit Mediumship', *South East Asia Research*, 20(4): 611–622.

Kirsch, A. Thomas. 1977. 'Complexity in the Thai Religious System: An Interpretation', *The Journal of Asian Studies*, 36(2): 241–266.

Lewis, I. M. 1971. *Ecstatic Religion: An Anthropological Study of Spirit Possession and Shamanism*. Harmondsworth: Penguin Books.

Muecke, Marjorie A. 1992. 'Monks and Mediums: Religious Syncretism in Northern Thailand', *Journal of the Siam Society*, 80(2): 97–104.

Norton, Barley. 2006. '"Hot-Tempered" Women and "Effeminate" Men: The Performance of Music and Gender in Vietnamese Mediumship', in Karen Fjelstad and Nguyen Thi Hien (eds), *Possessed by the Spirits: Mediumship in Contemporary Vietnamese Communities*. Ithaca, New York: Cornell Southeast Asia Program: 55–76.

Pattana Kitiarsa. 1999. 'You May Not Believe, But Never Offend the Spirits: Spirit-medium Cult Discourses and the Postmodernisation of Thai Religion', PhD dissertation, University of Washington.

———. 2005. 'Beyond Syncretism: Hybridisation of Popular Religion in Contemporary Thailand', *Journal of Southeast Asian Studies*, 36(3): 461–487.

———. 2012. *Mediums, Monks, and Amulets: Thai Popular Buddhism Today*. Chiang Mai: Silkworm Books.

Tambiah, Stanley J. 1970. *Buddhism and the Spirit Cults in Northeast Thailand*. New York: Cambridge University Press.

Terwiel, B.J. 2012. *Monks and Magic: Revisiting a Classic Study of Religious Ceremonies in Thailand*. Second revised edition. Copenhagen, Denmark: NIAS Press.

Turner, Victor. 1969. *The Ritual Process: Structure and Anti-Structure*. Chicago: Aldine Publishing Company.

Weber, Max. 1985. *The Protestant Ethic and the Spirit of Capitalism*. London: Unwin Paperbacks.

Wijeyewardene, Gehan. 1986. *Place and Emotion in Northern Thai Ritual Behaviour*. Bangkok: Pandora.

Wilson, Constance M. 1997. 'The Holy Man in the History of Thailand and Laos', *Journal of Southeast Asian Studies*, 28(2): 345–364.

CHAPTER 4

Reorganisation and Realignment of Spirit Mediumship and Spirit Possession in Chiang Mai, Northern Thailand[1]

Kazuo Fukuura

Introduction

*A*s globalisation has proceeded, various sorts of new religious phenomena seen around the world have generally been considered as evidence of the failure of expectations associated with Weberian sociology of religion. Thailand, a Theravada Buddhist country in mainland Southeast Asia, is a site of some of this evidence. This chapter documents how popular religion has been involved with ongoing processes of modernisation in Northern Thailand. It illustrates how internal relationships among spirit mediums have been maintained and developed, and how spirit mediumship has extended out from local societies and engaged with the nation-state and globalisation. In this chapter, I emphasise the importance of focusing on religious practices per se, including their performative aspects in particular contexts in the contemporary world. I also elucidate how religious creativity can 'transform existing cultural practices in a manner that a community or certain of its members find of value' (Lavie, Narayan and Rosald, eds. 1993: 5).

For these purposes, this chapter focuses on the reorganisation and realignment of spirit mediums and their religious practices in Chiang Mai in the early 21st century. After presenting general information about mediumship

---

[1] I gratefully acknowledge financial support from JSPS KAKENHI (Grant Numbers JP17K03280 and JP20K12458), Witoon Buadaeng's able assistance while I was conducting fieldwork, and the anonymous reviewer for their valuable comments and suggestions.

in Chiang Mai, I explore how and why mediums have created new rituals concerning the 13th-century Three Kings of Lan Na and established the Assembly of Spirit Mediums in Lan Na. I share Chiang Mai mediums' remarks about this Association and also recount how it subsequently became obsolete, reflecting on the local creativity and independent character of Chiang Mai mediumship. I also consider tensions within the reorganised forms of spirit possession in Chiang Mai by comparing a male medium for the Hindu deity Shiva, who now also has followers in Phuket and Bangkok, with another male medium for a local spirit of the traditional Northern Thai city-state, who emphasises the importance of preserving Chiang Mai mediumship as an indispensable basis for Lan Na or Northern Thai cultural identity.

Spirit mediumship in Chiang Mai

Spirit worship and mediumship in Chiang Mai from an historical perspective

While a variant of Theravada Buddhism has historically been a major religion in Chiang Mai, the centre of the Lan Na kingdom from the end of the 13th century until the beginning of the 20th century, spirit worship has also been widely practised. Throughout its history, belief in and rituals for the guardian spirits of the city-state were an important basis of political power for the kings of Chiang Mai (Anan 1999). Although one hundred years have passed since the city's integration into Siam, these beliefs and rituals constituting the city's traditional religiosity still persist among *khon mueang*, 'the people of the city-state', as Northern Thais call themselves. During the Lan Na period, several calendrical rituals for the guardian spirits of Chiang Mai were developed and some are still practised as components of the locality's cultural heritage (Sommai and Doré 1992). Importantly, all of these can be seen as examples of religious syncretism, as many also feature Buddhist chanting for the guardian spirits of the city in their ritual procedures.

After the integration of Lan Na into Siam at the beginning of the 20th century, these rituals for the guardian spirits were strictly regulated, as they were directly associated with the former polity. As a result, most of these rituals came to be performed by villagers or local government officials in a small way, away from the gaze of the central administration. Furthermore, spirit possession and animal sacrifice were severely limited in their performance, and the basic nature of these rituals was forced to become much more Buddhistic. Since then, in contrast to regions or countries where mediumship has been officially recognised, the Chiang Mai administration has not given it any official backing. In this context, by the middle of the 20th century, traditional spirit worship and spirit mediumship were rendered powerless and confined within rural villages.

Since the 1970s, however, and concomitant with social development and urbanisation, this tendency has changed drastically. In the 1970s, traditional spirit worship in rural areas started to decline in a setting in which unequal development and modernisation of social life in Northern Thailand favoured spirit belief in other forms. In contrast to the decline in rural spirit rituals, 'modern' spirit mediumship increased in urban areas, especially in Chiang Mai. By means of trance séance rituals, this rise in urban spirit rituals responded to needs created by the social, political and economic situation. In addition to traditional spirits linked to myths and historical domains, so-called 'modern' spirits such as those of kings in Northern and Central Thai history, as well as Hindu deities of Central Thai origin also emerged, which suggests that the traditional pantheon of tutelary spirits had been gradually undermined. In the 1980s, mediums supplemented their traditional practices such as healing with rituals for new services that enable individuals to realise their desires in fields such as business consultancy and the divination of winning lottery numbers (Irvine 1984; Tanabe 2002). In the 1990s, while the local people employed cursing rites against the despised military junta in Bangkok, or against unwanted condominium construction, businessmen frequently came to mediums in Chiang Mai in efforts to secure financial success (Morris 2000).

My fieldwork since the beginning of the 21st century has shown that mediumship in Chiang Mai comprises all the features cited above, and that traditional spirit worship in rural areas has not further declined to any significant degree. Throughout the recent developments of mediumship, the historical dimensions of traditional religiosity have been called back and now function as alternative ways to address problems in the everyday lives of ordinary people. In addition, spirit mediumship has also operated as a tacit ground for Northern Thai identity politics in pursuit of religio-cultural hegemony, in lieu of the erstwhile religio-political autonomy that the region enjoyed in the era before the nation, capitalism and globalisation began to influence its development.

Chiang Mai professional mediums and their spirits

While spirit mediumship is the sole activity of some professional mediums, many also engage in other business activities. Most Chiang Mai spirit mediums are from the middle and lower classes. Though the majority are female, there are significant numbers of male mediums. They range in age from children to elders. Though it has been argued that vulnerable women, who are believed to have a weaker *khwan* (life essence or soul) than men, become mediums in order to gain power and authority (Tanabe 2002: 54), both female and male mediums have created gender-inclusive communities for decades. Furthermore, mediums' master-disciple relationships have not been bound exclusively by gender. Nowadays, apprenticeship lineages, charisma and the ability to fund rituals are regarded as more significant than a medium's gender. Generally, Northern Thai people call spirit mediums *khao song* (the spirit enters), *rang song* (the body that is entered by the spirit) or *ma khi* (the horse that is ridden [by the spirit]). In this last expression, the spirit medium is deemed to be ridden and controlled by the possessing spirit.

Most people who become mediums first have experienced some form of illness of unknown origin and sought the assistance of a spirit medium, who has diagnosed their condition not as a disease but rather as a 'call' from the spirits. The diagnosing medium then recognises the patient as a new disciple (*luk sit*), and the latter begins to perform ritual practices that guide them as they begin to accede to the idea that they are possessed. Most possessing spirits are male and range from traditional spirits to tutelary spirits of high rank (*phi jao nai*). The former include guardian spirits of villages (*phi suea ban*), matrilineal ancestor spirits (*phi pu ya*), and tutelary spirits of the traditional city-state (*phi suea mueang*), while the latter include diverse spirits such as those of kings and other personages from Northern Thai history, myths and legends, Hindu gods and goddesses, historical figures from the Central Thai Rattanakosin kingdom such as King Chulalongkorn, Kuan Im (Guan Yin) of Chinese Buddhism and the spirits of hill tribes.

On the top of a spirit medium's altar is a tray for *khu*, or *phi khu* (literally, 'teacher' or 'spirit of teacher'). This tray, called *khan khu* (NT: teacher's tray), is not for the possessing spirit, but for the transcendental teacher. This transcendental teacher is the spiritual being whom the spirit worships, and its existence is presumed to secure the authenticity and charisma of the possessing spirit's ritual practices.[2]

---

2   In Northern Thailand, this belief is also widely held by traditional healers as well as in the domain of traditional handicrafts and skills such as silversmiths and traditional musicians.

The mediums' religious practice is twofold. First, they perform spirit possession séances for their devotees on a regular and often daily basis. When a medium begins a séance, they call on their possessing spirit to enter them. Then, upon entering trance, the medium puts on clothes associated with the particular possessing spirit, who listens and responds to the stories and issues related by the devotees. During a séance, mediums may be possessed by their spirits without any music or dancing (Fukuura 2012).

Mediums also perform various kinds of collective rituals. Changing the host medium and ritual site, these collective rituals are performed frequently in one or other Chiang Mai neighbourhood throughout the year, except during the Buddhist Lent retreat season. On these occasions, normally more than one hundred mediums gather together and dance to the loud accompaniment of traditional Northern Thai music. The ritual sites include several historical locations important for spirit worship in and around the old city area of Chiang Mai, as well as mediums' houses in Chiang Mai district and other nearby areas. The most common form of such rituals is the *yok khu*,[3] or to worship the transcendental teacher (or occasionally called *wai khu*, meaning to pay respect to the transcendental teacher), and most mediums organise one of these rituals every year. Through the performance of these collective rituals, spirit mediums develop and maintain informal networks of practitioners in and around Chiang Mai (Fukuura 2011). As of 2020, along with traditional spirits, tutelary spirits of golden boy (*kuman thorng*),[4] kings and personages from Northern Thai history, Hindu gods and goddesses, and spirits of hill tribes attract attention in collective rituals.

Phi meng, phi mot: *Matrilineal ancestor spirit cults*

Alongside the collective rituals arranged by professional mediums, another type of religious tradition in Northern Thailand features collective spirit possession. These are the special matrilineal descent cults such as *phi meng*

---

3   *Yok khu* and *wai khu* are sometimes written as *yok khru* and *wai khru* to accord with the spelling of these expressions in Central Thai. In this chapter I use *yok khu* and *wai khu* to reflect the common pronunciations in Northern Thailand.

4   Generally, the golden boy is the spirit of an infant who died in the womb and is considered to have supernatural power to make devotees lucky and wealthy. Fetishes for this belief range from embalmed and dried corpses of stillborn infants to dolls that represent the spirit. The latter are often found on the altars of mediums. For more details on child spirits in Thailand, see Megan Sinnott's chapter in this volume.

(Mon spirits) and *phi mot*.[5] Generally, the former have a higher status than the latter in Northern Thai matrilineal society, and each is categorised as having its own type of matrilineal ancestor spirits.[6] Normally, descendents of these matrilineal ancestor spirits perform a collective spirit dance ritual once every few years, and these spirit dances are commonly accompanied by several theatrical sequences, including animal sacrifices, possessions, and games.[7] Since the end of the 20th century, the popularity of these cults has grown, and some mediums of these special lineage spirits have joined the community of professional mediums.

Pillar of the God Indra and a group of spirit mediums

Chiang Mai contains a monument called Inthakhin, or the Pillar of God Indra, in Wat Chedi Luang temple in the city's historic centre. This monument is a variant of the *lak mueang*, the traditional city-state pillar found in the Tai-speaking areas of mainland Southeast Asia, which symbolises the city's guardian spirit as well as its political authority. Chiang Mai's pillar, one of the most important in Thailand, is related to a local myth of city's construction (Fukuura 2022). As the integration of Lan Na into Siam proceeded, traditional rituals for the guardian spirits of the city-state, including the ritual concerning Inthakhin, were strictly regulated by authorities in Bangkok (Anan 1999).

Notwithstanding this, there are some cases in which spirit-oriented religious traditions were maintained and subsequently revived. Today, they play an important role in the politics of culture in the locality vis-à-vis the nation-state. Indeed, a group of spirit mediums worships the tutelary spirit of the pillar, and they know its historical significance. This group was established in the period after World War II, when a spirit medium, who had long been a cook at the Chiang Mai court and was possessed by *Jao Phor* Lak Mueang (the Lord Father of the Pillar of Mueang Chiang Mai), reconfigured and restored the pillar's obsolete ritual from a Buddhist point of view, even as

---

5 In Central Thai *mot* literally means 'ant'. However, given that this religious practice goes back several centuries to the Lan Na era, there has been some debate about about the meaning of the term *mot* in ritual contexts. In any event, *phi mot* and *phi meng* are generally regarded as maintaining good relationships with each other.

6 These special matrilineal descent groups normally consist of 10–100 households (Tanabe 1991: 192).

7 Prevailing opinions support the idea that the cult of the Mon spirit and its theatrical sequences were derived from ethnic Mon people and their *kalok* dance. See Halliday (2000 [1917]).

he created a new spirit possession ritual at the spirit shrine at the northeast corner of the old city area (Chaeng Si Phum) (Tanabe 2000: 309–310). Since that time, negotiating with the Buddhist-cum-national value in the former ritual in order to take advantage of the relationship with the local government, this group of mediums has maintained and developed the latter ritual as one of the most significant collective spirit possession practices in mediumship in Chiang Mai, without any official support from the municipality or province. Being deeply involved in the rituals for the guardian spirit of the pillar, the group has actively developed its religious practices and has at least several hundred informal members (Fukuura 2011).

Merging genres among religious traditions of spirituality

Over the course of the city's long history, Theravada Buddhism, spirit worship, and spirit mediumship have combined into a loosely configured syncretic religious system. There is a recent merging of genres and growing interconnectedness among these religious traditions (Fukuura 2017). Older matrilineal spirit cults have sometimes merged with newer forms of spirit mediumship. Although formerly practised independently, matrilineal cults and mediumship rituals are sometimes merging at the local community level and being reorganised to produce a single, collective performative ritual. Here, professional spirit mediums play the leading roles in most ritual sequences, even when these mediums live in different neighbourhoods or are not related to the descent groups by birth or even by marriage. Indeed, the participation of these professional spirit mediums is now taken for granted. Some members of one cult told me that worship in their matrilineal ancestor spirit cult in this way was better, as they could hold a ritual that fulfils two objectives simultaneously, namely, worshipping their ancestor spirits and organising a collective ritual of mediumship within which their ancestor spirits serve as host of the day. In connecting these two cults, many come to consider both as forming indispensable elements that equally represent the religious traditions of Chiang Mai. In short, the practice of these rituals has enabled people who are engaged in spirit possession in Chiang Mai to become increasingly aware of their own religio-cultural traditions.

Some Buddhist monks are now frequently involved with some aspects of spirit mediumship and possession. Indeed, some worship their own transcendental teachers, which makes it possible for them to continue their magical practices. Though special relationships between these two kinds of religious practitioners were reported three decades ago by Muecke (1992), collaborations between monks and mediums seem to have developed even more significantly since then. Spirit mediums often visit these monks in their monasteries, where they deliver letters of invitation to collective rituals to be held in the near future. Some monks had been spirit mediums before they entered the monkhood. Moreover, the most striking observation is that some monks are more or less active as spirit mediums who retain connections with their spirits even after their formal ordination, and maintain close ties with their master mediums.[8] Normally, monks in Northern Thailand are not supposed to be possessed by spirits, nor should they join in dancing rituals associated with spirit possession. However, though they never dance, some monks continue to feel indebted to their spirits. When some monks hold annual rituals to pay respect to their transcendental teachers, mediums are often invited to these events, and they typically share in the celebration by dancing with lively music on the background.

Reorganisation of mediumship: Three Kings ritual and the Assembly of Mediums

While the Inthakhin pillar and the northeast corner of Chiang Mai's old city area have been important sites for spirit worship for centuries, there are some cases in which a site has been selected for a newly created spirit ritual in order to develop and enhance the sense of cultural identity in those localities. This is the case of the novel Three Kings ritual. At the navel of the old city area of Chiang Mai, a public square is decorated with statues of three historical Northern Thai figures: King Mangrai, the founder of Chiang Mai; King Ngammueang of Phayao; and King Ramkhamhaeng of Sukhothai. These images were installed in September 1983.[9] The statues depict these three kings discussing the layout of the new city of Chiang Mai at the end of the 13th century. In the process of founding the city, Mangrai had invited Ngammueang and Ramkhamhaeng to examine both the site and the town plan (Sarassawadee 2005: 57). Thus, as the area around this square is related to the city's construction and is considered to be historically and politically

---

8   As to Northeastern monks who are possessed by spirits and retain spiritual relationship with mediums, see Visisya Pinthongvijayakul's chapter in this volume.

9   See Johnson (2011: 514).

significant, the square is often the main site for important rituals such as the calendrical ritual to maintain the good fortune of Chiang Mai.

Three Kings ritual

In 1996, a large ceremony to celebrate the 700th anniversary of the founding of Chiang Mai was held at the square. As part of the celebration, hundreds of mediums were possessed by their various spirits during the first-ever performance of the Three Kings ritual. The ritual requires a huge financial outlay, as it gathers about a thousand participants. It has been deemed to be the biggest collective mediumship ritual in Chiang Mai. Different from other collective rituals of mediumship that are held according to the Northern Thai lunar calendar, the Three Kings ritual is held annually at the end of the international month of April.

Like other collective mediumship practices, the Three Kings ritual offers spirit dances throughout the day. Nonetheless, it differs in other ways. First, its ultimate purpose is to pay respect to the most important kings in the history of Northern Thailand. Second, it consists of three independent rituals that proceed simultaneously. While the mediums directly worship the kings by offering their dancing under the main tent, two chosen matrilineal descent groups of *phi meng* and *phi mot* do so indirectly by practising rituals for their ancestor spirits under shrines installed in the same square. Third, these matrilineal cult rituals are performed openly, even though they are normally practised in secret and solely by the descendants.

As a whole, the mediums for the Three Kings and the two descent groups could be considered the representatives of the local communities. Putting more emphasis on local values and cultural identities in the localities, the Three Kings ritual confirms a communitarian trend in the recent reorganisation and realignment of spirit mediumship in Chiang Mai.

The Three Kings ritual held in April 2004

In April 2004, I observed the performance of the Three Kings ritual. The eve of the ritual began with Buddhist chanting. Many tents were set up in the square and about 170 mediums were on hand. In front of a big ceremonial tower made of flowers (*bai si*), mediums in white clothes then performed a four-hour ritual to invite the souls of the Three Kings (*anchoen winyan*

Figure 4.1. The Three Kings Ritual in April 2004: the statues became an altar for spirit mediumship rituals. **Colour** p. 317.

banphaburut khorng sam kasat), who are collectively regarded as the ancestors of Northern Thai people.

The next day, the ritual continued and there were about one thousand participants. At the entrance to the ritual space, a banner proclaimed: 'Please join in the traditional ceremony, worship the charisma and ritual of making oblations/King Mengrai [also called Mangrai], King Ngammueang, and King Ramkhamhaeng'.[10] As the mediums offered their dancing to the Three Kings under the main tent, the two matrilineal descent groups practised their rituals independently on two separate pavilions, including their characteristic theatrical representations of historical memory that celebrate social relations as established during the Lan Na period, such as *khong chang* (NT: to capture an elephant) or *hae bokfai* (NT: fire rocket procession). There were also demonstrations of Northern Thai traditions, such as the nail dance and the sword dance. At the height of the festivities, the host mediums performed ceremonial acts of respect for the Three Kings.

As a whole, the three independent rituals deepened the connections among three communities. The first community was created by the practices of the mediums engaged in the ritual of worshipping the Three Kings, who have now come to be regarded as the new tutelary spirits of Chiang Mai. The

---

10 *choen ruam ngan prapheni waisa barami phithi buangsuang/sadet pu phaya Mengrai maharat phaya Ngammueang phor-khun Ramkhamhaeng maharat*. *Waisa* is Northern Thai meaning 'to pay respect and to worship sacred beings'.

Figure 4.2. Participants dancing at the end of the Three Kings ritual in April 2004. **Colour** p. 318.

second and third communities emerged from the two cults of the matrilineal descent groups. As these latter groups publicly demonstrated how familial ties are maintained, they played the role of representatives of every descent group in Chiang Mai. These communities thus performatively combined into one ritual system from which a new ritual community has emerged as an irreducible totality.

Organisers and the ritual

The organiser of the original 1996 ritual was a university professor from an established family in Lampang, a city about a hundred kilometres south of Chiang Mai. Lampang is an important city in the history of Northern Thailand, as it was the home of King Kawila, who restored Lan Na rule in Chiang Mai at the end of the 18th century after more than two hundred years of Burmese rule. This organiser was a ritual officiant for his matrilineal descent group. The founding year is significant, since 1996 marked the seven hundredth anniversary of the city. Big sponsors were on board and the provincial governor, descendants of the ancient royal families and other very important guests attended. The organiser recognised the importance of praising the city's ancient founder and preserving spirit possession rituals as integral to Northern Thai religious traditions. The ritual's organisation was didactic: placards were used to indicate which spirits were in the shrines and the main tent as well as to provide explanations of each spirit, and there was also a curated exhibition of ritual instruments and practices.

In 2001, the ritual was held once more at this same organiser's initiative. Subsequently, trouble arose between him and the Chiang Mai mediums: a cultural confrontation regarding how to practise the ritual. After that, the first organiser pulled out of the ritual completely, and, since 2002, Chiang Mai mediums have organised the ritual. Financially supported by rich devotees and assisted by fellow participants, a female medium took charge. The ritual performed in the Chiang Mai style came to emphasise the ritual practices themselves, without the use of any didactic placards for the audience. The Chiang Mai mediums created opportunities for cultural empowerment for those who wished to be thus associated. While this organiser criticised her predecessor, she nonetheless also shared his belief that the local people should not forget the traditions of their own culture. Her leadership lasted until 2009.

Crisis of the ritual and the Assembly of Spirit Mediums in Lan Na

In 2010, due to sickness of a few family members, the second organiser of the Three Kings ritual could not secure adequate funds to hold the event. Hearing this news, other mediums discussed how they might assist. They decided to establish the Assembly of Spirit Mediums in Lan Na, and this assembly became the third organiser of the ritual for the following few years.

Formally, this group was named 'The Assembly that Preserves the Tradition of *Mot* Spirits, *Meng* Spirits, and Deities in Lan Na' (*chomrom suepsan tamnan Phaya Mot Phaya Meng Thepphajao Lanna*). According to the assembly's regulations, regardless of their type of possessing spirit, all mediums could become members after submitting the necessary papers. The assembly issued a membership card with a photograph. It had approximately seven hundred members in 2013, mostly from Northern Thailand. A core member explained to me that the assembly aimed to mobilise all spirit mediums living in the former Lan Na region.

A temporary assembly committee was set up, including a chair (*prathan chomrom*), two vice chairs (*rorng prathan*), and a secretary (*lekhanukan*). In addition, others were responsible for various tasks associated with the Three Kings ritual. An important purpose of the assembly was defined as fostering mutual aid among members – especially raising funds for family members of deceased mediums – though its main objective was to ensure that the Three Kings ritual ran smoothly. While assembly members considered holding an election for the role of the chair, it never occurred. The assembly started with a temporary executive committee, but its real driving force seemed to be Medium A, who was appointed as temporary chair. He was in his seventies and his possessing spirits were Hindu Gods, such as Shiva. He was deemed to have many virtues and, as he had rich devotees who lived in Phuket, in

Southern Thailand, he could direct significant funds to the ritual, at least for a few years.

Opponents and proponents

Though organisation of the Three Kings ritual by the assembly seemed to run smoothly for a few years,[11] in fact it faced problems from the very beginning. Opinions were divided among the mediums as to whether they should be united formally and continuously, or only on an ad hoc basis for important ritual events at the traditional city-state level. According to interviews conducted in 2012, there were both opponents and proponents of the assembly.

Generally, opponents preferred a 'local' spirits way of doing things. For example, one male medium in his fifties, a craftsman of traditional handicrafts, emphasised that though he went to the Three Kings ritual every year, he did not like the assembly, saying that the chairman was not from Chiang Mai or even Northern Thailand, but rather from Central Thailand, and that his possessing spirits were Hindu Gods who contrasted dramatically with local spirits. On the other hand, proponents emphasised the importance of mutual aid among the members and thus supported the assembly's 'translocal' approach. For example, a male medium in his sixties said that although he rarely attended assembly meetings, he had signed up for it and had his membership card. Appreciating the methods used by the assembly, he also supported its ability and willingness to pay for such things as medical consultation fees or funeral fees for association members.

Attitudes towards the assembly did not necessarily depend on what kinds of possessing spirits a medium had. Some mediums with local spirits supported the assembly, and some with translocal spirits opposed it. Anyway, it is obvious that Chiang Mai mediums were divided, even though most of them appreciated that the assembly had had the important role of organising the Three Kings ritual.

Stagnation of the Assembly

By 2013, it had become apparent that the values and attitudes of Medium A did not always coincide with those of other mediums. A considerable num-

---

11 According to a medium, in 2011, the Chiang Mai municipality sent a few persons in plain clothes to participate in the evening ritual, the one held on the eve of the practices and which preceded the following day's main events.

ber of mediums had started to distance themselves from the assembly and its activities. As a result, it became impossible to organise a full-scale Three Kings ritual and, as time passed, its pageantry dwindled until, in 2013, only a single tent was available for ritual dancing. Finally, in 2014, the mediums had to be content with just making offerings (*thawai*) to the Three Kings, without any dancing or other performative ritual. A committee member said that because there was no formal leader, mediums had to give precedence to their own annual collective rituals, and he pointed out that in 2014 nobody in the assembly was responsible for securing funding. This man will return to the discussion, and I will refer to him as Medium B.

To complicate matters, the Thai military launched a coup just after the ritual in May 2014. In the follow-up, soldiers were stationed on Three Kings square for months and Chiang Mai municipality did not give permission to use the square for the ritual.[12] Moreover, as it had become impossible to affiliate in the name of the assembly, the mediums could not collect funds through it to hold the ritual. Seven years later, as of 2021, there is still no clear idea as to when the ritual might be able to resume.

Concurrently with these many twists and turns concerning the ritual, huge social change had been going on in Thai society, including in the Northern region. Policies of the Thaksin administration (2001–2006) became unprecedently popular, especially in the North and Northeast regions, where their genuinely positive impact on underprivileged people's lives was undeniable. However, those at the centre of the old established power hierarchies became hostile to Thaksin. As a result, coups d'état in 2006 and 2014 split Thai society into two sides: namely, those who support Chiang Mai natives Thaksin and his sister Yingluck, and those who oppose them. As Thai citizens, spirit mediums in Chiang Mai have also been more or less involved with the broader social change, and not a few have expressed their moral support of the so-called Red Shirts, a pro-Thaksin social and political movement. In addition, when considering social welfare elements of the assembly's own action plan in the midst of these dramatic social changes, it is plausible to say that although they did not have any explicit political agenda, the mediums tried performatively to create an alternative public sphere for themselves.

---

12 There is another difficulty involved in renting out the square: the square is always crowded with tourists, as it is part of the weekly pedestrian tourist market precinct.

Significance of the Three Kings ritual and the Assembly

Generally, the example of the ritual and the assembly demonstrate the local creativity and independent character of Chiang Mai mediumship. While the Three Kings ritual is a new invention, Chiang Mai residents recognised its value by virtue of its rich historical connotations that celebrate local identity. Throughout their attempts to develop the ritual performatively, the mediums have understood what they have developed: by practising a polyphonic ritual consisting of three different and concomitant rituals under the same impetus,[13] they have been able to create a new ritual community as an irreducible totality, which for a while was a strong tool for the construction of broader cultural identity politics.

Though the attempt to formalise the community seems to have failed, it enabled mediums to recognise the importance of maintaining the religio-cultural essence of spirit possession as a Northern Thai cultural asset. In addition, the fact that mediums who serve matrilineal spirits as well as professional mediums associated with a wide range of spirits were included in the assembly as equals demonstrates the sociality created by the effectiveness of the polyphonic ritual. Though descent spirit cults had been derided as provincial and less elaborate than professional spirit mediumship, mutual recognition on the basis of common Lan Na historical roots made their integration possible.

By the way, in an August 2019 interview, a medium explained that he could not say anything about whether the assembly had included mediums of historical personages from the Central Thai Rattanakosin kingdom, such as King Chulalongkorn. If such mediums had openly displayed their ritual practices in Chiang Mai, they would have been arrested by the local authorities. In short, such beings are deemed to be disturbing and against the social order, at least in Northern Thailand. In a similar vein, the medium added that the local authorities had actually summoned a medium who is possessed by a few Northern Thai kings.

Concurrently with this heterogeneous reorganisation of spirit mediums, diversification of local social life has been in line with the broader social changes in Thai society, brought about by capitalism and the influence of globalisation. Significantly, two different inclinations toward realignment

---

13 In addition, occasionally, some practitioners move among the three sites to interplay in the different ritual events.

are observed among the spirit mediums who were reorganised through the creation of the new ritual and the assembly. One emphasises translocal values and is represented by Medium A, former chairman of the assembly. The other prefers to support more purely local values and is represented by Medium B. In the remainder of this chapter, I explore the contrasting tendencies of Mediums A and B and their religious activities, with information gained through interviews conducted mainly in August 2017 and March 2018.

Medium A: Realignment of mediumship with translocal values

The first case study concerns the religious practices of Medium A. He is an elderly man who lives in the San Sai district of Chiang Mai province. This district is neighboured by the Doi Saket district to the east and adjoined by the Chiang Mai district to the south. He was chair of the assembly for a few years. He has worked as a professional spirit medium for nearly forty years, and turned 75 in 2017. He can be described as a 'translocal' medium, as all of his possessing spirits are Hindu gods: Ganesh, Vishnu, Brahma, and Shiva,[14] whose interest in Northern Thai spirit mediums had been unknown until relatively recently. He has a large number of devotees who live in the southern province of Phuket as well as in Bangkok.

Life story and calling of spirits

Medium A was born in Central Thailand. When he was 18 years old, he went to Chiang Mai, where he worked as a mechanic. Since then, he has spent most of his time in Northern Thailand. He has married several times and has a number of children. At the final stage of his professional life, he managed a hotel in Chiang Mai. It was during that time that he experienced his first spirit possession. On a merit-making day for commemorating the end of the Buddhist Lent retreat, he vomited, jumped in the air, and began to speak the so-called 'god's language' (*phasa thep*). In the evening, he was possessed by the spirit once again. His colleagues' opinions were divided: some said that he was possessed by the spirit of the deceased owner of the hotel, while others disagreed. He was sick for four months. As he pointed

---

14 When I was allowed to join in his annual rituals in March 2018, these deities possessed him successively.

Figure 4.3. Medium A possessed by Shiva at his annual ritual in March 2018. **Colour** p. 318.

out, he was sick in the head. He went to consult a medical doctor at a big hospital and had an examination of his brain. They found nothing abnormal. He resigned from managing the hotel and moved to a village in Chiang Mai, where the spirit started to come to him and possess him more regularly. The spirit told him that he must stop eating animal meat and practise ascetic meditation, and he complied. One day, he felt a pain in his head. He saw a bright light of deep blue and could not hear any sounds around him. He thought he had died. Then, his headache vanished, and he felt relaxed. After six months of experiencing possession, he started the ritual of walking on fire. He says that Shiva possesses him, and that this deity is the chair of the Council of Gods and is greater than all the kings in the universe. Shiva possesses him three times a day. Medium A does not have a human teacher-master. He says that the Vedic scriptures are his teacher.

'Gods' residence' and other sites

Medium A's house stands on disproportionately huge premises for a spirit medium. It is named Gods' Residence (*thewalai*), and two main shrines are dedicated to several Hindu gods and goddesses. Most of these shrines are for the dedicated purpose of worshipping deities from the Hindu pantheon, including the four gods that possess him. A separate temple is designated for possession rituals, and he has also established a meditation centre. There is also an alms canteen and living facilities for guests who are interested in practising meditation.[15] In addition to this complex, he has sites for religious activities in Phuket and Bangkok. According to his devotees, the shrines, the buildings, and the land were all donated by his rich devotees, most of whom were businessmen.

---

15 He explained that the design of the residence came to him while he was possessed by the Hindu deity Visukarm (Vishvakarma), who is believed to be a son of Brahma and is the patron deity of craftsmen and architects. He said that while four other Hindu gods possess him regularly, this deity possesses him only in regard to determining architectural matters.

Belief in Theravada Buddhism

Though Hindu Gods are his possessing spirits, Medium A is a devout Buddhist. According to him, in this world there is only one religion, which is the religion of the Buddha, of Prince Siddhartha. This religion has a clear history, and that is to achieve enlightenment by oneself: the teaching does not have to refer to any 'god' in order to prove the existence of god by oneself. He said that any religion that refers to 'god' would be a cult, and merely a philosophy, he said.

Devotees

Medium A's income comes from offerings from his devotees, who generally can be categorised as middle or upper class. Actually, this medium is proud of his high-status devotees, who include a former Royal Thai Air Force general from the royal family, the incumbent mayor of Phuket, and the president of a hotel chain.

As a whole, his high status as a spirit medium cannot be detached from his close relationship with devotees in Phuket and Bangkok, where he frequently travels to perform rituals. In Phuket, for example, he performed one ritual to install a Brahma shrine in a hotel, another to improve a real estate business, and so on. Phuket municipality has invited him several times to conduct *feng shui* rituals for Chinese gods during the Chinese New Year period. Though no Chinese gods possess him, he has acquired knowledge of Chinese geomancy through his Sino-Thai family lineage. Phuket politicians have relied on his ritual power to win elections. In 2011, when the Assembly of Lan Na Spirit Mediums had just been set up, Medium A and 40–50 other Chiang Mai mediums went to Phuket to participate in a week-long ritual. According to one participant, its purpose was to build a new spirit shrine.

Medium A said his devotees have sent him to perform rituals in the United Kingdom, France, Indonesia, Malaysia, Singapore, Hong Kong, Taiwan, and Macau, but he has never been to India. In addition, he told me that a few university scholars in Chiang Mai led their students to study at his residence.

Realignment of mediumship with translocal values

After the stagnation of the Assembly of Spirit Mediums in Lan Na, Medium A seems to have kept Chiang Mai mediums at arm's length. He has incorporated more and more of the values of translocal, contemporary Thai society. Throughout the interview, he seemed to denigrate most of the mediums in Chiang Mai for engaging in only 'small business' at the local level, and praised the scale and importance of his devotees, who he said were doing 'big business'. Medium A and his religious practices function as a focal point for people of the middle and upper classes who desire religious guarantors of success in their social lives. At the same time, he recognises the importance of worshipping the Three Kings.

Medium B: Realignment of Northern Thai mediumship with local values

The second case study concerns the religious practices of Medium B, a middle-aged man who lives in the Chiang Mai city area. He turned 47 in 2017 and has worked as a medium for more than thirty years. He is considered to be a 'local' medium, as his possessing spirit is a native to Chiang Mai. He is known as one of the de facto leaders in the group of spirit mediums and has about twenty disciples who, as spirit mediums, have received ritual trays (NT: *hap khan*) from him in acknowledgment of his role as their teacher and guide, thus creating an important subgroup among Chiang Mai mediums. His most important disciple is the wife of a local government administrator. He explains that there are no rich people among his devotees and says that his possessing spirit helps poor people.

Life story and calling of spirits

As a child, Medium B lived with his maternal grandmother, a medium with several possessing spirits, including *Jao Phor* Sing Dan (the Lord Father of Lion Protecting Checkpoint), a guardian spirit of the historical city-state. In addition, his great-grandmother had been the teacher-medium of a famous medium who, in her nineties, was the teacher-medium of the second organiser of the Three Kings ritual. In 1984, when he was a thirteen-year-old and had just returned from school, Medium B was possessed for the first time by *Jao Phor* Sing Dan. After he was first possessed by the spirit, Medium B prepared a ritual tray to accept his calling as a spirit medium. He started dancing in collective rituals of mediumship in 1986.

He was ordained as a novice and later as a monk at monasteries in Chiang Mai district and Doi Saket district, respectively. His spirit asked him to become ordained, because it believes that much merit-making will let everybody die faster, which it considers a good thing. Medium B finished his studies and got a certificate in automobile repair from a vocational college. After that, he studied cultural studies in a public university, because he wanted to expand his horizons in terms of culture, to which he had been introduced at the local level by his family members. He also wanted to earn a Bachelor's degree.

Statues of two lions at Khuang Sing

On a terrace at the 'head' of the old city to the north of Chiang Mai stand the figures of two white lions. One is called Sing Dan, or the Lion that Protects the Checkpoint, the other is called Sing Du, or the Ferocious Lion. This area came to be known as Khuang Sing, which means 'the ground of lions'. When King Kawila re-established the independence of the city of Chiang Mai from Burmese rule at the end of the 18th century, he rebuilt several sacred places and objects, including the statues of two lions. The lion figures were considered auspicious symbols for Chiang Mai, and troops gathered at this location in preparation for war during the king's time (Sarassawadee 2005: 134–135). Just after the Thai New Year in April, the governor of Chiang Mai province regularly performs libation rituals at several important sites, including Khuang Sing.[16] Generally, local administrations tend to cooperate when they are asked to help local rituals and festivals that are deemed to be historically authentic and that have continued since ancient Lan Na times. According to Medium B, there is a budget of 12,000 baht (about US$360, as of August 2017) per year from the Fine Arts Department of the Ministry of Culture for taking care of the Khuang Sing monument.

---

16 In April 2018, the then-Chiang Mai governor visited many important sites: the statue of King Kawila, the White Pagoda near Chiang Mai municipality, the Shrine of City Pillar (Chaeng Si Phum), the Shrine of King Mangrai, statues of the Three Kings, the Lord Father and Lord Mother of the Victory Gate (Chang Phueak Gate), the Shrine of Lord Father Khamdaeng near Chaeng Hua Lin, the statues of two White Elephants, Wat Suan Dok temple, the statues of the two Lions at Khuang Sing, and the statue of King Rama V (Chiang Mai province organised annual libation rituals of sacred national treasures in B.E. 2561 *jangwat chiang mai jat phithi song nam sing saksit khu-ban khu-mueang prajam pi 2561* thainews.prd.go.th/website_th/news/print_news/TNART6104170010010, accessed May 23, 2018)

Figure 4.4. Khuang Sing ritual in June 2018. **Colour** p. 319.

Khuang Sing ritual

Medium B explains that a collective ritual at Khuang Sing has been carried out for at least one hundred years. Currently, as the host medium, he manages this ritual, which is held in Northern Thailand's ninth lunar month. The main objective of this ritual is to make offerings to the guardian spirit of Chiang Mai. In previous times, Medium B's maternal grandmother performed the *wai khu* ritual in her house to show respect to the transcendental teacher, and then went to the merit-making ritual at the White Elephants monument at Chang Phueak, on the same north side of the old city area as the Khuang Sing monument. In the afternoon, she came to the collective ritual at Khuang Sing.[17] On that occasion, just one traditional musical band was employed for both rituals. Today, the ritual held at the White Elephants monument is obsolete.

It is important to note that the name of the possessing spirit of Medium B is Sing Dan, the same as the Lion Protecting Checkpoint at Khuang Sing. Actually, his grandmother had also been possessed by the other lion, Sing Du, though lately, there is no medium for this being. Therefore, when possessed, Medium B could be considered to become an incarnation of the guardian spirit of the lion.

Relationship with the local government

As mentioned above, after the integration of Lan Na kingdom into Siam, local spirit worship at the traditional city-state level was strictly regulated, as it had contributed to constructing authenticity of the Northern Thai kingship and provided it with royal authority. Therefore, throughout most of the 20th century, the local provincial administration in Chiang Mai, as an organ of the Bangkok state, did not provide significant funds or staff for collective

---

17 This explanation corresponds with the ethnographic literature of Wijeyewardene based on his observations in the 1970s (Wijeyewardene 1986: 130–131).

mediumship rituals. However, times have now changed. In 2016 and 2018, I observed the Chiang Mai governor's banner and the deputy-governor present at the Khuang Sing ritual, although the local government continued the policy of not funding the ritual. Nonetheless, judging from the banner at the ritual site entrance, it would be right to say that the governor of Chiang Mai province was the de facto chair (*jao phap*) or sponsor of the ritual.

In August 2017, Medium B explained the relationship of the Chiang Mai provincial administration to the Khuang Sing ritual:

> Recently, I invited the deputy-governor of Chiang Mai province to the ritual. The deputy-governor is in charge of lighting incense sticks and candles at the beginning of the ritual because Khuang Sing is one of the important places worthy of worship among several localities in Chiang Mai province. A [Chiang Mai provincial] governor who moves to another province to work must first come and say goodbye to Khuang Sing. Khuang Sing is considered to be the force (*det*) of Chiang Mai city for luck and progress. The incumbent deputy-governor of the province has been part of the ritual for two successive years up until 2017.

Relationship with the local community

When the ritual was held in July 2018 with the attendance of the deputy-governor of Chiang Mai province and his wife, a dignitary from the army, deputy chairman of Chang Phueak subdistrict, and a female descendant of the Chet Ton dynasty (King Kawila's descendant), there were dozens of local people in uniform bearing an emblem of the 'Khumsingh (NT: community of lions) Conservation Club' (*chomrom anurak khumsing*). Throughout the day, they had been working hard behind the scenes to prepare for the event.

According to interviews with several members of the club in August 2018, the governor attended the ritual in person in 2014, and even though he could not come every year, the deputy-governor had come in his place. Every year, the male chair of the Khuang Sing community, who is an ardent admirer of Khuang Sing and its historical value for Chiang Mai, writes a letter inviting the governor to preside at the ritual's opening ceremony. He also goes to Chiang Mai municipality and subdistrict office of Chang Phueak to ask for their support. The conservation club was established in 2016 by the local people who love the monument and its historical significance. The membership list includes the names of a few spirit mediums who have been engaged in the ritual at this site for a long time. The committee's 20 or so members serve for three years; key posts include the chair (*prathan*), vice chair (*rorng prathan*), secretary (*lekha*), treasurer (*heranyik*), public relations officer (*pracha-samphan*) and advisor (*thi-prueksa*). The ritual is supported by donations from local people and local administrators in their private capacity, including offerings of food and drink from the former. Though the club meets only a few times each year, they communicate with one another every day through social network service. Generally, they aim to invigorate their communality by promoting belief in Khuang Sing monument, and its ritual is their common cause.

Realignment of mediumship with local values

Since he and his grandmother are possessed by the same spirit, Medium B has devoted himself to Khuang Sing-related activities for a long time, and has incorporated more and more of the values of this local, communitarian society. In my interview, he said that he knows that historically several calendrical rituals in Chiang Mai had been held at the traditional city-state level, and that some of them had featured spirit possession and animal sacrifices. Then, he made it clear that he dreams of reviving these traditions someday. It seems that his inclination to respect the historically constructed cultural autonomy and authenticity of Chiang Mai has the capacity to pursue hegemony in terms of religio-cultural aspects. Thus, Medium B and his group, negotiating skilfully and performatively with the local society, are trying vigorously to realign their religious practices with local values.

Conclusion

This chapter has focused on the reorganisation and realignment of spirit mediums and their religious practices in 21st-century Chiang Mai, Northern Thailand. First, I explained how mediums have created and managed new rituals and assemblies, which demonstrates local creativity and the independent character of Chiang Mai mediumship. The mediums demonstrated that invented rituals or traditions could work impeccably as strong tools in broader cultural identity politics. Second, I introduced two different mediums and their religious practices, providing an examination of their different orientations. Medium A has aligned his mediumship with translocal values, and his religious practices function as a focal point for middle- and upper-class people from throughout Thailand who seek religious guarantors for their economic activities and social lives. In contrast, Medium B has aligned his mediumship with local values, and his religious practices are solely community-based and oriented to revitalising the religious and ritual traditions of Chiang Mai. These two contrasting personalities present, in microcosm, tensions that are inherent to the larger social challenges faced by Thai society, which is ever more influenced by capitalism and globalisation. In short, the two mediums enable their devotees to reconfigure, negotiate with, and sometimes overcome these challenges in the midst of commercialisation and sociocultural homogenisation.

If this study is considered in relation to how Chiang Mai mediumship has been developing since the 1970s, it becomes evident that the religious tradition has broadened its boundaries and capabilities by drawing on and amplifying its potential to adapt intrinsically to the social environment of the times. As a whole, the examples of recent reorganisations and realignments of mediumship in Chiang Mai should not be regarded as mere religious hybridisation. Rather, they are something new that has emerged out of the creative inheritance, maintenance, and development of the religious traditions, and they demonstrate the creativity of mediumship and its ritual practices to adapt to, negotiate with, and influence the social environment of this ever-changing local society today.

References

Anan Ganjanapan. 1999. 'Phithi wai phi mueang lae amnat rat nai Lanna (Wai Phi Muang and the State's Power in Lanna)', in Princess Maha Chakri Sirindhorn Anthropology Centre (ed.), *Sangkhom lae Watthanatham nai Prathet Thai (Thailand: Culture and Society)*. Bangkok: Princess Maha Chakri Sirindhorn Anthropology Centre: 149–161.

Fukuura, Kazuo. 2011. 'A Ritual Community: The Religious Practices of Spirit Mediums Who Worship the Spirit of the Chiang Mai City Pillar', *SOJOURN: Journal of Social Issues in Southeast Asia*, 26(1): 105–127.

⸻. 2012. 'Adapting Popular Religion: The Séance Practices of Spirit Mediums and their Devotees in Chiang Mai, Northern Thailand', *Japanese Review of Cultural Anthropology*, 13: 61–81.

⸻. 2017. 'Reconfiguring Lan Na Religiosity: Interconnectedness of Religious Actors through Spirit Possession in Chiang Mai, Northern Thailand', in *Proceedings of the 13th International Conference on Thai Studies*: 336–346.

———. 2022. 'From Ritual Traditions to Spirit Mediumship: The Evolution of Pillar Worship in Chiang Mai, Northern Thailand', in Holly High (ed.), *Stone Masters: Power Encounters in Mainland Southeast Asia*. Singapore: NUS Press.

Halliday, Robert. 2000 [1917]. *The Mons of Burma and Thailand. Volume 1: The Talaings*. Bangkok: White Lotus Press.

Irvine, Walter. 1984. 'Decline of Village Spirit Cults and Growth of Urban Spirit Mediumship: The Persistence of Beliefs, the Position of Women and Modernization', *Mankind*, 14(4): 315–324.

Johnson, Andrew. 2011. 'Re-centreing the City: Spirits, Local Wisdom, and Urban Design at the Three Kings Monument of Chiang Mai', *Journal of Southeast Asian Studies*, 42(3): 511–531.

Lavie, Smadar, Kirin Narayan and Renato Rosaldo (eds). 1993. *Creativity/Anthropology*. Ithaca and London: Cornell University Press.

Morris, Rosalind C. 2000. *In the Place of Origins: Modernity and its Mediums in Northern Thailand*. Durham and London: Duke University Press.

Muecke, Marjorie A. 1992. 'Monks and Mediums: Religious Syncretism in Northern Thailand', *Journal of the Siam Society*, 80(2): 97–104.

Sarassawadee Ongsakul. 2005. *History of Lan Na*, trans. Chitraporn Tanratanakul, ed. Dolina W. Millar and Sandy Barron. Chiang Mai: Silkworm Books.

Sommai Premchit and Amphay Doré. 1992. *The Lan Na Twelve-Month Traditions*. Chiang Mai: Faculty of Social Sciences, Chiang Mai University, Chiang Mai and Centre National de la Recherche Scientifique, Paris.

Tanabe, Shigeharu. 1991. 'Spirits, Power and the Discourse of Female Gender: The *Phi Meng* Cult of Northern Thailand', in Manas Chitakasem and Andrew Turton (eds), *Thai Constructions of Knowledge*. London: School of Oriental and African Studies, University of London: 183–212.

———. 2000. 'Autochthony and the Inthakhin Cult of Chiang Mai', in Andrew Turton (ed.), *Civility and Savagery: Social Identity in Tai States*. Richmond: Curzon: 294–318.

———. 2002. 'The Person in Transformation: Body, Mind and Cultural Appropriation', in Shigeharu Tanabe and Charles F. Keyes (eds), *Cultural Crisis and Social Memory: Modernity and Identity in Thailand and Laos*. London: RoutledgeCurzon: 43–67.

Wijeyewardene, Gehan. 1986. *Place and Emotion in Northern Thai Ritual Behaviour*. Bangkok: Pandora.

CHAPTER 5

"We Will Never Get Rich if We Follow Buddhism"
The Rise of Brahmanism in Cambodia from 1979 Until Today

Paul Christensen

Introduction[1]

Cambodia is still afflicted by its troubled past. After independence in 1953, armed battle started with American bombings on Eastern Cambodian territory in 1968, eventually engulfing the entire country from 1973 to 1975. The situation for Cambodians worsened significantly during the Khmer Rouge's brutal four-year regime from 1975 to 1979, which was followed by Vietnamese occupation and ongoing fights with remnants of the Khmer Rouge. Following the end of the war in 1989, the country opened up for international investment and tourism, becoming one of the fastest growing economies in Southeast Asia during the 1990s. Nevertheless, the majority of the population has seen little benefit from this growth, and Cambodia remains one of the least developed ASEAN partner states.

When I started my research in Cambodia in 2012, I was interested in understanding how spirit mediums shaped the process of local reconciliation after decades of conflict and turmoil. I came to understand the historical roots of contemporary spirit mediums' social and religious positioning in Cambodia (Christensen 2020). Today, most Cambodians stress that Brahmanism (*brahmaṇya sāsanā*) and Buddhism (*braḥ buddha sāsanā*) belong to one religious system, which they call 'Cambodian Buddhism' (*braḥ buddha sāsanā khmaer*). As it is advanced by key representatives of the Ministry of Cults and Religion, this can be even regarded as the 'official' definition of the religion.

---

1   While using the ALA-LC transliteration system, exceptions are made for Khmer words when no written record is available, such as names of specific spirits.

Nevertheless, a differentiation between the two elements is generally made in terms of the effects of the rituals. Buddhist rituals focus on merit-making (*dhvoe puṇya*) that has a karmic effect in this or the next life, while 'Brahmanist practices' focus on providing and distributing spiritual power (*pāramī*) that can be used to influence the here and now. As described by Guillou (2017a), Cambodians differentiate clearly between Brahmanism and Buddhism in specific contexts, including as spirit rituals. From this perspective, Brahmanism forms a loose category for everything religious considered non- or pre-Buddhist, referring to the era of Indian religious thought when the Khmer Empire was at its most powerful.[2] While Buddhism is regarded as the national religion and superior in terms of morality, Brahmanism and *pāramī* (spiritual power)[3] are regarded as potent, even dangerous, forces. During my research, some spirit mediums made it clear to me that they saw themselves as Brahmanists rather than Buddhists. These mediums placed statues of spirits and of the Buddha on the same level in their shrine (*pāy sī*)[4], and they even dared condemn the 'corrupt' ritual practices of Buddhist monks, whom they regarded as lacking any spiritual power (*pāramī*).

In this chapter, rather than adopting the local/official definitions of 'Cambodian Buddhism', I deliberately adopt the categories used by spirit mediums to stress how they delineate between the two practices. In so doing, I attempt to illustrate how the differentiation between Buddhism and Brahmanism is not only highly situational, but also has become increasingly important, especially for Brahmanist actors themselves, in order to meet the expectations of their clients. Unlike the comparatively well-documented development of Buddhism in Cambodia (Marston and Guthrie 2004; Harris 2005; Kent and Chandler 2008; Harris 2012; Davis 2015), the revitalisation of Brahmanism, which can be observed throughout the country, has received less attention from the country's contemporary scholars.

---

2 In contemporary Cambodia, the term 'Brahmanism' refers to the religious system of the time before the spread of Buddhism (13th century). It was imposed during the 1910s as a category comprising spirits and magical practices to differentiate it from a 'purified' Buddhism without such influences (see below).

3 According to Guillou (2017b), *pāramī* is a powerful energy dwelling at places which manifests itself as a personified entity (e.g. in bodies of mediums). Spirit mediums today prefer to call their spirits (mainly *anak tā*) *pāramī*, as the Buddhist connotation of the term (as one of the perfections of the Buddha) is more prestigious.

4 Originally, *pāy sī* referred only to a particular construction of banana leaves as part of a temporary spirit shrine (Ang 1986: 86–87). Today, the meaning has changed and the entire shrine of spirit mediums is also called *pāy sī*.

Before providing explanations for these interpretations, using the emic categories throughout, the chapter examines the development of Buddhism and of Brahmanism in particular. As Brahmanism's increasing popularity is attributable to its (near) immediate economic benefits, I illustrate how it can also be understood as a 'prosperity religion' (Jackson 1999). In an ethnographic account of a medium's 'optimised' ceremony to increase the output of spiritual power of the ritual's patron, I illustrate how Brahmanist practice has re-emerged from the shadows. I conclude that, despite attempts by successive rulers of Cambodia – notably the French, the Khmer Rouge and the Vietnamese – to undermine, or even eradicate 'irrational' religious practices, modern religiosity in Cambodia has become increasingly 'enchanted'.

The differentiation of religions until 1979

Historical records suggest that there was relative harmony between the different religious trends of pre-existing spirit cults, Indian religions and the ongoing impact of Buddhist ideas in the Khmer Empire from the 8th to the 15th centuries (Pou 1987–1988: 340). From the start of the subsequent Middle Period, kings firmly established Buddhism, and the Hindu gods were substituted by high deities in the Buddhist cosmology (Pou 1987–1988: 341; Ang 1993; Edwards 2007: 98). This Middle Period ended when Cambodia, desperate to escape Vietnamese and Siamese rule, became a Protectorate of France in 1863 (Chandler 1972).

The vital role of spirits in the practice of Cambodian Buddhism (Leclère 1899) was first contested at the beginning of the 20th century, when Buddhist leaders, inspired by the Western imaginary of 'world religions', began to promote rationalist reform to modernise Buddhism (Guillou 2017a: 71). The distinction between modern (*samăya*) and ancient (*purāṇa*[5]) became crucial in a process that Guillou (2017a) calls 'religionisation'. Members of the predominantly urban[6] modernist movement sought to purify Cambodian Buddhism of 'superstition' (*jaṃnya chveṅ*, 'faith on the left'), which included

---

5   Rather than terms like *yogavacara*, "esoteric" or "tantric" (Bizot 1976; Crosby 2000; Harris 2005), I prefer the contemporary and vernacular term *purāṇa* to refer to unreformed Buddhism; see for example Marston (2008a).
6   In these urban contexts, spirit mediums shifted their practice to astrology and fortune-telling, which they could base on 'rational calculation' rather than on consultation with spirits. This separation of mediums possessed by spirits (*grū pāramī* or *grū cūl rūpa*) in the countryside and the astrologers (*grū dāy*) in cities still exists today (see Poonnatree, this volume).

all spirit practices (Hansen 2004: 58ff). In the process, the concept of *sāsanā* was transformed from a loosely defined reference to common origins, customs, and language to the Khmer equivalent of 'religion', which was mainly referred to as *buddha-sāsanā* (Guillou 2017a). At the same time, the notion of Brahmanism, or *brahmaṇya-sāsanā*, was used to describe all elements of Cambodian Buddhism that did not correspond to this purified definition of religion.

In the course of the dispute between largely rural traditionalists and largely urban reformists, the latter were more effective in interacting with the French, who supported their vision of a 'pure' Buddhism; a vision which they directly connected to the *dharma* from texts as the *Pāli* Canon. In contrast, *purāṇa* Buddhism became a counter model to French constructions of modernity, and its leaders viewed themselves as neo-traditionalists who could fuse the new with the old (Marston 2008a). The majority of Cambodians adhered to this form of Buddhism, which was well integrated in local village society (Kalab 1968; Keyes 1994; Bertrand 2004; Kent 2008). To a great extent, *purāṇa* Buddhism laid the foundation for what Brahmanism would later become for the spirit mediums I refer to here: a neo-traditional movement opposed not only to reformist Buddhists but to Buddhism itself.

Soon after the outbreak of the American war in Vietnam, bombs began to fall across Cambodia from 1965 to 1973 (Kiernan and Owen 2006). Millions of refugees searched for shelter in the cities, from which they would be expelled shortly after the Khmer Rouge took the capital in 1975. The Khmer Rouge regime was led by *angkār* ('the organisation'). Like spirits, *angkār* was presented as an all-powerful entity that could observe and overhear, give orders to, and judge people (LeVine 2010: 34–35). *Angkār* attempted to eliminate all religious practices, especially Buddhist, portraying monks as beggars from an irrational and unproductive institution. However, investigations on the impact the Khmer Rouge had on non-institutionalised religious practices are in their infancy. O'Lemmon (2014: 48) and Bennett (2015: 98ff) describe how Khmer Rouge soldiers consulted *anak tā*,[7] or tutelary spirits, for protection. My findings also suggest that the Khmer

---

7 *Anak tā* (transcripted: *neak ta*), which denotes the most popular spirits in Cambodia, is a broadly defined category of tutelary spirits. These are the spirits of powerful, deceased individuals (historical figures such as the founders of the village or soldiers), Hindu deities (e.g., Yāy Mao, reminiscent of Kali), and mythological persons or animals. Their shrines can be found in every village and city throughout the country. They are understood to be social beings capable of engaging with humans (Christensen 2020; Ang 1986; Guillou 2012).

Rouge feared the powers of some spirit mediums and therefore avoided harming them. Indeed, due to her spiritual powers, one medium I talked to was even promoted to the role of Khmer Rouge regional leader. In short, the regime's attacks had a much more significant, indeed devastating, impact on the Buddhist *sangha* than they did on local spirit cults and its practitioners (Gyallay-Pap 2002; O'Lemmon 2014:48).

Religious revitalisation: From 1979 until today

> Buddha and ghosts, prayers at the temple and invocations to spirits, monks and mediums are all part of what is essentially a single religious system, different aspects of which are called into play at different, appropriate times. (Ebihara 1968:364)

The times, it seems, are indeed appropriate for the rise of Brahmanism in Cambodia. I now turn to the reasons for this.

After Vietnamese troops defeated the Khmer Rouge in 1979 and forced them to flee to the northwest of the country, the revitalisation of religion was not considered a priority by the newly established People's Republic of Kampuchea (PRK). While the new government favoured the reformist branch of Buddhism (Marston 2008a), it restricted the number of re-ordinations, thereby limiting the Buddhist revitalisation. Indeed, only a few thousand monks had been (re-)ordained by the end of the PRK-era in 1989 (Gyallay-Pap 2002).

The revitalisation of spirit practices may have remained rural and local in this period, but it was also unrestricted. With the close connection of spirits to the land, spirit practice grew in importance during the PRK-era. The *anak tā* were seen as having retreated to the forests during the Khmer Rouge regime and, like the thousands of people who returned to their home regions after working under the command of *angkār* in other districts, were regarded as having returned to their shrines. Some spirit mediums also started working again. With a lack of Buddhist monks and the haunting presence, all over the country, of those who had lost their lives under the Khmer Rouge, people turned to the spirits for their religious concerns. However, it should be noted that the spirits of the dead were not nearly as important as they are in post-conflict Vietnam (Kwon 2006, 2008), since in Cambodia, they are believed to have been reborn some years after their death. Other spirits, such as the *anak tā* with their *pāramī* (spiritual power) soon became sources of moral guidance and help in times of resettling and survival, especially for those who became seriously ill and could only be healed with the help of the spirits – a typical event in the biographies of most spirit mediums. The mediums of this early period of Brahmanist revitalisation were often called on to heal the sick or to help find a lost (and possibly still living) relative. However, offerings were limited and, due to their ambiguous status, being a medium was typically seen as a burden rather than a privilege.

By 1989, the Vietnamese withdrawal from Cambodia was complete, and religious restrictions were lifted. Prime Minister Hun Sen and his People's Revolutionary Party of Kampuchea (renamed to Cambodian People's Party [CPP] in 1991) reconciled with Buddhist leaders, and religious revitalisation began in earnest: thousands of monks were ordained, existing monasteries were renovated, new ones were built, and Buddhist rituals were re-established[8] or invented.[9] Even in areas where pockets of Khmer Rouge fighters remained, the re-introduction of Buddhism was relatively smooth. *Purāṇa* Buddhism, the major religious practice before the crisis, quickly re-established itself, providing a common ground for villagers to resume links with the pre-war past (Zucker 2006, 2013).

Like royal rulers up until 1975, the CPP sought to legitimate political power through religious authority in the 1990s. Since staging a coup that ousted his royal Co-Prime Minister Norodom Ranariddh in 1998, Hun Sen has continued this strategy: he has maintained strong relationships with the *saṅgharājas* or Supreme Patriarchs from both orders of Buddhism,[10] and has engaged in the type of religious patron-client relationships common throughout the long tradition of *purāṇa*-Buddhism in Cambodia.[11] In this

---

8   For example *bhjuṃ piṇḍa*, the 'ceremony of the dead', was re-established. See Holt (2012) and Davis (2015).
9   For example, the 'Day of Tying Anger' which later became the 'National Day of Remembrance' was first held on 20 May 1984 to celebrate the defeat of the Khmer Rouge. See Hughes (2006) and Bennett (2015:218).
10 As in Thailand and Laos, the Cambodian Buddhist monkhood consists of two orders. The majority of Cambodians belong to the *Mahānikāy*, while the *Dhammayut* order has only a few monasteries under its control. Nonetheless, each order has its own *saṅgharāja* or Supreme Patriarch.
11 Hun Sen has sought to represent himself as being 'destined' to be the righteous ruler over the country; as the reincarnation of King Jayavarman VII (Ledgerwood 2008: 219), the legitimate successor of the kings from Oudong (Guthrie 2002), more precisely the reincarnation of King Sdech Khan (Norén-Nilsson 2013) or of the late King Sihanouk. After King

system of personal patronage, money is passed 'upward' in exchange for protection (Zucker 2013:101): Cambodian elites patronise monasteries, which they support not only to receive support from monks but also to secure their worldly positions, and to make merit that counteracts the karmic consequences of their bad deeds in this or former lives (Keyes 1973).

On the grounds of the new monasteries, places for *anak tā* are also generally included. By 2002, more than 50,000 monks were living in monasteries again (Gyallay-Pap 2002: 111). The demand for spirit practices also increased. However, Bertrand reports that in the late 1990s, people in rural areas showed ever greater interest in engaging with the embodied forms of their preferred spirits, but complained of a shortage of mediums (2004: 158–159). In the late 1990s and early 2000s, Brahmanism and Buddhism underwent multiple processes of both approximation toward and differentiation from one another. For instance, some Buddhist monks were willing to be a 'body' (*rūpa*) that spirits would enter, as well as to perform magic rituals (*dhvoe vedamanṭ*). At the same time, some tutelary spirits, *anak tā*, transformed from chthonic to more visually iconic forms: their former manifestation in stones, termite mounds, trees and mountains were sometimes reconceptualised into the form of human-shaped statues. This adaptation of Buddhist ideas is described as Buddhicisation by scholars of Cambodian Buddhism (Ang 1986; Forest 1992; Guillou 2017a) and other regions in Southeast Asia (Ladwig 2016; Brac de la Perrière 2017). Here I argue that Cambodian Buddhism is also defined by processes of 'Brahmanisation'. In order to stress the mutual influence of Buddhism and Brahmanism, I prefer the term 'hybridisation' (Pattana 2005).

Economic growth began to take off in Cambodia in the late 1990s with an orientation away from the export of agricultural products and toward textile and garment industries that harnessed the supply of cheap labour, especially that provided by women. The economy was 'liberalised',[12] leading both to increased social inequality and to growing hopes and expectations for the future, something I witnessed in (competitive) rituals of spirit possession. In this context, at the beginning of the 2000s, a new spirit of optimism

---

Sihanouk's death in 2012, Hun Sen claimed that he been 'chosen' by the king to protect the royal family (Strangio 2014: 126).

12 Here, liberalisation describes a process of internationalisation and privatisation rather than an 'open' market economy, because investments and share purchases remain highly regulated by the ruling elite.

emerged among members of the private sector, where the number of small and medium-sized enterprises or start-ups increased constantly.

My data suggests that the number of spirit mediums began to rise in parallel with the developments toward a 'liberalised' form of market economy, and the hopes and expectations for the future that came with it. The main literature on religious and social revitalisation in Cambodia mentions spirits, but does not emphasise their relevance (Marston and Guthrie 2004; Hansen and Ledgerwood 2008; Kent and Chandler 2008). The lack of mediumship that Bertrand (2004) reported from the late 1990s was soon remedied. It is fair to say that by the 2000s, both religions had been fully reconstituted. Under the premise that different parts of one religious system – Cambodian Buddhism – come into play at appropriate times, I will now look at how Brahmanism can be defined today, and what its key components are.

Following the reformist critique that it does not belong to Buddhism, most Cambodians call spirit practice 'Brahmanist'. Nevertheless, these same actors also stress that it does belong to 'Cambodian' or *purāṇa* Buddhism. Indeed, the revitalisation of Buddhism and the broad acceptance of *purāṇa* have weakened the reformist critique that was strong in the first half of the 20th century, and along with the absence of official critique, have allowed these practices to flourish. Today, only few monks actively reject 'superstitious' practices in the name of 'purifying' the *dharma* (Guillou 2017a). Without a textual basis, (Cambodian) Brahmanism is, even more than Buddhism, a category of negotiation and context. It is not at all in opposition to Buddhism, but is rather intertwined with it. Indeed, most official Buddhist ceremonies contain rituals dedicated to spirits, such as the *Kruṅ Bālī* ritual for the Earth Goddess that begins most Buddhist ceremonies (Guthrie 2004). All forms of non-Buddhist practices, such as spirit mediumship and (morally ambiguous) magic (*vedamant*) are labelled 'Brahmanist', while Cambodians constantly debate whether magic should be considered a part of Cambodian Buddhism.

The elites' increasingly open use of, and absence of critique of, spirit mediums is comparable to similar developments in Thailand (Jackson 2016), Burma (Brac de la Perrière, Rozenberg, and Turner 2014) and Laos (Evans 2002). The Cambodian media is controlled by members of the ruling party, who themselves use spiritual practices to legitimate their power as the kings had done in the past (Norén-Nilsson 2013), as well as to use the services of mediums or fortune-tellers who are willing to provide them with protection or predictions about the future (Christensen 2016). It is an open secret that members of the elite also pay spirit mediums to work exclusively for them. Hun Sen's wife, Bun Rany, is known as the main sponsor of a medium in Kampong Thom Province who holds sway over a huge, boat-shaped monastery complex (*Wat Sompov Meas*) with ordained Buddhist monks. This contrasts with elite behaviour in countries such as Vietnam or Indonesia, where politicians' use of mediums would undermine their credibility (Endres and Lauser 2011; Sorrentino 2018; Bubandt 2014; Christensen 2014).

Despite being understood as non-Buddhist, Brahmanist practices are popular across society; mediums today have urban and rural clients from across the entire social spectrum in every province of the country. Depending on client demands, mediums may position themselves as more 'Brahmanist' – to speak the language of the spirits (*bhāsā khmoc*), become possessed or offer immediate results after a ritual – or as servants of devout Buddhist spirits – to stress the importance of virtue and merit-making.

This flexibility is a key factor in the increasing popularity of Brahmanist rituals today. Although *purāṇa* Buddhism allows for a broad range of rituals, including the blessing of vehicles, soldiers or spirit shrines (see below), and even though monks still perform spirit possession rituals,[13] their practice remains oriented toward merit-making and moral guidance, and they emphasise that their rituals cannot harm or disturb others. In contrast, Brahmanist rituals promise this-worldly rewards and can blur the moral codes Buddhist monks are bound to uphold.[14] Whereas in Buddhist thought, wealth is a reward for good deeds that must be collected during various life cycles, the spirit mediums define their practice as individual, flexible and immediate. Rather than offering salvation through merit-making, mediums typically offer assistance with personal requests such as help passing an exam, finding a partner, becoming pregnant, or reconciling between parties at odds. This help is delivered through the use of *pāramī*, which is granted by the spirits (*anak tā*). However, the most common requests are for a better life, primarily

---

13 Often referred to as *braḥ saṅgḍh ceḥ sro dẏk* ('monks who know how to perform *sro dẏk*'). *Sro dẏk* is a ritual where monks or mediums sprinkle water on the practitioner's body to purify and bless them.

14 'Buddhism can explain transcendental questions such as one's general existence in this life and the next. But the folk religion can give reasons for and means of coping with the more immediate and incidental, yet nonetheless pressing, problems and fortunes of one's present existence' (Ebihara 1968: 442).

in health or financial terms. In this chapter, I therefore focus on Brahmanist practices associated with competition, profit, and prosperity.

Today, most spirit mediums (*grū pāramī*) are consulted for business reasons. Clients rush to a spirit medium's shrine (*pāy sī*) in the morning to 'donate' a typically fixed sum of money in exchange for hand-painted *yantra* designs, which should provide magical power to protect against any dangers, or for blessed incense sticks, which should attract customers, before hurrying off to open their own business. Clients told me the cost of these blessed objects was minor compared to their possible effects; effects which are ever present in the stories about shops or stalls that did booming business on the days that the spirits decided to help them. Other rituals may be used to make a person more attractive, in order to give them the upper hand over their competitors, for example, in a job interview. This can be done by applying gold foil to a client's face. When the face is completely covered, the medium will rub it 'into' the skin, while reciting mantras in spirit language (*bhāsā khmoc*). Donations for such a treatment range from 10,000 to 30,000 Riel (US$2.50–7.50), which clients view as a rational investment given the possible beneficial outcome. Ang (1986) states that before the war, these rituals (*sneh°*) were considered *aṃboe*, literally as 'acts' or 'actions', but used colloquially to mean amoral action or 'black magic'. Today, rituals to influence others are openly offered by spirit mediums, who nonetheless state that these can only provide morally proper effects, as the spirits cannot harm others without a 'good' reason.

This desire to be better off now – without having to 'wait' for the consequences of merit-making (which can happen after rebirth as well) – has been sparked by economic growth and the new atmosphere of optimism which has developed in parallel. This situation corresponds to what Jackson has described as 'prosperity religion' (1999) and reflects the intertwined correspondence between economic liberalisation, societal modernisation and religious re-enchantment. This situation has recently been documented in many Southeast Asian contexts (Pattana 2008; Endres and Lauser 2011; Foxeus 2017). In the following section, I illustrate the connection between prosperity and re-enchantment by looking at the example of Bun Ly, a spirit medium from Southwest Cambodia.

Contemporary Brahmanist practice

Few people in Cambodia today would define themselves as Brahmanists rather than Buddhists, but Bun Ly does. He is a self-assured medium and organiser of spirit ceremonies that involve up to 15 simultaneously possessed mediums (each by a different spirit) and attract dozens of visitors. Bun Ly has also inspired others to become mediums, who then feel obliged to follow him to ceremonies throughout Cambodia. In performing new variations of existing rituals, he is not only a practitioner but an inventor of Brahmanist practice. By focusing my anthropological research on him and his work (Christensen 2020), the logic of how and by which means Brahmanist practice is conducted and perceived in contemporary Cambodia becomes clear.

When I met him in 2012, Bun Ly lived in a small house which had two shrines, next to the house of his wife and children. He had lived there since 2005, when his wife excluded him from their shared living space after he closed down his business to become a spirit medium. Recounting this event, Bun Ly stressed his efforts to escape his destiny. He had loved running his own construction company, which had several machines and employed about two dozen workers. Lacking orders and facing financial difficulties, however, Bun Ly became exhausted and desperate. His possessing spirit, Lok Tā Eysey,[15] offered him help in both physical and financial forms, if Bun would become his *rūpa* (body). He had resisted for several months, but things continued to get worse, and his company and indeed his health became seriously endangered. He finally agreed to the spirit's wish in a dream, in which he also negotiated an agreement to retain a 20 percent share of the income from the medium work, promising to donate the rest to charity or spend it on spiritual offerings.

After building his first shrine, thereby bringing Lok Tā Eysey's spirit to its new home and possessing his body permanently, he used the strategies he had learnt as a business owner and manager in his new career as a medium. That is, he saw himself as self-employed and tried to win *anak dhaṃ* ('big people') as clients. To convince his clients of his 'Chinese' roots (symbolising a certain business acumen), he erected a second Chinese-looking shrine that he rarely

---

15   The title *lok tā* ('honourable grandfather') is often used as a synonym of *anak tā*, while a female spirit would be addressed as *yāy* (grandmother). Eysey is derived from the Khmer name for Shiva (*braḥ Eysor*) and is mostly presented in his ascetic form – with a long white beard, a kettle and walking stick, vested in tiger fur. Locals do not connect him to the Indian God.

used. Unlike others, he also made contact with other mediums in the area and set up social networks (*khsae*) among the members of his new profession.

Since Brahmanist practice relies on the will and desires of spirits, and only the mediums have access to these spirits, the arrangement does appear to offer mediums a great deal of interpretive flexibility. Bun Ly's spirit had a striking idea: conduct as many *ḷoeng anak tā* ceremonies as possible. Normally held between harvest and planting season each year, the ceremony is to 'praise' (*ḷoeng*) the *anak tā*. It is not only a thanksgiving ceremony, but also an opportunity to meet as a community after the long months of work in the fields. Working on behalf of his spirit, Bun Ly next adapted the ritual frame to make it more attractive to wealthy patrons. He would enable these patrons to be blessed by a number of spirits, which would increase the *pāramī* of the blessing. As a medium with business experience, Bun Ly was careful to calculate the costs and returns before organising meetings: he would consult possible donors, gather information about their requests, and search for spirit mediums who could meet their demands. When he had collected at least US$500 in offerings, he would start to organise a new ceremony. A number of decisions had to be made: about the musicians, the craftspeople who would set up a temporary shrine for the ceremony (as is common for *ḷoeng anak tā*), and which spirit mediums to invite.

In 2011, a police officer who worked along the Thai border sought Bun Ly's assistance in treating an unknown illness. In the process, the officer became possessed by a powerful *anak tā*, who was responsible for his health issues. Bun Ly cured the officer and later convinced him to construct a huge shrine in his own house and became a spirit medium himself. With the officer's help, Bun Ly developed connections with high-ranking police and military staff (patron-client relationships known as *khsae*), who would spend large sums on offerings in his rituals. During my research in 2012–13, Bun Ly conducted at least seven *ḷoeng anak tā*, including four at the police officer's home. To illustrate the range of requests Bun Ly accommodated, I recount one of these ceremonies in detail, also showing the economic layers of the ritual practice and the different demands that clients bring to Brahmanist and Buddhist actors.

On the morning of 22 November 2012, I woke up in the house of my host, the border patrol officer/spirit medium. It was my second *ḷoeng anak tā* organised by Bun Ly at the newly built shrine.[16] A politician was one of the

---

16 During the first ceremony, when a politician had asked for protection from the Thai military, he learned that the spirit needed individual worship such as specific music to grant his wish (Christensen 2016).

major patrons of this ceremony, and he may have also been there because of the first ritual that day – a flag raising ceremony in front of the house to which several of the 20 mediums present had invited their spirits and shouted nationalist slogans. Monks from a nearby monastery, who had been invited to receive the *dāna*,[17] arrived during the ritual. While this was bad timing for the organisers, as they did not want the monks actually to witness Brahmanist practice, they calmly completed the flag ritual. The participants in the *dāna*, mainly women from the surrounding area, entered the first floor, which was overlooked by a huge shrine. Most of the mediums did not take part in the Buddhist *dāna*. When I asked Bun Ly, the self-declared Brahmanist, why he invited monks to every ceremony, he answered: 'Otherwise, people would call me crazy'. To avoid any moral ambiguity, Bun Ly understood that even the most Brahmanist public ritual needed Buddhist legitimation. At the *dāna*, the monks were presented expensive offerings in the name of the host family, as well as normal offerings made by local women who were regular visitors to the monastery. After three hours, Bun Ly announced that the ceremony was over, and that the monks wanted to stay on a little to rest. Once the donors had left, the mediums re-entered the first floor, and the monks were then asked to bless the shrine. As I had never seen monks bless a shrine of a spirit medium before, and as the blessing was conducted only after most regular monastery visitors had left, I suspect that the end of the ceremony had been announced so that the blessing could be done without them witnessing it. When it was completed, Bun Ly proudly announced that the power (*pāramī*) of the shrine had been increased by the '*pāramī* of Buddha'. The mediums had refrained from becoming possessed for the four hours that the monks were there, but the 'main' part of the ceremony began while they were still getting on a truck to go home: ancient music (*bleng purāṇa*) started and the spirits that possessed the mediums' bodies began to dance.

In the ceremony, the 'highest' spirit which Bun Ly identified, a Chinese spirit in the body of a daughter of the host, was exclusively involved in the politician's matters. As the highest-ranked guest, he engaged in several activities, including carrying the host couple on a palanquin around the shrine and donating rice to villagers who had waited for the whole day, outside the house complex, for

---

17 Monks are treated to a meal and are presented with gifts (mostly utensils for daily use) to gain merit.

this gift. These deeds can be interpreted as *pāramī*-creating (as distinct from merit-making), as they were only conducted when mediums were around; mediums cannot transfer merit, but rather provide access to *pāramī*.

Another sponsor of the ceremony was a high-ranking police officer who arrived with his family in the late afternoon. He wanted to consult Bun Ly on a personal matter, as well as ask for help to get promoted to provincial police chief. He also asked for physical protection, since there were other candidates for the lucrative position. The officer had donated a lot of money to Bun Ly before the ceremony and agreed to triple the donation if promoted. A few weeks later, the officer died in an accident, an event that Bun Ly ascribed to the spirit mediums of other candidates who had provided more powerful *pāramī* than he had been able to.

The organisation of the *ḷoeng anak tā* was always tied with the concerns of patrons, who 'donated' money in return for spiritual help from the *anak tā*. The costs were not always covered by the donations, but if *anak dhaṃ* ('big people') were involved, there was an opportunity to make a good profit. Bun Ly was always taking a financial risk. By acting as manager and medium, he collected the clients' demands and connected them to matching spirits/mediums, and, in the process, all of them became part of his *khsae*. Of course, this was not the only reason for such an event. After the patrons had been blessed, local villagers were invited to come to enjoy the spirit-rich atmosphere. In making donations to the poor villagers, the patrons could also gain merit. At the same time, these villagers also asked the mediums for blessings, healing and charms, which were provided immediately.

After the fourth *ḷoeng anak tā* at the Thai border, Bun Ly and the border patrol officer/spirit medium argued over money and stopped working together. At one of my last meetings before I left Cambodia in 2013, and before I gave him one of my regular donations which were an obligatory prerequisite to asking questions of the spirit, Bun Ly informed me that he had re-negotiated his share of the profits with his main spirit, Lok Tā Eysey, and that he could now keep 50 percent. He proudly told me that this was much more than one can get in Buddhist practice, stating, 'We will never get rich if we follow Buddhism'.

Conclusion

The example of the *ḷoeng anak tā* illustrates how Buddhism and Brahmanism can work together in practice, and the role that Brahmanism has for practitioners today. An aspect of Cambodian religious practice which has turned out to be particularly appropriate for these times, Brahmanism has undergone a 'quiet' revitalisation. The difference between *purāṇa* ('ancient') and *samăya* ('modern') is essential to understanding how Cambodian religious practice has developed, and how it operates today. The ancient *purāṇa* turns out to be more appropriate for economic development and other 'modern' concerns than the text-based *samăya* movement which, in contrast, is based on the study of the Pāli Canon. The rewards of merit-making are mostly related to the next life and are therefore significantly less explicit or immediate; today's Brahmanist practices promise the individual (near) immediate, this-worldly rewards. This difference, I argue, is the primary factor in their revitalisation (see also Christensen 2020). This becomes clear when looking at the requests of the clients in the *loeng anak tā* example. *Pāramī* is considered not only a powerful form of assistance for a person who is seeking a promotion or, as in the case of the border patrol guard or the politicians, against possible Thai attacks (Christensen 2016); it is also morally questionable, since it involves potential harm to others. On the basis of *pāramī* – the morally ambiguous power of spirits – clients negotiate and demand things that would not be otherwise possible. In this respect, *pāramī* becomes a catalyst for negotiating politics, finances, safety and worldly power (*aṃṇāca*) (Gyallay-Pap 2007; Kent 2007; Marston 2008b), and the mediums, clients and actors interested in *pāramī* clearly differentiate it and its effects from Buddhism, which is considered less suitable for practical, this-worldly assistance.

In this chapter, I have demonstrated that Brahmanist practice can be understood as a prosperity religion, at least to some extent, as its effects are suitable in the aspirations for prosperity. However, clients also adopt Brahmanist practices for a range of other issues: to be healed, for advice on difficult issues, and for help with personal relationships, finding a partner, or passing exams. Nevertheless, most clients consult the spirits – through their mediums, of course – to ask for financial help. Tracing Cambodia's ancient and recent history – the rationalisation of Buddhism in the colonial period and the Khmer Rouge's subsequent attempts to eliminate it, as well as the needs, hopes and demands that Cambodians have today and in a future that is shaped by liberalisation ideologies – it becomes clearer how and why Brahmanist practices have gained such prominence. I argue that this forms a re-enchantment of Cambodian society, in which the relations between Cambodian Buddhism and spirit practices have been, and indeed are being, constantly renegotiated.

Notes

Acknowledgments: This article is based on two chapters of my dissertation (Christensen 2020). I am grateful for the valuable comments and suggestions made by the editors Peter A. Jackson and Bénédicte de la Pèrriere and the reviewers from NIAS Press, which helped me to clarify some points and to improve the quality of the article.

References

Ang, Chouléan. 1986. *Les Êtres Surnaturels dans la Religion Populaire Khmère*. Travaux et Recherche Bibliothèque Khmère. Paris: Cedoreck.

———. 1993. Recherches récentes sur le Culte des Mégalithes et des Grottes au Cambodge. *Journal Asiatique*, 281(1–2): 185–210.

Bennett, Caroline. 2015. 'To Live Amongst the Dead: An Ethnographic Exploration of Mass Graves in Cambodia', PhD dissertation, University of Kent.

Bertrand, Didier. 2004. 'A Medium Possession Practice and its Relationship with Cambodian Buddhism: The Grū Pāramī', in John Marston and Elizabeth Guthrie (eds), *History, Buddhism, and New Religious Movements in Cambodia*. Honolulu: University of Hawai'i Press: 150–169.

Bizot, François. 1976. *Le Figuier à Cinq Branches: Recherches sur le Bouddhisme Khmer I*. Publications de l'École Française d'Extrême-Orient 107. Paris: École Française d'Extrême-Orient.

Brac de la Perrière, Bénédicte. 2017. 'About Buddhist Burma: Thathana or Religion as Social Space', in Michel Picard (ed.), *The Appropriation of Religion in Southeast Asia and Beyond*. New York: Palgrave: 39–66.

Brac de Perrière, Bénédicte, Guillaume Rozenberg and Alicia Turner (eds). 2014. *Champions of Buddhism: Weikza Cults in Contemporary Burma*. Singapore: NUS Press.

Bubandt, Nils Ole. 2014. *Democracy, Corruption and the Politics of Spirits in Contemporary Indonesia*. Abingdon, Oxon, New York: Routledge.

Chandler, David. 1972. 'Cambodia's Relations with Siam in the Early Bangkok Period: The Politics of a Tributary State', *Journal of the Siam Society*, 60(1): 153–169.

Christensen, Paul. 2014. 'Modernity and Spirit Possession: Horse Dance and its Contested Magic', in Volker Gottowik (ed.), *Dynamics of Religion in Southeast Asia: Magic and Modernity*. Amsterdam: Amsterdam University Press (AUP): 91–113.

———. 2016. *Spirits in Cambodian Politics:* Global South Studies Center, University of Cologne.

———. 2020. *Geister in Kambodscha: Existenz, Macht und rituelle Praxis* (Spirits in Cambodia: Existence, Power and Ritual Practice). Göttingen: University Press Göttingen.

Crosby, Kate. 2000. 'Tantric Theravāda: A Bibliographic Essay on the Writings of François Bizot and Others on the Yogāvacara Tradition', *Contemporary Buddhism*, 1(2): 141–198.

Davis, Erik W. 2015. *Deathpower: Buddhism's Ritual Imagination in Cambodia*. New York: Columbia University Press.

Ebihara, May. 1968. 'Svay, a Khmer Village in Cambodia', PhD dissertation, Columbia University.

Edwards, Penny. 2007. *Cambodge: The Cultivation of a Nation, 1860–1945*. Honolulu: University of Hawai'i Press.

Endres, Kirsten and Andrea Lauser (eds). 2011. *Engaging the Spirit World: Popular Beliefs and Practices in Modern Southeast Asia*. New York: Berghahn Books.

Evans, Grant. 2002. 'Revolution and Royal Style: Problems of Post-Socialist Legitimacy in Laos', in Cris Shore and Stephen Nugent (eds), *Elite Cultures: Anthropological Perspectives*. New York: Routledge: 189–208.

Forest, Alain. 1992. *Le Culte des Génies Protecteurs au Cambodge: Analyse et Traduction d'un Corpus de Textes sur les Neak Ta*. Paris: L'Harmattan.

Foxeus, Niklas. 2017. 'Possessed for Success: Prosperity Buddhism and the Cult of the Guardians of the Treasure Trove in Upper Burma', *Contemporary Buddhism*, 18(1): 108–139.

Guillou, Anne. 2012. 'An Alternative Memory of the Khmer Rouge Genocide: The Dead of the Mass Graves and the Land Guardian Spirits [Neak Ta]', *South East Asia Research*, 20(2): 207–26.

———. 2017a. 'The (Re)configuration of the Buddhist Field in Post-Communist Cambodia', in Michel Picard (ed.), *The Appropriation of Religion in Southeast Asia and Beyond*. New York: Palgrave: 67–93.

———. 2017b. 'Khmer Potent Places: Pāramī and the Localisation of Buddhism and Monarchy in Cambodia', *The Asia Pacific Journal of Anthropology*, 62(2): 1–23.

Guthrie, Elizabeth. 2002. 'Buddhist Temples and Cambodian Politics', in John L. Vijghen (ed.), *People and the 1998 National Elections in Cambodia: Their Voices, Roles and Impact on Democracy*. ECR Publications 44. Phnom Penh: Experts for Community Research (ECR): 59–73.

———. 2004. 'A Study of the History and Cult of the Buddhist Earth Deity in Mainland Southeast Asia', PhD dissertation, University of Canterbury, Christchurch.

Gyallay-Pap, Peter. 2002. 'Khmer Buddhism Resurfaces', in John L. Vijghen (ed.), *People and the 1998 National Elections in Cambodia: Their Voices, Roles and Impact on Democracy*. ECR Publications 44. Phnom Penh: Experts for Community Research (ECR): 109–116.

———. 2007. 'Reconstructing the Cambodia Polity: Buddhism, Kingship and the Quest for Legitimacy', in Ian Harris (ed.), *Buddhism, Power and Political Order*. London, New York: Routledge: 71–103.

Hansen, Anne R. 2004. 'Khmer Identity and Theravāda Buddhism', in John Marston and Elizabeth Guthrie (eds), *History, Buddhism and New Religious Movements in Cambodia*. Honolulu: University of Hawai'i Press: 40–62.

Hansen, Anne R. and Judy Ledgerwood (eds). 2008. *At the Edge of the Forest: Essays on Cambodia, History, and Narrative in Honor of David Chandler*. Ithaca: Cornell Southeast Asia Program.

Harris, Ian. 2005. *Cambodian Buddhism: History and Practice*. Honolulu: University of Hawai'i Press.

———. 2012. *Buddhism in a Dark Age: Cambodian Monks under Pol Pot*. Honolulu: University of Hawai'i Press.

Holt, John Clifford. 2012. 'Caring for the Dead Ritually in Cambodia', *Southeast Asian Studies*, 1(1): 3–75.

Hughes, Rachel Bethany. 2006. 'Fielding Genocide: Post-1979 Cambodia and the Geopolitics of Memory', PhD dissertation, University of Melbourne.

Jackson, Peter A. 1999. 'Royal Spirits, Chinese Gods, and Magic Monks: Thailand's Boom-Time Religions of Prosperity', *South East Asia Research*, 7(3): 245–320.

———. 2016. 'The Supernaturalization of Thai Political Culture: Thailand's Magical Stamps of Approval at the Nexus of Media, Market and State', *SOJOURN Journal of Social Issues in Southeast Asia*, 31(3): 826–879.

Kalab, Milada. 1968. 'Study of a Cambodian Village', *The Geographical Journal*, 134(4): 521–37.

Kent, Alexandra. 2007. 'Purchasing Power and Pagodas: The Sīma Monastic Boundary and Consumer Politics in Cambodia', *Journal of Southeast Asian Studies*, 38(2): 335.

———. 2008. 'Peace, Power and Pagodas in Present-Day Cambodia', *Contemporary Buddhism*, 9(1): 77–97.

Kent, Alexandra and David Chandler (eds). 2008. *People of Virtue: Reconfiguring Religion, Power and Morality in Cambodia Today*. Copenhagen: NIAS Press.

Keyes, Charles F. 1973. *The Power of Merit* [revised]. Bangkok: The Buddhist Association of Thailand.

———. 1994. 'Communist Revolution and the Buddhist Past in Cambodia', in Charles F. Keyes, Laurel Kendall and Helen Hardacre (eds), *Asian Visions of*

Authority: Religion and the Modern States of East and Southeast Asia. Honolulu: University of Hawai'i Press: 43–73.

Kiernan, Ben and Taylor Owen. 2006. 'Bombs over Cambodia', *The Walrus*: 62–69.

Kwon, Heonik. 2006. *After the Massacre: Commemoration and Consolation in Ha My and My Lai*. Berkeley: University of California Press.

———. 2008. *Ghosts of War in Vietnam*. Cambridge: Cambridge University Press.

Ladwig, Patrice. 2016. 'Religious Place Making: Civilized Modernity and the Spread of Buddhism among the Cheng, a Mon-Khmer Minority in Southern Laos', in Michael Dickhardt and Andrea Lauser (eds), *Religion, Place and Modernity: Spatial Articulations in Southeast Asia and East Asia*. Leiden: Brill: 95–124.

Leclère, Adhémard. 1899. *Le Buddhisme au Cambodge*. Paris: E. Leroux.

Ledgerwood, Judy. 2008. 'Ritual in 1990 Cambodian Political Theater: New Songs at the Edge of the Forest', in Anne R. Hansen and Judy Ledgerwood (eds), *At the Edge of the Forest: Essays on Cambodia, History, and Narrative in Honor of David Chandler*. Ithaca: Cornell Southeast Asia Program: 195–220.

LeVine, Peg. 2010. *Love and Dread in Cambodia: Weddings, Births, and Ritual Harm under the Khmer Rouge*. Singapore: NUS Press.

Marston, John A. 2008a. 'Reconstructing "Ancient" Cambodian Buddhism', *Contemporary Buddhism*, 9(1): 99–121.

———. 2008b. 'Wat Preah Thammalanka and the Legend of Lok Ta Nen', in Alexandra Kent and David Chandler (eds), *People of Virtue: Reconfiguring Religion, Power and Morality in Cambodia Today*. Copenhagen: NIAS Press: 85–108.

Marston, John A., and Elizabeth Guthrie (eds). 2004. *History, Buddhism, and New Religious Movements in Cambodia*. Honolulu: University of Hawai'i Press.

Norén-Nilsson, Astrid. 2013. 'Performance as (Re)Incarnation: The Sdech Kân Narrative', *Journal of Southeast Asian Studies*, 44(1): 4–23.

O'Lemmon, Matthew. 2014. 'Spirit Cults and Buddhist Practice in Kep Province, Cambodia', *Journal of Southeast Asian Studies*, 45(1): 25–49.

Pattana Kitiarsa. 2005. 'Beyond Syncretism: Hybridization of Popular Religion in Contemporary Thailand', *Journal of Southeast Asian Studies*, 36(3): 461.

———. (ed.) 2008. *Religious Commodifications in Asia: Marketing Gods*. London: Routledge.

Pou, Saveros. 1987–1988. 'Notes on Brahmanic Gods in Theravadin Cambodia. Colette Caillat Felicitation Volume', *Indologica Taurinensia*, XIV: 339–351.

Sorrentino, Paul. 2018. *A l'Épreuve de la Possession: Chronique d'une Innovation Rituelle dans le Vietnam Contemporain*. Paris: Société d'ethnologie.

Strangio, Sebastian. 2014. *Hun Sen's Cambodia*. New Haven, London: Yale University Press.

Zucker, Eve M. 2006. 'Transcending Time and Terror: The Re-emergence of Bon Dalien after Pol Pot and Thirty Years of Civil War', *Journal of Southeast Asian Studies*, 37(3): 527.

———. 2013. *Forest of Struggle: Moralities of Remembrance in Upland Cambodia.* Honolulu: University of Hawai'i Press.

CHAPTER 6

Lottery Mania in Burma/Myanmar
Prosperity Buddhism and Promoting
the Buddha's Dispensation[1]

Niklas Foxeus

Since the 1990s, Burma has witnessed the emergence of Buddhist cults that focus on wealth acquisition, business success, finding a good job or promotion, and a search for the winning lottery numbers. In these forms of 'prosperity Buddhism', people seek to acquire wealth through Buddhist practices and ritual technologies. In this period, illegal lotteries have enjoyed widespread popularity in Burma. Monks, professional spirit mediums and possessed ordinary people predict winning lottery numbers, indirectly (using coded language) or directly (giving the actual numbers), through contact with spirit entities who are known for promoting and maintaining the Buddha's dispensation (P. *sāsana*).[2] These supernatural beings include guardians of treasure troves, especially the children therein, and Buddhist esoteric masters (*weizzā*), especially Bo Min Gaung (Bho Min Khaung). Alternatively, the winning lottery numbers (the actual numbers or in coded form) can also be found by devotees during dreams or meditation. Monks can also predict the winning lottery numbers during sermons (using coded language).

---

1   I would like to thank Bénédicte Brac de la Perrière, and Peter A. Jackson for their constructive criticism and helpful suggestions on earlier drafts of this chapter. This chapter was mainly written when the author was a Royal Swedish Academy of Letters, History and Antiquities Research Fellow. It was also funded by the Swedish Research Council under Grants numbers 2012–1172, and 2019–02601.
2   The Buddha's dispensation (P. *sāsana*) is understood as Buddhism as grounded and institutionalised in society – namely, the material dimension in terms of Buddhist edifices, Buddhist texts, relics, and the like; and an embodied dimension – observance of the monastic discipline by the monks, and the practice of meditation, scriptural learning, and observance of morality and other practices by both the monks and the laypeople.
  In this chapter, 'P.' is an abbreviation for Pāli. All foreign words are Burmese, unless otherwise indicated. The term 'karma' will be used instead of the Pāli *kamma*, since the former has been adopted into English.

Following the global spread of capitalism after the end of the Cold War in the early 1990s, 'occult economies' (Comaroff and Comaroff 1999, 2000) have emerged through an interplay of religion and capitalism, and are integral to the prosperity religions and cults that have emerged throughout the world, including Southeast Asia (see Jackson 1999a, 1999b; Pattana 2008; Taylor 2004; Foxeus 2017, 2018). Such prosperity cults create 'new religious subjectivities that relate to the assertion of personal agency, the quest for predictability, and the management of anxiety' (Taylor 2004: 87). The development of novel cults of that kind in Burma/Myanmar should be situated in the social, political and economic transformations the country has undergone since the 1990s. In 1988, the planned economy of the socialist government under General Ne Win (1962–1988) collapsed and the military junta SLORC-SPDC (1988–2011) seized power and implemented modernisation projects, including a limited market economy. In 2011, a semi-civilian and semi-democratic government under President Thein Sein began to implement democratic reforms and a further liberalisation of the market economy (Jones 2014). In interplay with these changes and globalisation, forms of prosperity Buddhism that are intrinsically linked to consumer culture began to evolve (see Foxeus 2017, 2018). After 2011, access to merchandise increased dramatically and an evolving consumer culture created new desires and shaped identities; consumption became increasingly a 'moving spirit' (Comaroff and Comaroff 2000: 293–295; *cf.* Taylor 2004: 86) in urban Burma. In this context, as well as in other parts of the contemporary world (Comaroff and Comaroff 2000: 295–299; Pattana 2005; Vanchai 2011), lotteries have been imagined as a useful way to realise growing expectations of prosperity.

In contrast to a previous study that examined lottery number prediction in coded language by Burmese monks (Rozenberg 2005), this chapter will discuss how winning lottery numbers are predicted directly, orally or through gestures, in an uncoded way by mediums and devotees. It will highlight how wealth acquisition in 'occult economies' is moralised insofar as these are linked to an in-built redistribution mechanism that benefits both the individual and the community, and how these cults seek to maintain the Buddha's dispensation in the face of the rapid changes that Burma is currently undergoing, a legacy of the preservation of Buddhism among ordinary laypeople that goes back to the colonial period.

This chapter is based on fieldwork carried out in Burma over several periods during 2013–2017, mainly in the Mandalay area but also in Yangon and at the pilgrimage site Mt Popa in Central Burma. I interviewed hundreds of people, mainly devotees, but also some ritual specialists, monks, and others in structured and semi-structured interviews regarding the novel interrelated cults of treasure trove guardians and the esoteric master Bo Min Gaung. Most interviewees were women. This chapter deals with cults of the guardians of the treasure trove in two pagoda clusters (mainly nine pagoda compounds) situated outside Mandalay in Upper Burma, and focuses on the Nagayon Pagoda among these pagodas.

Illegal lotteries in Burma

As in Thailand (see Sunisa and Vanchai 2014; Vanchai 2011), Burma's legal lotteries (like the state lottery) are 'passive', that is, lottery tickets have pre-printed numbers. Beyond these, illegal 'active lotteries' invite gamblers to select the numbers they wish to bet on. The Burmese illegal lotteries belong to the latter category and are based on the draws of state lotteries: the Burmese and the Thai state lotteries.[3] The novel prosperity cults that predict the winning lottery numbers are exclusively linked to the illegal lotteries.

The two most popular illegal lotteries in Burma are the three-digit 'Thai' lottery (*khye*), which is based on the bi-monthly draws of the Thai state lottery in Bangkok, and the two-digit lottery based on the draws of the Burmese state lottery. According to Guillaume Rozenberg, who made the first study of these lotteries in the early 2000s, the three-digit lottery seems to have begun in Lower Burma in the 1980s, while the two-digit lottery began around 1996. These lotteries have been widely popular since the mid-1990s (Rozenberg 2005). However, after Aung San Suu Kyi and the National League for Democracy (NLD) came to power in March 2016, the government tried to eradicate corruption. In order to operate, the illegal lotteries run by laypeople have depended on bribery of local police authorities, but once the latter seem to have rejected bribes, the betting offices of illegal lotteries situated in the safe haven of Mandalay monasteries have suffered.[4] According to some informants (Mandalay, 2017), about 50 per

---

3   In Thailand there are similar illegal lotteries based on the draw of the Thai state lottery (see Sunisa and Vanchai 2014: 1635).
4   The laypeople running these betting offices bribed local police officers at various administrative levels. In that way, they would, among other things, be informed by the local police in advance about planned raids of a central police force from the capital.

cent of the betting offices situated in monasteries had closed down between 2016 and 2017. However, they thought that the number of gamblers had not decreased. In 2014, I visited a 'lottery monastery' in central Mandalay. I was not allowed to take any photographs. Inside the walls surrounding the monastic compound, a ticket office faced the monastery. Through its windows, I saw a row of computers with clerks seated in front of them; some people outside were standing and making their bets. In front of the office, I saw a smiling Muslim and a monk who had just learned the results of their bets on the two-digit lottery. It was not the monk's lucky day. He therefore gave me his worthless lottery ticket as a sample.[5] In 2017, I visited another monastic lottery ticket office situated in central Mandalay that was less technologically advanced. At that time, there were still a couple of lottery monasteries operating, but at the time of my fieldwork in July–August 2019, all such offices had been closed and removed.

The person who establishes, manages and is financially responsible for a lottery is called a *daing gyi*.[6] He/she is the manager and the banker of the lottery; gives salaries to his/her underlings and calculates the lottery prizes, but remains in the shadows. Many who work in the organisation do not know his/her identity. Those selling the lottery tickets, who might be betel nut vendors, trishaw drivers, or others belonging to lower socio-economic groups, are mostly called *commission-sa*, the 'eater of the commission'. They may go from house to house and sell lottery tickets or those they trust may call them to make a bet by phone. They may also sell tickets at an office. In 2014, one *commission-sa* estimated that about one hundred *commission-sas* serve each *daing gyi*. The one who bets on the lottery is called *hto tha*, 'better/gambler'. According to several people at that time (2014), the illegal lottery had increased over the preceding two years.

According to several sources involved in the sale of lottery tickets, about 70–80 per cent of the people in their respective areas bet in illegal lotteries. This probably holds for the rest of Mandalay. The draw for the two-digit lottery is held twice a day, Monday through Friday, at 12 p.m. and at 4:30 p.m. Draws for the three-digit lottery are held twice a month in Bangkok: on the first day of the month and on the 16th. In Burma, many learn about the

---

5   The lottery office of that monastery had already closed down when I enquired about the matter in 2017, as well as other monastic betting offices I heard of in 2014.

6   The information presented below is based on interviews in 2014 with a *daing gyi* and others involved in the lottery.

results of the draw in Bangkok from Skynet and other satellite TV channels. Depending on the *daing gyi*'s financial resources, an upper limit of the amount for betting might or might not be established. One can win large amounts of money in this lottery. In the two-digit lottery, one gets 80 times of the amount one has bet; in the three-digit lottery, one gets 550 times of the amount.[7]

New cults since the 1990s: Esoteric masters and guardians of the treasure trove

The global phenomenon of 'occult economies' refers to a conjunction of global capitalism and local religion that can be encountered in certain religious cults that some people turn to in their quest for economic success (Comaroff and Comaroff 2000). Such prosperity religion is expected to bring wealth, health and general success (Jackson 1999a, 1999b; Pattana 2008; Taylor 2004; Foxeus 2017, 2018). Burmese prosperity Buddhism provides Buddhist means for the acquisition of wealth and prosperity that should benefit both the Buddha's dispensation and the individual's quest for material gratification. At the same time, these novel cults are seeking to create what is perceived by many Burmese people as a Buddhist identity of a higher status by differentiating these cults from the 'traditional' cult of the 37 Lords. The latter is a spirit (*nat*) cult that tends to be regarded by urban people as a lower-status or even non-Buddhist cult that promotes unrestrained greed and that embraces values that represent the very opposite of normative Buddhist morality (see Brac de la Perrière 2011, 2012, 2016; Foxeus 2017).[8]

The quest for prosperity and wealth has long been an integral part of so-called karma Buddhism (see Spiro 1982 [1970]; he refers to it as '*kammatic* Buddhism'). In connection to Buddhist merit-making rituals, Buddhists can make mundane and/or supramundane wishes, including a wish for wealth that might be realised in an indeterminate but mostly remote future, depending on the karmic capital of the giver. However, the novel prosperity

---

7 Much of my information about the lotteries is similar to that of the findings in Guillaume Rozenberg's research in Lower Burma in the early 2000s (see Rozenberg 2005: 27–32). However, there are also some notable differences.

8 The novel cults of prosperity Buddhism seek to differentiate themselves from the *nat* cult spatially by being situated within pagoda compounds, by prohibiting the use of alcohol and offerings of meat, by an emphasis of Buddhist morality, and through projects that promote and maintain the Buddha's dispensation (see Foxeus 2017).

cults promise and pilgrims expect rather immediate results, mostly within a few weeks. Karmic discourse (in terms of achieving success entirely through one's karmic history) tends to be downplayed in these cults. Instead, they emphasise that a collaboration (see below) with the spirits aiming to promote and maintain the Buddha's dispensation is the condition for the successful pursuit of material gratification, including finding the winning lottery numbers. While 'traditional' Burmese Buddhism, focused on merit-making and monks, includes a degree of 'soft prosperity Buddhism', the novel cults cultivate a 'hard prosperity Buddhism' that is entirely focused on gaining wealth and prosperity for their devotees.[9] This chapter reserves the label 'prosperity Buddhism' for cults promoting the hard form. Many of the novel cults of prosperity Buddhism are closely linked to institutionalised Burmese Buddhism (pagoda compounds, the *sangha*, etc.). Donations received from pilgrims serve as an important source of funding for the maintenance, renovation and expansion of the pagoda compounds where the rituals for the novel cults are performed. That is probably the reason why the lay authorities (*gawpaka ahpwe*) responsible for the pagoda compounds have permitted and even encouraged the efflorescence of these novel cults.

In urban Burma, people from all walks of life, socio-economic classes and occupations engage in manifold non-institutionalised forms of prosperity Buddhism. People turn to these pragmatic forms of religion for their perceived efficacy: they are expected to bring quick results (*cf.* Taylor 2004). Devotees wish for success in business, to find the winning lottery numbers, and the like. If their wish is granted, they must support the Buddha's dispensation financially and/or by embodying Buddhist practice (see below). These Buddhist activities are referred to as *thathana-pyu*, 'promoting and maintaining the Buddha's dispensation'. The spirits in the novel cults are thought to be linked to the 'treasure trove' (*thaik*), and the most popular ones are *nagas*, 'serpent spirits,' in particular *naga medaw*, a generic name meaning the '*naga* mother'. However, in most cases there is a specific one that is worshipped, and therefore Naga Medaw will be used below in such cases. Mya Nan Nwe is a popular named *naga* spirit. Other spirits enjoying cultic support are of Shan origin, notably Saw Mun Hla and her siblings.[10]

---

9   I borrow this analytical dichotomy from Jørn Borup (2018: 276).
10 Saw Mun Hla, a Shan queen of the famous King Anawyatha (r. 1044–1077), has recently been refashioned as a guardian of the treasure trove after about 40 years of informal inclusion in rituals for the 37 Lords (see Brac de la Perrière 1989: 173, personal communication).

Other popular spirits are Buddhist demons called *yakkha/bilu*. All of these beings are imagined to guard treasure troves filled with gems and jewels buried beneath pagodas and intended for the next Buddha, Arimetteyya (or *Metteyya*). The *weizzā*s, semi-immortal, accomplished esoteric Buddhist masters, especially Bo Min Gaung, and these guardians are viewed as being engaged in the project of maintaining the Buddha's dispensation.[11]

In the early 1990s, the military government SLORC-SPDC (1988–2011), ritual specialists, and devotees were the agents behind the emergence of the cult of the guardians of the treasure trove. A new kind of shrine (*thaik nan*, 'treasure trove palace') was dedicated to these spirits, statues of which were built and installed in pagoda compounds during state-led pagoda renovation campaigns (Brac de la Perrière 2011, 2012; Foxeus 2017, 2018). Many of the figures in the evolving pantheon of the cult of the guardians of the treasure trove were recently invented, especially the children from the treasure trove, frequently derived from the dreams or mystical encounters of ritual specialists, monks or devotees (Brac de la Perrière 2011, 2012; Foxeus 2017, 2018).

In the Mandalay area, devotees of the cult of the guardians of the treasure trove go to pagoda compounds, most of which are old, which contain the architectural innovation of 'treasure trove palaces' in the form of large temples housing statues, a 'dance floor' for possession rituals and a traditional Burmese orchestra (see Foxeus 2017).[12] When two clusters of pagoda compounds near Mandalay were renovated in the 1990s, treasure trove temples were added. Since then, these pagodas have become popular pilgrimage sites due to the new temples.[13] Cluster One is situated in villages to the south of

---

11 A *weizzā* is believed to be a human who has achieved a superhuman state and is endowed with supernormal powers through a combination of Buddhist meditation, morality, and esoteric practices. After having attained the mystical transformation (*htwek-yap-pauk*), they depart for a hidden realm from where they are assumed to be able to communicate with (through telepathic messages or omens) and possess their devotees to promote the Buddha's dispensation and to save the suffering sentient beings. In that state, they are something akin to gods. Bo Min Gaung has been the most popular accomplished esoteric master (*weizzā*) since the 1940s. He passed away in 1952 at the pilgrimage site Mt Popa, but his devotees believe he underwent a mystical transformation at that time. Many believed that his consciousness departed to the mystical forest Mahāmyaing (see Foxeus 2011, 2016).
12 Treasure trove temples are otherwise usually small shrines. In Burma, a pagoda compound is mostly surrounded by a wall and contains a pagoda (P. *stūpa*) with relics, and temples and shrines. Buddhist monasteries are situated in separate compounds.
13 Pagoda Cluster One consists of Kangyima Pagoda; Paw Taw Mu Pagoda, Aung Buddha Pagoda, Shwe Kyay Si Than Kya Pagoda, and Kan Ku Gyi Pagoda. Pagoda Cluster Two consists of Shwe Sa Yan Pagoda, Ka Wun Pagoda, Nagayon Pagoda, and Zamaṇi Thaik. Kangyima

Mandalay and Cluster Two is to the southeast. Although all the pagodas are situated in villages, almost all pilgrims are urban traders, businesspeople, and the like from Mandalay. Many of those visiting these pagodas also go to a temple dedicated to the esoteric master Bo Min Gaung, built after 1988 and situated in a large pagoda compound in Amarapura south of Mandalay, and attend the annual celebration of his 'exit' (*htwek pwe*) at Mt Popa in September.[14] All of these temples tend to be crowded 1–3 days before the twice-monthly draw of the (Thai) three-digit lottery.

Predictions of lottery numbers directly: Mediums and devotees

As in Thailand and China (see Sunisa and Vanchai 2015), the winning numbers in Burma are assumed to 'be out there' to be interpreted and found through religious means. Rozenberg's study (2005) of illegal lotteries exclusively examines monks who predict the winning lottery numbers. In these cases, the lottery numbers were predicted indirectly by coded language. The audience picked up a phrase from the monk's sermon and followed a traditional Burmese system of correspondences between syllables, numbers, weekdays, and so forth as they tried to decode it. Such decoding procedures were also common in the cults I have investigated (see above), but what seems to be a recent innovation in these cults is that the numbers are frequently given directly and uncoded, especially by mediums possessed by child guardians of the treasure trove.[15] Frequently, devotees also get the uncoded lottery numbers from guardians of the treasure trove through their own dreams. There are also other procedures. In the following, I will give some examples of how ritual specialists (mediums) and possessed ordinary people/devotees (non-specialists) give the winning lottery numbers directly and uncoded to others.

Pagoda and Paw Taw Mu Pagoda were renovated in the beginning of the 1990s and the treasure trove temples were built shortly thereafter. Aung Buddha Pagoda was renovated in 1999, and the treasure trove temples were built in 2000 and 2002. The treasure trove temple at Ka Wun Pagoda was built in 2000 and the one at the Nagayon Pagoda in 2012. The temple at the nearby Zamaṇi Thaik was constructed in 2008.

14 For more on Bo Min Gaung's exit, see Foxeus 2011.

15 Rozenberg (2005) did not report lottery number prediction by spirit mediums (*nat kadaw*) in the cult of the 37 Lords at the time he was in the field in the early 2000s. Such predictions emerged at some later point within that cult.

The current Burmese Buddhist complex variety of categories of ritual specialists – novel and older ones, some of which assume overlapping roles – represent a transformation that is part of a general restructuring of the religious field in Burma that has developed since around the early 1990s, partly due to new economic opportunities, modernisation and urbanisation (see Brac de la Perrière 2011, 2012; Foxeus 2017, 2018). At the novel temples (pagoda clusters One and Two), there are mainly two categories of practitioners, the boundaries between which are occasionally blurred: semi-professional female mediums (*hsayama*) and devotees.[16] The semi-professional mediums serve as ritual specialists and perform rituals for and give instructions to their clients. In performing possession rituals, they serve as intermediaries/mediums between the spirits and their clients. The supernatural beings, it is thought, seek to establish contact with certain human beings because of an earlier connection in previous lives (*thaik hsek*) and exhort them to serve as mediums. Their careers usually begin with such an exhortation from a spirit guardian of the treasure trove, which frequently is combined with a mystical encounter with Bo Min Gaung. Most of these mediums seek to distinguish themselves from the *nat kadaw* ('wife of the spirit'), spirit mediums in the older, institutionalised cult of the 37 Lords (see Brac de la Perrière 2016), which they perceive to be a lower form of religious practice.

Many devotees (predominantly women) claim that they were called by the spirits. They perform their own possession rituals, but do not serve as intermediaries between the spirits and the human beings. Instead, they perform the possession rituals as a kind of self-therapy for their own benefit: to get healthy, to obtain success in business, to get a better job, or, of course, to find the winning lottery numbers. They have no clients, but some of them are clients to established mediums (*hsayama*).[17] Other devotees (men and women) are merely clients to the mediums and do not perform possession rituals.

However, the careers of the two most prominent female mediums (*hsayama*) at the Nagayon Pagoda (Cluster Two)[18] were atypical. They repre-

---

16 By calling themselves *hsayama*, lit. 'female teacher/master', they seek to distinguish themselves from the cult of the 37 Lords, where the mediums are called *nat kadaw*, 'wife of the spirit'. The former word is primarily used for a schoolteacher, but it is also a label for a female medium or cult leader within the novel cults.

17 For more on their role in contrast to professional spirit mediums, see Foxeus 2017, 2018.

18 This pagoda is situated in the village Mondaw and can be reached by a dirt road from the more famous Shwe Sa Yan Pagoda, a trip that takes about 45 minutes by motorbike. The latter pagoda is located about 22 km southeast of Mandalay. The Nagayon Pagoda is situated near a river

sented a kind of ad-hoc medium whose vocation did not begin by being called by the spirit, which is usually the case. Instead, pilgrims/devotees encouraged them to serve as mediums and ritual specialists. Formerly, they were sellers of ritual offerings (*kadaw bwe*) at that pagoda. One of them began that business in 2008 and, in her spare time, she swept the pagoda and changed flowers in the vases in front of the Buddha statues. Soon some pilgrims, whose numbers began to increase from around that time, asked her to make offerings on their behalf. At first she refused, because she did not know how to perform such rituals. She and others even asked mediums from a nearby city to come and work there, but they declined. Eventually, she submitted to the demands not of the spirits, as other mediums had, but of the pilgrims. Several lottery-predicting mediums at that pagoda began their careers in this way, and new cults developed around them and the services they provide.

In the following, possession rituals will be described. For the devotees, the spirits are the agents who are acting and speaking while the mediums merely serve as bodily vessels for the spirits. The following descriptions are made from the vantage point of an outside observer. When the mediums – they are mostly female – are possessed by the children from the treasure trove, they speak in a child-like high-pitched voice, pout their lips, crack jokes, tease their clients, give moral lessons and ask for toys, soft drinks, lipstick and candy. Most importantly, they also ask for donations intended for *thathana pyu* ('promoting and maintaining the Buddha's dispensation'). They also instruct their clients to engage in Buddhist practice, do *thathana pyu* on their behalf, and thereby share merit with them. Moreover, these child spirits predict lottery numbers in an uncoded way. At the Nagayon Pagoda, these events are joyous occasions that take place during the weekends, mainly in a large man-made 'cave' that was built in 2009. The cave is situated next to the pagoda and its most prominent contents are statues of the Shan spirits Saw Mun Hla and her siblings, and the seven child spirits who protect a treasure trove that is assumed to be situated beneath the pagoda. At the same time, noisy possession rituals are performed nearby, in a large temple next to the pagoda. While the mediums in the cave are possessed and behave and speak like children, clapping their hands, offering candy to others from a plastic tray, and so on, onlookers frequently laugh heartily. Although the female mediums

---

and could formerly be reached only by boat, but due to the increasing number of pilgrims, a dirt road was recently built that connects it to the more famous Shwe Sa Yan Pagoda.

Figure 6.1. The seven children from the treasure trove, Nagayon Pagoda. **Colour** p. 319.

are older than most of their clients, they address them as 'grandpa', 'grandma', 'older sister', or 'older brother', because the spirits possessing them are supposed to be 4–6-year-old children. The devotees are usually equipped with notebooks in which they write down the lottery numbers. Sometimes the mediums, while possessed by spirits, reveal embarrassing details about their clients. Furthermore, people possessed by the guardians of the treasure trove frequently employ Burmese gambling vocabulary that has developed within the illegal lotteries. In the following, I will point out some of this terminology.

In possession rituals that I recorded in December 2014 at the Nagayon Pagoda, a female medium was possessed by the children from the treasure trove. She was seated in front of the statues of these children in the cave temple situated within the pagoda compound. First, she recited some texts and then she became possessed saying the following to a man in his late 30s and his wife:

> I'm happy! Grandpa, you come here often! We have been generous to you. You must come here often, OK? And your business is good, right? … Grandpa, bet on these! I will give you three sets of numbers: 7-2-1; 7-2-3; and 5-3-4. They will come out as the winning numbers. Bet on these three sets of numbers with the same amount of money. You do not need to do "R", you know, right? You do not need to do "R." Bet on them!
> … These numbers will surely hit the jackpot.

'R' refers to the English word 'round', and is a technical word in gambling jargon meaning that one should bet on all combinations of a set of digits. In the above example, the client should thus bet on the numbers in exactly the order she recited them. Moreover, there is indeterminacy. While possessed, the medium gave three sets of numbers, but did not say when they would hit the jackpot. At yet another session, she was possessed by another spirit and said the following to a woman:

5–4 and 3–3. Bet more and more on 3–3! They will come out as the winning numbers, especially this [coming] week. If they turn out to be the winning numbers, you must come here immediately.[19]

To 'bet more and more' is also derived from gambling jargon: *hsa-do-ne-laik-deh*, which means to double the bet on each occasion. Again, the mediums, possessed by the spirits, do not say which numbers will win in a certain draw. They only speak about probability. The numbers will be winning sooner or later, but nobody knows exactly when. While possessed, the medium said only 'especially this [coming] week.' This is the two-digit lottery and there are ten draws every week (Monday–Friday); she said this on a Sunday.

In the novel possession cults, ordinary female devotees become possessed by a variety of guardians of the treasure trove. When they are possessed by the child guardians spirits, while performing possession dances in the treasure trove temples at the two clusters of pagodas, they display similar childlike behaviour. They smile and laugh, suck on lollipops, become defiant, quarrel among themselves and with the audience, play football, eat candy and offer candy to the audience. One possessed woman even snatched a feeding bottle filled with milk from a woman feeding her baby at the edge of the dance floor. In this state, they frequently predict lottery numbers with their fingers. One woman, while possessed by the children from the treasure trove at the Nagayon Pagoda in October 2013, raised her fingers to indicate winning two-digit lottery numbers, and she also wrote them on the floor with her fingers. She showed the numbers 6–9, 1–7, 6–4, and 5–7. Later, after being possessed, she explained that two of these pairs would win, but she did not say when.

Predicting that a certain number will win in a specific draw, which a few did, is riskier, but is quite unusual in these cults. It is mostly thought, as well as supported by how the possessed mediums articulate the matter, that the numbers will eventually be winners. One man said that he stopped betting on numbers acquired in this way after failing to win a single time in three months. Thereafter, he concluded that the numbers were wrong. However, the majority of the devotees blame neither themselves nor the spirits if they do not hit the jackpot. They must continue betting. The numbers are correct, they think. Their trust in the spirits thus mostly prevents them from concluding that the numbers are erroneous. The uncoded prediction of lottery

---

19 That is, to present offerings to the spirits and to promote Buddhism (see below).

numbers is thus characterised by indeterminacy, although there are some factors that circumscribe it, including instructions such as 'especially this week.'

Prosperity Buddhism: Promoting and saving the Buddha's dispensation

Burmese prosperity Buddhism is constrained by Buddhist morality and duties. Many of my informants claimed to have achieved business success and acquired wealth through the guardians of the treasure trove or Bo Min Gaung, or both. At the same time, in return for receiving such help, the cults require them to reciprocate. This is understood in two ways. First, devotees must return to the temple and present offerings to the spirits. For instance, those who have received help from Saw Mun Hla return to the temple and offer a shawl and a *kadaw bwe*, that is, a tray with coconuts and bananas. Second, they must engage in *thathana pyu*, 'promoting and maintaining the Buddha's dispensation' (P. *sāsana*). This may entail giving donations to the pagoda and alms to the monks, building or repairing pagodas, or engaging in Buddhist practice, including observing Buddhist morality (traditional Buddhist merit-making activities) and sharing karmic merit with the spirits. All these acts are perceived as serving to maintain and expand the Buddha's dispensation in society. Individual religiosity is thus viewed as being closely intertwined with the communitarian project of maintaining the Buddha's dispensation. This intimate relationship between the individual and public spheres characterises the novel cults.

The relationship between humans and spirits is perceived to be based on co-operation. If the devotees share merit with the guardians of the treasure trove, the karmic status of the latter, it is thought, will be improved and they will reach a higher level in the Buddhist cosmology, spanning from heaven to hell. Moreover, many devotees believe they have a *thaik hsek*, a 'connection to the treasure trove', based on their previous lives. To gain karmic merit is the motive for these spirits to help human beings to become successful in business. However, if the human beings fail to perform their duty, the spirits may cause them problems related to business or health, including premature death (see Foxeus 2017, 2018). The mediums, while possessed by child spirits, often put this in a joking manner: 'Grandpa, as soon as you send us loving kindness and share merit with us, we will help you. Soon you will have your thumbs up, OK?' Clients are repeatedly asked to engage in Buddhist practice and morality. As for prosperity, the general idea is that the more you give, the more you will get. The mediums, possessed by children, use the language of children when articulating that idea: *gyi-gyi-ya-khyin-yin, gyi-gyi-pay-ba*, 'If you want to get big, give big!' A medium, while possessed by a child spirit, jokingly explained promoting Buddhism (*thathana pyu*) in the following manner to a female client, who had failed to bring soft drinks:

> You may think that *thathana pyu* is only building pagodas or giving large donations (*hlu*), right? But *thathana pyu* is also donating (*hlu dan*) soft drinks to us. After you give donations to us in these ways, and if you would get an abundance of gold and silver, you will be satisfied, won't you? I will help you.
>
> Do *thathana pyu* for us, OK? If you get big, do big *thathana pyu* for us. If you get little, do small *thathana pyu* for us. … If you do *thathana pyu* by building or renovating pagodas, you will get a lot of merit so that we [too] can acquire merit, right?

There is thus a conditional relationship: the spirit only helps human beings to become wealthy or to get success in business if the latter promote Buddhism and engage in Buddhist practice. For instance, one possessed medium said, 'Do *thathana pyu*! Only thereby your money will increase. If you don't donate, your money won't increase.' One medium, possessed by a child spirit, offered protection to a female client's business enterprise, provided she promoted Buddhism and shared merit with them, saying, 'Grandma, I will help you to sell the stuff in your shop. I will shoot those who speak ill of you with my slingshot.' Buddhist morality and proper behaviour are also emphasised as a condition. A possessed medium said to a young man that if he wanted to get a job and earn money, he must stop dreaming about girls. Only if he stopped running after girls and instead did *thathana pyu* for the spirits, would the spirit help him to obtain money and to get a job. The possessed medium also said to him that the girls are less interested in him than in his money. Moreover, possessed mediums asked their clients not to be greedy, not to drink alcohol and not to lie. In this way, they admonish them to observe the Buddhist moral precepts. If they fail to do so, the spirits will not help them to get success in business. A possessed medium said the following to a client, 'Don't be greedy! If you are greedy, you won't get anything!' Moreover, the clients should not share the winning numbers with immoral people, who, presumably, would not use the money for Buddhist causes. All this emphasises the Buddhist identity of these cults.

The conditional relationship between devotees and spirits thus stipulates that one can acquire wealth only if one promotes Buddhism, observe Buddhist moral precepts, meditate, and tell rosary beads. This is a recurrent idea in the various forms of Burmese prosperity Buddhism. Several cult leaders (*bodaw*) said that the reason why Bo Min Gaung and the guardians of the treasure trove help people to get success in business is to enable them to promote and maintain the Buddha's dispensation.[20] One female devotee, who was 39 years old (in 2015) and ran her own shop, often performed the novel possession rituals for the guardians of the treasure trove. She said that when she is possessed and predicts winning lottery numbers, she only gives the numbers to others (devotees or spectators) if they promise that they will promote the Buddha's dispensation if they win. Moreover, if people break the Buddhist moral precepts, they will not get money for either their private consumption or for promoting Buddhism. There is thus a moral basis and condition for economic success. These two domains – the private (gaining prosperity) and the public (promoting the Buddha's dispensation) – are closely interrelated.

The moral dimension of the Burmese cults of prosperity Buddhism resembles I.M. Lewis' concept of 'central possession religions' that serve to maintain public morality (Lewis 2003 [1971]). In other cultures, spirits and their mediums voice public opinion and serve as vehicles of social control of individuals (Lewis 2003 [1971]: 123–146). In Thai spirit cults, for instance, spirits may 'call attention to such social ills as negligence in religious observance and deviation from traditional behavioural norms', and interventions by spirits can be interpreted by exorcists as being such admonitions, and 'prescribe appropriate behavioural reforms' (Golomb 1985: 237).

In the Burmese cults, devotees who have achieved success in business or hit the jackpot in the lottery both ascribe their success to the spirits and frequently devote considerable economic resources to Buddhist purposes. They build or renovate pagodas, hold lavish merit-making ceremonies, especially by giving food to the monks; they engage in Buddhist practice and observe Buddhist morality (see Foxeus 2017, 2018). For instance, one man in his forties working

---

20 A *bodaw* is a male leader of a cult of mainly Buddhist esoteric masters (*weizzā*), like Bo Min Gaung, but also of the guardians of the treasure trove. Usually, they do not become possessed by spirits.

as a carpenter said (in 2015) that for every 500,000 kyat he earns, he donates 300,000 for Buddhist ends. He explained that Naga Medaw gives him work so that he can earn money. For that reason, he must give something in return, that is, karmic merit from Buddhist merit-making. He and his wife have built two pagodas and one monastery, and shared merit with Naga Medaw. If they do not give offerings to Naga Medaw and do not promote Buddhism, they will run into economic difficulties. There are also success stories. One woman who was 45 years old in 2014 worked as a diamond dealer and lived in a palatial building in Mandalay. In her youth, she was poor and sold palm tree roots and boiled beans on the roadside. After she got married, she realised that she had a connection to the treasure trove (*thaik hsek*). She began turning to Naga Medaw and made wishes to her. Her business improved and she often received the winning lottery numbers from the guardians of the treasure trove. Eventually, she became wealthy – mainly, as she explained, through the money she won on the illegal lottery – and built her grandiose residence. In one year, she hit the jackpot 18 times in the three digits lottery, that is, 18 times out of the 24 annual draws. She received the lottery numbers from the guardians of the treasure trove and attributed her success to them. In return, she spends huge amounts for Buddhist causes and shares merit with the spirits. She has donated 10 million kyat several times; and she showed me her donation letters. Moreover, she gave a monk four acres of land worth about 300 million kyat. Many others credited spirits for success in business and lottery victories that enabled them to build their own houses.

Moralisation of wealth acquisition and 'occult economies'

Burmese prosperity Buddhism thus serves to maintain Buddhist traditions, morality and other values. Predicated on a moralisation of wealth acquisition, devotees are required to support the Buddha's dispensation in return for help from the spirits, lest they face difficulties. This in-built reciprocating mechanism compels devotees, who have a connection to the spirits and have gained some material benefits through them, to redistribute financial gains by donations for Buddhist ends and/or by embodying Buddhism through practice, whereupon they must share merit with the spirits (see also Foxeus 2017, 2018). This system, in which karmic merit is exchanged for money/wealth/prosperity, does not seem to be part of the 'traditional'

Buddhist imaginary.[21] Through the agency of spirits, economic gains are realised much more quickly than is possible via 'traditional' forms of merit-making. In these Buddhist prosperity cults, there is an assumption that it is only possible for devotees to become wealthy and successful if they remain a virtuous Buddhist who responsibly 'promotes and maintains the Buddha's dispensation' (*thathana pyu*). This mechanism seems to be a rather recent transformation of the meaning of merit-making, while the acts of merit-making have basically remained the same. Without the fundamental exchanges between the laypeople and Buddhist institutions (especially the monks) that acts of karmic merit-making entail, Buddhism – at least as it has been known in its institutionalised form historically and in contemporary Southeast Asia – would probably not have managed to survive in either earlier historical periods or in the contemporary era (*cf.* Borup 2018: 257).

The conditional relationship between supporting Buddhism and receiving help from the spirits to become wealthy does not seem to be evident in other Buddhist countries, such as Thailand (Jackson 1999a, 1999b; Pattana 2005), Vietnam (Taylor 2004) or Taiwan (Weller 1996). Such cults typically require a return gift to be presented to a spirit or the like, if the wish is granted, but nothing corresponding to a duty to promote Buddhism (*thathana pyu*). As demonstrated above, the Burmese cults require both. By contrast, what are portrayed by Robert Weller as amoral prosperity cults of greedy ghosts in Taiwan seem to represent a complete inversion of the moral Buddhist Burmese cults, which partly serve the community's interest in maintaining the hegemonic Buddhist order in society. Taiwan's individualistic and amoral cults apparently reflect that country's similarly amoral capitalist market and business enterprises, which promote egoistic greed (Weller 1996). To understand the 'boom-time religions of prosperity' in Thailand in the 1990s onward, Peter A. Jackson (1999b: 252) claims that one needs to adopt a 'post-Buddhist frame'.

Burma's colonial legacy can account for this difference, which seems to be unique to Burmese forms of prosperity Buddhism. The novel cults fit into a broader Burmese historical pattern going back to the colonial period of saving, maintaining, and protecting the Buddha's dispensation (*thathana pyu*) in times of rapid change in society (Turner 2014), as in the recent period of political and economic liberalisation (2011–2021). The king had been the

---

21 For more on traditional merit-making, see above.

foremost patron and defender of the Buddha's dispensation, but with the abolition of the monarchy in 1885, the monarch's responsibility shifted to the laypeople, including Buddhist lay associations (Turner 2014), Buddhist esoteric (*weizzā*) congregations and cult groups (Foxeus 2011). Since then, most Buddhist movements, associations and cults have emphasised the duty to do *thathana pyu*, including the contemporary Burmese forms of prosperity Buddhism (Foxeus 2011, 2016, 2017, 2018). These novel cults entail a transformation of Buddhist practice and imagining, including the environment of the pagoda compounds (novel iconography, temples, and noisy orchestras), and have, in effect, transformed the Burmese religious field (*cf.* Taylor 2004: 12). Although inventing new practices and imaginings, the novel cults seek to preserve 'traditional' Buddhist merit-making and other Buddhist practices. Moreover, they constrain individualist quests for material gratification by imposing a collective dimension that emphasises community and the preservation of the Buddha's dispensation.

These interlinked strategies – the moralisation of wealth acquisition and the call to promote the Buddha's dispensation – could thus be said not to represent ways of opposing processes of modernisation and social and economic change but rather strategies to cope with the challenges they pose to the perpetuation of the Buddha's dispensation. They serve as what seems to be a specifically Burmese mechanism to transform Buddhist practice and imagination, thereby making Buddhism more relevant in the contemporary world.

In this way, these novel cults contribute to a reproduction of the Buddhist order at a time when some urban Buddhists may, when struggling with economic difficulties, experience a diminished relevance of 'traditional' Buddhism to their everyday lives. Some Buddhists I interviewed expressed frustration with the explanations monks tend to give for the economic misery they suffer in their present life: that their suffering is determined by their bad karma from previous lives (*ateit kan*), and the best way to improve their lot was to donate lavishly to monks so that they, due to the karmic merit thereby acquired, may expect better conditions primarily in their future lives.[22] In contrast, the novel cults' focus on the present life addresses these

---

22 Some women, who had previously turned to the cult of the 37 Lords and had given lavishly to monks but had remained poor, reported that 'traditional' monks had given such explanations to them. They were now followers of the controversial monk Ashin Nyāna, who recognises only one life, denies the existence of supernatural beings, and claims that giving donations to monks does not improve their lot (see Foxeus 2020).

lay concerns and supplements 'traditional' Buddhism. To some degree, the relevance of the latter is reinforced by supplementary cults like these.

In a sense, these novel cults represent an affirmation and an embrace of the cultural signifiers of modernity and the transformation that processes of modernisation bring about in the everyday lives of urban Buddhists. Many young people turn to these cults wishing for iPhones, fancy motorbikes, or success in exams. The cults of prosperity Buddhism, including those of the mischievous children from the treasure troves, serve as resources for imagining 'alternative modernities' (Gaonkar 2001; Comaroff and Comaroff 2000: 311). That is, they represent a local 'cultural' dimension of modernity and likewise a 'creative adaptation' or synthesis of local culture and religion, on the one hand, and of capitalism and consumer culture, on the other, in which 'people "make" themselves modern' (Gaonkar 2001: 18) on their own terms. In this way, spirits cults are becoming an integral feature of modern urban Buddhist identities.

The novel forms of prosperity Buddhism have been shaped by changes in Burma's social, economic and political situation since the early 1990s. At that time, Burma shifted from a socialist dictatorship (1962–1988), which had implemented a planned economy that was devastating for the economy of the country, to a military dictatorship (1988–2011), which sought to establish a limited market economy and promote Buddhism. Occult economies, through which supernatural forces are harnessed to gain success in economic activities, represent a conjunction of capitalism and religion emerging at the intersection of the global and the local (Comaroff and Comaroff 1999: 283–284, 297; 2000: 310–317). Comaroff and Comaroff suggest how, especially in postrevolutionary societies (like Burma and Vietnam), new material desires and expectations emerge.[23] Capitalism and the new economic opportunities create, they maintain, a sense of both hope and hopelessness, promise and despair. However, the roots of the latter primarily lie not in poverty but in the perception that vast wealth is in the hands of the few, and the fear of being left out of the perceived promise of prosperity (1999: 281–284, 2000: 318). In Burma, the perception of this affluence of the few – especially a clique of crony capitalists privileged by the former military junta (Jones 2014) – combines with images of luxurious

---

23 The situation in Burma is comparable to that of Vietnam in the political and economic senses (see Taylor 2004: 5–6).

consumer products from media, social media, the Internet, shopping malls, advertisements in the streets, and so on. This situation has created new desires, for instance, for merchandise that serve as markers of social status, such as expensive iPhones or Japanese motorbikes, as well as frustration and despair (for not being able to purchase such expensive products).[24]

The lottery with its promise of prosperity and wealth is an important technology within Burmese occult economies. It is a trope of creating wealth from nothing (Comaroff and Comaroff 1999: 281; 2000: 313), which has been an attractive prospect not only for those with limited financial resources but also for others, including the middle classes. Success stories such as the formerly poor woman who hit the lottery jackpot 18 times during one year (see above) nourish 'fantasies of abundance' and of 'beating capitalism at its own game' (Comaroff and Comaroff 2000: 297). Such stories serve as models for others of the possibility of instantly becoming wealthy through the novel cults. In these cults, an imaginary of material abundance has become linked to indigenous figures – especially the guardians of the treasure trove and the esoteric master Bo Min Gaung – associated with supernormal powers and the ability to conjure wealth.

The majority of my informants from the temples dedicated to the guardians of the treasure trove belonged to the lower middle classes. However, a considerable number also belonged to the middle classes, mainly jade dealers and real estate agents, and a few were wealthy people belonging to the upper middle classes. Many of these relatively wealthy people, including ministers and military officers and owners of big companies and education centres, went to the Bo Min Gaung temple in Amarapura. A majority of all these people of various socio-economic classes played the illegal lotteries. This social complexity deviates from the norm in Western societies, where the poor are over-represented in lottery participation (Beckert and Lutter 2012).[25] One reason for this might be that most people in Burma, including the middle classes, are rather poor in comparison to other countries, and cannot easily afford luxury products that are available on the global market.

---

24 A telecommunication revolution occurred in Burma after 2011, with access to the Internet for many. Shopping malls, trendy restaurants, and karaoke clubs had already emerged in the 1990s (see Skidmore 2004), but their prevalence has virtually exploded in recent years and urban areas have transformed considerably.

25 A similar social complexity within lotteries can be found in Thailand (see Sunisa and Vanchai 2015).

Moreover, the incorporation of technical gambling language – known to many in urban areas – and gambling practices into the Buddhist rituals of the prosperity cults demonstrates the degree to which the novel cults are shaped by new socio-economic practices. Such close relationships between novel prosperity cults and economic practices were also observed in Vietnam by Philip Taylor (2004: ch 3; see also Jackson 1999b; Pattana 2005). In Burma, spirits may be considered supernatural bookmakers who provide a sense of certainty in a risky game that is determined entirely by chance.

Compared to other forms of gambling, lotteries are characterised by an extremely low probability of winning and the lowest pay-out ratio, and much research has attempted to resolve the conundrum of why people nevertheless buy lottery tickets (Vanchai 2011: 16). For the devotees, the *raison d'être* that also contributes to the expansion of these cults is that they provide a sense of control and predictability of something that is essentially beyond control (*cf.* Sunisa and Vanchai 2015: 1635).[26] As uncertainty tends to characterise everyday life in modernity, especially in times of modernisation and change, religious practice and imagination that can provide a sense of predictability and control demonstrate how modernisation and economic development, contrary to the old sociological modernisation-secularisation paradigm, can contribute to the proliferation of religious cults (*cf.* Taylor 2004: 11–12, 83–87; Jackson 1999b: 288–289, 292; Comaroff and Comaroff 2000: 314).

The direct, uncoded prediction of lottery numbers documented here differs radically from Rozenberg's (2005) observations of coded predictions by monks in the early 2000s. Today, coded predictions are still common, but direct, uncoded predictions have become widespread, especially in the cult of the guardians of the treasure trove. Although the latter might appear to be riskier, since the lotteries are illegal, spirits that predict uncoded lottery numbers are, however, less liable to be held accountable in a criminal investigation than monks.

Conclusion

Modernisation and the further liberalisation of the market economy that were implemented following the opening up of Burma in 2011 have thus entailed an increase and flourishing of Buddhist practice. In contrast to prosperity cults

---

26 It is also common among Thai and Chinese gamblers to develop 'superstitious beliefs' as a way to deal with uncontrollable outcomes of gambling (Sunisa and Vanchai 2015: 1635).

in some other Buddhist countries in the region, these cults are perceived to be intrinsically Buddhist and constitute an articulation of Buddhist identity, including by differentiating these cults from the *nat* cult of the 37 Lords. The possession rituals and the mediums predicting lottery numbers are situated in temples located within Buddhist pagoda compounds. Although the reasons for establishing betting offices of the illegal lotteries in monastic compounds were probably entirely pragmatic, this Buddhist framing has probably enhanced the perception of the Buddhist nature of this enterprise. Wealth acquisition is thus conditional: it requires a moral foundation and benefits both the individual and the community. Part of the wealth that is acquired through hitting the lottery jackpot must be redistributed for Buddhist ends. Devotees turn to these novel cults to gain wealth and prosperity, which enable them to promote and support the Buddha's dispensation. That is a legacy that goes back to the colonial period. The cults require devotees to become pious Buddhists who observe moral precepts, engage in Buddhist practices, and donate lavishly to the monks and for the pagodas. For that reason, these cults are individualistic in a rather restricted sense. As Burma's rapid changes between 2011 and 2021 were leading many to fear that the Buddha's dispensation was under threat, the novel cults protected and maintained the Buddhist order. From the point of view of the devotees, the cults served both their own egoistic interest in material gratification and the communal interest of preserving the Buddha's dispensation.

References

Beckert, Jens and Mark Lutter. 2012. 'Why the Poor Play the Lottery: Sociological Approaches to Explaining Class-Based Lottery Play', *Sociology*, 47(6): 1152–1170.

Borup, Jørn. 2018. 'Prosperous Buddhism, Prosperity Buddhism, and Religious Capital', *Numen*, 65: 256–288.

Brac de la Perrière, Bénédicte. 1989. *Les Rituels de possession en Birmanie: du culte d'Etat aux cérémonies privées*. Paris: Éditions Recherche sur les Civilisations.

———. 2011. 'Being a Spirit Medium in Contemporary Burma', in Kirsten W. Endres and Andrea Lauser (eds), *Engaging the Spirit World: Popular Beliefs and Practices in Modern Southeast Asia*. New York: Berghahn Books: 163–183.

———. 2012. 'Spirits versus Weikza: Two Competing Ways of Mediation', *Journal of Burma Studies*, 16(2): 149–179.

———. 2016. 'Spirit Possession: An Autonomous Field of Practice in the Burmese Buddhist Culture', *Journal of Burma Studies*, 20(1): 1–29.

Comaroff, Jean and John L. Comaroff. 1999. 'Occult Economies and the Violence of Abstraction: Notes from the South African Postcolony', *American Ethnologist*, 26(2): 279–303.

———. 2000. 'Millennial Capitalism: First Thoughts on a Second Coming', *Public Culture*, 12(2): 291–343.

Foxeus, Niklas. 2011. 'The Buddhist World Emperor's Mission: Millenarian Buddhism in Postcolonial Burma', PhD dissertation, Stockholm University.

———. 2016. 'Vidyādhara (weizzā/weikza)', in Michael Payne (ed.), *Oxford Bibliographies in Buddhism*. New York: Oxford University Press.

———. 2017. 'Possessed for Success: Prosperity Buddhism and the Cult of the Guardians of the Treasure Trove in Upper Burma', *Contemporary Buddhism*, 18(1): 108–139.

———. 2018. 'Spirits, Mortal Dread, and Ontological Security: Prosperity and Saving Buddhism in Burma/Myanmar', *Journal of the American Academy of Religion*, 86(4): 1107–1147.

———. 2020. 'Leaving Theravāda Buddhism in Myanmar', in Daniel Enstedt, Göran Larsson, and Teemu T. Mantsinen (eds), *Handbook of Leaving Religion*. Leiden: Brill: 116–129.

Gaonkar, Parameshwar Dilip. 2001. 'On Alternative Modernities', in Parameshwar Dilip Gaonkar (ed.), *Alternative Modernities*. Durham: Duke University Press: 1–23.

Golomb, Louis. 1985. *An Anthropology of Curing in Multiethnic Thailand*. Urbana: University of Illinois Press.

Jackson, Peter A. 1999a. 'The Enchanting Spirit of Thai Capitalism: The Cult of Luang Phor Khoon and the Post-Modernization of Thai Buddhism', *South East Asia Research*, 7(1): 5–60.

———. 1999b. 'Royal Spirits, Chinese Gods, and Magic Monks: Thailand's Boom-Time Religions of Prosperity', *South East Asia Research*, 7(3): 245–320.

Jones, Lee. 2014. 'The Political Economy of Myanmar's Transition', *Journal of Contemporary Asia*, 44(1): 144–170.

Lewis, I.M. 2003 [1971]. *Ecstatic Religion: A Study of Shamanism and Spirit Possession*. Third Edition. London: Routledge.

Pattana Kitiarsa. 2008. 'Buddha Phanit: Thailand's Prosperity Religion and its Commodifying Tactics', in Pattana Kitiarsa (ed.), *Religious Commodification in Asia: Marketing Goods*. London: Routledge: 120–143.

Rozenberg, Guillaume. 2005. 'The Cheaters: Journey to the Land of the Lottery', in Monique Skidmore (ed.), *Burma at the Turn of the 21st Century*. Honolulu: University of Hawai'i Press: 19–40.

Skidmore, Monique. 2004. *Karaoke Fascism: Burma and the Politics of Fear*. Philadelphia: University of Pennsylvania Press.

Spiro, Melford E. 1982 [1970]. *Buddhism and Society: A Great Tradition and its Burmese Vicissitudes*. Berkeley: University of California Press.

Sunisa Pravichai and Vanchai Ariyabuddhiphongs. 2015. 'Superstitious Beliefs and Problem Gambling Among Thai Lottery Gamblers: The Mediation Effects of Number Search and Gambling Intensity', *Journal of Gambling Studies*, 31: 1633–1649.

Taylor, Philip. 2004. *Goddess on the Rise: Pilgrimage and Popular Religion in Vietnam*. Honolulu: University of Hawai'i Press.

Turner, Alicia. 2014. *Saving Buddhism: Moral Community and the Impermanence of Colonial Religion*. Honolulu: Hawai'i University Press.

Vanchai Ariyabuddhiphongs. 2011. 'Lottery Gambling: A Review', *Journal of Gambling Studies*, 27: 15–33.

Weller, Robert P. 1996. 'Matricidal Magistrates and Gambling Gods: Weak States and Strong Spirits in China', in Meir Shahar and Robert P. Weller (eds), *Unruly Gods: Divinity and Society in China*. Honolulu: University of Hawai'i Press: 250–268.

CHAPTER 7

Looking for Fortune in the City
The Enchantment of Divination, Magic and Spirit Rituals in a Cambodian Urban Culture

Poonnatree Jiaviriyaboonya

Introduction

A group of Khmer university students broke out in laughter when I told them about my ethnographic research on divination and magic in Phnom Penh. They reflected that Cambodia might not be the right place to find such practices, especially in the capital city. The fortune-tellers in Phnom Penh, from what they experienced, are 'cheaters'. Most fortune-tellers they had met were uneducated, unemployed and without prospects, and that is why they had turned to fortune-telling. The students suggested that if I wanted to find the authentic form of divination, I should go to a rural village. Khmer people in the countryside still love and use divination, magic and spiritual cults to eliminate danger or resolve problems. In the city, they continued, the popularity of magic and supernatural beliefs had decreased and probably faded out because, 'Cambodia is now modernised and the country is more developed than before.' They went on to say that highly educated people are sceptical about fortune-telling and they tried once again to convince me that Phnom Penh was not the right place to look for genuine and reliable fortune-tellers. In contrast, the students stated that in neighbouring Thailand, the use of magic and other religious traditions is increasing and gaining in popularity; these practices are widely represented in Thai TV series that are very popular in Cambodia. Thai television characters use black magic and sorcery to attack their enemies, to attract an admiring lover, or to maintain familial relationships.[1]

---

1 I should emphasise that Thais and Khmers have different assumptions about the authority, originality and authenticity of traditional religious practices. Each country projects the stereotype that the ethnic other is the source of magic. I have observed that members of

Although the Khmer university students stated that they disagreed with such divinatory services, they also acknowledged that they consult fortune-tellers when they encounter various life crises or uncertainties about their studies, future careers or well-being. They also participate in the annual Khmer and Chinese ghost festivals, where they make merit for their ancestors and for homeless spirits, thus enhancing and cultivating their fortune and preventing supernatural forces from causing bad luck. When they or their parents were suffering from illness, and could not recover through modern medical treatment, they sought alternative diagnoses from fortune-tellers for an alternative diagnosis and took their parents to Buddhist monks in various monasteries to receive a water blessing, believing it might cure their sickness.

What surprised me was, despite their denials, that university students and other educated and 'modern' urban residents try to make sense of their lives through divination, magic and spirit rites. It seems that there is a dramatic contrast between discourses of modernity as being disenchanted and the lived experiences of the participants in these discourses: a wide range of modern lifestyles and urban experiences rely upon enchanted rituals. Furthermore, the resurgence of such religious practices in the capital city of Cambodia is vastly diverse and complex: spanning localities from markets to temples, and including both the wealthy and the poor. The popularity of divination, magic and spiritual beliefs is rising in Phnom Penh, despite the city's fame within the country as a centre of modern education, the market economy, rural–urban migration, cosmopolitanism and globalisation.

Several scholars have examined the revival movements of Cambodian religious traditions that highlight the reinvention of both orthodox and less-orthodox Buddhist practices (Ang 1988; Marston and Guthrie 2004; Kent and Chandler 2008). However, these studies have situated the resurgence of urban religious practices on the periphery of anthropological studies of Cambodia. There is a notable lack of in-depth ethnographic research on religious phenomena such as divination, magic and spirit cults in the urban environment, as well as on their broader influences on the lived experience of urbanites. Furthermore, to date, no religious studies scholars have explored how the revival of urban divination practices might factor into

numerous Thai youth groups in Bangkok think that Khmer people are experts in using black magic and spirit cults, while Khmer students in Phnom Penh express the converse belief: that Thais are experts in such practices. See also Baumann (2016) to further explore issues related to Thai stereotyping of Khmer magic.

explanations of the existential concerns of Cambodians who are remaking their lives within the context of an industrialising and globalising city. Finally, we lack understanding as to how contemporary practices such as divination might relate to Khmer 'tradition', given that the Khmer Rouge destroyed so many traditional cultural forms only a few decades ago.

This chapter attempts to fill these gaps in the anthropology of Cambodian religion by reporting the findings of ethnographic research that focuses on the resurgence of religious practices in an urban Cambodian setting. The ethnographic data sheds light on the understandings and circumstances of Khmer people who utilise various religious technologies for specific issues in well-defined situations. The data are drawn from 14 months of fieldwork in Phnom Penh undertaken between January 2015 and March 2016. This fieldwork included in-depth interviews, informal discussions and participant observation of the everyday-life activities of the research interlocutors, who were fortune-tellers and their clients. Both the fortune-tellers and their clients who were interviewed were rural–urban migrants who sought alternative technologies to cope with the uncertain circumstances in the urban environment. The experience of the fortune-telling client is here presented in the form of a case study of a young woman who moved from the countryside to the city to pursue education and seek employment. Practices of divination, magic and spiritual beliefs came into play when this student encountered situations of uncertainty generated by historical rupture, dislocation and rapid social change.

Conflicting dreams: Disoriented experiences of a university student from the countryside

Four years before I met her, Sovanna, a 24-year-old student, left her home village in Battambang Province and migrated to Phnom Penh, thereby taking a first step toward fulfilling the ambitious desire to make her dreams come true. Her original plan was to complete a B.A. in Economics at a well-known university and then return home to work in her family's small agricultural equipment business. Like other rural migrant students, Sovanna saw Phnom Penh as an educational hub where she could study international languages, computer skills and modern technology. Living in the city also introduced Sovanna to a multicultural community that included many resident foreigners who were willing to exchange their cultural ideas and practices with local people. Soon after she arrived in Phnom Penh, Sovanna was offered part-time work as a general manager in her auntie's electronics sales company. The richness of knowledge, resources and social connections to which she was exposed magnified this student's desire to stay in the city after graduation and build a career there, instead of returning to her home province.

Sovanna reflected that her life in Phnom Penh was like that of a bird. Living in the big city allowed her to fly anywhere she wanted, just like a bird, without the constraints of familial obligations. Living in her home village could be compared to being in a nest where her mother always fed her, but where mobility was constrained. In the city she had more freedom, but had to feed herself. Despite celebrating her freedom, however, the difficult living conditions in the city taught her a valuable lesson: she had to become self-sufficient. Sovanna was proud of the independent life she had managed to carve out in the city; where she had adjusted quickly to the new environment without needing to ask her parents for financial support. She also differentiated herself from the majority of urban university students, who, in her assessment, were spoiled as a result of their parents' willingness to give them money all the time. This safety net enabled them to avoid applying themselves to their studies. Sovanna saw that a lot of her city-born friends liked to spend their leisure time shopping at the malls. Sovanna could not lead such a life, since she had to work full time in order to save money to pay her school fees.

She also shared her opinion of the moral values of young migrants from the countryside who, she claims, try to work hard, exercise consistent discipline in their studies, and view work as the vehicle for achieving their dreams. Explorations through social media, especially Facebook and Instagram, enabled Sovanna to learn about successful people, including Jack Ma and Bill Gates. These two famous billionaires represented, for Sovanna, the epitome of success since, despite coming from a poor background and lacking a higher education degree, they had each achieved their ambitious dreams as a result of their intelligence, creative ideas, hard work and discipline.

The independence and freedom she experienced while living in the city allowed Sovanna to imagine she could make her own decisions about her future career and follow her own desires and aspirations. In other words, the student considered herself free to choose the academic discipline and subsequent career that would best guarantee her future success. After four years in the city, Sovanna made a big decision: sometime soon, she would open a coffee shop. She enjoyed the idea of being a barista for a while and, as she had learned from the story of successful business icons, she had to think about her future career differently from other students. Her pathway towards business success would necessarily be different from that of her classmates, most of whose dreams did not extend beyond becoming an employee and working in an office. Sovanna planned to open a coffee shop by the time she was 28, meaning within the following four years. But despite her strong passion and belief in her ability to realise her dream, she reflected that, to invest in a business, she needed to develop her knowledge, capacity and relevant social connections, all of which could be accomplished by pursuing higher education in a foreign country. After four years of living in Phnom Penh, the future that Sovanna imagined for herself was broader than what she had dreamed of when she first arrived in the city. She came to realise that a B.A. in Economics was not enough to achieve her new life dreams and goals in the capital.

Sovanna's plans for studying overseas were already well in train when I first met her. She was investigating the possibilities of studying in either Thailand or the US and had already researched several school programs and scholarship schemes. Soon after I met her, however, she shared her concerns about her parents' grave and chronic health problems, and the large obstacle that her parents' disabilities placed in the way of her dreams. If she proceeded with her plans to study abroad, her parents might suffer or even die while she was away, causing her lifelong regret. But if she stayed in Cambodia to care for them, she might entirely miss the opportunity to make a better life for herself.

This dilemma plunged Sovanna into a serious life crisis. I could imagine and understand why she sometimes seemed very disoriented and overwhelmed. She could not decide whether to study abroad or continue her life in Cambodia. Both options had positive and negative outcomes. On the one hand, studying abroad might enable her to realise certain opportunities, but she would have to leave her severely ill parents behind. On the other hand, if she decided not to leave the country and study locally so as to take care of her parents, her own self-development might suffer, since she would have to endure the corruption and other limitations that characterise Cambodian education. It was very difficult for this young Khmer student to know whether to follow tradition and be a grateful and dutiful daughter, or to enjoy her freedom and independent life, like the bird, or perhaps even the renowned billionaire, she dreamed of becoming.

In the process of coming to a decision, Sovanna thought that she might not receive a clear answer about her life options from her family members or friends. They may not fully understand the difficulties surrounding the scenarios she contemplated. Owing to this constraint, she decided to experiment with other sources of decision-making assistance. The idea of consulting a fortune-teller occurred to her frequently.

Exploring divination in Phnom Penh

Khmer people usually call fortune-tellers or diviners *grū dāy*, which literally means a teacher or a person who applies his/her divination skill(s) 'to guess' or 'to read people's fortune'. Phnom Penh residents often assume that the most authentic and reliable divination practices are to be found in rural areas, not in the city. They consider Siem Reap, for example, as a place where cultural traditions have been preserved since the Angkor Empire dominated Southeast Asia in the 9th to 12th centuries. A historical scholar, Ian Harris (2005: 60), also supports the view that Khmer folk religious practices involving divination, astrology and magic can be traced back to the Angkorean Empire. However, the historical literature does not explain how or even whether divination and astrology played a significant role in peoples' everyday lives at that time. The existence of divination was not recorded until the colonial era (1863–1953). Evidence from French archives indicates that royal astrologers (*horā*) assisted the Cambodian King for many tasks, including the famous prediction of a lunar eclipse in 1934 (*Bulletin De Soit Communiqué* 1934). Furthermore, royal astrologers also helped the king and the royal families predict the fortune of the country in the coming year based upon their interpretations of symbolic meanings and actions performed during divinatory rituals in the Royal Ploughing Ceremony (*brahrājabidhī puṇyacrātbrahnanggǎl*).

Returning the discussion to Phnom Penh, various forms of divination practices have become especially well developed. Various types of divination are offered to urban clients based on old scriptures (*câkgambīra*), card-reading (*meol bhea*), numerology (*lekha prāṃbīrtua*) and mediumistic divination (*cūl rūpa*). To be consistent with the local classifications, I use the term 'divination' to refer to a range of fortune-telling practices in Cambodia based on various cosmological beliefs, traditions, functions and interpretations that are embedded into and reflect upon the Khmer people's everyday-life experiences. Divination gives rise to seeing not only the future, but also unknown events and situations in both the past and present. It also exposes occult realms, forces, and principles that normally are invisible to ordinary people (Poonnatree 2018).[2]

Numerology or astro-numerology is a fortune-telling technique that applies astrological understandings and formulas of numerological calculations to decipher an individual's fortune. The numerological formulas (*lek atta* or *lek prumpi tua*) include numbers of seven or sometimes nine digits, depending on the fortune-teller's specific tradition and training. Calculations based on an individual's birthdate provide a group of numbers that the fortune-teller can read, interpret and then transform into concrete explanations that are delivered to clients. In contrast, mediumistic divination offers an entirely different method of reading fortune. A mediumistic fortune-teller/diviner (*nak cūl rūpa*) divines through his or her connection with spirits. Most mediumistic diviners offer consultation services in their homes. Sometimes they are able to heal clients by using traditional healing methods. A traditional healer who might also have a spiritual divining skill is called a *grū meol*, which means 'a teacher or a master who can look and see'. In Kampong Thom and Battambang Khmer the terms *nak cūl rūpa* and *grū meol* are used in reference to mediumistic fortune-tellers or spirit mediums. In popular understandings, a *grū meol* is a healing expert who can detect and subvert occult forces that cause affliction. Traditional Khmer healers know how to perform certain ritual actions, such as blowing, chanting and blessing while placing certain sacred objects on specific parts of the client's body. My research interlocutors explained that most *grū meol* reside in villages throughout Cambodia.

Sovanna sought out various divinatory techniques to make sense of her past, present and future. She hoped that one or other fortune teller would

---

2   In English the literal meaning of 'fortune-teller' is 'a person who is supposedly able to predict a person's future, for example, by palmistry, a crystal ball or similar methods.' The term 'divination' refers to 'the practice of seeking knowledge of the future or the unknown by supernatural means' (*Oxford Online Dictionary*, 'Fortune-teller', en.oxforddictionaries.com/definition/fortune_teller; *Oxford Online Dictionary*. 'Divination', en.oxforddictionaries.com/definition/divination; accessed 28 October 2014. In the Cambodian context, 'fortune-teller' has been defined slightly differently from the English literal meaning. This article follows the local definition using the term 'divination' since it encompasses a broader range of meanings and functions of a kind that one can find in Cambodia. Divination entails seeing not only the unknown future but potentially also the past and present, as well as occult realms, forces and principles that normally are invisible to ordinary people.

help her find a clearer direction for her life journey and resolve the agonising conflict between her personal dreams and the traditional expectations of a daughter who had parents with long-term health problems. Sovanna felt comfortable engaging with fortune-tellers; she had consulted with mediums in Battambang and Banteay Meanchey provinces while she was a teenager.

The *nak cūl rūpa* she consulted claimed to be able to divine Sovanna's fate through their connection with spirits, and the spiritual divination performed on her behalf addressed Sovanna's concerns about her parents. The *nak cūl rūpa* explained that Sovanna's anxiety, concern and uncertainty about her present life crisis, as well as her indecisiveness, were the outcome of a past transgression of tradition: Sovanna had failed to show sufficient respect to her ancestors. The proposed remedy, however, was not specific enough to guarantee a cure for her parents and thus did not relieve her of the sense that she ought to be doing something more to help them. Furthermore, Sovanna reflected that some *nak cūl rūpa* could predict their clients' lives accurately, but watching the process of being possessed by the spirits was, as she told me, 'dangerous and scary' for a young person such as herself.

The spiritual divination did not help Sovanna decide whether to stay in Cambodia or go overseas. As a result, she decided to seek out a card reader, a popular divinatory technique in Phnom Penh. She went to a Vietnamese *meol bhea* specialist at Psar Kandal, a popular market in the capital city. Sovanna believed the card reading was quite accurate because the fortune-teller successfully identified her emotional state as very stressed, distressed and depressed. Still, the cards did not reveal the kind of insights that could help her come to a decision.

After several more fortune-telling consultations, Sovanna was still no closer to making a decision and her options remained the same: either follow her ambitions and aspirations to study abroad, return home to care for her parents, or invest in a coffee shop and aim to be a successful businesswoman. One day, when I met her as she was in a disoriented emotional state, including expressing a sense of crisis about her sense of self, it struck me that Sovanna's life experience was similar to that of many young migrants who I had come to know in Phnom Penh. They also experienced indecisiveness in the face of conflicting life options, which led them also to wonder about their identities and sense of self.

Consulting numerology fortune-tellers in Phnom Penh

Hearing Sovanna speak about her attempts to manage her life crisis, I understood that she needed advice and assistance to address the sources of her anxiety. She next arranged an appointment with a numerology fortune-teller called *Grū* Bun, who offered divination services in Phnom Penh's Chbar Ampov area. On this occasion, I followed Sovanna to the fortune-teller's residence. We arrived at around 3 pm. When walking into the house, we saw a middle-aged woman who was waiting for a consultation. On the left side of the terrace, we saw a mirror-backed cabinet displaying various kinds of amulets and fabric talismans available for purchase, which was a clear sign that the fortune-teller *Grū* Bun offered a range of magical techniques.

Grū Bun could speak Thai fluently, since he used to be a monk and learned Buddhist doctrine when in Thailand. He seemed to be quite different from other fortune-tellers I had met: he was only 36 years old but was already well-known and had a backlog of clients who relied on his services. All other professional fortune-tellers I had met were older than 40; many were in their 60s. Every day, *Grū* Bun met between ten and fifteen clients from a variety of socio-economic backgrounds. There were restaurant owners, politicians, high-ranking military and police officers, jewellery shop owners, market traders, members of the Khmer diaspora who had returned to Cambodia, as well as university students. *Grū* Bun also had some 'VIP clients,' elite people who were members of the political or economic upper crust. He explained that some came in search of ways to get promoted, while others sought business success. *Grū* Bun observed that most university student clients were concerned about family, educational achievement and future career. Then he tried to correct the students' misunderstandings by telling them that divination and magical practices cannot guarantee that they will pass their exams. Instead of relying upon unseen powers, he encouraged these clients to concentrate on their studies with discipline and hard work in order to pass their exams.

Improvising divinatory traditions after the Khmer Rouge

The principal technique *Grū* Bun used to divine an individual's fortune was numerological calculations based on the client's day, month, and year of birth.[3]

---

3 Numerological divination techniques are commonly found across Southeast Asia and especially in Cambodia, Thailand and Burma. Although *Grū* Bun did not explain in detail the origin of the belief in the power of an individual's birthdate, I discovered later from the famous Thai divination book *Sat Haeng Hon* (*The Astrologer's Teachings,* Parinya 2000) that

Grū Bun claimed that his numerological technique was unique and distinct from card-reading divination because the numerological calculation is capable of providing information about exactly what will happen to a client for a whole year, as well as also indicate happenings in each month of the coming year.

Grū Bun and other fortune-tellers I have met in Phnom Penh encountered challenges and obstacles as they tried to establish their divinatory authority. The rupture of cultural traditions during the civil war dramatically reduced both the knowledge available and the means by which it traditionally had been communicated. Khmer religious practitioners and scriptures related to Buddhism and supernatural ritual were seriously compromised and often destroyed during the Pol Pot era from 1975 to 1979 (Edwards 2007; Chandler 2008). After the fall of the Khmer Rouge in 1979, Theravada Buddhism was revitalised by government officials and various NGOs. Despite its name, the Ministry of Cults and Religion has never proposed a standard or official astrological practice, neither has it published any astrological handbooks for people interested in these matters. The official representatives of the Ministry of Cults and Religion have regarded divination as a form of supernatural practice that lies outside of the boundaries of appropriate government activities, which are limited to reviving 'religious' traditions, especially Theravada Buddhism.[4] As such, the state neither supports nor opposes supernatural ritual practices. Although the state Ministry of Cults and Religion prioritises Buddhism as the main focus of its policies, it also accepts the existence of folk beliefs such as *neak ta*, a form of tutelary spirit that safeguards and protects Buddhist sacred spaces such as monasteries and pagodas, and also looks after human residences and living spaces.

---

the strength of belief in the astrological significance of each of the seven days of the week was influenced by Hindu teachings of the *graha* or *navagraha*, a belief in nine deities who reside in nine astrological planetary domains: Surya (The Sun), Soma (the Moon), Mangala (Mars), Budha (Mercury), Brihaspati (Jupiter), Shukra (Venus), Shani (Saturn), Rahu (Shadow) and Ketu (Shadow). The Sanskrit titles of the first seven deities in this list are deployed in the Khmer and Thai languages as the names of the week's seven days, that is, *athit, jan, angkhan, phut, pharuehatsabodi, suk,* and *sao* (Thai Romanisation). The origins of each deity are associated with numbers that are also linked with various auspicious animals, and the fortune-teller/astrologer believes that these series of numbers signify the relative strength of each day, a detail that is important to the numerological divination technique.

4   Interview with Sok Mathea (pseudonym), Ministry of Cults and Religion, Phnom Penh, 2015. As I have observed Khmer scholars and university students communicate in everyday conversation, *apiya jaṃnya* is typically translated into English as 'superstition' or 'supernatural belief'. The expression *apiya jaṃnya* literally means 'invisible belief', which includes magic, divination and spirit mediumship.

A second challenge relates to knowledge transmission in the field of divination. Previous generations of skilled Khmer fortune-tellers refused to transmit their knowledge to the next generation. Khmer fortune-tellers believe that authentic divinatory knowledge, like astro-numerology, is a high privilege because historically it was preserved through oral transmission within royal families as well as by some educated Buddhist monks. For example, some Buddhist monks, including Som Korn, a famous monk who resides in Phnom Penh's Nak Kawann monastery, claim that some divinatory knowledge has been preserved since the civil war, but knowledge of the technique is both rare and kept private (NyoNyum 2015). Furthermore, a small number of specialists who have been trained by their former mentors or followed their own autodidactic learning from legitimate sources seem to be anxious about circulating their techniques to people they do not know. By comparison, the Astrological Association of Thailand plays a key role in standardising and popularising astrology and divination practices across that country. This national association was established in Bangkok in 1947 with the co-operation of members of the royal family and elite state officials. This is not the case in Cambodia, where a national astrology association has never been established. Although some members of the Cambodian royal family claim that they have preserved Khmer divinatory traditions, they serve few clients and share knowledge of their craft with even fewer people (Will Jackson 2014).

It was in the context of such problems and challenges that *Grū* Bun attempted to find his own way to establish his divinatory authority. He claimed that his divinatory technique is established from *kpuan* or formal knowledge, and that its methodologies of divination and astrology have been meticulously developed from a range of document-based formulae or published handbooks. His numerological divination skill was developed through self-study and research into divination books and other sources, as well as through his own experiences while consulting with satisfied clients for almost ten years. *Grū* Bun gained access to relevant source materials after he was ordained as a monk in Cambodia's Takeo Province and subsequently when pursuing his monkhood in Thailand and Laos. These materials include books written by different famous fortune-tellers, published in Khmer, Thai, and Burmese. He cannot read Burmese, but claims that some Cambodian numerological symbols are taken from ancient Burmese traditions, and that in any case the Khmer and Thai sources are more reliable.

Although many Khmer divinatory traditions were destroyed by the Khmer Rouge, some repertoires of this field were preserved by individual practitioners, especially Buddhist monks.[5] *Grū* Bun's most comprehensive source originated from Siem Reap and was given to him by a monk. The Khmer divinatory tradition tends to focus on astrological perspectives on the Khmer New Year and calendrical system, as well as different kinds of magical *yantra* designs and their spiritual powers. *Grū* Bun argued that such traditional practices, however, were inadequate to establish his own authority and reputation as a professional practitioner. Therefore, he scoured well-known Thai divination books for additional insights and found much of value in the *Patithin Nueng Roi Pi* (100-year calendar) (see Figure 7.1), *Tamra Phrommachat* (see Figure 7.2) and *Tamra Phlu Luang*. *Grū* Bun has been especially influenced by the first two of these books, with the *Tamra Phrommachat*, in particular, being a must-read handbook for students of Thai astrology.[6] This book covers a range of astrological techniques including the predictions of individuals' lives using various astrological approaches, such as twelve-year animal zodiacs, birthdates and spiritual divination.[7] The *Tamra Phrommachat* also introduces a manual that outlines horoscope analysis that can inform considerations regarding the compatibility of a pair of individuals (usually applied in choosing soulmates) and introduces rituals to eliminate bad luck, unusual situations and natural disasters. Importantly, the book also guides readers to perform certain actions, especially during 'auspicious times'. *Grū* Bun considered the *Tamra Phrommachat* to be his 'teacher'. The book introduced him to the fundamental concepts of Thai astrology and divination, which he used as approaches and tools to reimagine and improvise the authority of the Cambodian divinatory tradition.

---

5   Som Korn, a Buddhist monk at Nak Kawann monastery, is an example of the many fortune-tellers and astrologers who claim to have preserved astrological books from the Khmer Rouge's devastation policy (Poonnatree 2016; NyoNyum 2015).
6   *Tamra Phrommachat* literally translates as 'The Scripture of the Lord Brahma's Lineage'. This text contains various astrological techniques, many of which suggest Hindu religious influences. All divinatory traditions featured in this book were originally written by an unknown astrologer in the Ayutthaya period (1351–1767) ('Intangible Cultural Heritage', ich.culture.go.th/index.php/th/ich/folk-literature/252-folk/462--m-s, accessed 2017). In the time of King Rama IV (r. 1851–1868), these practices were compiled and integrated with new techniques and then officially published in the text's current form. *Tamra Phrommachat* was first translated from Thai to Khmer in 1971, before the Khmer Rouge, and has been reissued several times since the revolution that overthrew the Pol Pot regime in 1979.
7   The spiritual divination offered in *Tamra Phrommachat* includes, for example, information on the belief in guardian spirits who protect newborn babies, called *Mae Sue* in Thai.

Figure 7.1. Cover of the Thai divination book *Patithin Nueng Roi Pi* (100-year calendar). **Colour** p. 320.

Figure 7.2. Cover of the astrological book *Tamra Phrommachat*. **Colour** p. 320.

The fortune-telling session: Elements of a numerological method

Grū Bun started the fortune-telling session for Sovanna by lighting two tall candles that stood behind his chair. Various images and statues could be seen on an altar behind him, including the Lord Buddha, the Chinese Bodhisattva Guan Yin, a hermit, and images of child spirits (*kumaradeba*) and two famous Thai monks: *Somdet* To (*Somdet Phra* Phutthajan, 1788–1872) and the legendary figure of *Luang Pu* Thuat (c. 1582–1682). *Grū* Bun came to know of these famous monks during his monkhood in Thailand. That experience led him to explore and utilise a source of magical power from famous

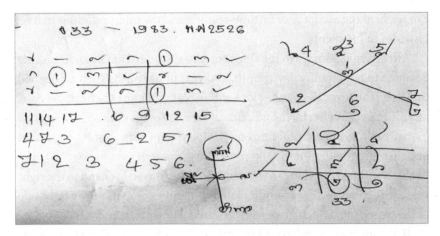

Figure 7.3. An example of the numerological tables and chart that were calculated from my own day, month and year of birth. In order to communicate more easily with this researcher, *Grū* Bun wrote down the Thai words and explained the meaning of the numbers on each direction of the cross chart. These words signify wealth (*sap*), power (*amnat*), debts (*nī*) and transportation/travelling (*jorn*). Photo: Poonnatree Jiaviriyaboonya.

Thai Buddhist monks (*keji ajan*). Belief in the power of Thai magic monks is widespread in Cambodia, especially among educated Khmer Buddhist monks and lay fortune-tellers who formerly were monks. They show a high degree of respect to Thai magic monks because of their moral character, such as the sense of compassion and strict discipline of Buddhist doctrine.

Moreover, *Grū* Bun explained that the sacred gods, goddesses, deities and spirits that he venerates have *pāramī* (spiritual power) to improve his divination skill and protect his life from danger, especially from the dangers that black magic might otherwise would have caused. Bertrand (2001, 2004) explains the concept of *pāramī* in the context of divination and spiritual healing practices as denoting a benevolent supernatural power that can be represented in the form of a god or deity that respects and practises Buddhist morality. Building on Bertrand's definition, *pāramī* can be considered as a kind of mystical potency that depends on certain forms of morality, including the association of goodness and purity with individuals who obey Buddhist precepts and believe in karmic causation. Broadly in line with Bertrand's definition and the case of *Grū* Bun, we can understand *pāramī* as a benevolent spiritual power that has been transferred from the gods and spirits to the fortune-teller. *Grū* Bun believes that the power of *pāramī* can enhance the efficacy of his divination, because this benevolent form of authority can reaffirm the accuracy of fortune-reading and the interpretations that he provides to his clients.

After paying homage to the spirits on the altar, *Grū* Bun began by asking Sovanna to tell him the day, month, and year of her birth. Then he opened the Thai 100-year calendar book (*Patithin Nueng Roi Pi*) to check the date, month and year of her birth and calculate the age of his client. He then drew a small table with seven columns on the left side of a sheet of A4 paper and put a Khmer number in the top row of each column (see Figure 7.3), and Arabic numbers elsewhere in the table. Then he moved his hand to the right side of the paper and drew another table with three columns on the right side of the paper, into which he quickly inserted Khmer numbers.

Grū Bun then commenced his calculation of Sovanna's fortune. After drawing a table, he wrote the number 24 on the right corner of the paper, which equated to Sovanna's age. He then multiplied this number by 12 and then divided by 7. This calculation helped him diagnose the specific ailment Sovanna suffered from. *Grū* Bun explained how the number 1 could affect Sovanna's life. Then, he diagnosed the reasons for her emotional and physical illnesses:

> Now you are suffering a great deal from headache and foot pain because you are very stressed. ... I can see why you feel like this. ... From the number [number 1], there might be a termite nest in your house. Also, the guardian spirits of your house [in Battambang] are displeased because the termite nest is actually occupying their residence. ... This might be the reason why your mother has gotten sick, but I have to see your mother's day, month and year of birth before I can explain more.

Inter-subjective communication between the fortune-teller and his client

Based on observations of this numerological fortune-teller and his young client, one can discern that the fortune-teller applies his numerological technique as a tool to visualise the student's life journey, in which outcomes such as wealth, power, security, fortune, sickness and debt are not predetermined, but rather are seen to be shaped in relation to morality, auspiciousness, spiritual power and obligation. The symbolic meanings of a range of numbers are decoded in accordance with sophisticated calculation formulae, knowledge of astrology and traditional belief in spirits.

During the consultation session, the fortune-teller diagnosed his client's parents' physical illness while also delivering emotional support for the client herself. We can infer that the student used the fortune-telling consultation as a platform to express her experiences of frustration and suffering at not being able to find someone in the urban neighbourhood to listen to her story. After the physical and emotional diagnoses, *Grū* Bun started talking about the student's current situation while also suggesting resources and opportunities in the city that she might avail herself of in the near future:

> As you turned 24 this year, you will have more money and also the opportunities to study or work in foreign countries. Your future husband has a similar working interest and he will come from the same career.

He forecast the future occurrences for Sovanna from January until December of the coming year:

> The first month [January 2016], you plan to do something? You plan to study abroad, right? This month you want to do a lot of things but you cannot follow most of your plans because you are concerned a lot about your mother … . She is sick now.

Then Sovanna told the fortune-teller about her goals for the year:

> I'm planning to pursue an M.A. in business management in Thailand or in the United States, but I haven't been able to make a decision right now because I am thinking a lot about my parents, especially my mother, as you said. It's correct, my mother is sick and I have to take care of her.

The fortune-teller responded:

> Let me finish this first: from January to May, your fortune is in the middle, not too high and not too low and it will be good until June. You won't have much money these months; you have to be patient until July. Your life will be good from July until December. and you will meet a man and start a relationship with him in November. … A man born in the year of the Dog should be the best for you. Those who were born in the years of the Rabbit and Dragon are also good, but you have to eliminate men who were born in the years of the Monkey, the Goat, the Horse, or the Cow.

Sovanna replied:

> Actually, someone has tried to approach me, but I think it's not a good time to think about a relationship or married life. I just want to focus on

> my studies, my work, and I still think a lot about my parents' well-being. … That's all for myself right now. … I just want to know when I can go to study abroad and open a coffee shop.

Grū Bun suddenly looked at the numbers he had written in the tables, and then explained:

> Yes, I didn't say that you have to think about love and married life right now, your fortune told me that you will meet the real soulmate in five years from now. … You don't need to be in a hurry, because you still have plenty of time to think about that.

Interestingly, after the fortune-teller had laid out a highly specific scenario about marriage, Sovanna responded by mentioning her experiences and expressing her own contrasting intentions in this regard. In response to her clarification, the fortune-teller refined his comments with more ambiguous statements about her time to get married. The exchange was flexible and allowed the student to show the fortune-teller her priorities. He then addressed the student's plans to study and open a coffee shop in Phnom Penh:

> You can do it later this year, around March to May. … You will see. A male relative will give some financial support to help you invest in the coffee shop, and you can also have a chance to travel to the foreign country within these two months as well. And I think a good time for you to study in the USA is in two years' time.

Two months after the fortune-telling session, Sovanna reflected that she felt more positive about her life. Concerns and anxieties were relieved because the fortune-teller's advice and decisiveness helped the student prepare her mind for her next steps. She decided to begin study for a Masters degree in 2016, instead of waiting until 2018 as the fortune-teller had indicated. She managed to get a visa to enter the USA and booked an air ticket for March in that year. When she arrived, she would take a short course in English and work in a restaurant until the school year began. She decided that this was a sensible plan and also one that the fortune-teller supported, as he had anticipated travel to a foreign country in March or April 2016.

During the consultation, the fortune-teller *Grū* Bun did not prescribe a fixed menu of advice. Instead, he manifested his attentiveness on the dilemma faced by his client; the obligations imposed by family membership versus her dreams of mobility inspired by Internet business celebrities. His advice was based on solid principles as well as supernatural laws. At the same time, however, it was flexible and accommodating to his client's interjected clarifications and interpretations.

The fortune-teller fully reaffirmed the student's desires for individual mobility. He affirmed that it is possible for the student, as a relative newcomer to the city, to achieve her ambitions and dreams while also advising her about accessible resources and possible opportunities in the city. Although Sovanna's capacity to invest in her own business was still constrained by her limited experience and inadequate financial resources, the fortune-teller contributed to lowering her anxiety by saying that the plan to open a coffee shop in the city was still possible since she would receive financial assistance from a relative in the near future. At the same time, the fortune-teller articulated traditional social values by reminding the student about her obligation, as a daughter, to show moral responsibility to look after her parents and especially her mother, who was still suffering from a severe disease. The fortune-telling consultation allowed the student to consider her choices and reflect on whether she should follow her desires to study abroad or look after her parents in Battambang.

The fortune-teller proposed a way around this dilemma by suggesting that the student's overseas study could come later. His reading of her fortune also kept open a space between her dreams of mobility and traditional expectations in suggesting that although she would meet a prospective husband in the near future, her real soulmate might not arrive for another few years.

Discussion and concluding remarks

Buttressed by the ethnographic data presented above, this study argues that the resurgence of divination, magic, and spiritual cults in Phnom Penh needs to be considered in relation to cultural diversity and social mobility, as well as the uncertainties and limitations engendered by historical crises in Cambodian society. Contemporary urban-based divinatory repertoires are not direct continuations of past tradition. Instead, I argue that various urban agents are creatively improvising hybrid Khmer religious practices that include divination, magic and spiritual rites. After the Khmer Rouge, Khmer fortune-tellers have attempted to revive and reestablish divinatory authority by considering Thai astrology as an important source of knowledge. *Grū* Bun insists that his numerology technique has been developed through and inspired primarily by Thai numerology. His technique relies upon Thai astrological handbooks including *Patithin Nueng Roi Pi* (100-year calendar), *Tamra Phrommachat* and *Tamra Phlu Luang*. Khmer sources of knowledge were an insufficient foundation for comprehensive numerological techniques and, as such, *Grū* Bun decided to supplement local repertoires with Thai handbooks. Contemporary Khmer divination techniques are being improvised through a process of creative reinvention of urban religious authority and knowledge, all within a context of historical rupture, ongoing turbulence, and profound socio-cultural change in the capital city.

The resurgence of divination in Phnom Penh also reflects the agency and aspirations of vulnerable individuals who attempt to establish a reliable way of knowing the world and, thereby, to secure and control their lives within uncertain circumstances. During my research, I met numerous Khmer fortune-tellers who are attempting to establish their divinatory authority independently and without any governmental support. They attempt to reestablish divinatory repertoires within the contexts of rupture, uncertainty and change that characterise Cambodia's post-revolutionary era. *Grū* Bun is one among the many Phnom Penh fortune-tellers who have attempted to solidify their claim to divinatory authority by employing selected foreign sources of knowledge. Thai astrology has had an especially large impact on the resurgence of astrology and divination in contemporary Cambodia. The ethnographic evidence suggests that the reinvention of divinatory authority in post-Khmer Rouge Cambodia has been influenced by Thai astrological tradition.

In addition, the ethnographic account explains why the demand for and popularity of Khmer religious traditions involving divination, magic and spiritual veneration are rising and expanding across Cambodia, especially in urban contexts. Young rural–urban migrants who embrace modern education are particularly likely to avail of various occult technologies to cultivate their fortune or look for solutions to life issues.

As can be seen from the inter-subjective communication between fortune-teller and client, divination offers a therapeutic service that enables a person facing moral dilemmas at a time of indecision to air concerns and articulate conflicting desires with a stranger. The inter-subjective experiences of the fortune-teller and his client not only revealed the client's existential problems but also pointed to possibilities for her relief. During the consultation, Sovanna expressed anxieties about the dilemma between her personal aspirations and socially imposed moral responsibilities. She was uncertain about her role and subjectivity and, given conflicting values and the multiple life scenarios on offer, her decision-making became fraught. As a result, her 'self' and 'subjectivity' entered a condition of crisis. In the course of the consultation, the fortune-teller rebuilt the migrant student's horizons of possibility and contextualised her imagination of her own life scenarios. The student was thus enabled to reprioritise her options, choose between her dreams, and to discover 'who' she is. In fact, the student's final decision reflected her intention to be liberated from familial obligations and social expectations. After the consultation with *Grū* Bun, Sovanna decided that an overseas education could improve her socio-economic status. Instead of following the fortune-teller's suggestion about the auspicious time to study abroad in two years' time, Sovanna made a decision by herself and changed her plan to study in the current year of 2016.

Khmer university students, as reflected by Sovanna's experience, tend to see studying overseas as a giant step forward in their pursuit of the life they dream of. Imagining an adventurous life in a foreign country frees Khmer rural–urban migrant students from out-of-control situations, the suppressed socio-economic structure, social expectations and the moral code of conduct expected of a dutiful daughter. The perspective of valuing a life overseas as a major achievement is very important to Khmer university students, who are about to transform their identities from one of a student to one of a full-time employee or a young entrepreneur. Such a turning point inspires the young Khmer generation to actively navigate and enthusiastically explore various opportunities from diverse channels. While encountering the challenging conditions of rural–urban mobility, Khmer university students perceive life overseas as offering alternative opportunities they could receive from a modern way of life.

In considering the achievements Sovanna proposed to measure her life by, notions of traveling overseas and of the foreign play key roles in understanding the symbolic meaning embedded in her story-telling. The value Cambodian youths ascribe to studying overseas has been fetishised by the power of capitalist culture. As Schroeder (2008) argues, fetishisation denotes the process of permeating an object or idea with power. A fetishised object or idea is usually related to sexual gratification, desire and worship. Fetishisation can be considered as a cultural, psychological and social technique to reconceptualise things as being 'larger than life, animate, or sexually desirable' (*ibid*). Schroeder's definition of fetishisation is applicable to this chapter's examination of how modern desire and aspiration influence ideology, perceptions, value judgements and behaviours of migrant Khmer university students. Indeed, the ethnographic data presented here suggests that the power of fetishisation not only shapes Khmer youths' cultural values but also influences Khmer fortune-tellers' reinvention of divinatory techniques.

The resurgence of local religious practices in Cambodian urban society contrasts with the expectations of scholars like Horton (1971) and Reid (1993), not to mention Weber (1905), who have argued that the social influence of local beliefs including spirit cults, magic and divination will decline as ideas and institutions associated with 'modernity' become more ubiquitous. Consistent with these scholars' expectations, local spiritual practices offering abstract norms of reciprocal and interpersonal relations were disenchanted in the 16th and 17th centuries within the economic fluctuations and population mobility that took place in Southeast Asia (Horton 1971; Reid 1993). This chapter, however, provides ethnographic evidence supporting the conclusion that local religious practices are rising and expanding in urban neighbourhoods. The resurgence of divination, magic and spirit cults in Cambodia's capital city supports the argument presented by, among others, Jackson (1999), Taylor (2007) and Hefner (2010), that local religious practices in Southeast Asian countries are not fading into oblivion but, rather, are continuing and changing in response to modernisation, industrialisation and the capitalist market economy. Such religious repertoires have been revived and reinvented in the form of technological resources utilised to assist the life journeys of urban Khmer who are, for example, uncertain of their obligations with respect to tradition and customary practices. As such, however, the discussions on the improvisation of the divinatory authority and the inter-subjective communications between the fortune-teller and his client demonstrate the creative ways urban Khmer experience and re-enchant the urban world. It also shows how vulnerable individuals, especially young migrants to urban areas, actively cope with uncertain and insecure circumstances and, at the same time, attempt to improve their lives through their use of religious technologies.

References

Ang, Chouléan. 1988. 'The Place of Animism within Popular Buddhism in Cambodia: The Example of the Monastery', *Asian Folklore Studies*, 47(1): 35–41.

Baumann, Benjamin. 2016. 'The Khmer Witch Project: Demonizing the Khmer by Khmerizing a Demon', in Peter J. Bräunlein and Andrea Lauser (eds), *Ghost Movies in Southeast Asia and Beyond: Narratives, Cultural Contexts, Audiences*. Leiden/Boston: Brill: 141–183.

Bertrand, Didier. 2001. 'The Names and Identities of the Boramey Spirits Possessing Cambodian Mediums', *Asian Folklore Studies*, 60(1): 31–47.

———. 2004. 'A Medium Possession Practice and its Relationship with Cambodian Buddhism: The Grū Pāramī', in John Marston and Elizabeth Guthrie (eds), *History, Buddhism, and New Religious Movements in Cambodia*. Honolulu: University of Hawai'i Press: 150–169.

Bulletin De Soit Communiqué. 1934. (Khmer archive, no title), January 10.

Chandler, David P. 2008. 'Cambodia Deals with its Past: Collective Memory, Demonisation and Induced Amnesia', *Totalitarian Movements and Political Regions*, 9(2–3): 355–369.

Edwards, Penny. 2007. *Cambodge, the Cultivation of a Nation, 1860–1945*. Honolulu: University of Hawai'i Press.

Harris, Ian Charles. 2005. *Cambodian Buddhism: History and Practice*, Honolulu: University of Hawai'i Press.

Hefner, Robert. 2010. 'Religious Resurgence in Contemporary Asia: Southeast Asian Perspectives on Capitalism, the State, and the New Piety', *The Journal of Asian Studies*, 69(4): 1031–1047.

Horton, Robin. 1971. 'African Conversion', *Africa*, 43(3): 85–108.

Intangible Cultural Heritage. 2010. 'The Myth of Phra Chao Ha Phra Ong [the Five Buddhas]'. ich.culture.go.th/index.php/en/ich/folk-literature/252-folk/221-the-myth-of-phra-chao-ha-phra-ong (Accessed 18 November 2021).

Jackson, Peter A. 1999. 'The Enchanting Spirit of Thai Capitalism: The Cult of Luang Phor Khoon and the Postmodernisation of Thai Buddhism', *South East Asia Research*, 7(1): 5–60.

Jackson, Will. 2014. '7 Questions with Prince Ravivaddhana Sisowath', *Phnom Penh Post* (4 April). www.phnompenhpost.com/7days/7-questions-prince-ravivaddhana-monipong-sisowath (accessed 18 November 2021).

Kent, Alexandra, and David Chandler (eds). 2008. *People of Virtue: Reconfiguring Religion, Power and Morality in Cambodia Today*. Copenhagen: NIAS Press.

Marston, John, and Elizabeth Gunthrie (eds). 2004. *History, Buddhism, and New Religious Movements in Cambodia*. Honolulu: University of Hawai'i Press.

NyoNyum. 2015. 'Cambodian Life Navigation' (in Japanese and English). n.p.

Parinya Nimprayoon. 2000. *Sat Hang Hon 1* (in Thai). N.p. Chomrom Phayakorn Sat.

Pattana Kitiarsa. 2012. *Mediums, Monks, and Amulets: Thai Popular Buddhism Today*. Chiang Mai: Silkworm Books.

Poonnatree Jiaviriyaboonya. 2016. 'Khmer Ways of Seeing and Being: Life-Experiences of Fortune-tellers and their Clients in Cambodian Urban Culture', The Biennial Asian Studies Association of Australia (ASAA) Conference. 5–7 July. The Australian National University, Canberra, Australia.

———. 2017. 'The Influences of Thai Divination on Present Cambodian Fortune-telling Practice', 13th International Conference on Thai Studies, 'Globalized Thailand? Connectivity, Conflict, and Conundrums of Thai Studies'. 15–18 July, Chiang Mai, Thailand.

———. 2018. 'Khmer Ways of Seeing: Migration and Divinatory Improvisation in Phnom Penh', PhD dissertation, The Australian National University, Canberra.

Reid, Anthony. 1993. *Southeast Asia in the Age of Commerce 1450–1680. Vol. Two: Expansion and Crisis*. New Haven: Yale University Press.

Schroeder, J.E. (2008). 'Fetishization', in W. Donsbach (ed.), *The International Encyclopedia of Communication*. doi.org/10.1002/9781405186407.wbiecf026 (accessed 18 November 2021).

Taylor, Philip. 2007. *Cham Muslims of the Mekong Delta: Place and Mobility in the Cosmopolitan Periphery*. Copenhagen: NIAS Press.

Weber, Max. 1958 [1905]. *The Protestant Ethic and the Spirit of Capitalism*, trans. Talcott Parsons. New York: Scribner.

CHAPTER 8

Spirit Bodies, Angel Dolls and Baby Corpses
Transformations of Child Spirit Practices in Thailand

Megan Sinnott

The distinction between life and death is overrated; within Thai cultural spaces, the realm between the living and the dead is full of activity, including the sounds of children crying, playing and laughing.[1] The spirits of deceased fetuses, infants and young children are particularly enticing spectral beings, and they are not as threatening as other spirits undoubtedly are. These child spirits can be entertaining and loveable. Without the rootedness of a biological form – a body – these spirit babies and young children roam an ultimately unknowable and invisible spectral realm, drifting in the in-between space after death and before rebirth, lacking the karmic force from their unlived lives to move smoothly to the next mortal incarnation. Ritual practices, primarily the making of offerings suitable for a child (such as toys and snacks) allow for human interaction and communication with the child spirits. Like all roaming spirits (*phi re-rorn*), these children depend on the living to give them sustenance and make merit for them so that they may ultimately move onto their next birth, their next body and their next life.

There are many names in Thai for these child spirits, including the traditional terms *kuman thorng* ('golden child' literally, but usually denoting a figurine that represents a child spirit), *luk krok* (preserved fetal remains), *rak yom* (child spirit amulet composed of wooden fragments held in sacred oil),

---

1 This paper is based on fieldwork and documentary research on the topic of Thai spirit beliefs from 2009 to 2019. My deepest thanks to my research collaborator, Nantiya Sukontapatipark. Rather than focusing on one specific location, as is typical of anthropological research, I chose to survey spirit beliefs across the country, looking for commonalities and the emergence of meta or national-level belief systems. I interviewed both spirit mediums and child spirit propitiators, as well as visiting child spirit shrines across the country.

or simply *phi dek* – 'child spirit'.² These child spirits are playful, mischievous, helpful and often unpredictable – not so different from their living biological counterparts in the human world. The child spirit in question may be a fetus, an infant or even a toddler; little, if any, distinction is made between these developmental stages. What unites these spirit beings is that their lives were cut short before they truly began – before they could enter sociality and pursue moral action, or merit, that would steer their future births and incarnations within the Buddhist worldview.

The Thai pantheon of spectral beings also occupies this space: these spirits of ancestors, trees, forests, fields, and tutelary beings of all varieties are separated from the biological living, but cannot properly be understood as dead. The Thai term *phi* encapsulates both a sense of a 'ghost' (a trace of a deceased being *or* monstrous entity that may or may not have been a living being) and a spirit (a supernatural being, including nature spirits that cannot be properly understood as a ghost; that is, a spirit is a trace of a previously biological being that now is deceased). All spirits, whether ghosts of previously living beings or near-eternal nature spirits, are without physical form in this plane of existence; they have no biological body.

Within Buddhist tradition, beings flow through a cycle of life, death, interstitial existence as a ghost or *pret* (a being that expiates negative actions that the being acquired in life, or *bap*, through a period of suffering existence in a different realm) and then rebirth as the cycle renews. Within this Buddhist worldview are beings, including Indic deities, that ostensibly are subject to the cycles of death and rebirth, yet have such cosmically long lifespans that they are perceived to be essentially eternal. Indigenous nature spirits and tutelary spirits typically are not understood as either ghosts or

---

2 *Luk krok* seem to bear the most similarity to the fetal body, which is fundamental to the traditional *kuman thorng* belief. *Luk krok* are preserved, desiccated fetal remains, typically kept by the fetus's mother as a connection to her lost child. Most informants agreed that *luk krok* did not require ritual specialists to empower the object, as the mother-child bond itself was the source of the connection between the fetal spirit and the mother. However, some informants associated *luk krok* with 'black magic' practices. As with all folk traditions, there exists a range of understandings and explanations for these spiritual entities. The variation in folk spirit belief is also evident in the *rak yom* amulet. Child spirit propitiators I interviewed generally explained *rak yom* as an amulet composed of two wooden fragments in sacred oil held in a small jar. However, according to an expert on Thai folk tradition, Professor Lom Pengkaeo, the wooden figures in the amulet typically are in the form of a child, but the traditional belief was that the spirit inhabiting the amulet may be a child or any other spirit (Field notes, 7/5/2011).

traces of previously living beings, but as near-eternal beings of a supernatural realm. Unlike most of these spirits or ghosts, however, many people seek out child spirits, invite them into their homes, offer them toys and snacks, and form loving familial relationships with them. Communication with these and other spirits is conducted through the material world; in addition to offerings that please a particular spirit, propitiators provide the most valuable of all material offerings: a physical form. Spirit mediums offer spirits the use of their physical body for a discrete period of time, during which the spirit may enjoy such pleasures as dancing, eating sweets and speaking in a childlike voice while communicating directly with their followers. Mediums of child spirits may also engage with an adult spirit guardian of the child spirit, which engages in adult activities such as smoking or drinking. For most people, however, the experience of spirit possession is neither desired nor attainable. Instead, a substitute habitance is provided for the child spirit. The form that these substitute bodies take for the propitiation of child spirits is the subject of this chapter. The material forms that 'house' the child spirit are not secondary to the relationship with the spirits or their meanings for the propitiators; in fact, the very malleability of these material bodies demonstrates the vitality of these spirit propitiation practices in the face of rapid social and economic change in Thailand.[3]

In spite of Max Weber's premature claim that the modern world brings increasing rationality and thus 'disenchantment', ghosts and spirits are ever-present in the contemporary, thoroughly modern Thai landscape, as evidenced by the ubiquity of spirit shrines and offerings that dot both the countryside and the country's cities. Thais from all class backgrounds, including Weber's ostensibly rational bourgeoisie, recognise the presence of spirits in everyday life. Spirits guard houses, haunt strangers as well as loved ones, animate the landscape, and befriend living mortals. Spirits are propitiated, worshipped, loved, feared and dreaded. Spirits are so central to the everyday experiences of many people that any account of religion and culture in Thailand is not complete without an accounting of how the spirit world informs both personal experience and ideological structures. While Buddhist doctrine, a quintessentially rational system of thought, provides such important structural elements to Thai spirit beliefs as the concepts of karma and rebirth, the spirit world has a kind of

---

3 For more on the shifting ontologies regarding the materiality of spirits, or *phi*, in the region, see Ladwig (2011).

mutability that no orthodoxy or formal religious system can fully contain. The material forms, or substitute bodies, of child spirits have transformed and diversified in recent years, and the introduction of the *luk thep*, (literally 'child deity' or 'angel child', which in this context always takes the form of a doll) is one of the most dramatic reconceptualisations and re-embodiments of the child spirit. This chapter will explore the shift away from traditional historical materialisations of the child spirit from the preserved body of the infant, to forms of mass-produced figurines, and to the highly commodified *luk thep* dolls that appeared in recent years.

Spirit practices are often thought of as 'traditional' practices and/or religious forms, and so they connote a kind of stasis or a historical remnant of a past way of life. Of course, there is truth to the claim that some forms of spirit belief are fading, especially among younger generations, as I found over the course of my fieldwork. Over the past decade of research on the topic, I have spoken with older spirit practitioners around the country who mourn the loss of cultural knowledge, accumulated over generations, regarding ritual practices and corresponding belief systems. However, it is also true that new forms of spirit practice are flourishing in Thailand, and that these both build on older traditions and shift in order to secure their relevance in light of new sensibilities and concerns. When spirit practices appear in clearly modern settings, such as the factory floor (Ong 1987), the associated spirit beliefs become relevant as a form of speaking back to modern capitalist exploitation. Likewise, migrant labourers employed in transnational factories in Thailand and abroad may use the language and symbolism of the spirit world to speak back to the disruption and loss of the new economic order (Mills 1995). Spirit beliefs are thus mobilised against new forms of extractive social control, giving meaning to these newer ways of life and providing avenues of agency for otherwise marginalised people. Transformed and adapted spirit beliefs are a valuable resource, and otherwise marginalised people use them to resist or mediate the oppressive capitalist system that they inevitably are enmeshed within. However, spirit practices also thoroughly reflect changing sensibilities *of* the dominant world economic and social order, and particularly of the newly ascendant middle-classes in Thailand and elsewhere in Asia.

Spirit beliefs in all their variation are not only a concern for the working class or marginalised populations; new forms of spirit belief thrive in modern Thailand, thanks to the enthusiastic participation of the urban middle classes. The revitalisation and transformation of child spirit beliefs constitute one such set of practices that, while rooted in deeply traditional beliefs about the magical powers of fetal remains, are able to embrace the possibilities that capitalism brings to the material world. To begin understanding this phenomenon of the growth of child spirit practices, it is important to grapple with how and why spirit practices seem to be so malleable, innovative and diverse. I argue that spirit practices in Thailand are not bound by orthodoxy or formal organisation, which opens a nearly infinitely broad institutional space for innovation and transformation. In addition, traditional spirit practices are relatively individualistic affairs; propitiators choose their preferred practices and patronise their preferred mediums or shrines. While spirit practices in pre-capitalist agrarian Thailand were more community affairs (e.g., Davis 1984, Tambiah 1970), capitalism's ethos of individualism and mobility allows for the growth of nationally circulating spiritual possibilities.

Émile Durkheim (1912) has famously argued that religious beliefs are templates for and reflections of social structure, and in this regard Thai spirit systems do not disappoint. Spirits in Thai cultural practices are understood to exist in a type of social hierarchy that mirrors human society (Chalartchai 1984). Indic deities and national-level tutelary spirits, such as those of royal historical figures, have relatively high status in relation to local spirits, family ancestral spirits and abstract nature spirits. Buddha is the highest spirit, always at the top of spirit shrines in both Buddhist temples and people's homes. Spirit shrines arrange spirits in a rough order of high prestige deities and spirits on the top shelves to lower prestige spirits that may have more personal, intimate significance, such as child spirits, on the lower shelves. Representation of the spirit world, as with any mytho-religious structure, mirrors and thereby reinforces social organisation and hierarchy. However, capitalism is in the business of responding to and creating desire for commodities, and the popularity of a commodity and the social practices surrounding it enable new imaginings of value. The changing material forms of the objects of child spirit propitiation, together with the growing popularity of collecting valuable child spirit embodiments, may not affect the ranking of spirits on household shrines, but could indicate the lack of absolute relevance of this hierarchy. The fluidity of spirits within a hierarchy is demonstrated by the rise of popularity of the *Mae* Nak shrine in Bangkok, discussed below. Justin McDaniel (2011:245) observes that the spirit of an ordinary 19th-century village woman who died in childbirth is now a 'standard object of worship', existing alongside famous monks, Indic deities and Buddha images. While child spirits may be lowly in the grand hierarchy of spirit beings, they allow for two things that, ironically, capitalism can market: uniqueness and intimacy. Child spirit practices allow for the attainment of unique, and therefore valuable, objects of propitiation. Since the spirit is a child, a more intimate, non-threating and family-like connection is possible than with a higher-status deity; the growing popularity of unique and individualised body-substitutes for child spirits (*luk thep* dolls) is a clear example of the ability of a new capitalist order to provide sacred commodities that are individualistic, intimate, and markers of social status. Anyone may practise spirit beliefs, and anyone may gain a following if they demonstrate expertise that is convincing and satisfying to followers. A common language and ontology frames these belief systems, but within those parameters a tremendous range of practices may emerge, flourish, expand, dwindle and be once again re-invigorated by a changing population.

Adopting, propitiating and worshipping child spirits has a long tradition within Thailand (Hardacre 1997, Moskowitz 2001). While there are interesting cross-fertilisations across Asia, the practice of child spirit 'adoption' in Thailand has a long, yet not well-known history. The worship of *kuman thorng*, or 'golden child (boy)', is usually traced to the well-known legend in the 17th-century Thai epic poem *Khun Chang, Khun Phaen*. In this epic the heroic warrior *Khun* Phaen kills his treacherous lover and cuts a fetus from her pregnant belly, which he roasts over a fire to dry and preserve the corpse. This corpse then becomes a kind of powerful amulet or talisman; a *kuman thorng* (Baker and Pasuk 2010a: 316–328, 2010b: 1174–1198). The *kuman thorng* he has created assists *Khun* Phaen in military battles and seductions, both particularly masculine pursuits. Whether this legend is the origin of these practices, or reflective of them, is not known, but the practice of preserving and propitiating the bodily remains of fetal, infant, or small child corpses is widespread and deeply historical. Preserving such remains and, if possible, covering them with gold leaf, resonates with the practice of covering sacred objects in gold leaf, including Buddha images and other sacred images within the panoply of Thai objects of devotion. A mother might preserve her stillborn fetus in desiccated form as a personal object, or they may be trafficked as powerful spiritual talismans by believers in the *kuman thorng* traditions. In Buddhist temples throughout Thailand, one can find the occasional shrine to the bodily remains of these fetuses/

infants/children. While the most popular child spirit shrines with preserved remains I have witnessed are located within Buddhist temples, smaller, more local shrines with manufactured images of child spirits (versus preserved remains) are found throughout the country. I speculate that preserved fetal remains that many people associate with dark magical powers need the spiritual cleansing, and respectability, that Buddhist temples provide for the shrines on their premises. Propitiators make offerings of snacks, soda, toys and other objects associated with childhood. In return, propitiators ask for blessings or make specific requests of child spirits. Typically, propitiators ask for prosperity, fertility, protection, success in business or school, or any general blessing. They make merit for themselves by caring for the spirits. In so doing they provide the spirits themselves, which otherwise do not have the means to make merit, with an opportunity to serve and protect their living propitiators and thereby accumulate the merit that eventually will pave the way for their auspicious rebirth.

In recent decades, the more individual and sanitised practice of 'adopting' a child spirit as a family member has grown in popularity, particularly among urban, educated, middle-class Thais. Referring to the spirit as a son or daughter, and oneself as a spirit's parent, can neatly be woven into tradition, as *Khun* Phaen calls his child spirit 'son' or 'spirit son' throughout the text (e.g., Baker and Pasuk 2010a: 328). However, while the practice of preserving and trafficking in children's remains has fallen out of favour, is considered by many to be unsettling, and is in fact a criminal offence in black-letter law, neither remains nor the shrines containing them are contested or removed. The unease with the practice of propitiating spirits associated with human remains reflects the broad social discomfort with spirit members of a broader category, 'malevolent spirits', and with those who seek to contact and manipulate these dark powers. An historical shift is appearing in which division between the lower, malevolent spirits and the good, higher order spirits is defined through the use of the term *thep*, (derived from the Sanskrit/Pali term *deva*, 'deity') referring to an angelic, 'good' spirit or deity, versus the term '*phi*'.[4] *Phi* has shifted from a more neutral traditional term

---

4   This claim is based on anecdotal evidence (Fieldnotes), as well as conversations with Professor Lom Pengkaeo, an expert on Thai folk traditions. More research is needed to gather the kind of data that would provide compelling support for my claim, which is that in recent decades, the term *phi* has been increasingly replaced with the term *thep* in vernacular references to revered local spirits. For example, tracing documentary references to the terms in magazines, newspapers, etc., would help substantiate this claim.

encompassing many types of otherworldly beings to a more direct reference to the kind of ghostly beings that might be featured in horror films – the monster or haunting ghost of someone who has been violently killed, or some such. This distinction between the terrorising ghost/monster *phi* and the benevolent and heavenly *thep* is embedded in the recent innovations of child spirit beliefs. The *kuman thorng* of the *Khun* Phaen legend, the traditional label to describe child spirits or *phi dek*, is being replaced with the sanitised and heavenly *luk thep*, translated as 'angel child' or 'divine child'. *Luk thep*, like other forms of individualised child spirit practice, are adopted into the family to be loved and cared for in exchange for the spirit's ability to provide otherworldly protection and support. The transition from the term *phi* to the more angelic *thep* is part of a process in which traditional practices and beliefs are modernised, cleansed, and made respectable for a new, transnationally oriented bourgeoisie.

The language of 'adoption' (*rap liang*) shifts the focus of the practice from one of necromancy and consorting with 'dark powers' to one of care-taking and family devotion. Although the past practice might have been an acceptable way for mothers to maintain a connection to their lost baby, today's popular media almost always present the practice as one of nefarious actions by those who foolishly engage in dark magical arts. In the transformed contemporary popular practice, rather than reflecting a biological bond formed between a parent and the spirit of their deceased fetal or infant child, the adoption bond allows for spirits not associated with a bodily corpse to be incorporated into the family. This more explicitly sentimental approach to child spirit propitiation has partially replaced the previous more transactional approach, which depended on the infant's corpse to embody a child spirit that was both protective and useful. Child spirit practices are no one thing, and perhaps can be best understood as falling along a broad spectrum, with the more impersonal amulet collecting at one end, moving to more personal, individualistic relationships with a spirit and its embodiment, at the far end where one can find purely disembodied spirits in an intimate personal relationship with their propitiator ('mother', 'sister', etc.). Along the way, transactional and sentimental connections may mix, and the creation of the images may come from a variety of sources. Many of the images are empowered with the spirit of the child by a spiritual practitioner or monk and, like similar images, are placed on shelves to receive offerings, and possibly be returned to the temple or religious practitioner if no longer wanted.[5] Clearly one would not contemplate discarding an actual child in such a manner, yet treatment of the abandoned spiritual object demonstrates that while the relationship may be intimate, the child spirit's potentially dangerous supernatural power must be managed.

An example of the unease with which the general public approaches the traditional practice of trafficking in preserved infant remains can be found in several news stories. For example, on 18 May 2012, the Thai press reported that Thai police confiscated a box of infant remains carried by a man traveling from Thailand to Taiwan. The remains had been desiccated and covered in gold leaf, which led to sensational international coverage of the regional practice. Operating on a tip, the police searched the man's hotel room and found the remains packed in his luggage.[6] Police officers told reporters of hearing the sound of children's crying at the station, leaving the police officials uneasy about and even fearful of the 'evidence' they held.[7]

At the time, I was visiting Buddhist temples, in search of well-known child spirit shrines. When the story broke, I noticed a reticence of locals to acknowledge the location or even existence of these shrines. I knew that the popular Mahabut Buddhist temple in the outskirts of Bangkok, known primarily for the famous and much-visited *Mae* Nak shrine, also houses a lesser-known shrine for 'Baby Ae' (*Luk* Ae or *Norng* Ae), the remains of a small child installed at the temple decades ago.[8] As I wandered around the large temple grounds, asking local vendors and temple employees about the location of the Baby Ae shrine, I was met with uncomfortable denials: 'No shrines like that here...' I did eventually find it and the large pile of donations to the child spirit at the shrine indicated that it was visited often by believers. As I prepared this chapter, I looked for an image of the Baby

---

5   Religious objects, including spirit shrines and spirit images/objects, are often discarded on temple grounds or other sacred places, such as at the base of a tree (often a Bo Tree or Bodhi Fig Tree, *Ficus religiosa*) that is understood to house powerful spirit entities. These locations are best suited to contain the spirit entities and their unruly power. Informants told me of returning their child spirit objects to the spirit practitioner who empowered them for the propitiator.

6   *Bangkok Post* May 18 2012, www.bangkokpost.com/print/294023, accessed May 21 2012. www.cnn.com/2012/05/18/world/asia/thailand-fetuses-black-magic/index.html, accessed October 21 2012.

7   See the following YouTube video for an interview with the police officers by the reporter. Rong-Ot Sarakham (pseudonym). www.youtube.com/watch?v=OkaejdcX3x4&feature=youtube_gdata_player, accessed 12 October 2012.

8   The story of '*Norng* Ae', or Baby Ae, was told in a popular ghost magazine, *Khon Hen Phi*, or 'People Seeing Ghosts' (*Luang Phi* 48 2012).

Figure 8.1. *Kuman thorng* Shrine at Wat Pradu, Samut Songkhram Province. **Colour** p. 321.

Ae shrine on the temple's website. Pictures of the numerous shrines to other spiritual entities at the temple were displayed on the temple's website, such as the *Mae* Nak and tree spirit shrines, but there was no mention of the Baby Ae shrine. Contemporary sensibilities in Thailand (in conformity with the transnational 'modern') relegate the traditional practice of preserving the infant's material body to the realm of distasteful 'black magic', leading to the practice being dismissed as a perhaps embarrassing reminder of the persistence of 'superstition' that has long been derided by reformist Buddhist monks.

Rather than bodily remains, the material object of devotion is increasingly likely to be a symbolic substitute for the body, such as a stylised plastic, ceramic or metal figurine. These figurines are mass-produced and rather interchangeable from an aesthetic point of view; they symbolically provide a body for a child spirit, or a materialisation of the otherwise non-material spirit. Some propitiators even use an ordinary toy, stuffed animal or doll as the material manifestation of a child spirit. Some interviewed propitiators have rejected the materiality of the child spirit in its entirety and maintain a purely abstract and directly personal relationship with the non-material entity of the spirit. The newest form of child spirit materialisation, the *luk thep* dolls, were introduced in Thailand about ten years ago, perhaps longer, as there is no firm date to when the first regular doll was transformed into a spirit body. While Mananya Boonmi, a Thai woman who goes by the nickname *Mae* Ning, is often credited with the creation of the first *luk thep* dolls, production of the dolls is widespread and international. *Luk thep* dolls often have the cute cartoonish appearance of the cabbage patch dolls of the late 1970s, but sometimes assume the more realistic and individual mien of so-called 'reborn dolls' that were found in the United States in the early 1990s, and more recently on eBay (White 2010). Like *luk thep* dolls, reborn dolls are industrially manufactured dolls converted by an artist to have an individual look and realistic feel, and are marketed internationally via eBay and other websites as being 'up for adoption'. While the adoption of reborn dolls internationally may have different cultural contexts than the adoption of *luk thep* dolls, in that the *luk thep* are clearly tied to the long-standing tradition of child spirit propitiation, and reborn dolls are not, the sudden popularity of *luk thep* and their correspondingly high price reveal a wider global connection to the practice of producing and adopting lifelike baby substitutes. *Luk thep* perhaps are a kind of 'craze' or fad that started in 2015 and peaked in early 2016, and have largely faded from the news, although they are still widely available.

Luk thep are currently available for purchase on eBay and other internet shopping sites, where prices range from approximately US $150 up to US $700 or more. The Thai practice of child spirit propitiation was able to seamlessly absorb the transnational commodity sensation of lifelike and individualised baby dolls and transform them into a way to continue the spirit practice with new sensibilities and forms of materialisation. In recent decades, Thailand has experienced a growth in prosperity cults and commercialised religiosity that scholar Pattana Kitiarsa calls 'Buddha *Phanit*' or 'Buddha-business'. Pattana describes the rise of Buddha *Phanit* (also written as *phuttha phanit*) as a situation in which, 'popular Buddhism has converged with the market economy, consumers' practices and the quest for personal and cultural identities' (2008b: 121). The commodification of Thai Buddhism and Thai spiritual practices is the larger context in which the particular practice of child spirit dolls has emerged (Jackson 1999; Pattana 2008a, 2008b, 2012). These 'cults' are extensions of the larger belief and religious structure, but are characterised by an openness to individual invention, mass participation, and are aimed at the attainment of wealth and general prosperity (Pattana 2008b:129).

The *kuman thorng*, or child spirit, has shifted from a personal spirit emanating from bodily remains to an abstracted entity embodied in a substitute 'body' of an inanimate object or figurine. The current trend is for the substitute body to take the form of a more personalised and individualised commodity that once again evokes the child's body, but one with no physical relationship to the living body of an actual fetus, infant, or child. In support of my claim that these newer embodiments of child spirits have largely severed their relationship to actual biological bodies, almost none of the dozens of propitiators I interviewed in the course of this research discussed the assumed once-mortal existence of the spirit. How did they die? Who were they and who were their parents and family? I said 'almost' above because one interviewee speculated that the child spirit she adopted, for which she provided a simple stuffed animal as a bodily form, was the aborted fetus of a relative. This intensely personal relationship to a particular child spirit is typically in relation to abortion, and more on this will be said in a moment. However, I theorise that the appeal of the *luk thep*, and other more abstracted forms of child spirit materialisation, lies in its distance from the physicality of the biological body and its association with death. The practice of child spirit propitiation is not based on mourning the loss of a child's life, and is not expressed through sadness or grief. Rather, the practice of adopting child spirits is founded on the idea of giving the spirit a means of entering social relationships through the provision of a material form. Of course, funereal practices mark the death of lost infants and fetuses, and new communal practices of mourning unknown infant death and fetal loss through abortion have emerged in recent years. The belief in fetal ghosts is widespread throughout East and Southeast Asia and is experiencing a wave of popularity and innovation (Florida 1999, Hardacre 1997, Hughes 1999, LaFleur 1993, Moskowitz 2001, Oaks 1994, Ohnuki-Tierny 1984, Pinit Ratanakul 1999).[9] While the emergence and growth of interest in mass propitiation of aborted fetal spirits is a new and related phenomenon in Thailand, its specific relationship to abortion would require more discussion than allowed in this essay.

Here, we are focusing on the practice of adoption of child spirits, not their mourning. Death and its markers have been excised from the revised and transformed tradition, as has any direct relationship to the individual death of an infant. The child spirits are simply another form of being, existing in the interstices between life and death, and can be engaged in social relationships and moral action through their materialisation. As noted above, spirits, or *phi*, have an ambiguous ontological position. Spirits, including child spirits, *exist* as disembodied beings. They may be a manifestation of a previously living being that is now dead, but simultaneously exist as an elemental force,

---

9   Moskowitz (2001) served as a primary source for this list of research on fetal ghosts.

a kind of power than can be channelled and communicated with through ritual. Spirits are part of Buddhist cosmology in which death and life flow in an endlessly repeating cycle, yet they are simultaneously perceived as near timeless, operating on an unknowable time frame. For example, for some propitiators, 'their' child spirit ages along with them, while for others, the spirit exists forever at a particular age. For most propitiators, the age of the spirit is unclear and ultimately unimportant. For these believers, the timeless essence of the child *is* the spirit, not so much the actual frozen age at the time of death. All child spirits engage in mischievous behaviour and enjoy sweets and toys, just as young biological children do, even as they demonstrate their (adult) potential to affect the outcome of events that their adopted family is particularly interested in, such as success in school and business.

The materiality of the body and its physical remains have transformed into a more abstract representation of the child spirit, and in place of ownership and control of an otherworldly power, the metaphor of loving adoption and child-care is characteristic of the current practice. I have argued elsewhere (Sinnott 2014) that changing class concepts of family and parenthood are reflected in the rise of child spirit practices in Thailand. In a sense, the practice of child spirit propitiation has gone mainstream. Middle-class, educated propitiators describe their parent-child relationship with their *luk thep* doll. The spirit is invited to take part in family meals and activities, is gifted toys and snacks, and at times talked to lovingly, personally and intimately. The term *luk thep*, or angel child, further dissociates the current practice from its necromantic predecessors. As mentioned above, angel, or *thep*, is a term usually used for divine beings within Thailand's diverse Buddhist/Hindu/Chinese pantheon, including spiritual beings within indigenous Thai belief systems that were formally called *phi*. While wealthy propitiators can afford the more socially prestigious *luk thep* dolls or other expensive figurines, all propitiators have the potential to form an intimate family relationship to a *thep*, a being more divine than a lowly ghost. The move to the *luk thep* dolls is perhaps a predictable adaptation and middle-class sterilisation of a practice that had at one time been closely associated with bodily remains, and therefore death.

Both the preserved and visible infant corpse and the commodified, cute, and at times realistic-feeling *luk thep* doll are objects of spiritual devotion. What does this transition mean for the ways in which desire is culturally structured in Thailand in the realm of spiritual practices? Not only have the objects changed in recent decades, but the meaning of the child-parent relationship and the instrumental value of children and spirits have also shifted. While the corpse of an infant elicits unease, embarrassment, and also devotion for some, *luk thep* practices are seen as childish and excessive by many other Thais. A more traditional figurine, or *kuman thorng*, appears to be an acceptable middle ground for some propitiators.[10] The multiple manifestations of child spirit propitiation illustrate the fluidity and adaptability of a deeply historical yet also highly contemporary belief system. The emergence of a large, educated middle class and the embrace of capitalism in Thailand are the two most obvious factors in the shifting contours of the practice.

Thailand is a dramatic example of rapid capitalist transformation in the contemporary world. Within a few decades, Thailand transformed from a largely agricultural and aristocratic status-based society to one firmly embedded in the rules and discourses of capitalist accumulation and economic class. However, capitalist trajectories of desire are not monolithic (Rofel 2007), and the cultural basis of capitalism also exists alongside and is intertwined with other cultural economic systems. The logic of child spirit practices reveals itself at the intersections of capitalist cultural modes and other uniquely local traditions and beliefs. Transactions with the child spirit are personal and intimate, and the relationship between spirit and propitiator is familial, one of parent and child. Yet this relationship is also guided by an abstract system that includes concepts like karma, sacrifice, and a hierarchy of spectral and biological beings. The capitalistic buying and selling of bodies and their labour is almost mirrored in the traditional acquisition of spirit relationships. The spirits may be bought (although termed 'rented', *chao*) from well-known temples, monks or other spiritual practitioners with reputable skills in empowering objects with spiritual beings and their power. Child spirit amulets or figurines are typically empowered with the power and essence of the child spirit. Monks or other spirit practitioners perform these ceremonies, although some of these objects come with instruction sheets on how to perform the empowerment ritual oneself. Some child spirit propitiators bypass ritual specialists altogether and simply invite a child spirit, perhaps one they met in a dream, into the body substitute. Not all child spirit bodies are equally enmeshed in capitalist valuation. These spirit

---

10 A reviewer of this essay astutely notes that this unease may be best described as 'uncanny'. Uncanny is a Freudian term that Nicholas Royle (2003) describes as an eerie feeling that something is both strange and familiar, leading to an unsettling uncertainty over the reality of a thing.

substitute bodies (amulets, figurines, dolls) are treated similarly to other magical ritual objects; offerings of specific foods and objects particular to the spirit are made at regular times, and placement is usually on a shrine shelf in the home. As such, these objects embody impersonal magical power that one might find in any amulet, yet they also may be treated as an intimate family member and, for some propitiators, as a unique being capable of compassion, care-taking and care-giving.

An example of the blending of capitalist exchange with the logic of spirit adoption can be found in the dramatic events that unfolded in November of 2010, when 2002 fetal remains were found in a crematorium at Wat Phai Ngoen, a temple in Bangkok. Apparently, local abortion providers had secretively deposited fetal remains in the temple's crematorium building. This grisly finding was transformed into an opportunity to provide the public with spectral children for adoption through the marketing of special figurines of various sizes and prices.[11] The temple began providing annual mass merit-making rituals for the fetuses, and for aborted fetuses in general, as well as the opportunity to adopt a fetal spirit empowered in figurines labelled the '*kuman* 2002' collection, referring to the remains of 2002 fetuses, or *kuman*. Three different figurine models were offered with a wide range of pricing. The figures have a doll-like quality and represent chubby babies in pleasing postures. After being propitiated en masse through ritualised offerings at the temple, these figurines were ready to be adopted and brought home to meet their new family. The Buddhist temple's participation in the propitiation of child spirits adds a degree of respectability to the practice, and embeds the practice in Thai Buddhist merit-making rituals. Merit is made for those adopting a spirit (the spirits are cared for) and also allows the child spirits to accumulate merit as adopted members of a family. Traditional beliefs, Thai Buddhism, and capitalism work together in the reforming of the practice.

It would be hard to deny that capitalism is at work in the marketing of child spirits at this temple, or elsewhere in Thailand. The sense that the traditional practice of propitiating child spirits has been appropriated by a devouring capitalist system is hard to avoid. Capitalism is often, rightly so, perceived as an obliterating, colonising force and, as such, when its traces are found in

---

11 For an example of international news coverage, see: www.bbc.com/news/world-asia-pacific-11785333.

Figure 8.2. Sign advertising special *kuman thorng* figurines available for adoption at Wat Phai Ngoen, Bangkok. **Colour** p. 321.

religion and spirit beliefs it is easy to conclude that the practices and beliefs are somehow lessened or cheapened by their commodification. I resist this temptation and ask instead: which cultural meanings are associated with the transformed practices? If commodified objects like the temple figurines just described, or the *luk thep* dolls, are objects of desire – compelling forms that inspire delight and interest – how can we understand them as substitutions for the physical remains of human infants?

First, the capitalist market played a role in the transformation of child spirit beliefs from centring on physical remains to commodified realistic or cute doll-like objects. The market mechanism provided space for this shift. Capitalism, obviously, is structured by the soulless drive of mass production and profit motives. However, capitalism both responds to and produces desire – and desire is always embedded within cultural meaning. Yes, capitalism might provide the possibility of these material forms, but what gives these material objects the sense of the otherworldly, even the sacred? If contemporary middle-class sensibilities do not allow for the propitiation and exchange of bodily remains as objects of devotion, then capitalism can provide a substitute form – a realistic, widely available infant-like body-like object that is thoroughly removed from any association with death.

The flexibility of late capitalism is often, and rightly in my view, associated with the pernicious durability of the economic system that has produced great wealth along with vast poverty and alienation. However, capitalism also has an unruly aspect: as a nonhuman abstraction, it is not beholden to any particular orthodoxy and can mould itself to fit diverse cultural sensibilities. The market provides alternative forms of belief and devotion, and is indifferent to traditional hierarchies and power structures that struggle to maintain dominance in a rapidly transforming world. The hierarchy of spiritual entities, with *thep* 'deities' posited at the apex and local *phi* 'spirits/ghosts' at the bottom, may be formally maintained. However, fetal ghosts, the ghost of a legendary village woman who died in childbirth (*Mae* Nak), and spirits of other commoners, like that of popular female country singer Pumpuang Duangjan (1961–1992), can be and have been reframed as *thep*.[12] Access to these *thep* is marketed to the general public, and their rise in the Thai pantheon is reflective of their popularity and resonance with followers; the hierarchy may be more fluid and adaptable than anyone imagined. The unruly nature of late capitalism is curiously similar to the unruly and uncontainable world of spirit beliefs. While there is a general consensus about the nature of spirits and how to treat them, tremendous innovation is possible within that structure. In the Thai context, there is no orthodoxy per se regarding spirits or central control of the ritual practices. *Thep*, the category of higher spiritual beings, is a fluid category. Not only *thep* but also the spirits of ancestors, forests, fields, and the innumerable spectral beings of the spirit world are resources for spirit propitiators. Village mediums who channel local spirits (possibly called *phi* or *thep* interchangeably, depending on audience and context) may gain prestige and a wide following. Older, fading spirits may be revitalised by a charismatic and skilful medium. Child spirits are particularly variable: while these spirits are linked with living beings, an unformed child or fetus, their power can be imagined in any number of creative ways. The child spirit may be a comforting companion or sibling to a lonely child. The child spirit may be a powerful ally in business, as well as helping with the mundane task of protecting the family from general harm. Anyone may form a relationship with a child spirit, and if they choose to provide a substitute body for their child spirit, they may obtain a realistic body-like doll, or simply use a stuffed animal or any other found object. The *luk thep* doll may be used to demonstrate the wealth and status of the adoptive parent, but it is not the only way to participate in this widespread practice of adopting child spirits. While capitalism cannot provide mass-produced infant corpses, thank goodness, it can provide satisfying substitutes that are not tinged with the stigma of necromancy and death.

While the market system may be a primary force in the efflorescence of child spirit practices in Thailand and their shift from bodily remains to market-provided substitutes, other factors are also at play in this shift. The medicalisation

---

12 For more on the deification of country singer Pumpuang Duangjan and her shrine complex at Wat Thapkradan, in Suphanburi Province, see Pattana (2012: 57–79).

of the body in recent decades in Thailand has shifted attitudes towards human remains. The medical approach to the body, concepts of hygiene, and public health also stigmatise the practice of preserving infant remains. In addition, changing middle-class concepts of parenthood may further stigmatise the original practice[13]. If parenthood is increasingly understood as a sentimental project in which children are valued as rights-bearing human beings, does the instrumental practice of using child remains as talismans create unease? The loving adoption of the representation of a child avoids these negative associations and foregrounds the idea of a modern, middle-class family. If we focus on the significance of the body itself, the *luk thep* doll moves closer to a realistic, if sentimental, image of the body. The impersonal stock figurines are largely interchangeable, devoid of particular or unique characteristics of the spirit itself. They provide a physical form for the spirit, but in themselves have little significance, other than the antique *kuman thorng* images that are collected by wealthy aficionados of the practice. In contrast, *luk thep* dolls are personalised and invite sentimental and emotional attachment, and are notable for their visibility; people display their *luk thep* dolls prominently at home and even bring them along on their travels; the international press had a field day when it was learned that some people buy airline tickets for their *luk thep* dolls.[14] As a result, the individual bodily remains of the fetus, infant, or child have been relegated to the margins, where they are associated with uncultured superstition and black magic. The spark of excitement, stimulation and arousal of the material, physical body of the child is too encumbered with the distaste that such remains evoke for many. The impersonal amuletisation of the child spirit in the form of figurines is still popular, but the material embodiment of the spirit in these bland, mass-produced figurines fails to fully capture what Lacan calls the dignity of the thing (quoted in Ruti 2012: 127–147) – that otherworldly spark that animates our excitement and curiosity, that once was found in physical remains. The *luk thep* dolls ironically return to the more evocative images of the actual body, yet their relentless cuteness is cleansed of physicality, death, and human remains.

Spirit practices in Thailand centre on the body – the physical body of a spirit medium, the preserved body of the infant, or the substitute body

---

13 For more on changing middle-class sensibilities on parenthood and childhood, see James and Prout (1997) and Zeliser (1985). For specific focus on historical shifts within Buddhist conceptions of childhood, see Gross (1996).

14 For example, see BBC news on *luk thep*: www.bbc.com/news/world-asia-35416537.

of an otherwise inanimate object. Communication with the spirit world, neither living nor dead in the biological sense, depends on the provision of a material form, and through this material form sociality and moral action are made possible. Material forms, or bodies, are central to spirit practices, so the substance of the substitute body is significant for understanding shifting attitudes towards the physical world and its relation to the ethereal world of the spirits. If the infant corpse as an object of spiritual desire is no longer tenable in contemporary, capitalist Thailand, and bourgeois sensibilities do not allow for the incorporation of death and its markers into the practice of child spirit adoption, then rather than describing market-provided bodily forms as inferior substitutes for the traditional or 'authentic' material bodies of the child spirit, they should be acknowledged as unruly innovations that the spirit world can truly appreciate.

References

Baker, C. and Pasuk Phongpaichit (eds). 2010a. *The Tale of Khun Chang Khun Phaen*. Chiang Mai: Silkworm Books.

———. 2010b. *The Tale of Khun Chang Khun Phaen: Companion Volume*. Chiang Mai: Silkworm Books.

Chalartchai Ramitanon. 1984 [2527]. *Spirit Lords* [phi jao nai]. Bangkok: Chiangmai University.

Davis, R. (1984). *Muang Metaphysics: A Study of Northern Thai Myth and Ritual*. Bangkok: Pandora.

Durkheim, É. 2019 [1912]. *The Elementary Forms of the Religious Life*, trans. Joseph Swain. Overland Park, KS: Digireads.

Florida, R. 1999. 'Abortion in Buddhist Thailand', in D. Keown (ed.), *Buddhism and Abortion*. Honolulu: University of Hawai'i Press: 11–29.

Gross, R. 1996. 'Child and Family in Buddhism', in H. Coward and P. Cook (eds), *Religious Dimensions of Child and Family Life: Reflections on the UN Convention on the Rights of the Child*. Waterloo: Wilfrid Laurier University Press: 79–98.

Hardacre, H. 1997. *Marketing the Menacing Fetus in Japan*. Berkeley: University of California Press.

Hughes, J. 1999. 'Buddhism and Abortion: A Western Approach', in D. Keown (ed.), *Buddhism and Abortion*. Honolulu: University of Hawai'i Press: 183–198.

Jackson, P. 1999. 'Royal Spirits, Chinese Gods, and Magic Monks: Thailand's Boom-time Religions of Prosperity', *South East Asia Research*, 7(3): 245–320.

James, A. and A. Prout (eds). 2007. *Constructing and Reconstructing Childhood: Contemporary Issues in the Sociological Study of Children* (2nd edition). London, Falmer Press.

Ladwig, P. 2011. 'Can Things Reach the Dead? The Ontological Status of Objects and the Study of Lao Buddhist Rituals for the Spirits of the Deceased', in K. Endres and A. Lauser (eds), *Engaging the Spirit World: Popular Beliefs and Practices in Modern Southeast Asia*. New York: Berghahn Books: 19–41.

LaFleur, W.R. 1993. *Liquid Life: Abortion and Buddhism in Japan*. Princeton, N.J., Princeton University Press.

McDaniel, J. 2011. 'The Agency between Images: The Relationships among Ghosts, Corpses, Monks, and Deities at a Buddhist Monastery in Thailand', *Material Religion*, 7(2): 242–267.

Mills, M.B. 1995. 'Attack of the Widow Ghosts: Gender, Death, and Modernity in Northeast Thailand', in A. Ong and M. Peletz (eds), *Bewitching Women, Pious Men: Gender and Body Politics in Southeast Asia*. Berkeley: University of California Press: 244–273.

Moskowitz, M. 2001. *The Haunting Fetus: Abortion, Sexuality, and the Spirit World in Taiwan*. Honolulu: University of Hawai'i Press.

Ohnuki-Tierney, E. 1984. *Illness and Culture in Contemporary Japan*. Cambridge, Cambridge University Press.

Ong, A. 1987. *Spirits of Resistance and Capitalist Discipline*. Albany, State University of New York Press.

Pattana Kitiarsa. (ed.). 2008a. *Religious Commodifications in Asia: Marketing Gods*. New York, Routledge.

———. 2008b. 'Buddha Phanit: Thailand's Prosperity Religion and its Commodifying Tactics', in Pattana Kitiarsa (ed.), *Religious Commodifications in Asia: Marketing Gods*. New York, Routledge: 120–143.

——— 2012. *Mediums, Monks, and Amulets: Thai Popular Buddhism Today*. Chiang Mai, Silkworm Books.

Pinit Ratanakul. 1999. 'Socio-medical Aspects of Abortion in Thailand', in D. Keown (ed.), *Buddhism and Abortion*. Honolulu: University of Hawai'i Press: 53–66.

Rofel, L. 2007. *Desiring China: Experiments in Neoliberalism, Sexuality and Public Culture*. Durham: Duke University Press.

Royle, N. 2003. *The Uncanny*. Manchester: Manchester University Press.

Ruti, M. 2012. *The Singularity of Being: Lacan and the Immortal Within*. New York: Fordham University Press.

Sinnott, M. 2014. 'Baby Ghosts: Child Spirits and Contemporary Conceptions of Childhood in Thailand', *TRaNS: Trans-Regional and National Studies of Southeast Asia*, 2(2): 293–317.

Tambiah, S.J. 1970. *Buddhism and the Spirit Cults in North-east Thailand*. Cambridge: Cambridge University Press.

White, M. 2010. 'Babies Who Touch You: Reborn Dolls, Artists, and the Emotive Display of Bodies on eBay', in J. Staiger, A. Cvetkovich and A. Reynolds (eds), *Political Emotions: New Agendas in Communication*. New York, Routldge: 66–89.

Zeliser, V.A. 1994. *Pricing the Priceless Child: The Changing Social Value of Children*. Princeton: Princeton University Press.

CHAPTER 9

Oneiric Encounters
Materialisations of the Invisible Present in Northern Thailand

Irene Stengs

This chapter is based on ethnographic material collected in the late 1990s in the context of my research on the veneration of King Chulalongkorn (r.1868–1910), a project mainly conducted in Bangkok and Chiang Mai (Stengs 2009). Spirit mediumship and spirit possession were not a specific focus, but came in inevitably since spirit mediumship formed an important instance within the wide variety of cultural and religious practices in which the veneration of the king manifested itself. In fact, at the time, the number of spirit mediums in Chiang Mai and vicinity known to have received the spirit of King Chulalongkorn was so large that such mediums could have been a topic of research in itself. This particular popularity of King Chulalongkorn might have been a distinguishing feature of Northern or Lan Na Thai spirit mediumship for some time. According to Pattana Kitiarsa, 'in Northern Thai spirit cults, mediums claim to be the mouthpieces of great kings of historical records, Ramkhamhaeng, Naresuan, Taksin and Chulalongkorn' (2012: 28). To Pattana's observation another distinguishing Northern Thai feature may be added, namely, the significance of Lan Na historical narratives, trajectories and self-understandings in shaping the form and style of local spirit mediumship. I will bring in three entangled, localising dimensions of Northern Thai forms of spirit mediumship, dimensions which will be given ethnographic substantiation further below: (1) the explicit and purposeful use of local materials and crafts; (2) King Chulalongkorn's commitment to and appreciation of Northern Thailand and Chiang Mai in particular; and (3) the spirit of King Chulalongkorn's Chiang Mai consort, *Chao* Dara Rasami.[1]

---

1 Dara Rasami became the king's princess consort (*chao chom*) in 1886. In 1909, King Chulalongkorn promoted her to the rank of high queen (*phra ratchachaya*).

This contribution takes as its point of departure that dreams, trance and visions are the joint basis of all possession-related practices and experiences, and that spirit mediumship is one particular instance within this perspective. Other authors (Baird 2014; Pattana 2012) have argued that in Thailand there are no clear, demarcated boundaries between (magic) monks (*keji ajan*), who are believed to possess the ability to magically empower amulets and tattoos, and spirit mediums (*rang song, khon song jao*).[2] I want to take this argument one step further by bringing in a perception of 'possession' as a continuum of possibilities, practices and modalities, all entailing some form of contact with the invisible. Herewith, I connect with Roberte Hamayon's (1993) plea for an understanding of possession as a mode of direct contact with the spirits.[3] Hamayon maintains a firm distinction between the shaman and *shamanising* individuals who are 'void of ritual value for the community'. My suggestion is that all forms of contact with the invisible are socially relevant, and for that matter equally relevant for a scholarly understanding of society. 'Professional' spirit mediumship appears in this perspective as one of the polar ends of such possible contacts, in the sense that this form of possession is most elaborate and with the most established ritual. This makes me also connect with Erick White's call to move beyond a perspective that foregrounds 'spirit cults' and instead examine (professional) spirit mediumship in relation to 'modalities of possession' (2014). Of course, we may ask whether connections with the invisible in the form of dreams and visions qualify as 'possession'. To avoid a clash over definitions, I suggest speaking of 'practices that render the invisible materially manifest' for the wide range of possible forms, situations and actions in which encounters with the spirit world happen.

My understanding of such encounters, as practices of world-making and creative intervention, is strongly influenced by what is generally referred to as the material turn in anthropology and religious studies (Bynum 2011;

---

[2] Baird, for instance, writes that 'Theravada Buddhist monks are often ideologically imagined as separate from spirit mediums, but in reality, the boundaries between the two are frequently blurred' (2014: 57). Also White on one occasion observed monks 'both behaving as if in a state of possession and being treated by individuals as if possessed by *thep* [deity]' (2014: 86, note 60). According to Pattana, 'both [magic monks] and urban spirit mediums provide mediumship, performing relatively similar functions, albeit in different settings and on different social scales' (2012:107). Pattana is specifically referring here to the enormous scale of the cult around the magic monk *Luang Phor* Khun (see also Jackson 1999). During my research, however, I met quite a few magic monks with no celebrity status.

[3] Hamayon's primary concern is the Western tendency to understand or reduce 'shamanism' to a physical and psychological state of certain individuals.

Houtman and Meyer 2012; Bennett and Joyce 2013). I am interested in how the imaginations, imaginaries and social memory around, in this case, King Chulalongkorn and, more broadly, Lan Na history and identity, materialise in 'things'. This leads to an interest in how 'thingly' properties such as bodies, artefacts, places, technologies, smells and clothing become accessible to the senses; hence, my exploration moves beyond a perspective of materialisation as mere 'representation'.

I hope to contribute to an understanding of *why* these imaginaries and imaginations matter, or, in other words, what the eventual materialisations do. Thais are born into a lifeworld in which the invisible (spirits, gods, stories, memories) comes naturally and influences such human conditions as affliction, affluence, happiness and so on. The invisible manifests itself in 'oneiric' everyday life experiences like dreams, visions, fantasies and trances. People's dealings with what could be called 'oneiric spaces' involve a logic of doubling: to testify to the invisible's presence, a visible, material double is created (Mbembe 2017; Meyer 2017, 2015). This material double can be manipulated in ways that favourably influence the unseen. Unlike 'imaginary' and 'social memory', 'oneiric space' involves an ontological aspect: it takes the unseen seriously as an autonomous part of the world, a part that forces itself, favourably or unfavourably, upon both individual and society.

The ethnographic material for this chapter is mainly derived from four case-studies in which encounters with the spirit of King Chulalongkorn were central. The principal people involved are:

- the abbot of Wat Doi Chang, a temple located on the outskirts of the city of Chiang Mai, who had a spiritual connection (*yan*) with King Chulalongkorn;[4]
- *Khun* Suwan, a female Chiang Mai cotton trader who had a spiritual connection with *Chao* Dara Rasami; and
- Two female spirit mediums, *Mae* Wan, a spirit medium in Saraphi, a district just southeast of Chiang Mai, and *Mae* Yai, a spirit medium living in the Chiang Mai city centre.[5]

---

4   Thai dictionaries translate *yan* as intuition or insight. White's suggestion is 'sixth sense' (2014: 449). It is a special insight, often including clairvoyance, clairaudience also regarded as a supersensory or magical insight that results from intensely focused meditation.

5   For reasons of privacy all names, including that of the temple, are fictitious.

The abbot's authentic teakwood King Chulalongkorn statue

An important dimension in the self-presentation of Northern Thailand (Lan Na), internally or outwards-oriented, consists of the region's traditional arts and crafts: dancing, cooking, paper umbrella making, fan painting, mulberry papermaking, silk weaving, chiselled metalwork and, of particular relevance in the context of this chapter, woodcarving and teak architecture. In this image of a region of authentic craftsmanship, Northern Thai identity appears as distinct from that of other Thai regions. Paradoxically, it simultaneously is an indispensable part of Thai national identity, providing a romantic view of the nation's past in the form of cultural artefacts. Authentic craftsmanship developed into a major ancillary of the tourism industry and delivers products that appeal to both foreign and Thai tourists (see for instance Cohen's 1998 article on Ban Thawai). The significance attributed to Lan Na craftsmanship articulates the growing cultural and political value attributed to 'heritage' (*moradok*) and 'historical authenticity' (*boran*).

The research site that opened my eyes to the relevance of this dimension is the Wat Doi Chang temple.[6] At the time of my research in the 1990s, the abbot of this temple was regularly visited by the spirit of King Chulalongkorn in the form of dreams and visions, in which the king instructed him on all kinds of issues, most of which were framed in the context of charity initiatives. The centrepiece of the temple is a gilded statue of Chulalongkorn, resembling the image of the then-young king in a widely reproduced photograph taken during the 'second coronation' on 16 November 1873. Contrary to my first impression, the 'matter' under the radiant gold-leaf 'surface' is not a cast image: instead, it is carved from a solid trunk of teak wood. The proof of this quality is only revealed at the rear side of the statue, where the craftsman had left a part unfinished. The statue is placed in a *wihan*, a temple building constructed for the purpose, with the name 'Prince Chulalongkorn Wihan' (*wihan luang chao fa chulalongkorn*).[7]

---

6 I draw here from the ethnographic material of earlier publications (Stengs 2009, 2012).

7 The name was chosen because the gilded statue depicts the king/prince at the moment of his coronation. The name is also an analogue of the name of the temple's stupa, which is *chedi chao fa*. For an image of the second coronation photographic portrait of King Chulalongkorn see link: second coronation portrait King Chulalongkorn, www.pbase.com/johnglines/image/153864440.

The abbot told me the story of the statue's creation. At some time in 1992, he had a vision of Chulalongkorn in golden attire, wearing a golden crown and seated on a golden throne. The voice of the king instructed him to create a gilded statue in his image, and to start a charity project for orphaned hill tribe boys. The abbot immediately began to search books for portraits of King Chulalongkorn, in order to identify what he had seen. It turned out that the scene in his vision was identical to that in the king's 'second coronation' portrait. This photograph provided the guidance necessary for the making of the statue. Had the abbot not recorded his story, one would have assumed that the coronation portrait had been the inspiration for the statue. Yet, the abbot claimed that he was not inspired by this photographic image, but rather by the oneiric vision. He discovered the portrait only later, in his search for the right image to fulfil his duty to have the statue made. The fact that the statue was not created on the abbot's own initiative, but on that of the king himself adds to the statue's spiritual value.

The success of the gilded King Chulalongkorn statue – the fact that it indeed took shape and that people also donated sufficient money to the temple to support the charity project for the orphaned youths – helps to explain the lay sponsoring of other wood-carved images at the temple. These images include larger-than-life-sized statues of the warrior kings Naresuan (r. 1590–1605) and Taksin (r. 1767–1781). These royal statues are placed left (Taksin) and right (Naresuan), just behind the entrance of the Chulalongkorn *wihan*, almost as if guarding the Chulalongkorn statue. A significant dimension for understanding the prominence of the warrior kings is that the abbot drew many followers from the nearby Kawila Army Barracks, some of whose higher-ranking military officers and their wives figured prominently in temple ceremonies. Other wood carvings at the monastery include several over-one-metre-tall Chulalongkorn portraits carved into blocks of wood, all placed on ledges to the left and right of the Chulalongkorn statue. Not long after I had found my way to the monastery, a small, temporary workshop was established there. Woodcarvers were busy transforming solid blocks of local wood into representations of Chulalongkorn portraits. All portraits copied well-known photographs or paintings of the king.

With regard to the gilded statue, we may conclude that the unfinished spot gives proof of its unique material properties. The importance attributed to authentic local materials and craftsmanship received further materialisation in the royal statues of Taksin and Naresuan, as well as in the Chulalongkorn portrait blocks. In this context, the temple workshop literally localised the statues and portraits as it authenticated both the material and the carving process as distinctively Northern Thai. The images' extraordinary size provided another material confirmation of the temple's identity as genuinely Lan Na.

Returning to the combined presence of the three kings – Chulalongkorn, Naresuan and Taksin – the temple reflects the strong nationalist sentiments upon which the King Chulalongkorn cult draws. Together, the statues depict the Northern region as an integral part of the Thai nation. Returning to Pattana's (2012) observation of these kings' popularity in Northern Thai spirit cults, we may note that their presence, in the form of authentic pieces of Northern Thai craftsmanship, testifies somewhat paradoxically to both the region's distinct identity and its national importance to the initiators, in what could be labelled 'regional national pride'.

The vision which inspired the abbot was from the spirit world. Lan Na craftsmen under his supervision created a material double of that part of the spirit world. This material doubling transformed the temple into a location where the spiritual power of King Chulalongkorn could be accessed and influenced, something that would not have been possible without the material presence of the statue.

Khun Suwan's Lan Na style 'Vimanmek' mansion

The 1990s were a period of rapidly growing popularity of newly built *boran* (old, antique) style teakwood houses in Chiang Mai as well as more broadly in Thailand. I met Suwan, a well-to-do female cotton cloth trader in Samphaeng Road in Chiang Mai city, through a befriended artist, the former spouse of her brother. Suwan had asked my artist friend to make a painting based on a Chulalongkorn photograph. What set Suwan apart from many other King Chulalongkorn worshippers at the time is that she had a teakwood house built that, as she told me, was motivated by a vision she once had while meditating (*nang samathi*) some twenty years earlier (if she remembered correctly, that must have been in the late 1970s) of King Chulalongkorn's famous teakwood Vimanmek Palace (Dusit Park 1901) in Bangkok. In the vision, Chulalongkorn instructed her to build him a house that resembled the palace. The king wanted her to do so, as Suwan told me, because he did not like condominiums or sky-high buildings, but rather wanted Chiang Mai to consist entirely of this style of teakwood houses.

At the time, she was not in the financial position to materialise the king's instructions, but over the years her business of locally manufactured cotton cloth grew to become an established enterprise. This made her wealthy enough to have an impressive house constructed, where she lives herself, although it is not really a palace and is different from Vimanmek, resembling instead a Lan Na style mansion. The building is constructed from the timber of at least twenty locally demolished original 'old' village houses. The king had instructed her not to paint the house, but to keep it in brown, the natural colour of teak. At the time of our conversation, Suwan was in the process of constructing a new side wing. During her meditations, she received instructions regarding the appropriate style and shape of the new wing.

Suwan's spiritual relationship with the former king entailed another local dimension: her veneration of Chulalongkorn's consort, *Chao* Dara Rasami. *Chao* Dara Rasami (1873–1933), the daughter of *Phra Chao* Inthanon – later Inthawichayanon (r. 1870–1897), the vassal ruler of Chiang Mai – was Chulalongkorn's only wife from Chiang Mai. Suwan dedicated one of the two upper-floor rooms to Chulalongkorn and *Chao* Dara Rasami. The room contained an antique bed, two large portraits – one of King Chulalongkorn and one of *Chao* Dara Rasami, each portrait with a Lan Na style *khantoke* wooden table in front of it[8] – other portraits of King Chulalongkorn, one other portrait of *Chao* Dara Rasami, and, at the other side of the room, an altar with statuettes of various monks, and a statuette of King Naresuan. Apart from the bed, the room breathed the atmosphere of a *horng phra*, a religious space used for prayer or mediation. On the day Suwan showed me this room, the *khantoke* table in front of the King Chulalongkorn portrait was filled with food offerings including rice, green curry, minced-pork salad (*lap*), fresh herbs, various fruits, water and cognac, items widely believed to be much liked by the king. The *khantoke* table for *Chao* Dara Rasami was empty. Upon asking why *Chao* Dara Rasami's table was empty, I was told all offerings were placed on the Chulalongkorn table because it was a Tuesday, Chulalongkorn's birth day in the Thai astrological system, but that the minced-pork salad and fresh herbs in fact were dedicated to his consort. Upon my question, how she knew about *Chao* Dara Rasami's preference for *lap*, Suwan told me that one day, after offering food, the people working

---

8   A *khantoke* table is a low, round pedestal tray meant for serving food in ceremonial settings, in particular.

in the kitchen downstairs had heard Suwan's voice saying that she had ordered them to make *lap kham mueang* (Northern style meat salad) for *Chao* Dara Rasami. Although Suwan asserted that it had not been her who had instructed them to do so, three people had independently heard her giving this instruction. Moreover, not long after, a distant relative (a 'cousin') of *Chao* Dara Rasami came to her house: in her meditations, the cousin had learned about the existence of this room, and she also told Suwan that *lap kham mueang* was one of *Chao* Dara Rasami's favourite dishes.

When we entered the room, Suwan immediately pointed out another *Chao* Dara Rasami portrait, based on a photograph that I had seen often, including at the abode of the spirit medium *Mae* Wan (see below) and at Wat Doi Chang.[9] It is an image of the princess, seated at her dressing table, turning her head to the camera, while combing her very long hair, the extraordinary length of which is only revealed by the reflection in the mirror in front of her. Suwan said, 'she was a real Chiang Mai queen. See her clothes, a *phasin* – precisely one as I am wearing'. Indeed, Suwan was wearing a very similar striped *phasin*, a traditional Northern Thai style ankle-length skirt that women nowadays seldom wear in everyday life. Interestingly, she added, 'same colour', although the portrait was in sepia. Later, my artist friend told me that Suwan, the oldest daughter in a modest rice farming family, considers herself to be the reincarnation of 'a Northern queen'.

The importance Suwan attributed to *Chao* Dara Rasami in part reflects a growing general interest in the princess in Chiang Mai since the 1990s. The city celebrates *Chao* Dara Rasami Day on 8–9 December every year. Most of the commemorative activities – paying homage to the princess, and a ceremonial procession including elephants, and dance performances – take place at her former residence (*phra tamnak dara rasami*) in Mae Rim, on the outskirts of the modern city of Chiang Mai, where she lived from 1910, after King Chulalongkorn passed away, until her death on 9 December 1933. In 1999, the building was restored by Chulalongkorn University to become Daraphirom Palace Museum. In front of the building, a statue was erected based on one of the photographs *Chao* Dara Rasami posed for after she was promoted to the rank of 'High Queen'. Furthermore, Suwan articulated a broader interest in King Chulalongkorn and his wives, particularly among

---

9   The temple had at least three photographs of *Chao* Dara Rasami; two from the series described below and one of *Chao* Dara Rasami as High Queen. The one that served as inspiration for Suwan's portrait can be seen at tinyurl.com/renk28f4.

women. *Chao* Dara Rasami's name would be raised in nearly every conversation with women about King Chulalongkorn. In Chiang Mai there was a general sense of local pride in their hometown woman having been Chulalongkorn's wife. She was, I was often told, one of the king's favourites. He was attracted to her because of her beauty and because of her distinctive Lan Na style of dress and language. Many referred to the photograph described above as visual proof.

In her analyses of the portraits of *Chao* Dara Rasami, Leslie Woodhouse argues that the photographs were indeed intended to highlight the consort's 'exotic appeal' (2012: 17). The photographer had been Erb Bunnag, another royal consort. In fact, the inspiration for the portrait in Suwan's room is part of a series of seven (?) images '*Chao* Dara Rasami letting down her hair'. Woodhouse shows how *Chao* Dara Rasami, unlike her fellow royal consorts, had chosen not to wear her hair in the 'short-cropped "flank" [Siamese] style' that was then the fashion among women in Bangkok, but rather maintained her knee-length hair, wound in a bun, and continued to wear Northern style *phasin*. She had also instructed the ladies of her entourage to do so, as well as to use the Lan Na language (*ibid*: 22).[10] Within the ethnically homogeneous elite environment of the Siamese court, *Chao* Dara Rasami's otherness were both proof and confirmation of urban elite ideas about the lower ranking of rural (*chao ban nork* or *lao*) people in the hierarchy of Siamese civilisation.[11]

Relevant for my account here are King Chulalongkorn's perceived concern with preserving Chiang Mai's Lan Na style architecture, the importance attributed to *Chao* Dara Rasami as the king's consort from Chiang Mai, and the latter's explicit connection with Lan Na culture in terms of dress and food preferences. Lan Na identity becomes manifest through the specific materialisations of buildings, bodies, food and dress. The material double of Suwan's vision of Vimanmek connects the spirit world, Lan Na history and local culture.

---

10 Discussing Woodhouse's arguments on the significance of cultural and political motives for understanding *Chao* Dara Rasami's continuing popularity here, would lead too far from the central topic of this chapter.

11 *Chao* Dara Rasami and her entourage were called Lao by the Siamese, which was a derogatory term. As Woodhouse points out, long hair may 'indicate' femininity for Westerners, but for Siamese 'this hairstyle instantly declaimed one's ethnicity as "Lao"' (2012: 22). Davis opens his chapter on 'The Muang' with the observation that 'the Northern Thai do not call themselves Lao, nor do they liked to be called Lao by outsiders' (1984: 23).

The spirit of King Chulalongkorn visits (*sadet prapat ton*) Chiang Mai

Mae Wan, like so many spirit mediums in Chiang Mai and elsewhere in Thailand, was a medium for spirits of a variety of categories.[12] First of all, there were the tutelary spirits *Chao* La, *Chao* Noi and *Chao* Pi, the first being the most prominent as the one who possessed *Mae* Wan nearly every day (except for Buddhist holy days and Wednesdays).[13] Popular among *Mae* Wan's entourage, he was consulted for healing, fortune-telling and providing all kind of remedies for a variety of problems. A second category of spirits who visited *Mae* Wan were holy monks (*arahan*), namely *Somdet* To (1788–1872), *Luang Pu* Thuat (1582–?) and *Khru Ba* Sri Wichai (1878–1939). A third category was royalty: the spirit of King Chulalongkorn. By mouth of *Mae* Wan, *Chao* La told me (as did some of *Mae* Wan's regular clients) that the spirits of the monks and the spirit of King Chulalongkorn all came to possess *Mae* Wan for the first time in 1992. *Chao* La further told me that he serves as King Chulalongkorn's 'guide', using the English word, organising the preparations necessary to lead the king's spirit to *Mae* Wan's abode. The possessions always took place in this abode, the *tamnak*, a purpose-built building in *Mae* Wan's garden, next to her house. The *tamnak*, literally 'royal abode or residence', consisted of a larger empty space for the medium's followers (*luk sit*) to sit, with a platform at the rear end for *Mae* Wan during possession, and another elevation for the statues of the monks and of King Chulalongkorn, as well as some other holy images. Later, a fourth category of spirits appeared, 'Chulalongkorn's Northern wives': *Chao* Dara Rasami and the further unknown, *Mae* Bua Khiaw. To me, the historicity of *Mae* Bua Khiaw remains unclear. I have been told that she was from Wiang Kalong in Chiang Rai. However, I never witnessed *Mae* Wan possessed by these female spirits, and indeed, as confirmed by the medium herself, their appearances

---

12 For this case-study I draw from the ethnographic material of an earlier publication (Stengs 2009).

13 The reason for that is, in the words of *Mae* Wan, that '*Chao* La knows that I need some rest, too. He makes me tired and that's why he does not come on Wednesdays. I also need some time for shopping and visiting relatives'. To this purely practical explanation another dimension might be added. In an article on Northern Thai spirit mediums by Jack Bilmes, it is mentioned that 'the spirit was not available on holy days nor on *wan sia* (inauspicious days), which in that year happened to fall on Wednesdays' (1983: 233). Apparently, there is a more general association of Wednesdays with inauspiciousness. A folk wisdom has it that cutting one's hair on a Wednesday might bring bad luck, so most barbers will be closed these days.

were rare. A photograph of *Chao* Dara Rasami adorning one of the walls was the only indication that she is, or had been, a presence here.

The spirit of King Chulalongkorn, on the other hand, was *Mae* Wan's second most frequent possessing spirit, behind *Chao* La. Chulalongkorn's spirit would arrive every two weeks on a Sunday, unless that happened to be a Buddhist holy day (*wan phra*) or a religious festival. If such was the case, the session was held on a Saturday or delayed for one week. During the possession, the king himself would use a calendar to determine the day and time of the next session. This schedule was convenient for worshippers who were constrained by urban life calendars that leave little free time on weekdays for spiritual consultations.[14] The spirit of *Chao* La was similarly accommodating: he always possessed the medium during the lunch hour. Many regular visitors who worked near the *tamnak* used their lunch break to consult *Chao* La.

Sometimes elements in the spirit medium sessions were evoked to emphasise the local, Northern Thai context as distinctive from the Bangkok or central Thai background of King Chulalongkorn. Usually, while receiving Chulalongkorn's spirit, the medium was helped by an assistant to get dressed in a white, rather official-looking, jacket, wide blue trousers, white stockings and a brown, Western-style man's hat.[15] But during the Thai New Year (*songkran*) season in April, the king, like the major part of Chiang Mai's population, dressed in Lan Na style, that is, in the indigo blue *mor hom* farmer's shirt and trousers with a *pha khao ma* chequered loincloth. Usually, in contrast to *Mae* Wan or *Chao* La, both of whom spoke Northern Thai (*kham mueang*), King Chulalongkorn's spirit spoke Standard (Central) Thai (*phasa klang*). On occasion, the king deliberately used Northern Thai or *kham mueang* expressions, which were always received with great appreciation by the primarily Chiang Mai audience.

Of a different nature were the references the spirit of king Chulalongkorn would make to his qualities as a benevolent power, bringing prosperity and progress. Elsewhere, I have analysed the cult of King Chulalongkorn from the perspective of 'narrated portraits' (2009). With this approach, I aimed at highlighting the inextricable connection between narratives and images:

---

14 A similar observation has been made by Apinya (1993) for the Thammakai. At the Thammakai temple, *wan phra* always falls on a Sunday. See also Guelden (2007) and Baird (2014). But see White for somewhat different observations (2014: 120).

15 A popular photograph depicts Chulalongkorn wearing such a hat.

the king's portraits provided the material proof and confirmation of stories about the king's deeds and qualities, while at the same time these stories needed continuous materialisation in the form of copies of the portraits, including embodied re-enactments of these images. I identified four dominant narrated portraits: 'King Chulalongkorn modernised Thai society', 'King Chulalongkorn visited the countryside', 'King Chulalongkorn saved Thailand from becoming a colony' and 'King Chulalongkorn abolished slavery'. When the spirit of Chulalongkorn visited Mae Wan, the latter two narratives were basically absent. Apparently, this part of the king's image was less meaningful to the medium and her entourage, most probably because of the predominant interest in immediate prosperity. As with most spirits, the spirit of the king frequently gave lottery predictions by 'hiding' numbers in his monologues.[16] These gifts connect well with the benevolent influence attributed to Chulalongkorn, which made him a source of *khwam-jaroen* or progress. In the sessions, the king's general appearance was an enactment of a combination of the narrated portrait 'King Chulalongkorn modernised Thai society' and 'King Chulalongkorn visited the countryside' (*sadet phrapat ton,* 'made a royal excursion'). During every session, the king spoke about the prosperity (*khwam-jaroen*) he had brought to the country, with a few illustrative examples like the introduction of electricity, railways and roads. Sometimes air-conditioning was included in the list. In addition to his achievements in the past, the king usually changed the subject by addressing the positive influence of his current spiritual presence on the direct environment of the *tamnak*. The *tamnak*, in other words, served as an instance of 'the countryside'. The following quotation illustrates the fusion of both narrated portraits: 'since *pu* (grandfather) made a royal excursion (*sadet phrapat ton*) to the *tamnak* of Mae Wan, there has been prosperity (*khwam-jaroen*)'.[17] Examples of this recent progress were the asphalting of roads in the entire neighbourhood, the connection of the area to the water mains, and

---

16   Such a hidden message might be formulated as follows: King Chulalongkorn or King Rama V (*ror. ha*) had come (*khi ma*) with King Rama VI (*ror. hok*) to eat four ducks (*pet*, resembling the sound of the Thai word for eight, *paet*, and eggs representing the round shape of zero). Hence the numbers 5, 6, 4 8 and 0 could be divined from the king's discourse.

17   Referring to himself as *pu* (grandfather) or *phor* (father) and to the audience as *luk-lan* ([grand]children), the spirit of the king followed the dominant paternal discourse that frames the relationship between Thai kings and their subjects as one between (grand)parents and (grand)children. The 'children' affirmed this relationship by referring to King Chulalongkorn as *pu piya* (beloved grandfather) or *phor piya* (beloved father).

the presence of a telephone in the *tamnak*. In one session, Chulalongkorn's spirit claimed credit for initiating the planting of the now-famous trees along the road from Chiang Mai to neighbouring Lamphun Province.

We can conclude that in the *Mae* Wan spirit medium performances with the spirit of Chulalongkorn, the king appeared as a harbinger of progress who displayed a special commitment to Chiang Mai. Progress and prosperity, of course, are among the achievements the king is generally venerated for. Although the spirit made references to the past, most important is the prosperity he brings here and now. His general concern with *Mae* Wan's residence and her entourage is further substantiated in Northern Thai cultural tokens such as clothing and expressions. Through the possessed *Mae* Wan – her body becoming a material double – King Chulalongkorn's spirit, otherwise a general guardian angel, becomes visible, accessible and capable of having a direct impact on the immediate environment and the people who approach him.

Mae Yai's *yok khru* ceremony[18]

Like *Mae* Wan, *Mae* Yai was a medium for spirits from several categories: the ancestral couple *Chao* Pu and *Chao* Ya; the siblings *Chao* Ka Fa (older sister) and *Chao* Ai (younger brother) – all tutelary spirits from Lampang, or actually from *Khelang Nakhon*, Lampang's traditional name, as *Mae* Yai told me. She was also the medium for a holy monk, *Somdet* To, and for the kings Naresuan and Chulalongkorn. One side of her *tamnak* – which was the upper floor of her wooden house – was filled with statuettes, among which the larger wooden, gilded Naresuan statue stood out because of its size, approximately one metre high, and its prominent position. The walls were covered with images of various monks, King Naresuan and King Chulalongkorn. One photograph depicted three girls in traditional-style red Chiang Mai dresses. The girls, in neat order behind each other, were kneeling while bowing deeply (*krap*) to make the royal salute (*thawai bangkhom*). A modest audience was looking at the girls. Above their heads hovered an opaque spot, or maybe a cloud. The photograph was taken on a *Chao* Dara Rasami Commemoration Day conducted at Mae Rim. On one occasion, *Mae* Yai asked me: do you see it [pointing at the 'cloud']? Isn't it exactly like

---

18 *Yok khru* is also sometimes written *yok khu* to accord with the common pronunciation in Northern Thailand. In this chapter I use *yok khru* to reflect the spelling of the expression in Central Thai.

a face? I took another look and, indeed, when looking from one specific angle, one could distinguish a face-like shape in the cloud, including two small holes or 'eyes'. In other words, *Mae* Yai explained, King Chulalongorn was watching over the event.

Mae Yai could distinguish which of the different spirits came to possess her, as their *winyan* (spirit or soul) evoked different feelings or sensations. For instance, *Mae* Yai herself weighed only 49 kilograms, but when possessed by *Somdet* To, she felt like she weighed 1000. This sensation was due to the enormous power and spiritual authority of the monk's mind, his *barami*. With the spirit of King Naresuan (*somdet phra* Naresuan), *Mae* Yai experienced a feeling of ferocity (*du*), which she explained derived from Naresuan's status as a military king. The spirit of King Chulalongkorn came with the feeling of being tender and smiling (*nim* and *yim*), and *Mae* Yai spoke of him in an affectionate manner as a beloved father [and] grandfather (*phor pu piya*).

In addition to statues and images, *Mae* Yai's *tamnak* displayed quite a few dried *bai si* (conical structures made from banana leaves decorated with flowers) of various sizes and shapes, kept from the previous year's so-called *yok khru* or 'to raise the teacher' ceremony. The *yok khru* ceremony is an annual ritual organised by a spirit medium to honour the spirit (*khru*, teacher) from which she derives her power in divination and healing. For this ritual, the medium invites all other mediums who derive their power from the same spirit, or, in other words, who belong to the same lineage of the teacher's spirit.[19] One day, *Mae* Yai showed me photographs of her *yok khru* ceremonies. The earliest had been taken in 1989, including many that featured *Mae* Yai's teacher medium, an elderly woman who had died some years before my first visit. The photographs showed people, all dressed in white, putting *phaen* (a white chalk mixture) on the *bai si* during an opening ritual called *boek bai si*. All of these participants, *Mae* Yai told me, were mediums. In their white clothes, these mediums looked very different from those

---

19 The *yok khru* ceremony resembles the *wai khru* or 'paying homage to the teacher ceremony' but is not exactly identical. *Wai khru* ceremonies include a moment when respect is paid to the 'original possessor of the knowledge', the teacher. Many Thai schools organise a *wai khru* ceremony at the start of the new school year. Important *wai khru* contexts are those of the performative and martial arts, astrology and traditional medicine. Musicians, actors, boxers, tattooists, dancers, artists and masseurs may regularly pay respect to their (mythical) teacher(s). The *yok khru* is, paraphrasing Baas Terwiel's account on tattoo teachers, an 'effecting or charging-up ritual', exerting a boost of spiritual or magical powers to all who feel in need of that (1994: 71–72).

attending *Mae* Wan's *yok khru* ceremony, and other spirit medium *yok khru* ceremonies I had seen. For those ceremonies, the mediums would change their everyday clothes in favour of colourful outfits at the moment their spirit, usually a noble tutelary spirit (*jao*) from a nondescript local past, was to possess them. The state of possession would further be indicated by the mediums' behaviour: dancing, smoking cigarettes and drinking liquor. There were no such scenes among the pictures of *Mae* Yai's *yok khru* ceremonies. From *Mae* Yai's explanation, I learned that the possessing spirits of these mediums were specific historical personae – monks, kings or one of the latter's relatives or consorts – and that actually none was a traditional local lord or *jao*. For example, one year the mediums present were: a male medium of the monk *Somdet* To; a male medium of the monk *Khru Ba* Sri Wichai; a male medium of King Taksin; a female medium of Kuan Im, the Chinese Mahayana Buddhist Goddess of Mercy; and a female medium (wife of the *Khru Ba* Sri Wichai medium) of a royal consort of King Chulalongkorn, Nang Rua Lom ('the lady of the capsized boat').[20] I was told that 'where she is present, everything will get wet', which statement I took as a token of both the consort's fate and of the truthfulness of the medium. Continuing the list, the assemblage also included a male medium of a 'grandfather' hermit (*pu ruesi*), a nondescript Brahman ascetic; a female medium of *Chao Mae* Camadewi, the queen and first ruler of Lampang, at the time part of the Northern Thai kingdom of Haripunchai (~600–700 AD); and a male medium for the younger brother of King Rama I (r. 1782–1809), called Chai Lek, whose history is unclear, at least to me.[21] Overall, according to *Mae* Yai, these mediums had white-collar jobs (government officials, bank employees) in Chiang Mai and surroundings. Another important guest that year had been a monk from Kamphaeng Phet (Wat Pa Dong) who also was a medium for *Somdet* To. *Mae* Yai explained how *Somdet* To's spirit could

---

20 Her official name is Queen Sunanda Kumariratana. On 30 May 1880, the queen, her daughter and her unborn child drowned when their boat capsized on their way to Bang-Pa In Palace, in Ayutthaya Province. Their deaths were all the more tragic as they might have been saved if it had not been forbidden for commoners to touch members of the royal family. After the tragedy, the king lifted the prohibition.

21 As has been noted in most studies on Thai spirit mediumship, male spirits may possess both male and female spirit mediums. To Peter Jackson's (2012) highlighting of the importance of cross-genderism in Thai spirit mediumship, I add that male spirit possession of female mediums is more common than the reverse. I never came across a male spirit medium possessed by an explicitly female or feminine spirit like Nang Rua Lom, for instance.

possess two mediums simultaneously: each medium receives a different *yan* (insight; sixth sense), and each *yan* carries its own specific characteristics and qualities of *Somdet* To.

Fortunately, I had the opportunity to attend *Mae* Yai's *yok khru* ceremony on 11–12 November 1998. In the remaining part of this chapter, I will concentrate on the possession-related practices that took place during this ceremony. As I will show, these practices articulate two forms of contact between this world and the world of the invisible, a distinction that corresponds to that between lay participant and spirit medium.

According to protocol, nine monks had been invited to open the ceremony, which was presided over by the *makkhanayok*, the lay liaison between monks and the laity. Everybody present was clad in white, except for the monks, a man dressed in orange, and me. That would change in the course of the evening, as thirty or so laypeople in everyday clothing, dropped in. The man in orange turned out to be a medium for King Taksin. The spirit of Taksin manifested itself sometime before the monks had completed their opening chants (I could not see the medium, as he was somewhere in the back), with the noise of chewing betel, spitting, pouring water, falling bottles, bowls and general mayhem. Immediately after the chanting, while the monks were on their way out, 'he' [Taksin] approached me to tell that he had not been executed by King Rama I, but had become a monk in Nakhon Sri Thammarat in the south of Siam, where he eventually died.[22]

As a matter of course, the spirit mediums and their appearing spirits formed the loci of attention, for me as well as for the lay participants. At a certain moment, however, I noticed a layman making strange movements with the upper part of his body, arms and head, while remaining seated. Soon, some others, men and women, also began to make such movements. An attendant explained that they were 'having an *ong*' (*mi ong*), an expression White (2014: 476) has translated as indicating their 'propensity for or susceptibility for possession'. The classifier *ong* may refer to a wide range of highly respected supramundane beings, such as the spirits of kings, queens,

---

22 According to official history, Taksin was beheaded after General *Chao Phraya* Chakri, later King Rama I, had seized power in 1782 (Terwiel 2005: 60). But it is also said that the king was placed in a velvet sack and then beaten to death with a sandalwood club, a way of executing exclusively reserved for royalty (Wyatt 1984: 145). A popular myth insists that a substitute died in the sack, and that Taksin was smuggled out of Thonburi to Nakhon Sri Thammarat, where, as one version goes, he continued to live in a palace specifically built for him; in another version, he lived as a monk in a cave in the nearby hills.

princesses or monks (*ibid.*: 352). From this we may conclude that all spirit mediums for such spirits in fact may be said to 'have an *ong*'.

I had seen such manifestations of *ong* among lay participants during earlier ceremonies, in particular, during the chanting session of an elaborate *pluk sek* (sacralisation) ceremony at Wat Don Chang on Chulalongkorn Day, 23 October 1998. That ceremony had been attended by hundreds of people and I saw at least twenty people making movements indicative of 'having an *ong*'. Every time I observed this behaviour, I also observed that other participants did not pay much attention, which may lead us to conclude that 'having an *ong*' was nothing unusual, as White's research also suggests.[23]

As *Mae* Yai's *yok khru* photographs only showed people dressed in white, the clothing indicating their spirit mediumship, we may also conclude that 'having an *ong*' was not regarded as being the same as spirit mediumship. This distinction was given concrete content in the difference in degree of specificity of contact with the invisible. Different from the *ong* of the laypeople, whose identity remained unclear, the spirits that manifested themselves through the spirit mediums were identifiable: their specific behaviour, food preferences and speech patterns enabled their precise identification as the spirits of historical/mythical personae, each of whom had a name and a life story.

Throughout the ceremony, the spirits would come and go. While present, they sometimes consulted an audience member, sometimes chatting among each other. Always, several mediums were possessed at the same time, each one by a different, identifiable spirit. To me, it was not always clear whether a medium was possessed or not, or when possessed, by which spirit. General indications of possession were: smoking, drinking or chewing betel.

---

23 White observed the manifestation of *ong* among possession-inclined people within the circles of professional spirit mediums. The above cases show that this development is not restricted to the Bangkok area, nor is it specific to urban spirit mediums in central Thailand. Moreover, White's suggestion that '*ong*-infused supramundane entities [such as kings or monks] cannot possess or displace the consciousness or agency of *ong*-infused human beings' (2014: 86, note 60) may explain why people instead spoke of *yan*, when explaining the abbot's spiritual relationships with kings Chulalongkorn, Taksin and Naresuan. As one *luk sit* (follower) of the abbot explained to me: he is not a *rang song*. A *rang song* needs to meditate before the *phra ong* manifests itself. The abbot just all of a sudden may become 'the *ong*' and speak *phasa thep* (the language of the gods/deities). These spiritual connections were explained to me from past-lives relationships between the abbot and each of these kings. On the other hand, the magic monk central to Pattana's study, Ajan Somsak, speaks of inviting 'one's superagency', *ong tham* (Dhammic entity/calling) (2012: 40). When possessed and in deep trance, practitioners would start speaking *phasa tham* (Dhammic language) (*ibid.*).

Sometimes, other attendants were also confused. For example, on one of the occasions that *Mae* Yai became possessed, there was uncertainty among the audience about whether the spirit was that of *Pu* In, King Naresuan or King Chulalongkorn. Clarity came when the spirit lit a cigar, well known to be favoured by King Chulalongkorn. '*Phor piya!*' the audience exclaimed in recognition, using the affectionate name for King Chulalongkorn as a 'beloved father'. Earlier that evening, the spirit of *Somdet* To had come to *Mae* Yai. A distinguishing feature of this spirit was his very old age, manifested in the medium walking with her body bending at 90 degrees and in need of support when moving.[24] The spirit of King Taksin also indicated his old age in this way, but he did not need any physical support.

One dimension of this spirit possession ceremony struck me in particular: the conviviality of the visiting spirits. Because most of the mediums were simultaneously possessed, each of them by a different spirit, the spirits met each other, so to speak, through their material doubles. As they chatted, they clearly displayed their appreciation of each other's company. I noticed, for instance, the spirit of King Taksin and the spirit of King Rama I discussing possible improvements of the *bai si*; there was a long conversation between the spirit of King Taksin, the spirit of King Naresuan (*phra jao dam*) and three other (for me unidentifiable) spirits conversing in *phasa thep* (the language of the gods/deities). At one moment, when the spirit of Chulalongkorn and the spirit of Rama I were quietly smoking cigars and drinking cognac together, chatting every now and then in *phasa thep*, I fully came to realise how totally self-evident these settings were for mediums and other participants alike. The temporalities allocated to these spirits' historical personae were of no relevance. Perhaps indeed, we could draw here on – as Michael Lambek (1998) suggests in his analysis of Sakalava (Madagascar) possession performances of royal ancestors – Mikhail Bakhtin's concept of the chronotope, 'particular configurations of time and space … that organise and emerge from particular cultural productions' (1998: 114). In Lambek's words, the chronotope of spirit possession performances 'brings together a cast of characters who establish their relationships to one another by means of greetings, gifts of drink, and the like, but who generally subsist side by side in a kind of "parallel play"' (*ibid.*: 116). Yet, I do not share Lambek's conclusion, that we are witnessing

---

24 This is a more common manifestation. Once I attended a classical *yok khru* spirit medium ceremony of local tutelary guardian spirits, and the most ancient spirit walked exactly this way (which was also explained to me as resulting from his age).

here 'the creative production of a kind of history', history in a new form, as distinct from occidental history (*ibid.*: 106).

Conclusion

The pantheon of Northern Thai spirit mediums is populated with spirits (mostly designated as *jao*) from a mythical or nondescriptive past, as well as with historical figures, royalty and monks in particular. In this worldview, these figures are a permanent and immanent part of the present. This presence manifests itself in visions, dreams and trance. Rather than understanding the spirits' presences during spirit possession sessions as 'realisations of the past' (Lambek 1998), I propose that they inhabit a specific dimension of the present made tangible, and hence prone to manipulation, by material doubling. The case studies demonstrate the amount of energy and creativity involved in realising these materialisations. They also demonstrate the wide range of forms and practices that such material doubling may entail: statues, mansions, dress, foods, speech, possessed bodies. At the same time, however, they are firmly localised, carrying distinctive Northern Thai features as essential elements of their materiality.

The ethnographic material presented in this chapter has shown that oneiric encounters with the spirit world may take a variety of forms and induce a variety of possession-related practices. Trance, a medium's condition when possessed by a spirit, is the main form in which the oneiric is encountered. Yet, also for laypeople, trance may be a condition that connects to the oneiric, as the people 'having an *ong*' demonstrate. In addition, through dreams and visions, either vocally or visually, people may receive clear instructions from the spirit world with regard to how to handle food, buildings, statues, dress or charity in order to deal properly with the invisible. My conceptualisation of the spirit world as an oneiric space – a space that unavoidably manifests itself in the here and now – clarifies that this world is equally as much part of everyday life as the visual and tangible, with an equal capacity to impact people's everyday life, work, financial situation, family relationships, and so on.

This perspective implies that understanding will be enhanced when scholars move away from conceptions that foreground time or history. The massive presence of historical figures, mythical or royal, in spirit mediumship does not relate to the past; it reflects a perception of the present. Paraphrasing the famous painting of Belgium surrealist René Magritte, '*Ceci n'est pas de l'histoire*' (this is not history).

References

Apinya Feungfusakul. 1993. 'Buddhist Reform Movements in Contemporary Thai Urban Context: Thammakai and Santi Asoke', PhD dissertation, University of Bielefeld.

Baird, Ian G. 2014. 'The Cult of Phaya Narin Songkhram: Spirit Mediums and Shifting Sociocultural Boundaries in Northeastern Thailand', *Journal of Southeast Asian Studies*, 45(1): 50–73.

Bennett, Tony and Patrick Joyce. 2010. *Material Powers: Cultural Studies, History and the Material Turn*. London and New York: Routledge.

Bilmes, Jack. 1995. 'On the Believability of Northern Thai Spirit Mediums', *Journal of The Siam Society*, 83(1–2): 231–238.

Bynum, Caroline W. 2011. *Christian Materiality: An Essay on Religion in Late Medieval Europe*. New York: Zone Books.

Cohen, Eric. 1998. 'From Buddha Images to Mickey Mouse Figures: The Transformation of Ban Thawai Carvings', in M.C. Howard, W. Wattanapun and A. Gordon (eds), *Traditional T'ai Arts in Contemporary Perspective*. Bangkok: White Lotus Press: 149–174.

Davis, Richard B. 1984. *Muang Metaphysics: A Study of Northern Thai Myth and Ritual*. Bangkok: Pandora.

Guelden, Marlane. 2007. *Thailand: Spirits Among Us*. Singapore: Marshall Cavendish.

Hamayon, Roberte N. 1993. 'Are 'Trance', 'Ecstasy' and Similar Concepts Appropriate in the Study of Shamanism?' *Shaman*, 1(1–2): 17–40.

Houtman, Dick and Birgit Meyer (eds). 2012. *Things: Religion and the Question of Materiality*. New York: Fordham.

Jackson, Peter. 1999. 'The Enchanting Spirit of Capitalism: The Cult of Luang Phor Khoon and the Post-modernization of Thai Buddhism', *South East Asia Research*, 7(1): 5–60.

———. 2012. 'The Political Economy of Twenty-first Century Thai Supernaturalism: Contemporary perspectives on Cross-Genderism and Limits to Hybridity in Resurgent Thai Spirit Mediumship', *South East Asia Research*, 20(4): 611–622.

Lambek, Michael. 1998. 'The Sakalava Poiesis of History. Realizing the Past Through Spirit Possession in Madagascar', *American Ethnologist*, 25(2): 106–127.

Mbembe, Achille. 2017. *Critique of Black Reason*, trans. Laurent Dubois. Durham and London: Duke University Press.

Meyer, Birgit. 2015. *Sensational Movies: Video, Vision and Christianity in Ghana*. Berkeley: University of California Press.

———. 2016. 'Mediating Affliction: Ghanaian and Nigerian Video-Movies as Oneiric Spaces of and for the Imagination'. Workshop Imaginaries of Affliction,

Healing and Medicine: Sickness and the Representation of Africa, Stellenbosch University, STIAS 19 – 23 September 2016.

Pattana Kitiarsa. 2012. *Mediums, Monks and Amulets: Thai Popular Buddhism Today*. Chiang Mai: Silkworm Books.

Stengs, Irene. 2009. *Worshipping the Great Modernizer: King Chulalongkorn, Patron Saint of the Thai Middle Class*. Singapore: NUS Press.

———. 2012. 'Sacred Singularities: Crafting Royal Images in Present-day Thailand', *Journal of Modern Craft*, 5(1): 51–68.

Terwiel, Baas J. 1994. *Monks and Magic: An Analysis of Religious Ceremonies in Central Thailand*. Bangkok: White Lotus Press.

———. 2005 *Thailand's Political History: From the Fall of Ayutthaya in 1767 to Recent Times*. Bangkok: River Books.

White, Erick. 2014. 'Possession, Professional Spirit Mediums, and the Religious Fields of Late-Twentieth Century Thailand', PhD dissertation, Cornell University.

Woodhouse, Leslie. 2012. 'Concubines with Cameras: Royal Siamese Consorts Picturing Femininity and Ethnic Difference in Early 20th Century Siam', *Trans Asia Photography, Women's Camera Work: Asia*, 2(2): 1–31. quod.lib.umich.edu/t/tap/7977573.0002.202/--concubines-with-cameras-royal-siamese-consorts-picturing?rgn=main;view=fulltext (Accessed 15 November 2021).

Wyatt, David K. 1984. *Thailand: A Short History*. New Haven and London: Yale University Press.

CHAPTER 10

Buriram's Possession Complex and the Growing Professionalisation of Village Mediumship in Thailand's Lower Northeast

Benjamin Baumann

A new language game

In this conceptual chapter I synthesise ethnographic material[1] with a recent paradigm shift in the anthropology of animism to outline a novel way of how mediumship in Thailand's lower Northeast may be approached anthropologically. The chapter mirrors my ongoing attempt to decolonise our thought when we[2] write about phenomena like possession and mediumship, as the most common analytical tropes we encounter in anthropological texts are still infused by a deeply Eurocentric philosophical undercurrent (Willerslev 2013: 41–42). The novel language I propose in this chapter is an attempt to work on an answer to the essential question posed by Eduardo Viveiros de Castro: 'What do anthropologists owe, conceptually, to the people they study?' (Viveiros de Castro 2014: 39) While I principally agree with Louis Dumont that we 'are caught between the Scylla of sociocentrism and the Charybdis of obscurity and incommunicability' and that 'our basic intellectual tools cannot be replaced or modified at one stroke' (Dumont 1986: 257), when we write about the worlds of our interlocutors

---

1 The ethnographic fieldwork in Buriram Province was financed with a grant from the German Research Foundation (DFG) and was part of the author's dissertation project, 'The Ritual Reproduction of Khmerness in Thailand' (Baumann 2017).
2 'We' refers more narrowly to the international community of scholars dealing professionally with phenomena in Thailand described as 'possession' and 'mediumship'. I think, nevertheless, that some of the points raised in this chapter may apply wherever anthropologists describe phenomena that anthropological jargon classifies as 'possession' or 'mediumship'.

we nevertheless need to continuously work on our analytic vocabulary to free it from implicit ontological assumptions about our world that are enshrined in the language we use when we talk about their worlds.

Non-professional mediumship by post-menopausal women used to be crucial for the reproduction of local cult lineages and collective sentiments of emplaced belonging in the lower Northeast. Socio-economic transformations of rural lifeworlds[3] have diminished the availability of these non-professional spirit mediums over the past couple of decades. Increasingly, the relatively recent phenomenon of professional mediumship is filling this gap and is booming not only in Buriram Province, but across Thailand.[4] Since 2011, I have observed and participated in various rituals performed by non-professional, semi-professional and professional mediums for various reasons and on behalf of different clienteles throughout Buriram Province, and I have talked to the ritual experts involved. On the basis of these experiences, I argue that these forms of mediumship and the possession phenomena they entail are emplacements of Southeast Asia's possession complex, which Kaj Århem identifies as an essential feature of the hierarchical animism in the region (Århem 2016a, 2016b).

The lower Northeast (*phak isan tai*) is vernacularly recognised as a distinct socio-cultural region with ambiguous frontiers and multiple centres. Thai common sense identifies the three provinces of Buriram, Surin, and Sisaket as forming the sub-region's heartland. The sub-region's only physical boundary is the Dangrek mountain range on the southern fringes of the three provinces, which also constitutes the international border between Thailand and Cambodia. Although Thailand's Northeast is commonly associated with the socio-cultural category Lao, the lower Northeast tends to be associated with the socio-cultural category Khmer (*khamen*), as a considerable portion of the local population speaks Northern Khmer as their first or second language (Baumann 2017).

I approach the emplacement of the possession complex in the region and the nonmodern ontology that renders it meaningful in everyday life from

---

3   'Lifeworld' here refers to the 'domain of everyday, immediate social existence and practical activity, with all its habituality, its crises, its vernacular and idiomatic character, its biographical particularities, its decisive events and indecisive strategies, which theoretical knowledge addresses but does not determine, from which conceptual understanding arises but on which it does not primarily depend' (Michael Jackson 1996: 7–8).

4   See Irvine 1982, 1984; Johnson 2015, 2016; Morris 2000; Pattana 1999; White 2014.

the perspective of 'new animism' (Harvey 2005). Rane Willerslev (2012) introduced this perspective as follows:

> Central to the approaches of new animism researchers is a rejection of previous scholarly attempts to identify animism as either metaphoric – a projection of human society onto nature as in the sociological tradition of Emile Durkheim – or as some sort of imaginary delusion, a manifestation of 'primitive' man's inability to distinguish dreams from reality, as in the evolutionary tradition of Tylor. (Willerslev 2012: 01/07, footnotes omitted)

New animism is part of a recent paradigm shift in anthropology that is commonly known as 'the ontological turn' (Holbraad and Perdersen 2017). Inspired by this paradigm shift, I argue that the social relevance of emplaced cults, the ubiquity of possession phenomena in everyday village life, and the flourishing of professional mediumship in the region are grounded in a nonmodern conception of collectivity (Baumann 2018, 2020a). This understanding of collectivity retains its lifewordly meaningfulness despite being constantly challenged by modernist conceptualisations of sociality that are articulated through the hybridisation of Buddhist and naturalist language games in Thailand's public sphere.

Drawing on Bruno Latour (1993), Philippe Descola defines a collective as 'a procedure of grouping, or "collecting", of humans and nonhumans into a network of specific interrelations' (Descola 2013: 422). Both authors distinguish the term 'collective' from 'the classic term "society" in that it does not apply solely to a group of human subjects who are thereby detached from the web of relations that link them to the nonhuman world.' (Descola 2013: 422). When I use the term collectivity here, it refers to the embodied sense of belonging to or being a member of a collective. As the boundaries between human and nonhuman being are in a collective not as elaborated as in a naturalist society (Latour 1993: 4, 11), I refer to the form of social being that characterises everyday lifeworlds in the lower Northeast as an animist collectivity. I draw on this analytic vocabulary, as it seems better suited to emphasise the contrasting ontological registers that distinguish animist, naturalist and Buddhist language games in contemporary Thailand (Baumann 2018, 2020a, forthcoming; Baumann and Rehbein 2020, 2022).

When talking about language games, we have to keep Ludwig Wittgenstein's inclusive understanding of language in mind (Wittgenstein 1982).

Language is for Wittgenstein, above all, a practice, deeply embedded in the pragmatics of everyday life and not a system of abstract signs and symbols (Winch 1992: 184). Wittgenstein's understanding of language encompasses all meaning-bearing activities so that ostensibly non-linguistic matters become elements of language, while he also stresses the ineluctability of language use and denies any pre-linguistic (i.e., meaningless) access to the world (Baumann and Rehbein 2022; Lütterfelds 1995: 109, 112). Language games need to be 'played' as they do not exist in the form of abstract rules or 'game manuals' outside their execution (Winch 1992: 183). As everyday practice, language games produce distinctive forms of life and thus the worlds in which discourses operate.[5] Peter Winch emphasises that everyday life is characterised by the parallel existence of multiple language games and a limited translatability between them.[6] To make things even more complicated, these multiple language games are played simultaneously but are not neatly separable; they rather co-exist in a disorderly fashion, crisscrossing in certain contexts, while remaining firmly distinct in others. Their mutual intelligibility decreases with their contextual specialisation and with differences in the ontological registers they articulate (Winch 1992: 183, 272–273).

I approach the relational logic that characterises conceptualisations of collectivity in animist language games via Marshall Sahlins' (2013) reformulation of Lucien Lévy-Bruhl's *law of participation* in order to outline a nonmodern social ontology[7] of everyday village life in Thailand (Baumann 2018, 2020). On this basis, I not only emphasise the relevance that mediumship and possession phenomena have for the reproduction of this social ontology, but I also introduce a typology of mediums who are active in contemporary Buriram's localised possession complex.

Non-professional and professional mediumship are just the most obvious ritualised manifestations of animist collectivity. Most rituals that

---

5 Whereas Foucauldian discourse analyses ask questions of power, Wittgenstein's linguistic phenomenology asks questions of meaning and its embodiment (Baumann forthcoming; Baumann and Rehbein 2022).

6 Peter Jackson emphasises this parallel existence of multiple language games as a characteristic feature of Thailand's contemporary socio-cultural configuration (Peter Jackson 2020).

7 Very briefly, social ontology refers to the interpretation a collective has of itself. This interpretation is embodied by every member of the collective through their socialisation into the language game that reproduces the collective. Social ontology, thus, refers to the ways a collective is meaningfully embodied as a characteristic form of collectivity by its members (Baumann and Rehbein 2020).

Buddhological common sense would label as 'non-Buddhist' reproduce animist collectivity as the social ontology of everyday life. These everyday rituals include: the 'calling of the *khwan*'[8] (*riak khwan*); its 'binding to the human body' (*su khwan, phuk khaen*); the 'calling of the rice's *khwan*' (*riak khwan khao*); the 'erection of a spirit shrine' (*yok san*); 'mending luck rituals' (*phithi sodor khror*); exorcisms (*lai phi*); 'votive offerings' (*kae bon*); 'making merit for the village' (*tham bun ban*); 'the planting of the first house post' (*pluk sao ek*); 'house warmings' (*khuen ban mai*); as well as aspects of local wedding ceremonies (*ngan taeng*) and funeral cultures (*ngan sop*). In addition, many rituals commonly identified as 'Buddhist' within local funeral cultures above all, also reproduce aspects of this social ontology.[9]

Animist collectivity also informs everyday conceptions of personhood, and local language games imagine the person in relational terms (Bird-David 1999; Sprenger 2016b; Tanabe 2002). This relational understanding of personhood co-exists with alternative conceptualisations that emerge from Buddhist and naturalist language games as well as their hybridisation (Peter Jackson 2020: 32). These alternative concepts of personhood have not only become mutually interdependent, but also hegemonic in the public sphere. In contrast to these more or less individualistic conceptions of bounded personhood, everyday language games imagine the human person itself as a social collective. In these language games, being – human and nonhuman – is a single ontological category that is distinguished merely by different grades of personhood (Sprenger 2016b: 78, 84). The Thai person is, accordingly, imagined as a configuration of human and nonhuman components that are united in 'mutualities of being' (Sahlins 2013: ix). Personhood is thus not an ontological given, but the result and expression of relationships (Baumann 2020a; O'Connor 2000; Sprenger 2016b, 2018).

---

8   *Khwan* are soul-like potencies that animate the human body. The human body is, however, not the only collective animated by *khwan*, as they also reside in certain animals (such as buffaloes and elephants), rice, house pillars, musical instruments, boats and ox carts (Terwiel 1980: 74). While *khwan* is not translatable to English, the German word *Lebensgeister* (*spiritus animales*) (Stengel 2013) captures at least some of the ideas villagers hold about *khwan*.

9   This is most obvious in the Buddhicised tradition of feeding the dead during the two weeks that the gates of the Buddhist hell are open each year. This Buddhicised form of ancestor worship takes place in central Thailand during the ritual known as *wan sat duean sip*. In the lower Northeast this ritual complex is known as *saen don ta*, in Cambodia as *pchum ben* and in Laos as *boun ho khao padap din* (Baumann 2017: 428; Davis 2016: 160).

Anthropology characterises such relational conceptions of personhood as 'dividualist'.[10] As opposed to the notion of the bounded individual as the cardinal value of Western modernity (Dumont 1986), the nonmodern dividual is relationally constructed, composite and essentially divisible (Bird-David 1999; Marriott 1976; Strathern 1988). While some scholarly accounts imply that Tai language games articulate dividual conceptualisations of personhood,[11] ethnographically founded descriptions of Thai dividuality are still scarce.[12] A reason for this absence may be that Thai dividuality is an aspect of everyday experience itself and, as such, is firmly situated in social practice. It appears so 'normal' and given that it is not consciously reflected upon in discourse and it cannot simply be understood through the lens of abstract analytic categories or assessed via talking to local interlocutors. This is especially true if these interlocutors are devout Buddhists who have been conditioned to rely on popular Buddhist idioms when they try to make sense of the rather abstract questions of anthropologists (Tannenbaum 1995: 9–11). The only way to develop a sense of Thai dividuality is through practical enmeshment in everyday lifeworlds (Baumann et al. 2020: 126).

Taking new animism to Thailand

Following Edward B. Tylor's influential minimum definition of religion as 'the belief in Spiritual Beings' (Tylor 1871: 383), most anthropological textbooks continue to place animism in the realm of (pre-)religion and portray it as the belief in an animate nature, where 'things' are endowed with 'souls'. Proponents of 'new animism' criticise this rationalist view as an attribution of modern dualities (like nature/culture, spirit/matter, body/

---

10 It may be argued that naturalist conceptualisations of the human person also acknowledge its dividuality in the sense of a participation of nonhuman beings like viruses, bacteria or internal parasites in human persons. However, the nonhumans that enter mutualities of being with humans in animist conceptions of collectivity are either of a sort whose existence is categorically denied by the natural sciences ('ghosts', 'spirits', 'demons', 'deities', etc.) or ontologically excluded from being able to 'enter' into a relationship with a human (stones, trees, places, etc.) (Baumann forthcoming).
11 Banks Findly 2016: 1; O'Connor 2000: 45–47; Richardson Hanks 1960; Tanabe 2002; Tidawan 2006: 150.
12 A recent and remarkable exception to the typical treatment of Thai dividuality is by Stonington (2020: 764-65), who emphasises the incoherencies that dividuality produces in Buddhist soteriology.

mind, etc.) onto nonmodern ontologies.[13] I use the word 'nonmodern' here not in the sense of 'premodern' but rather as 'different-from-modern', in order to distinguish between contemporary language games that rely on a naturalist ontological register in the generation of meaning (modern) and those that do not (nonmodern) (Baumann 2020b: 109).

'New animism' outlines a non-evolutionist alternative to this still-influential conceptualisation of animism. As a theoretical paradigm, new animism is not about the 'belief' in 'spirits' animating 'things' in 'nature', but about nonhuman-being-in-the-world and how nonhumans relate with humans to form animist collectives (Bird-David 1999). Many proponents of 'new animism' purge the evolutionist content that renders Tylor's conceptualisations of animism unsupportable by drawing on Descola's model of ontological multiplicity (Descola 2013). In Descola's typology of four ontologies (animism, totemism, analogism and naturalism), animism represents the antithesis of naturalism, which is identified as the hegemonic ontology of Western modernity (Viveiros de Castro 2014). With reference to this model, Århem succinctly explains the differences between naturalism and animism:

> As opposed to naturalism, which assumes a foundational dichotomy between objective nature and subjective culture, animism posits an intersubjective and personalised universe in which the Cartesian split between person and thing is dissolved and rendered spurious. In the animist cosmos, animals and plants, beings and things, may all appear as intentional subjects and persons, capable of will, intention and agency. (Århem 2016a: 3)

While Descola's (post-)structuralist typology of four ontologies has triggered a whole range of creative responses and some scholars argue that the valley-centred imperial states of mainland Southeast Asia manifest an analogic rather than animistic conceptualisation of the world, I will not discuss the limits of Descola's typlogy here in detail. It suffices to note that Anne Yvonne Guillou shows not only that important aspects of appreciating everyday understandings of collectivity in mainland Southeast Asia are missing in Descola's conceptualisation of analogism, such as the agency and potency of places, but also that these emplaced collectives seem to hybridise aspects of Descola's animistic and analogistic types (Guillou 2017: 392).

---

13 Århem 2016a, 2016b; Bird-David 1999; Descola 2013; Harvey 2005; Ingold 2006; Sprenger 2016a; Viveiros de Castro 1998, 2004, 2014.

In order to describe Thailand's animist social ontology and distinguish it from alternative social ontologies that also inform everyday village life, I follow Sahlins (2014) and subsume analogism, totemism and animism under the broad label animism here, as these three ontological ideal types are all about the participation of nonhumans in human existence, which is categorically ruled out, in one way or another, by doctrinal Buddhism and naturalism. The form of relational being that characterises these participations and the central role mediumship plays in the reproduction of emplaced social collectives is the distinguishing feature of the social ontology that shapes everyday life, and is essential to understanding the logic of Thailand's possession complex.

In his outline of Southeast Asia's possession complex, Århem also draws on Sahlins and suggests calling the paradigmatic Southeast Asian ontology, with its characteristic blending of analogistic and animistic features, 'hierarchical animism' (Århem 2016a: 14–15; Sahlins 2014).[14] In Århem's model, the proliferation of hierarchically ordered nonhumans that are venerated by human worship groups is the outstanding feature of this Southeast Asian variant of an animistic ontology. Hierarchical animism is 'most clearly manifest among the village-centered rice-cultivating and livestock-raising communities constituting the majority of indigenous societies in Southeast Asia' (Århem 2016a: 16). Pattana Kitiarsa calls Thailand's hierarchically ordered cosmology a 'parade of hybrid deities' among which the Buddha is supreme (Pattana 2012: 23–24). Pattana's depiction of Thai cosmology shows how the hierarchical logic of Southeast Asian animism usurps everyday Buddhism and informs human–nonhuman interaction not only in the agrarian peripheries, but also in the urban lowlands and even in the globalised centres of contemporary polities, such as Bangkok (Pattana 2002, 2005, 2012).

Outlining Thailand's mystic field

The ontological register of Thailand's animist language games overlaps with that of Buddhist language games in the mystic field, where proper conduct, the observation of taboos and above all the keeping of the Buddhist precepts are essential to gain the blessing of various nonhuman beings. This blessing

---

14 Århem's outline of Southeast Asian hierarchical animism implies that within this hybrid configuration the organisational logic of hill-dwelling collectives tends towards Descola's animistic pole, whereas the social logic of valley-dwelling collectives tends towards the analogic pole.

manifests in a field-specific form of 'cultural capital' (Bourdieu 1983) that I call 'mystic capital'. I draw here on Bradford Verter, who suggests that the fluidities of today's spiritual marketplace call for a new category of capital to be added along with Bourdieu's conception of 'religious capital' (Verter 2003: 151–152). While I reserve the term 'religious capital' for the field of state-patronised Theravada Buddhism and its intimate links to political power, the boundaries between Thailand's mystic and religious fields are rather methodological.

Fields are sociological abstractions, heuristic devices to contextualise forms of capital and power. They enable us to identify field-specific logics and language games, and thus to escape economic reductionism. Fields and field-specific language games overlap in everyday practice and the nonmodern logic of the mystic field frequently usurps the modern logic of a state-promoted Thai Buddhism that has been rationalised over the past 200 years in dialogue with naturalism (Gray 1986; Ladwig 2011; Larsson 2020; Terwiel 2012). I suggest this alternative analytic framework to overcome some of the ostensible paradoxes produced by scholarly attempts to fit the contrasting ontological assumptions characterising everyday practices under the encompassing label of 'Theravada Buddhism' (Baumann 2020b).[15]

Thailand's religious field slowly emerged as a sub-field of an encompassing mystic field through the growing institutionalisation of Theravada Buddhism in the region and it became hegemonic as it was wedded to morally righteous rulership and political power in Siam. However, the imagined boundaries between these two fields concretised only when the modernising monarchs Mongkut (Rama IV, r. 1851–1868) and Chulalongkorn (Rama V, r. 1868–1910) tied the articulation of national identity to a purified form of 'Thai Buddhism' that was purged of many mystic elements and increasingly identified as a 'religion' compatible with the modern values of 'progress' and 'development'. Both fields continue, however, to rely on reformulations of Brahmanical lore that smooth the mutual convertibility of field-specific language games in everyday life.

Until the middle of the 20th century, an imagined boundary between the religious and mystic fields was largely an urban phenomenon and not

---

15 White's (2014: passim) discussion of multiple 'Buddhist regimes' and Aulino's 'competing Buddhist practices' (Aulino 2019: 37) are just two recent moments when anthropologists have pointed out that it is misleading to cast the competing imaginations of Buddhism that exist in contemporary Thailand under the label Theravada Buddhism.

an established aspect of rural Thai habitus (Terwiel 2012). The acknowledgment of two distinct fields separated by a boundary was a form of cultural capital that functioned to differentiate 'civilised' urbanites from 'superstitious' country folk during the modernisation of the Siamese kingdom and its transformation into the Thai nation-state. Nonetheless, rural–urban migration and the growing urbanisation of Thai lifeworlds have firmly established the idea of Thai religion and a boundary between both fields as constitutive aspects of contemporary Thai habitus. The concretisation of this imaginary boundary in practice and discourse, as well as the hegemony of rationalised self-imaginations of Thai Buddhism in Thailand's public sphere, accelerate the mystic field's discursive association with 'primitivity' on the one hand and the 'evils of global capitalism' on the other (Peter Jackson 1999b, 2009, 2014). These associations enhance the practical convertibility of mystic into economic capital, which is one reason for the proliferation of professional spirit mediumship and other urban cults in contemporary Thailand (Johnson 2012; White 2014).

Applying aspects of Pierre Bourdieu's field theory to everyday interactions with nonhuman beings in contemporary Thailand allows us to make sense of their specificities, without drawing on the notion of an all-encompassing 'Theravada Buddhism' or indulging in unhelpful discussions of whether Thai religion is a 'syncretic' or 'hybrid' blend of animist, Brahmanist and Buddhist features (Peter Jackson 2020). Talking, instead, about religious and mystic fields and field-specific forms of capital and language games, allows us to stress the parallel existence of multiple and sometimes contradicting ontological assumptions in everyday life, their merging in certain situations as well as their contextual opposition. It also allows us to emphasise that Thai animism is not a religion but a social ontology and thus to look at mediumship and possession phenomena sociologically and link developments in the relationships between humans and nonhumans to social structure and the reproduction of political power and social inequalities in Thailand (Baumann 2020a).

The 'rules' of Thailand's mystic field allow for the easy convertibility of mystic into religious, economic or political capital, as various discussions of Thai 'prosperity religions' have shown (Jackson 1999a, 1999b; Pattana 2005, 2012). These discussions show also, how field-specific accumulation logics easily blend into each other and field-specific language games retain a high level of mutual intelligibility (Tannenbaum 1995). Wealth, sacrifice, and spiritual blessing are in everyday life linked in endless positive feedback chains that lead to a reification of mystic potency in the form of more wealth, rank and worldly power (Århem 2016a: 20). As Bernard Formoso observes of this imagined relationship:

> Accordingly, Thai Buddhists regularly make merit (*tham bun*) for the *winyan* of their dead parents, with the conviction that in so doing they can simultaneously uplift their own *karma* and that of the deceased. In return, they expect from their dead supernatural patronage in the form of protection, health and prosperity. (Formoso 2016: 124)

Accumulated mystic potency is a field-transcending protective force that guards social collectives against misfortune and various external dangers (Terwiel 2012: 112). While the specific ideas of mystic potency usually remain implicit in everyday language games in rural Buriram, Thailand's public sphere distinguishes a Buddhist-coded form of charisma (*barami*) from a form of power (*saksit*) that tends to be qualified as 'supernatural'. I am drawing here on Anderson's discussion of Javanese ideas of 'power' when I stress that local conceptions are radically different from the abstract and Western concept of instrumental power (Anderson 1972: 4).[16]

Drawing on Peter A. Jackson's register of multiple forms of Thai 'power', one may be inclined to identify the potency accumulated in the rituals of Thailand's mystic field as *saksit* (Jackson 2010: 33). Villagers in Thailand's lower Northeast sometimes use the word *saksit*, when they are asked to name the potency generated in the rituals of the local possession complex. However, the more frequently used concept is *khlang* or *khwam-khlang*. *Khwam-khlang* is usually translated as 'magical power' and it seems to be a more open concept than the two other forms of 'religious power' – *barami* and *saksit* – that are often invoked in accounts of Thailand's public sphere. While *khwam-khlang* needs to be added to Jackson's register of Thai notions of 'power', I prefer the word 'potency' to designate the existential reality of a mystic force that enables actions to become effective. The rituals of Buriram's possession complex are always about this form of potency, its concretisation and accumulation in specific bodies. Instrumental power (*amnat*) is a sec-

---

16 Questions of 'power', its contextual imagination and ontological quality have shaped the study of Southeast Asia like perhaps no other topic. Drawing on a long tradition of anthropological studies, there is still a lively debate about the characteristic forms 'power' can take in Southeast Asia.

ondary phenomenon, a mere result of the accumulation of mystic potency and its convertibility into field-specific forms of capital and/or power.

The neo-functionalist rationalism that dominates current studies of mediumship and possession phenomena in Thailand is thus not per se wrong when it stresses insecurity reduction and prosperity enhancement as the triggers of growth of urban spirit cults;[17] it simply fails to explicate what makes these practices culturally meaningful. In their aim for explanations, neo-functionalists translate these seemingly irrational practices into another cultural logic to make them plausible to people who think as they do. As such, their explanations remain on the analytic level of James G. Frazer's portrayal of magical practices in the *Golden Bough* (Wittgenstein 1967: 235) and they add little to understandings of the everyday meaning of possession phenomena in Thailand. In everyday language games, the acquisition of mystic potency automatically implies an increase in prosperity, security and well-being. In a world where security and prosperity are merely tangible manifestations of one's mystic potency, they cannot be regarded as the ultimate motivation of a person who becomes the active devotee of a deity/spirit and joins their cult.

This is also true for the practice known as *kae bon*, which is frequently portrayed as a prime example of the commodification of 'Thai religion'. Shrines overflowing with characteristic offerings like wooden elephants, or zebras and roosters made from concrete, seem at first glance to be misplaced in an ostensibly Buddhist temple or shrine. Yet they are increasingly visible in urban and rural configurations alike. The usual explanation behind this accumulation of what might be called 'votive offerings' is that worshippers are 'repaying' a nonhuman being for a wish that has been granted with an object that the nonhuman is known to have a particular liking for. What may look like the *do ut des* of exchange partners we know from commodity economies, is in fact one expression of the mutuality of being that characterises Thai notions of animist collectivity, notions that retain their meaningfulness in contemporary Thailand's many simultaneous language games.

While some of the relationships between humans and nonhumans established by *kae bon* and similar transactions may be terminated with a reciprocal offering afterwards, my impression is that these relationships between nonhumans and humans are frequently much more complex and persistent than

---

17 Johnson 2015; Mills 1995, 2001, 2012; Morris 2000, 2002.

many observers seem to recognise and practitioners are willing to admit. They seem rather to manifest a variant of what Marcel Mauss famously called 'the spirit of the gift', where givers give aspects of themselves as part of the gift, which the recipients accept together with the gift to become an aspect of their selves afterwards (Mauss 2002). The acceptance of a gift from a nonhuman, like the passing of an exam, thus generates a lasting relationship of mutuality between human and nonhuman that cannot easily be terminated as an aspect of the nonhuman has become an aspect of the human person. Despite the ostensibly non-binding character of *kae bon* transactions in contemporary Thailand, it is thus no coincidence that the human parties involved frequently revisit a shrine should a misfortune arise after they have reciprocated with the promised offering, to make sure that they have not angered the nonhuman party involved. Doubt about whether the relationship between human and nonhuman engendered by making a wish and its subsequent granting is really terminable characterises *kae bon* transactions.

Thai dividuality

While neo-functionalist analyses treat the accumulation of instrumental power and wealth as self-explanatory ends in themselves, my survey of Thailand's mystic field indicates that the accumulation of mystic potency is an essential aspect of an animist conceptualisation of personhood that remains practically meaningful in everyday life, despite the growing hegemony of naturalism. This nonmodern conceptualisation of personhood enables the unproblematic translation of the mystic field's animist accumulation logic into the intertwined language games of Thai Buddhism and neoliberal capitalism.[18] As Århem notes,

> In this perspective, the entire ... ritual economy can be interpreted as a means of constituting complete persons in a metaphysical environment of graded personhood – a progressive construction not of the body (as in Amazonian cosmology) but of the differentiated "soul" as both the basis for the spiritual matrix of bodily constitution and the ritually acquired external body manifest as wealth and prosperity. (Århem 2016a: 24–25)

While I have emphasised the tendency of the mystic field's animist logic to usurp the rationalised logic of state-promoted Theravada Buddhism in

---

18   Davis 2016; Durrenberger and Tannenbaum 1989; Formoso 2016: 129; Tambiah 1970; Tannenbaum 1995; Terwiel 2012.

everyday life, various Buddhist elements have also become central features of the mystic field and Buddhicised field-specific language games. The *modus operandi* of the mystic field is, thus, not consciously mastered by social actors self-identifying as Thai Buddhist. The 'objective' intentions (completing dividual personhood) of a professional medium's devotees are therefore not necessarily congruent with the devotee's conscious explications (i.e., to enhance well-being and prosperity) (Bourdieu 1987: 106; McDaniel 2011: 14). A Thai Buddhist may stress insecurity reduction or wealth accumulation as the personal reasons for becoming the devotee (*luk sit*) of a professional medium, when the underlying implicit logic for following a spirit medium is the chance to enhance one's 'mystic potency' through the mutuality of being with potent nonhumans. This 'non-verbalisable' urge to complete dividual personhood through mutualities of being with nonhumans is an aspect of Thailand's animist social ontology and develops from its embodiment as an implicit aspect of contemporary Thai habitus.

While neo-functionalists may be inclined to explicate the practical logic of this form of relational being with reference to Lucien Hanks' discussion of patronage and its political institutionalisation in Thailand (Hanks 1962, 1975), I approach everyday imaginations of personhood via Sahlins' reformulation of Lévy-Bruhl's 'mystic participation' (Baumann 2016: 148, 2018, 2020a: 51; Sahlins 2013).

Thai dividuality rests on the animist paradigm that a person only becomes complete through the establishment of mutualities of being with nonhuman sources of potency. Lévy-Bruhl captured the logic of this paradigm with his 'law of participation', which he portrayed as the nonmodern antithesis of Aristotelian logic. 'The law of participation' states that something can be both itself and something else simultaneously and thus denies the imagined universality of the Aristotelian laws of non-contradiction and the excluded middle (Baumann 2018: 131, 2020a: 50–51, 2020b: 119–120; Lévy-Bruhl 1966: 61). The law of participation is basically about ways humans and nonhumans participate in each other's existence in order to form the conglomerates Latour called collectives. The rationale behind the acquisition of mystic capital is thus not simply the maximising logic of the modern *homo oeconomicus*, but rather the animist logic of accumulating lasting relations of mutuality with sources of potency. Thai patronage is one way this form of relational being is institutionalised. Thai conceptualisations of kinship and mediumship are others and, in rural Buriram, patronage, kinship and mediumship are not neatly distinguishable (Baumann forthcoming).

Drawing again on Sahlins' terminology, we may finally say that animist collectivity is generated through 'mystic bonds'. Mystic bonds ensure that 'what one person does or suffers also happens to others. Like the biblical sins of the father that descend on the sons, where being is mutual, then experience is more than individual' (Sahlins 2013: 2). In Thailand's lower Northeast, these mystic bonds are established through the agency of nonhumans such as 'ancestor spirits' (*phi banphaburut*) or 'masters of the place' (*jao thi*), which, as members of animist collectives, participate simultaneously in the being of multiple human persons. It poses no problem for the logical coherence of this language game when a nonhuman being is affective in two different human bodies or at multiple places simultaneously. It also constitutes no paradox when interlocutors state that they do not believe in the existence of these nonhumans (*mai chuea wa phi mi jing*), but nonetheless do everything to establish lasting relations of mutuality with them. When analysing local language games, we have to keep in mind that although Aristotelian logic is no longer alien to local lifeworlds, everyday language games are not necessarily bound by it (Baumann 2020b).

Mystic bonds between persons that result in 'sins' descending on kin are omnipresent in local lifeworlds, and local language games refer to taboo violations, therefore, as wronging a class of nonhumans (*phit phi*). The mutuality of being that unites human and nonhuman members of animist collectives through mystic bonds has the effect that if one human member of a collective violates a taboo, the nonhumans may not necessarily punish the culprit directly, but rather may punish any other member of the collective. This relational form of being informs larger social collectives like villages, neighbourhoods, houses and cult-lineages, and also the concept of the human person itself. Thai dividuality then represents the smallest manifestation of animist collectivity in everyday life. As Richard O'Connor observes, 'society is like a person and, as this metaphor works both ways, the person is a society and the human body is its littlest container' (O'Connor 2000: 45).

The dividual person in Buriram's folk etiology

In Buriram's localised folk etiologies, the graded components of the dividual person are frameable with more abstract concepts like 'body elements' (earth, water, wind and fire) or more figuratively with the soul-like concepts *khwan*, *winyan*, *jit* and *jettaphut* (Richardson Hanks 1960: 301). The theory of four body elements as well as the soul-like concept *jettaphut* are probably localisations of Brahmanical lore in vernacular language games (Textor 1973: 377, 590, 773–777). The term *winyan* is the Thai form of the Pali-derived notion of life force or Buddhist moral consciousness known as *viññāṇa*. *Viññāṇa* is specific to Buddhist metaphysics, where it is not strictly the single, spiritual, immaterial counterpart to the material body – as the modern Western soul is commonly conceived – but rather is the body's animating force (Thompson 1996: 2). *Khwan, winyan* and *jit* are the most commonly encountered soul-like concepts throughout Thailand. Local language games in the lower Northeast add the word *plueng* (*braling*)[19] as the Khmer equivalent of the Thai *khwan* to this multiplicity of soul-like entities animating the human body. Local interlocutors use the local concept *boriphut* in the same way *jettaphut* (Pali: *catubhūta*) is used in Cambodia. Ghostified as *jettaphut*, all four base elements that constitute the human body have the potential to haunt a dead person's descendants (Davis 2016: 74).

While the socio-cultural origin of the different soul-like concepts remains unclear, their imagination in everyday life strongly overlaps. The specific terminology used in rituals throughout the region mirrors localised traditions and language games. However, all local language games that reproduce animist collectivity as the social ontology of everyday life acknowledge that various soul-like entities are graded aspects of the living human person, and that these entities have the capacity to wander or escape from the body and hence need to be bound to the human body at constant intervals to maintain the person's well-being.[20] The most important social function of the mediumship rituals of Buriram's possession complex is, therefore, the reordering of the graded components that form all meaningful social collectives.

Before I address mediumship as the possession complex's most important form of ritualised human–nonhuman interaction, let me re-emphasise the broad spectrum of rituals that reproduce animist collectivity as the social ontology of everyday life. Many of these rituals are performed by Buddhist monks and therefore classified by local interlocutors as essentially Buddhist (on this point see also Visisya in this volume). The 'mending of luck ritual' (*phithi sador khror*), which has many localised variants, is one among many rituals that reproduce animist collectivity while being classified vernacularly

---

19   *Braling* is the usual Cambodian Khmer word for this soul-like entity.
20   Banks Findly 2016: 73–76; Davis 2016; Formoso 2016: 121–126; Tanabe 2002: 44–49; Terwiel 1978.

Figure 10.1. Villagers sharing mystic potency during a *sador khror* ritual performed by Buddhist monks. **Colour** p. 322.

as Buddhist. What characterises these ritual complexes is the idea that mystic potency is generated by a ritual expert's recitation of potent texts (*suat mon*). This mystic potency concretises in the expert's body but is also able to travel through bodies. The most common medium used to facilitate the travel of mystic potency between social bodies is a thread of white cotton (*sai sin*) that the ritual experts hold in their hands during the recitation of potent spells (*khatha*) and Pali chants. This line of white cotton thread physically connects the ritual expert with members of the worship group and infuses the bodies thus connected with the mystic potency generated by the expert. Folk etiology conceives the human body as a storing unit of mystic potency that is literally recharged during these rituals. The ritually created boundaries of a charged body are stronger, which makes it less likely that a graded soul-like component of the dividual human person leaves the collective or that a malevolent nonhuman is able to enter it. During these rituals of the possession complex, members of localised worship groups literally participate in each other's existence through the sharing of mystic potency that travels not only through the *sai sin* cotton thread, but also through the bodies connected by the thread. The recharging even extends to members of the worship community who are not physically present, as long as they are re-presented during the ritual. This form of re-presentation can take various forms (High 2009). During the rituals I have witnessed, this was typically accomplished by tying to the white cotton thread a piece of paper with the name of the physically absent person written on it.

Death and the localised possession complex

These rituals seek to strengthen the ritual boundaries of animist collectives through the generation of mystic potency and its accumulation in certain bodies. Other rituals of the local possession complex aim to re-establish a healthy equilibrium among the human and nonhuman components of an animist collective (Aulino 2019: 73).[21] This includes the *riak khwan* 'calling' of lost soul-like components and their reintegration into the dividual human person (*su khwan*) as well as the expulsion of entities that cause disorder in the configuration of human and nonhuman components (*lai phi*). The objective of other possession complex rituals, like mediumship rituals, is the opening of channels that allow direct communication between the living and the dead. While Buddhist monks may be actively engaged in these rituals, the most important ritual specialists are mediums. Throughout Southeast Asia, mediums are publicly recognised as vehicles for dead ancestors and other nonhuman beings. The many ritual functions they perform are comparable with those of the typical Amerindian and Siberian shaman. Since mediumship is the much more common form of ritualised human–nonhuman interaction in the region, Århem (2016b: 293) suggests subsuming shamanism as an aspect of the 'possession complex'.

Local language games in Thailand's lower Northeast hold that the nonhuman constituents of the dividual human person disintegrate upon death. While most of these nonhuman components turn into free-floating entities, some remain attached to the place of death – ideally the dead person's family compound – where they are emplaced through various rituals that bind potency into place.[22] While this essential idea of animist collectivity is framed in different ways, the fundamental notion of nonhuman components of dead persons becoming emplaced in or around the family compound is a common trope of the possession complex, used by interlocutors to explain how mutualities between the living and the dead are established and maintained through rituals associated with the complex. One of my key informants, a lay village medium in her nineties, explained this localised imagination of animist collectivity in the following way: 'If a person dies a "good death" (*tai di*), then the *winyan* will stay in the house. One of the four *boriphut* goes to the temple, one goes to the funeral grove (*pa cha*), one stays in the house and one is reborn.'[23]

The exact process of how these nonhuman components of formerly living persons become aspects of an unspecified class of ancestral spirits through

---

21 While Aulino also stresses the importance that the notion of equilibrium has for the imagination of the Thai social body, her anthropocentric perspective ignores the role nonhumans play in Thai imaginations of collectivity.
22 Banks Findly 2016: 74; Davis 2016; Formoso 2016; 123–124; Stonington 2020.
23 Conversation with *Nang Mor* Koiram, April 2012.

rituals remains largely unelaborated in local language games. Nevertheless, there is no question that these nonhuman components have agency and join an already established mutuality of being that links dead ancestors with their living descendants in emplaced collectives that are associated with a distinctive class of houses (stem houses).[24] The disintegration of the human person into its nonhuman components upon death also explains why these 'ancestors' are usually not personalised as a specific deceased relative, but rather addressed with the de-personalised kinship categories *pu-ya ta-yai* (maternal and paternal grandparents), *banphaburut* (ancestors), *thuat* (classificatory great-grandparent), or *pakam* (matrilineal ancestor/teacher spirit [*khru*] of the ancestors) in local language games.[25] During the mediumship rites I observed in rural Buriram, unspecified ancestral spirits were usually addressed as classificatory great-grandparents (*thuat*). In this context, the category also functions as a reference to an 'authoritative past that is used to justify contemporary practice' (Walker 2006 198). Sometimes, individual ancestors are recognised by their descendants and addressed with their personal names.

The hierarchical relationships that link the living with their dead ancestors is, according to Århem, the characteristic feature of the possession complex's localisation in mainland Southeast Asia, which he conceptualises along an active-passive continuum, where the most active pole is associated with recognised ritual specialists. Although these recognised ritual specialists have, according to Århem, ceased their travel to the 'spirit world', they are able to mobilise and channel tutelary spirits and other nonhuman familiars to cure patients afflicted by nonhuman malevolence or bring back lost or wandering nonhuman entities, to complete the specific configuration of a collective's graded components (Århem 2016b: 294). The possession complex's paradigmatic medium acts in a more passive but yet instrumental and controlled mode as a mouthpiece and messenger of a possessing entity. Socially recognised mediums are seen as 'instruments' of nonhumans and

---

24 Stem houses host the shrine for the matrilineal ancestors who are essential for the matrifocal organisation of village life in Buriram Province. I adopt the term 'stem house' from Irvine's discussion of matrilineal cult-lineages in Northern Thailand (Irvine 1982: 286).

25 I use 'ancestral spirits' here as it has become the commonly used anthropological jargon term to refer to this class of nonhuman beings. Walker and others working on these nonhumans in Northern Thailand have pointed out that this term is problematic as it is not clear whether the terms used in local language games refer to 'spirits that belonged to the ancestors' or 'spirits of the ancestors' (Walker 2006: 198).

have the capacity to convey messages from one world to the other (Keller 2002). In local understanding, mediums are given this capacity by their nonhuman familiars and can activate this capacity by their own volition.

However, the ritual office as medium is usually preceded by a liminal period of 'sickness' or 'craziness', in which the medium was herself afflicted by episodes of involuntary spirit possession. In an adorcistic process, which sometimes takes the form of an initiation into a mediumship lineage (*khrorp khru*), the future mediums manage to establish a mutuality of being with the afflicting entity, turning it into a nonhuman aspect of their person (Tanabe 2002: 60). Lewis (2003: viii) describes adorcism as a domestication process, which turns an afflicting nonhuman into an established aspect of the medium's configuration of graded components. The prominent place these adorcisms occupy in professional mediums' personal narratives of their career underlines domestication as the characteristic logic of harnessing mystic potency in the regional possession complex.

At the extreme passive pole of Århem's model of the Southeast Asian possession complex are the victims of spirit affliction and ghostly haunting. Thailand's mystical etiology perceives involuntary possession episodes, in which victims lose control over their situation, as a state of illness that needs to be treated. Involuntary possession can have various ascribed reasons, but local etiology usually emphasises an imbalance in the dividual's configuration of graded components, either caused by being soft-souled (*jit orn*), the absence of a soul-like component (*khwan hai*), or by a malevolent entity's forceful penetration of the collective's ritual frontiers (*phi sing*). However, Thailand's possession complex also acknowledges this involuntary affliction as a possible first step of the afflicted person's career as a spirit medium. All mediums I met reported liminal periods of craziness (*pen ba*) that made them realise the permanent presence of a nonhuman (*mi ong*), which distinguishes most mediums from a possessed dividual.

Another form of affliction found at the most passive pole of the possession complex that Århem ignored is a person's transformation into a 'witch-like being' (Baumann 2014, 2016, 2020c). Most important for the possession complex's conceptualisation of witchcraft is that a possession by a witch-like being may be cured by an excorcism (*lai phi*), whereas a person's transformation into a witch-like being (*pen porp/pen krasue*) is final and incurable. These transformations manifest all the characteristic inversions that anthropology associates with witchcraft-related phenomena, as someone engaging actively

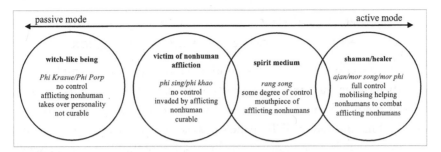

Figure 10.2. Graphic illustration of my re-conceptualisation of the Southeast Asian possession complex based on Århem (2016b: 294).

in magical practices becomes a passive victim of 'spirit affliction' after the breaking of a taboo associated with potent magical practices, like love magic (*sane ya faet*). Local conceptualisations of the witch-like beings produced by these taboo violations manifest the mutuality of being that relates humans and nonhumans in Thailand's possession complex most figuratively as the nonhuman leaves its human hosts during the night to search for impure food in order to stay alive (Baumann 2016, 2020c).[26] However, all stages between the possession complex's active and passive poles manifest mutualities of being between humans and nonhumans that characterise Thai conceptualisations of animist collectivity. These mutualities of being are either temporary or lasting, loathed or desired.

I summarise my reconceptualisation of the Southeast Asian possession outlined above in graphic form in Figure 10.2. Since the possession complex manifests as a continuum between active and passive poles, I draw on Århem's (2016b: 294) graphic conceptualisation, but alter it by introducing circles and by adding the fourth class of protagonists described above (witch-like beings). The short characterisation of these classes of protagonists indicates that the boundaries between the three classes on the right of the diagram are not fixed, as indicated by the intersecting circles, and that a movement from a more passive position of afflicted victim to the more active poles of spirit medium and shaman/healer describes the 'career' of many mediumistic ritual specialists in the region.

---

26 The witch-like *phi* known in Thailand are partly human and partly nonhuman. The nonhuman entity that has invaded the collective and turned the human person into a *phi* needs to feed off abjected bodily substances like faeces in order to retain its strength. The human body possessed would be the first to suffer if the *phi* cannot satisfy its characteristic craving for filth (Baumann 2016).

The growing professionalisation of village mediumship in Buriram's localised possession complex

In the final section of this chapter, I outline a typology of medium-like ritual experts active in Buriram's possession complex. My typology amalgamates various typologies of ritual expertise to capture the characteristics of this localised manifestation of Thailand's possession complex. Crucial for my typology are David Frankfurter's differentiation of 'local' and 'peripheral' community ritual experts (Frankfurter 2002: 162–163), Walter Irvine's discussion of 'traditional' and 'modern' Thai mediums (Irvine 1982: 337–344), and Pattana's distinction between rural and urban Thai mediumship (Pattana 1999, 2005, 2012). To this conceptual apparatus, I add my own ethnographic observations and propose the following inductively developed criteria to distinguish various types of mediums, namely: possessing entities and nonhuman familiars; immediate relationship between medium and client; social reach of the medium; medium's degree of professionality; category used by audiences to classify the gender of the medium; and, finally, the medium's age. Based on these criteria, I distinguish four types of medium-like ritual specialists active in Buriram's mystic field.[27] I refer to these four types of ritual experts as lineage mediums, village mediums, active devotees and professional mediums (see Figure 10.3).

Lineage mediums

I call the first type of ritual experts 'lineage mediums'. These non-professional mediums are the heads of *pakam*-cults, localised matrilineal ancestral cults that in my fieldwork area are essential for the reproduction of emplaced collectives and collective sentiments of belonging. *Pakam* is probably a Kui word.[28] Kui-speakers use the word *pakam* to designate a particular class of nonhuman beings (*khruba-ajan*) that reside in the leathern ropes made

---

27 There are, of course, many other ritual experts active in this localised variant of Thailand's mystic field. The four types I outline in this chapter are medium-like in the sense that their ritual expertise is linked to possession phenomena.
28 *Kui* is one of the socio-cultural categories used in a permanent exhibition in the *Lower Isan Cultural Centre* (*sun watthanatham isan tai*) in the provincial capital (Mueang Buriram) to name one of the four major 'ethnic groups' (*klum chatiphan*) of Buriram Province. 'The Kui' are known throughout the lower Northeast as mahouts and elephant catchers, although only a small minority actively ply these trades.

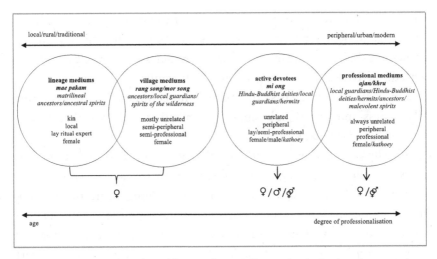

Figure 10.3. Types of medium-like ritual specialists active in Buriram's possession complex.

from buffalo hides that were formerly used to catch and domesticate wild elephants in the region (Wira 2544 [2001]: 87). Despite its probable Kui origin, most Khmer-speaking villagers conceive *pakam* as a Khmer word and use it to refer to a particular class of ancestral spirits, who are also imagined to have been elephant hunters.[29] Various utensils associated with elephant hunting like ropes, rifles and goads feature in the mediumship rituals of the *pakam* cult. The localised *pakam* cult in the sub-district (*tambon*) where I conducted fieldwork is a central aspect of cultural heritage of the Khmer-speaking population here.

Heads of the *pakam* cult are usually women who have inherited this ritual function from their mothers or matrilineal grandmothers. These cult leaders are known vernacularly as *mae pakam*. The core mediumship rituals of Buriram's possession complex are known as *len mae mot, len mor* or *len khru. Len mae mot* is the term used most commonly in the sub-district's local dialect. *Len* is a Thai word and is commonly translated as 'to play'. It is encountered in various contexts and as a prefix to leisure time activities like doing sports (*len kila*) or swimming (*len nam*), but is also used to emphasise the performative dimension of a practice like acting (*len lakhorn*). Combined

---

[29] The differentiation between 'ancestral spirits' and 'spirits that belonged to the ancestors' is especially complicated in the case of the *phi pakam*, which local interlocuters simultaneously identify as ancestor spirits (*phi banphaburut*) and teacher spirits of the ancestors (*khru khorng banphaburut*). However, interlocutors see no logical problem in the *phi pakam* being both.

with the Thai word for a female adept of mystic knowledge (*mae mot*), the vernacular designation *len mae mot* emphasises the performative dimension of mediumship including the gaiety and 'playfulness' commonly associated with the activities surrounding it, but also its significance in folk etiology.[30] It is important to emphasise that there is no contradiction between this 'playfulness' and the serious business of propitiating nonhumans in everyday village life (Irvine 1982: 307).

Usually, a village seer (*mor bun*) reveals that it is necessary to perform such a mediumship ritual. Village seers, who are mostly women, are visited when a sick person shows no signs of betterment after allopathic treatment. If the seer diagnoses the loss of a soul-like component, magical aggression, a taboo violation or the intrusion of a malevolent nonhuman, a *len mae mot* ritual has to be performed. As local community ritual experts, the *mae pakam* are part of the immediate neighbourhood; they only perform mediumship rites on behalf of their matrilineal cult-lineages and usually only within the confines of their own sub-district (*tambon*). During these rituals, the *mae pakam* act as lineage mediums and channel exclusively their own matrilineal ancestral 'spirits' (*phi pakam*). They are lay ritual experts and gain very little material benefit from their ritual expertise or their role as *mae pakam*. All *mae pakam* I talked to were over fifty years old and none took the role of *mae pakam* before she was forty. Although it is theoretically possible for men to assume this ritual office, no one I talked to remembered a case of a man acting as *mae pakam* and no masculine designation for this ritual office exists in local language games.[31] All *mae pakam* agreed that they were chosen by the *phi pakam* after the last medium in their matrilineal kinship group had died. The obvious sign of being chosen as a *mae pakam* is an inexplicable urge to dance (*ram*). Although most *mae pakam* were at first reluctant to assume the ritual office, the urge to dance soon became unbearable so that most finally accepted the

---

30 *Mamot* and *mamuat* are local Khmer equivalents that are also known in Cambodia. Irvine suggests that the fact that the word *mot* also means 'ant' in Thai is a residue of animal totems worshipped by the Mon (Irvine 1982: 293–294), but Sanguan considers this reading to be highly unlikely (Sanguan 1971: 220). However, Irvine's reference to 'ant spirits' in his discussion of the Northern Thai *phi mot* cults may not be totally misleading. I discuss the relevance that termite mounds – frequently misclassified as ant-hills – and the nonhumans associated with them have for the local possession complex in another publication (Baumann forthcoming). For the use of the term *mot* in Northern Thai spirit ritual settings see Fukuura's chapter in this book.

31 As *mae* means 'mother' in Thai, the designation automatically feminises this form of ritual expertise. I have never heard of a *phor* (father) *pakam*.

phi pakam's decision.[32] During a possession dance, the characteristic feature of the local possession cults, the *mae pakam* channel their elephant hunting ancestors. During the possession episodes, however, this form of ritualised dancing is subsumed under the performative category *len*.

Village mediums

As lineage mediums, the *mae pakam* are indispensable for the success of the *len mae mot* rituals, but they are not the main ritual officiant. The *mae pakam* are guided by a master medium (*rang song/mor song*), who leads the ritual performance and initiates the possession dance. The 'master medium' who presided over all mediumship rituals I observed in the sub-district is in her early seventies and belongs to the type of ritual expert I call 'village mediums'.[33] She is married, has three children and several grandchildren and worked her entire life as a farmer. After the birth of her third child, she became possessed for the first time. Although her family performed a propitiation ritual for the ancestors on her behalf, her condition did not improve afterwards. She felt like 'dying' after her initial possession experience and was frequently struck by blackouts. During this time, the nonhumans began to 'ask her whether they could stay with her' (*khao khor ma yu duay*). After three months of constant nonhuman presence within herself, she felt like she was going crazy (*pen ba*). However, she became used to the nonhuman presence and, after she accepted it, she felt much better. After villagers started to ask her for advice regarding their encounters with nonhumans, she finally became a village medium.

This story mirrors the classic tripartite structure of all *rites de passage* that is frequently described in the anthropological literature on mediumship and possession. The first recognition of nonhuman presence within the 'self' is usually treated as a period of sickness. Structurally, it signals the person's social seclusion and the entering of a liminal phase of transition, while the mediums themselves frequently describe this interstitial condition using idioms of 'craziness' or 'insanity'. The domestication of the nonhuman and

---

32 In another village, I encountered a case where a women refused to become a lineage medium although the *pakam* had obviously chosen her. This refusal caused a number of uncontrolled possession episodes of the women's youngest granddaughter, as the ancestral spirits were eagerly looking for a new host.
33 The following information was gathered during a conversation with this village medium in 2011.

its acceptance as meaningful aspects of the dividual self ends the liminal period and signifies social reintegration. As a medium, the formerly 'sick' person re-enters society endowed with a new social status.[34]

The village medium is not a *mae pakam*. As a village medium her repertoire of possessing nonhumans is much greater than the exclusive mutuality that connects the *mae pakam* with their matrilineal ancestors. Village mediums variously channel ancestors (*thuat*), masters of the land (*nia ta/jao thi*)[35] and undomesticated nonhumans associated with the wilderness outside the village's ritual frontiers ([*phi*] *charap*/[*phi*] *arak*).[36] While she shares no kinship ties with these possessing entities, they are all more or less emplaced, bearing references to the village and its immediate surroundings. The (*phi*) *charap* she also channels is one of the most dangerous nonhumans known in local language games. It is a chthonic nonhuman associated with salt licks and termite mounds (Baumann forthcoming). Although the village medium usually restricts her practice to the confines of her local district or *tambon*, her clientele is not exclusive or restricted to certain lineages or villages. She sometimes practises in different *tambon* and once performed a ritual in a different province. For her services, the village medium is paid a small sum in euphemised form as offerings to her tutelary spirit (*khru*). She is the *tambon*'s only one active village medium.

Village mediums fulfil the most important functions in village-based *len mae mot* rituals. They preside over the entire ritual complex, are responsible for the correct ritual set-up, including proper offerings and the construction of variously proportioned ritual structures (*bai si*). They are the first persons to be possessed and they invite the lineage ancestors to take possession of

---

34 Boddy 1989 1994; de Heusch 1971; Lewis 2003; Tanabe 2002; Turner 1967; van Gennep 1981.

35 *Nia ta* are the localised equivalents of the nonhuman beings known in Cambodian Khmer as *neak ta*. In his chapter here, Paul Christensen transcribes the term *neak ta* as *anak tā*. *Neak ta* are usually portrayed as 'guardian spirits' and are very similar to the beings known in Thai as *jao thi* (Baumann forthcoming). However, *neak ta* is a very inclusive category encompassing mythical and historical figures as well as anthropomorphised 'nature spirits' (Ebihara 2018: 175–178; Guillou 2017; Work 2019). In local language games, *nia ta* refers to a distinctive class of masters of the land, who are worshipped once a year during the *tham bun ban* rituals. The *nia ta* thus closely resemble the *phi pu ta* of Lao-speaking villages in the region.

36 I have bracketed the prefix *phi*, which in Thai language games indicates the uncanny character of a nonhuman being (Baumann 2016), as it is not used when local interlocutors speak Khmer, although the designation of the nonhuman beings (*charap* and *arak*) remains the same in both local dialects.

Figure 10.4. Village medium presiding over a *len mae mot* ritual. **Colour** p. 322.

the lineage mediums by initiating the possession dance. By initiating the possession dance, the village medium facilitates the possession of the lineage mediums, which is the necessary requirement for the reestablishment of the mutualities of being that connect the living with the dead in an emplaced animist collective. A collective possession dance is also the final stage of the *len mae mot* rituals in Buriram Province and it shows striking resemblances to Émile Durkheim's (1995: 228) description of ritual effervescence as the foundation of collective sentiments of belonging.

Active devotees

The third type of ritual specialists active in the local possession complex is not a recent but, according to my local interlocutors, nonetheless a growing phenomenon. I call this type 'active devotee'. Active devotees recognise the constant presence of a potent nonhuman being and have recently established a relation of mutuality with it. These nonhumans do not belong to the class of nonhumans encountered in everyday notions of dividuality or non-professional mediumship. Rather, they tend to be Hindu-Buddhist deities (*thep*), Brahmanical-type hermits (*ruesi*), honoured figures known from regional history (*jao*), child-like spirits (*kuman thorng*, see Megan Sinnott in this book) or figures from Buddhist mythology (*keji ajan*).[37] The recognition of this kind of nonhuman presence is also preceded by an initial period of 'sickness' or 'craziness', which is followed by the adorcistic stages of Thai mediumship described above. Most active devotees recognise a mutuality of being with more than one of these extraordinary and potent nonhumans, but regard one as their principal nonhuman familiar (*khru*).

---

37 It is interesting that I have not (yet) come across any medium in Buriram Province who channels the spirit of a Thai king. This in no way denies the possibility that such mediums exist. See Irene Stengs' chapter in this book.

Figure 10.5. Collective possession dance of active devotees of the Hindu goddess Mahakali. **Colour** p. 323.

Active devotees become medium-like when they channel their nonhuman familiars during larger and partly public *khrorp khru* rituals, which are simultaneously the most important ritual events for renewing the mutuality of being with the potent nonhumans classified as *khru*. *Khrorp khru* rituals are irregularly organised and are either internal affairs and part of 'paying homage to the teacher ritual' (*yok khru*) of a (professional) medium lineage (*sai khru*), or public events where different medium lineages meet to welcome new lineage members and pay respect to their human and nonhuman patrons within their lineage.[38] Collective possession dance (*ram*) in front of a statue depicting the nonhuman is the essential moment of the *khrorp khru* rituals in Buriram Province. It is simultaneously an offering to the nonhuman and a re-creation of the mutuality of *khru*–devotee being. The dances take place in front of altars on which images of the nonhumans are hierarchically ordered, with a Buddha statue on top. During these events, active devotees seem to compete for the nonhuman's, and possibly its followers', attention through a kind of look-alike contest.

Many active devotees I talked to have already started to convert the mystic potency created through their mutuality with a potent nonhuman, such as a Hindu deity, into economic capital by becoming professionally involved in the mystic field through fortune-telling and palm-reading (*du duang*). They become fully professional mediums, and securing their own sustenance is a nontrivial motivation when they agree to be possessed by their nonhuman familiars during the ritual services they provide for paying customers. Professionalisation also motivates them to engage actively in Buriram's mystic etiology and establish an entourage of followers (*luk sit*) who visit them frequently and acknowledge them and their possession entity as human and nonhuman patrons, respectively. All active devotees

---

38 Human and nonhuman patrons are both known as *khru*, which questions their analytic separability. The frequency and multiple meanings of the word *khru* in this context indicate the importance of what is usually termed 'patronage' for an understanding of Thai mediumship and animist collectivity.

are particularly interested in accumulating followers and mystic potency, which usually includes the observance of the Buddhist ethical precepts (*sin ha*), pilgrimages to potent Buddhist and non-Buddhist sites, participation in as many ritual events as possible and the collection of potent objects, which are displayed on their private altars.

I have met cis-gendered men and women who are active devotees in Buriram's possession complex, but trans women (*kathoey*) and gay men seem to be the majority. Older cis-gendered female semi-professional mediums in urban Buriram confirm that it is becoming more and more common that young transgender *kathoey* become active devotees and members in exclusive trans or gay mediumship lineages. Active devotees are young rather than old and come from both rural and urban backgrounds. Increasingly, *khrorp khru* rituals are organised in urban contexts, which opens them for participation by devotees without elaborate networks. Active devotees who started to convert their mystic capital into economic capital have usually no prior relationships to their clientele and increasingly rely on social media and public events like these to attract customers and convert them into followers. Being an active devotee is, for many practitioners, only a liminal phase on their way to becoming professional mediums and, finally, recognised healers.

Professional mediums

Professional mediums come into play whenever people afflicted by magical or nonhuman aggression have no access to the services of a lineage or village medium. The presence and growing number of professional mediums in rural Buriram indicates that lacking access to the services of these more traditional mediums is becoming a characteristic feature of contemporary rural lifeworlds. Professional mediums are about to replace the non-professional village mediums to become the most important ritual experts in Buriram's mystic etiology.

Professional mediums show many characteristics of urban mediumship as described by Pattana and, in Århem's typology, are closest to the shaman. Professional mediums manifest all characteristics of Frankfurter's 'peripheral ritual experts'. Most importantly, they are set off from the community and are beyond the reach of simple consultation. People have either to travel to consult them or book them to come to the village to perform a ritual. Professional mediums rarely perform in their natal villages, but rather are booked for rituals all over the province and in neighbouring provinces – especially Surin. Because of this 'symbolic outsiderness' they at times raise suspicion and are regarded as possible dangers. However, their outsider status contributes dialectically to their mystic potency (Frankfurter 2002: 162–163). One of the district's most well-known professional mediums is feared by most villagers, who suspect him[39] of practising malevolent magic (*len khorng*). However, they also approach him to purchase magical objects and, despite his youth, address him with the honorific title *ajan* and double it with *khru*, which both mean 'teacher'. This doubling of honorific titles is an indication of the degree of mystic potency he has accumulated in the eyes of his followers. Professional mediums in Buriram refer to themselves as *rang song* or *khru mot*. Their broad repertoires of possessing entities range from Hindu deities at one end of the spectrum to the dead ancestors of their clients at the other end. Which nonhuman they channel depends on the context of the ritual and on the affliction they are asked to treat. However, at a certain point during the ritual they will inevitably channel their *khru*, which also signifies their membership in a particular mediumship lineage. Although the most popular medium in the district talks about a mystical kinship bond that links him with his *khru*, whom he imagines as a Khmer warlord who fought for the Siamese against the Khmer in the 16th century, professional mediums are usually unrelated to the nonhumans they channel in the sense of biological descent.

One of the most important differences between older and younger mediums is, thus, their gender.[40] In contrast to the non-professional lineage and village mediums, as well as the semi-professional older urban mediums, who are all cis-gendered women, younger professional mediums are predominantly biologically male. While many show no obvious signs of transgenderism in everyday life and frequently self-identify as *gay*, villagers tend to classify them under the ambivalent gender category *kathoey*, which 'challenges Western notions of binary thinking and even the term "continuum" seems distorting and arbitrary' (Van Esterik 1999: 279) as *kathoey* are 'neither male nor female,

---

39 Although this medium is usually classified as *kathoey* by villagers, he does not look particularly feminine and would not pass as a trans woman in Western contexts. However, the classification of non-heteronormative genders and sexualities in Thailand, and especially in rural Thailand, is quite different from Western standards (Baumann et al. 2020: 120–122). While I know that he self-identifies as gay, I cannot say whether he self-identifies as *kathoey*.

40 For an extended discussion of the rise of gay and trans spirit mediums in Thailand and across the Buddhist societies of mainland Southeast Asia see Jackson and Baumann (2022).

Figure 10.6. An older female and a younger male medium, both channelling the spirit of a 19th-century heroine. **Colour** p. 323.

but both' (Morris 1994: 19). Although it cannot be elaborated here, I contend that this classification as well as the growing number of professional *kathoey* mediums hints at the intimate links between mystic potency and (gender) ambiguity in Thailand's mystic field (Baumann 2018, 2020b, forthcoming).

The most important characteristic of this new class of professional mediums is, nevertheless, that they make their living completely from their ritual services and their large following of disciples (*luk sit*), who provide for their human *khru* on a regular basis, but more importantly in a yearly ritual of paying homage to the 'nonhuman *khru*' (*phithi yok khru*). The extraordinarily expensive teak house recently built by a professional medium indicates that at least some people have succeeded in converting mystic into economic capital in Buriram's rapidly transforming mystic field.

Conclusion

Socio-economic transformations of rural lifeworlds, which manifest most dramatically in the permanent out-migration of women (Johnson 2018; Mills 1999), as well as the growing hegemony of a naturalist etiology in everyday village life, have led many families in the sub-district to abandon their *phi pakam* completely over the last 30 years (*thing pakam*).[41] Villagers mention various reasons for this abandonment of their ancestral spirits, but the most frequent explanation is the lack of interest of younger women in becoming actively involved in these 'superstitious' rituals and their favouring of purified imaginations of Buddhism. The same villagers express their regret for this decision and its irrevocability, as they recognise the continuing etiological relevance of mediumship in everyday life and the financial costs involved in obtaining professional replacements for non-professional lineage and village mediums.

---

41 *Thing* translates literally as 'to throw away', and *thing pakam* means 'to abandon the *pakam*'.

While the non-professional spirit mediums of the localised possession complex manifest a more 'traditional' form of mediumship than their professional counterparts, professional mediums rely on the same animist ontology and fill a void left by the discontinuation of lineage and village mediumship in rural communities. Even though many villages of the lower Northeast no longer have their own non-professional village mediums to channel ancestral nonhumans, the dead and other nonhumans have not ceased to interact with the villagers and dividual personhood remains a meaningful aspect of everyday life. It is the continuing meaningfulness of an animist social ontology and the mutuality of being that continues to link humans and nonhumans in emplaced collectives, which are essential for local etiologies and the reproduction of localised sentiments of belonging in the sub-region. To understand the mystic qualities of everyday life and social belonging in the lower Northeast, we have to look at Thailand's possession complex, its emplacement in specific localities and reconstruct the growing complexity of the mystic field in contemporary lifeworlds. The typology of ritual expertise outlined in this chapter may help to map the growing differentiation and professionalisation of Buriram's possession complex, without losing sight of the fact that these developments rely on the same animist language game and continue to reproduce animist collectivity as a meaningful social ontology of everyday life in the region.

References

Anderson, Benedict R. 1972. 'The Idea of Power in Javanese Culture', in Claire Holt (ed.), *Culture and Politics in Indonesia*. Ithaca and London: Cornell University Press: 1–69.

Århem, Kaj. 2016a. 'Southeast Asian Animism in Context', in Kaj Århem and Guido Sprenger (eds), *Animism in Southeast Asia*. New York: Routledge: 3–30.

———. 2016b. 'Southeast-Asian Animism: A Dialogue with Amerindian Perspectivism', in Kaj Århem and Guido Sprenger (eds), *Animism in Southeast Asia*. New York: Routledge: 279–301.

Aulino, Felicity. 2019. *Rituals of Care: Karmic Politics in an Aging Thailand*. Ithaca: Cornell University Press.

Banks Findly, Ellison. 2016. *Tending the Spirits: The Shamanic Experience in Northeastern Laos*. Bangkok: White Lotus Press.

Baumann, Benjamin. 2014. 'From Filth-Ghost to Khmer-Witch: Phi Krasue's Changing Cinematic Construction and its Symbolism', *Horror Studies*, 5(2): 183–196.

———. 2016. 'The Khmer Witch Project: Demonizing the Khmer by Khmerizing a Demon', in Peter J. Bräunlein and Andrea Lauser (eds), *Ghost Movies in Southeast Asia and Beyond: Narratives, Cultural Contexts, Audiences*. Leiden/Boston: Brill: 141–183.

———. 2017. 'Ghosts of Belonging. Searching for Khmerness in Rural Buriram', PhD dissertation, Southeast Asian Studies, Humboldt-Universität zu Berlin (microfiche).

———. 2018. 'Das animistische Kollektiv. Lévy-Bruhl, soziale Ontologien und die Gegenseitigkeit menschlicher und nicht-menschlicher Wesen in Thailand', *Zeitschrift für Kultur- und Kollektivwissenschaft*, 4(2): 129–166.

———. 2020a. 'Reconceptualizing the Cosmic Polity: The Tai Mueang as a Social Ontology', in Benjamin Baumann and Daniel Bultmann (eds), *Social Ontology, Socioculture and Inequality in the Global South*. New York: Routledge: 42–66.

———. 2020b. 'Same Same But Different: Eine romantische Dekonstruktion des paradoxografischen Trends in den Thai Studien', *polylog*, 43: 101–130.

———. 2020c. 'Thai Monsters. Phi Krasue: Inhuman Kiss (Mongkolsiri 2019)', in Simon Bacon (ed.), *Monsters: A Companion*. Oxford: Peter Lang: 101–109.

———. forthcoming. 'Masters of the Underground: Termite Mound Worship and the Mutuality of Chthonic and Human Beings in Thailand's Lower Northeast', in Holly High (ed.), *Stone Masters: Power Encounters in Mainland Southeast Asia*. Singapore: NUS Press.

Baumann, Benjamin, Danny Kretschmer, Johannes von Plato, Jona Pomerance, and Tim Rössig. 2020. 'Small Places Large Issues Revisited: Reflections on an Ethnographically Founded Vision of New Area Studies', *IQAS*, 51(3–4): 99–129.

Baumann, Benjamin, and Boike Rehbein. 2020. 'Rethinking the Social: Social Ontology,Ociocultures and Social Inequality', in Benjamin Baumann and Daniel Bultmann (eds), *Social Ontology, Sociocultures and Inequality in the Global South*. New York: Routledge: 6–22.

———. 2022. 'Was heißt eine Fremdsprache verstehen? Verstehen zwischen Sprachspielen, Lebensformen und sozialen Ontologien', in Cornelia Bading, Kerstin Kazzazi and Jeannine Wintzer (eds), *(Fremd-)Sprache und Qualitative Sozialforschung: Forschungsstrategien in interkulturellen Kontexten*. Heidelberg: Springer.

Bird-David, Nurit. 1999. '"Animism" Revisited: Personhood, Environment, and Relational Epistemology', *Current Anthropology*, 40(S1): 67–91.

Boddy, Janice. 1989. *Wombs and Alien Spirits*. Madison: University of Wisconsin Press.

———. 1994. 'Spirit Possession Revisited: Beyond Instrumentality', *Annual Reviews of Anthropology*, 23: 407–434.

Bourdieu, Pierre. 1983. 'Ökonomisches Kapital, kulturelles Kapital, soziales Kapital', in Reinhard Kreckel (ed.), *Soziale Ungleichheiten*. Göttingen: Schwartz: 183–198.

———. 1987. *Sozialer Sinn*. Frankfurt am Main: Suhrkamp.

Davis, Erik. 2016. *Deathpower: Buddhism's Ritual Imagination in Cambodia*. New York: Columbia University Press.

de Heusch, Luc. 1971. *Why Marry Her? Society and Symbolic Structures*, trans. Janet Lloyd. Cambridge: Cambridge University Press.

Descola, Philippe. 2013. *Beyond Nature and Culture*, trans. Janet Lloyd. Chicago and London: University of Chicago Press.

Dumont, Louis. 1986. *Essays on Individualism: Modern Ideology in Anthropological Perspective*. Chicago: University of Chicago Press.

Durkheim, Émile. 1995. *The Elementary Forms of the Religious Life*. New York: The Free Press.

Durrenberger, Paul and Nicola Tannenbaum. 1989. 'Continuities in Highland and Lowland Religions of Thailand', *Journal of the Siam Society*, 77(1): 83–90.

Ebihara, May. 2018. *Svay, A Khmer Village in Cambodia*. Ithaca and London: Cornell University Press.

Formoso, Bernard. 2016. 'Thai Buddhism as the Promoter of Spirit Cults', *South East Asia Research*, 24(1): 119–133.

Frankfurter, David. 2002. 'Dynamics of Ritual Expertise in Antiquity and Beyond: Towards a New Taxonomy of "Magicians"', in Paul Mirecki and Marvin Meyer (eds), *Magic and Ritual in the Ancient World*. Leiden, Bosten, Köln: Brill: 159–178.

Gray, Christine. 1986. 'Thailand: The Soteriological State in the 1970s', PhD dissertation, University of Chicago.

Guillou, Anne Yvonne. 2017. 'Potent Places and Animism in Southeast Asia', *The Asia Pacific Journal of Anthropology*, 18(5): 389–399.

Hanks, Lucien M. 1962. 'Merit and Power in the Thai Social Order', *American Anthropologist*, 64(6): 1247–1261.

Hanks, Lucien M. 1975. 'The Thai Social Order as Entourage and Circle', in William Skinner and Thomas Kirsch (eds), *Change and Persistence in Thai Society: Essays in Honor of Lauriston Sharp*. Ithaca and London: Cornell University Press: 197–218.

Harvey, Graham. 2005. *Animism: Respecting the Living World*. London: Wakefield Press.

High, Holly. 2009. 'The Spirit of Community: Puta Belief and Communal Sentiments in Southern Laos', in Andrew Walker (ed.), *Tai Lands and Thailand: Community and State in Southeast Asia*. Honolulu: University of Hawai'i Press: 89–112.

Holbraad, Martin, and Morten A. Pedersen. 2017. *The Ontological Turn: An Anthropological Exposition*. Cambridge: Cambridge University Press.

Ingold, Tim. 2006. 'Rethinking the Animate, Re-animating Thought', *Ethnos*, 71(1): 9–20.
Irvine, Walter. 1982. 'The Thai-Yuan Madman and the Modernising, Developing Thai Nation as Bounded Entities under Threat: A Study in the Replication of a Single Image', PhD dissertation, School of Oriental and African Studies, University of London.
———. 1984. 'Decline of Village Spirit Cults and Growth of Urban Spirit Mediumship: The Persistence of Spirit Beliefs, the Position of Women and Modernization', *Mankind*, 14(4): 315–324.
Jackson, Michael. 1996. 'Introduction: Phenomenology, Radical Empiricism, and Anthropological Critique', in Michael Jackson (ed.), *Things as They Are: New Directions in Phenomenological Anthropology*. Bloomington and Indianapolis: Indiana University Press: 1–50.
Jackson, Peter A. 1999a. 'The Enchanting Spirit of Thai Capitalism: The Cult of Luang Phor Khoon and the Postmodernisation of Thai Buddhism', *South East Asia Research*, 7(1): 5–60.
———. 1999b. 'Royal spirits, Chinese Gods, and Magic Monks: Thailand's Boom-Time Religions of Prosperity', *South East Asia Research*, 7(3): 245–320.
———. 2009. 'Markets, Media, and Magic: Thailand's Monarch as a 'Virtual Deity'', *Inter-Asia Cultural Studies*, 10(3): 361–380.
———. 2010. 'Virtual Divinity: A 21st-Century Discourse of Thai Royal Influence', in Søren Invarsson and Lotte Isager (eds), *Saying the Unsayable: Monarchy and Democracy in Thailand*. Copenhagen: NIAS Press: 29–61.
———. 2014. 'Ascendant Doctrine and Resurgent Magic in Capitalist Southeast Asia: Paradox and Polarisation as 21st Century Cultural Logic', DORISEA Working Paper Series, Volume 6. Göttingen: University of Göttingen.
———. 2020. 'Beyond Hybridity and Syncretism: Kala-Thesa Contextual Sensitivity and Power in Thai Religious and Gender Cultures', *Journal of Anthropology, Sirindhorn Anthropology Centre (JASAC)*, 3(1): 1–37.
Jackson, Peter A. and Benjamin Baumann (eds). 2022. *Deities and Divas: Queer Ritual Specialists in Myanmar, Thailand and Beyond*. Copenhagen: NIAS Press.
Johnson, Andrew Alan. 2012. 'Naming Chaos: Accident, Precariousness, and the Spirits of Wildness in Urban Thai Spirit Cults', *American Ethnologist*, 39(4): 766–778.
———. 2015. 'A Spirit Map of Bangkok: Spirit Shrines and the City in Thailand', *Journal for the Academic Study of Religion*, 28(3): 293–308.
———. 2016. 'Ghost Mothers: Kinship Relationships in Thai Spirit Cults', *Social Analysis*, 60(2): 82–96.
———. 2018. 'Deferral and Intimacy: Long-distance Romance and Thai Migrants Abroad', *Anthropological Quaterly*, 91(1): 307–324.

Keller, Mary. 2002. *The Hammer and the Flute: Women, Power, and Spirit Possession*. Baltimore and London: The Johns Hopkins University Press.

Ladwig, Patrice. 2011. 'Can Things Reach the Dead? The Ontological Status of Objects and the Study of Lao Buddhist Rituals for the Spirits of the Deceased' in Kirsten W. Endres and Andrea Lauser (eds), *Engaging the Spirit World: Popular Beliefs and Practices in Modern Southeast Asia*. New York: Berghahn Books: 19–42.

Larsson, Tomas. 2020. 'Royal Succession and the Politics of Religious Purification in Contemporary Thailand', *Journal of Contemporary Asia*. doi.org/10.1080/00472336.2020.1849775.

Latour, Bruno. 1993. *We Have Never Been Modern*, trans. Catherine Porter. Cambridge, Mass.: Harvard University Press.

Lévy-Bruhl, Lucien. 1966. *How Natives Think*. New York: Washington Square Press.

Lewis, Ioan M. 2003. *Ecstatic Religion: A Study of Shamanism and Spirit Possession*, third edition. London and New York: Routledge.

Lütterfelds, Wilhelm. 1995. 'Das "Durcheinander" der Sprachspiele. Wittgensteins Auflösung der Mentalismus-Alternative', in Eike von Savigny and Oliver Scholz (eds), *Wittgenstein über die Seele*. Frankfurt am Main: Suhrkamp: 107–120.

Marriott, McKim. 1976. 'Hindu Transactions: Diversity Without Dualism', in Bruce Kapferer (ed.), *Transaction and Meaning: Directions in the Anthropology of Exchange and Symbolic Behaviour*. Philadelphia: Institute for the Study of Human Issues: 109–142.

Mauss, Marcel. 2002. *The Gift: The Form And Reason For Exchange in Archaic Societies*. London and New York: Routledge.

McDaniel, Justin. 2011. *The Lovelorn Ghost and the Magical Monk: Practicing Buddhism in Modern Thailand*. New York: Columbia University Press.

Mills, Mary Beth. 1995. 'Attack of the Widow Ghosts: Gender, Death, and Modernity in Northeast Thailand', in Aihwa Ong and Michael G. Peletz (eds), *Bewitching Women, Pious Men: Gender and Body Politics in Southeast Asia*. Berkely: University of California Press: 244–273.

———. 1999. *Thai Women in the Global Labor Force: Consuming Desires, Contested Selves*. New Brunswick, NJ: Rutgers University Press.

———. 2001. 'Rural-urban Obfuscations: Thinking about Urban Anthropology and Labor Migration in Thailand', *City and Society*, 13(2): 177–182.

———. 2012. 'Thai Mobilities and Cultural Citizenship', *Critical Asian Studies*, 44(1): 85–112.

Morris, Rosalind C. 1994. 'Three Sexes and Four Sexualities', *positions: Asia Critique*, 2(1): 15–43.

———. 2000. *In the Place of Origins: Modernity and its Mediums in Northern Thailand*. Durham: Duke University Press.

———. 2002. 'Crises of the Modern in Northern Thailand: Ritual, Tradition, and the New Value of Pastness', in Shigeharu Tanabe and Charles Keyes (eds), *Cultural Crisis and Social Memory: Modernity and Identity in Thailand and Laos*. London: RoutledgeCurzon: 68–94.

O'Connor, Richard. 2000. 'Who are the Tai? A Discourse of Place, Activity and Person', in Yukio Hayashi and Guangyuan Yan (eds), *Dynamics of Ethnic Cultures Across National Boundaries in Southwestern China and Mainland Southeast Asia: Relations, Societies and Languages*. Chiang Mai: Ming Muang Printing House: 35–50.

Pattana Kitiarsa. 1999. 'You May Not Believe, But Never Offend the Spirits: Spirit-medium Cult Discourse and the Postmodernization of Thai Religion', PhD dissertation, Anthropology, University of Washington.

———. 2002. 'You May not Believe, but Never Offend the Spirits: Spirit-medium Cults and Popular Media in Modern Thailand', in Timothy J. Craig and Richard King (eds), *Global Goes Local: Popular Culture in Asia*. Vancouver: University of British Columbia Press: 160–176.

———. 2005. 'Beyond Syncretism: Hybridization of Popular Religion in Contemporary Thailand', *Journal of Southeast Asian Studies*, 36(3): 461–487.

———. 2012. *Mediums, Monks, and Amulets: Thai Popular Buddhism Today*. Chiang Mai: Silkworm Books.

Richardson Hanks, Jane. 1960. 'Reflections on the Ontology of Rice', in Stanley Diamond (ed.), *Culture in History: Essays in Honor of Paul Radin*. New York: Columbia University Press: 298–301.

Sahlins, Marshall. 2013. *What Kinship is – and is Not*. London: University of Chicago Press.

———. 2014. 'On the Ontological Scheme of Beyond Nature and Culture', *HAU: Journal of Ethnographic Theory*, 4(1): 281–290.

Sanguan Chotisukharat. 1971. 'Supernatural Beliefs and Practices in Chiengmai', *Journal of the Siam Society*, 59(1): 211–233.

Sprenger, Guido. 2016a. 'Dimensions of Animism in Southeast Asia', in Kaj Århem and Guido Sprenger (eds), *Animism in Southeast Asia*. London and New York: Routledge: 31–51.

———. 2016b. 'Graded Personhood: Human and Non-Human Actors in the Southeast Asian Uplands', in Kaj Århem and Guido Sprenger (eds), *Animism in Southeast Asia*. London and New York: Routledge: 73–90

———. 2018. 'Buddhism and Coffee: The Transformation of Locality and Non-Human Personhood in Southern Laos', *SOJOURN*, 33(2): 265–290.

Stengel, Friedmann. 2013. 'Lebensgeister – Nervensaft. Cartesianer, Mediziner, Spiritisten', in Monika Neugebauer-Wölk, Renko Geffarth and Markus Meumann (eds), *Aufklärung und Esoterik: Wege in die Moderne*. Berlin/Boston: De Gruyter: 340–368.

Stonington, Scott. 2020. 'Karma Masters: The Ethical Wound, Hauntological Choreography, and Complex Personhood in Thailand', *American Anthropologist*, 122(4): 759–770.

Strathern, Marilyn. 1988. *The Gender of the Gift: Problems with Women and Problems with Society in Melanesia*. Berkeley: University of California Press.

Tambiah, Stanley. 1970. *Buddhism and the Spirit Cults in North-east Thailand*. Cambridge: Cambridge University Press.

Tanabe, Shigeharu. 2002. 'The Person in Transformation: Body, Mind and Cultural Appropriation', in *Cultural Crisis and Social Memory: Modernity and Identity in Thailand and Laos*, Charles Keyes and Shigeharu Tanabe (eds), London: RoutledgeCurzon: 43–67.

Tannenbaum, Nicola. 1995. *Who can Compete Against the World? Power-protection and Buddhism in Shan Worldview*. Ann Arbor: Association for Asian Studies.

Terwiel, Barend. 1978. 'The Tais and their Belief in Khwans: Towards Establishing an Aspect of "Proto-Tai" Culture', *South East Asian Review*, 3: 1–16.

———. 1980. *The Tai of Assam and Ancient Tai Ritual: Volume I: Life-cycle Ceremonies*. Gaya: Centre for Southeast Asian Studies.

———. 2012. *Monks and Magic: Revisiting a Classic Study of Religious Ceremonies in Thailand*. Copenhagen: NIAS Press.

Textor, Robert. 1973. *Roster of the Gods: An Ethnography of the Supernatural in a Thai Village*. New Haven: Human Relations Area Files.

Thompson, Ashley. 1996. *The Calling of the Souls: A Study of the Khmer Ritual Hau Bralin*. Clayton, Australia: Centre for Southeast Asian Studies, Monash University.

Tidawan Vaseenon. 2006. 'Dynamics of Kinship and the Uncertainties of Life: Spirit Cults and Healing Management in Northern Thailand', PhD dissertation, Social Sciences, Brunel University.

Turner, Victor. 1967. *The Forest of Symbols: Aspects of Ndembu Ritual*. Ithaca and London: Cornell University Press.

Tylor, Edward B. 1871. *Primitive Culture: Researches into the Development of Mythology, Philosophy, Religion, Art, and Custom*. London: John Murray.

Van Esterik, Penny. 1999. 'Repositioning Gender, Sexuality, and Power in Thai Studies', in Peter Jackson and Nerida Cook (eds), *Genders and Sexualities in Modern Thailand*. Chiang Mai: Silkworm Books: 275–289.

van Gennep, Arnold. 1981. *Les rites de passage*. Paris: Édition A. et J. Picard.

Verter, Bradford. 2003. 'Spiritual Capital: Theorizing Religion with Bourdieu against Bourdieu', *Sociological Theory*, 21(2): 150–174.

Viveiros de Castro, Eduardo. 1998. 'Cosmological Deixis and Ameridian Perspectivism', *The Journal of the Royal Anthropological Institute*, 4(3): 469–488.

———. 2004. 'The Transformation of Objects into Subjects in Amerindian Ontologies', *Common Knowledge*, 10(3): 463–484.

———. 2014. *Cannibal Metaphysics: For a Post-Structural Anthropology*. Minneapolis: Univocal Publishing.

Walker, Andrew. 2006. 'Matrilineal Spirits, Descent and Territorial Power in Northern Thailand', *The Australian Journal of Anthropology*, 17(2): 196–215.

White, Erick. 2014. 'Possession, Professional Spirit Mediums, and the Religious Field of Late-Twentieth Century Thailand', PhD dissertation, Anthropology, Cornell University.

Willerslev, Rane. 2012. Laughing at the Spirits in North Siberia: Is Animism Being Taken too Seriously? *e-flux journal*, 36. www.e-flux.com/journal/36/61261/laughing-at-the-spirits-in-north-siberia-is-animism-being-taken-too-seriously/ (accessed 19 November 2021).

———. 2013. 'Taking Animism Seriously, but Perhaps Not Too Seriously?' *Religion and Society: Advances in Research*, 4: 41–57.

Winch, Peter. 1992. *Versuchen zu verstehen*. Frankfurt am Main: Suhrkamp Verlag.

Wira Thansanon. 2001 [2544]. *Sapthanukrom Chang*. Bangkok: Chulalongkorn University.

Wittgenstein, Ludwig. 1967. 'Bemerkungen über Frazers The Golden Bough', *Synthese*, 17: 233–253.

———. 1982. *Philosophische Untersuchungen*. Frankfurt am Main: Suhrkamp.

Work, Courtney. 2019. 'Chthonic Sovereigns?, "Neak Ta" in a Cambodian Village', *The Asia Pacific Journal of Anthropology*, 20(1): 74–95.

AFTERWORD

Rethinking Vernacular Religion across Mainland Southeast Asia

Erick White

The various contributions to *Spirit Possession in Buddhist Southeast Asia* advance a welcome and long overdue rethinking of spirit possession, divination, esotericism and the pursuit of well-being and worldly auspiciousness in mainland Southeast Asian religiosity. Many of the foundational scholarly frames, models and assumptions that continue to inform the study of these phenomena were first advanced in the 1960s and 1970s by a pioneering generation of anthropologists, historians and religious studies scholars grappling with questions surrounding orthodoxy, orthopraxy, religious diversity, syncretism and the localisation of world-historical religions such as Buddhism (see, for example: Spiro 1970; Tambiah 1970; Kirsch 1977; Terwiel 1979). New studies and new interpretations, however, increasingly challenge these early analyses and arguments, in part because much has changed since those seminal studies were first undertaken. Three changes are particularly noteworthy.

First, our empirical data is now much more fulsome, detailed, nuanced and wide-ranging. Despite one rare exception (Spiro 1967), the earliest scholarly investigations of spirit mediums, astrologers, fortune-tellers, lay esoteric masters, hermits, 'magicians', and other non-monastic religious virtuosos in mainland Buddhist Southeast Asia tended to be brief, unelaborated and impressionistic. Other than a few short articles (Textor 1962; Gandour and Gandour 1976), most discussions were included within books primarily focused on Buddhist monks, the Sangha, and the orthodox beliefs and practices stereotypically associated with them. A few supplemental pages on non-monastic religious actors were typically designed to cursorily sketch the outer margins of a religious world conceptualised as definitively centred on normative, establishment Buddhist actors and institutions. Occasionally, more sustained and extensive studies of non-monastic religious virtuosos (most typically spirit mediums) appeared, but these discussions were almost inevitably embedded within, and subordinated to, more general analyses of spirit cults, animism and popular religion, or in the context of discussions about how these phenomena relate to Buddhism (Nash 1966; Kirsch 1967; Tambiah 1970). Even among the generation of scholars working in the 1980s, studies that centred squarely on non-monastic religious virtuosos and their ritual practices typically were limited to the occasional stand-alone journal article (Schober 1980; Ferguson and Mendelson 1981; Wijeyewardene 1981; Irvine 1984; Jackson 1988). While a few books along these lines were published (Wales 1983; Heinze 1988; Brac de la Perrière 1989), growing interest in them by young scholars typically did not extend beyond dissertations (Irvine 1982; Yagi 1988; Cook 1989; Schober 1989). Even then, many of these dissertations included only a chapter or two that examined these 'marginal' religious figures as elements of larger religious developments and phenomenon.

Consequently, before the 1990s, few published studies focused solely on the non-monastic religious figures that take centre stage in the current volume, and studies that did exist were neither sustained nor in-depth. Scholars therefore had a very limited empirical understanding of the social, performative, literary, material and aesthetic cultures these figures inhabited. Beginning in the 1990s, however, this situation changed dramatically. A wealth of studies of all sorts of non-monastic religious virtuosos and their ritual lives began to appear. These religious actors increasingly become central objects of sustained study in their own right, with numerous articles, book chapters, multi-authored edited volumes and monographs about them regularly appearing in print (in addition to an increasing number of dissertations).[1] As a consequence, scholars began to accumulate an increasingly nuanced empirical understanding of these figures, as well as where and how they were located in the larger religious landscapes of mainland Southeast Asia. The authors and studies in this volume belong to this tradition of research, and they provide valuable contributions to its documentary and interpretive agenda.

---

1 It would be impossible to list all the relevant articles and book chapters. A select list of edited volumes and monographs about Buddhist Southeast Asia must include: Morris 2000; Cohen 2001; Pattana 2012; Brac de la Perriere, Rozenberg and Turner 2014; Rozenberg 2015; Guelden 2018a; Guelden 2018b; Patton 2018. Scholarship on such figures in Vietnam has also grown rapidly; key edited volumes and monographs include: Taylor 2004; Fjelstad and Hien 2006; Norton 2009; Phuong 2009; Endres 2011.

Second, the religious landscape of mainland Southeast Asia has changed markedly since those early seminal studies of the 1960s and 1970s, most of which either centred on rural, peasant society or took that world as their principal point of reference. Urbanisation has exploded. Nationalism and state-building have intensified. Capitalist development has remade agricultural economies and fostered globalised industry and trade. Civil society has grown in scale and complexity. Mass culture industries have reimagined and reorganised arts, leisure and entertainment. Transportation and communication infrastructures have expanded and multiplied, intensifying mobility and information flows both within nations and across the region. Globalisation and transnationalism have reframed and transformed cultural identity, transmission and exchange. Just as Buddhist monks, monasteries and the Sangha have been challenged and remade in light of all these developments, so have non-monastic religious actors and the rituals and beliefs surrounding them. All of the chapters in this volume explore these non-monastic religious virtuosos in light of some mix of these the major social, economic and cultural transformations that have social, economic and cultural transformations which have defined the past forty years, further clarifying their impact and significance.

And third, the theories concepts and analytic models that shape studies of spirit cults, spirit possession and worldly auspiciousness in mainland Southeast Asia also have changed dramatically since those seminal studies. Functionalism, structural-functionalism, symbolic hermeneutics and Weberian historicism have been challenged, even supplanted, by postmodernism, poststructuralism and postcolonialism, as well as a wealth of narrower analytic models and theories. Ideas about animism, syncretism, adaptation and systemic homeostasis, for example, have been displaced by concepts such as haunting, hybridity, assemblage and contingent cultural formations. To varying degrees, each of the chapters in this volume grapples with the challenge of which theoretical frames, conceptual tools and analytic models to employ in order to best understand mainland Southeast Asian non-monastic religious virtuosos – and their ritual, social and cosmological worlds – at the beginning of the 21st century.

In their introduction, Peter Jackson and Bénédicte Brac de la Perrière astutely summarise many of the important and novel contributions collectively advanced by the volume's authors by synthetically reading their chapters in dialogue with each other. The editors have also usefully foregrounded a series of new interpretive frames – the manifold dynamics of modern enchantment, an indigenous regional spirit possession complex, and the significance of spirit possession within the logic of the religious field – which in combination can fruitfully reorient and advance future scholarship about these non-monastic religious virtuosos and the religious worlds that have developed around them. Rather than simply reiterate their valuable observations, I instead focus the remainder of this afterword on several general challenges raised collectively by all of the contributions to this volume, including the introduction.[2] I will pose a series of conundrums that need to be addressed and questions that need to be answered if the full analytic, conceptual and theoretical promise of this volume's contributions is to be realised. Creatively looking ahead in this manner, however, ironically will often require returning to and rethinking anew foundational assumptions, frames and debates posed by the seminal pioneering scholarship of the 1960s and 1970s.

Vernacular religion as an amorphous object of study

Once one steps beyond the official, normative boundaries of orthodox world historical religions, precisely defining and demarcating one's religious object of study often becomes increasingly challenging. Without the benefit of an ecclesiastical establishment that normatively and definitively standardises official beliefs, practices, symbols and roles, defining, demarcating and labelling religious phenomena can become difficult. This is especially the case in that amorphous domain – of non-sectarian, vernacular religiosity primarily concerned with mundane, worldly well-being and auspiciousness – which is the primary focus of the case studies in this volume. In the past, the concept of 'spirit cults' often served as a shorthand for indexing this amorphous domain of religious life, although I would argue that, over time, this association has proved less useful and even distorting. As a result, scholars can find it

---

[2] Various authors in this volume also raise, albeit obliquely, more general theoretical and conceptual questions circulating among contemporary scholars of religion. How useful is the concept of 'belief' in making sense of everyday religious ideology and motivation? Will foregrounding embodiment fruitfully reorient our understanding of everyday religious practice? Will the conceptual deployment of ontology rather than religion or worldview insightfully revise our understanding of everyday religious difference and epistemology? While many of the chapters in this volume point toward the importance of answering these questions, few directly engage these debates. Therefore, I do not explore these particular intellectual challenges in my remaining comments.

difficult to precisely define and bound what sort of religious phenomena they are examining. Actors, activities and ideas fluidly mix and crystallise.

Sometimes the authors in this volume focus on a specific social group or community of practice. 'Spirit cults' is a frequently employed label, but other 'cultic' variations also appear ('Buddhist cults', 'prosperity cults' and 'devotional cults') as well as the language of movements and subcultures. At other times, the authors focus on the type of ritual activity under study, and so we encounter discussions of spirit possession, divination, sorcery, the veneration of teachers and 'magic', as well as more generic labels such as spirit worship, spirit rituals or spirit practices. Another strategy is to focus on the types of religious actors under study. From this angle, we hear about spirit mediums, astrologers, fortune-tellers, esoteric masters, brahmins and devotees, with the occasional recourse to a more generic language of spiritual practitioners, religious virtuosos or ritual specialists. Much of this language – except for the most generic – to one degree or another indexes religious phenomena that are generally treated as marginal, stigmatised or nonnormative from the perspective of official or ecclesiastical religious authorities (even if they are simultaneously quite common and even mainstream in their social prominence and cultural prevalence).

Discovering a cacophony of religiously 'subaltern' groups, activities and actors who are trafficking in the provision of worldly well-being and auspiciousness is not surprising in the study of Southeast Asian religion. Nor is it surprising to discover the degree to which they ambiguously overlap and interact with each other (as well as normative figures such as monks, institutions such as the Sangha, or rituals such as merit-making). Nonetheless, these various groups, activities and actors are not analogous with each other, nor are they necessarily related to one another analytically or even empirically. One can have spirit cults without spirit possession, and vice versa. Prosperity cults may or may not traffic in sorcery or divination. Astrologers, spirit mediums, esoteric masters, brahmins and sorcerers trade in subtly different forms of religious expertise and knowledge. While normative religious authorities might imagine all of this to be a shared stew of apotropaic, supernatural or superstitious foolishness, this non-sectarian domain of vernacular religiosity is in fact populated by relatively distinct lineages of belief, practice and authority.

Capturing this diversity descriptively and interpretively is important since these distinct groups, activities and actors have been transformed somewhat differently by the dynamics of modern enchantment in colonial and postcolonial Southeast Asia. Their unique historical and sociocultural trajectories in an age of modern enchantment, neoliberal occult economies and mass-mediated technological spectacles are therefore worth untangling and documenting with greater precision precisely so that they then can be more carefully compared across the 20th and 21st centuries. This more careful, comparative delineation of social and historical transformation is only hinted at in the individual chapters of this volume and the more general analytic framing of the introduction. More robust pursuit of this project in future studies, however, will deliver many benefits, as it conceptually delineates the great variety of actors, activities and forms of knowledge at play when religiously seeking worldly well-being and auspiciousness in mainland Southeast Asia.

Multiplying 'spirits' and pantheon politics

When referring to the nonhuman, 'supernatural' agents that interact with humans, including religious virtuosos, it is typical to reach for the English term 'spirit'. The authors in this volume do the same, even as they consistently reveal the substantive and classificatory diversity hidden behind that overly general term in Southeast Asia. We hear about the *nats, weikza, bilu, naga,* and *bobogyi* that populate the Burmese spiritual pantheon. We are introduced to the *pārami, anak tā,* and *keji ajan* of the Cambodian spiritual pantheon. The various *phi, jao* and *thep* who in combination constitute the Thai spiritual pantheon are explored in a variety of regional settings. And the diverse aristocratic and administrative figures that occupy the various ranks of Vietnam's Four Palaces are explored in great detail. These are just select, narrow windows into the much larger and more complicated richness of the religious pantheons present in Myanmar, Thailand, Cambodia and Vietnam.

It is not just the dizzying diversity of specific personas occupying Southeast Asian spiritual pantheons that stands out in these chapters, but the diversity of the types of 'spirits' within each pantheon. Indeed, a single generic type of 'spirit' within a pantheon can contain incredible diversity nestled within it. In Thailand, for example, it is not uncommon to discover that a single local community identifies not only *phi*, but many of its subtypes, such as *phi banphaburut* (ancestral spirits), *phi arak* (guardian spirits), *phi khru* (lineage teacher spirits), and *phi rai* (wrathful spirits). The same hidden diversity can lie within the types of spirits classified as *jao* and *thep*. Moreover, one frequently discovers specific religious personas fluidly shifting location across categorical types of 'spirits', as well as disagreements among Thais about where specific figures reside within the moral hierarchy of accessibility and efficacy that defines the pantheon (as Sinnott usefully notes in her chapter in the case of Thai child spirits and angel dolls).

These diverse, multiplying and fluid labels and logics have made it difficult to place a single country's religious pantheons – much less the entire peninsula's – into comparative perspective. Differences between the religious pantheons of the majority Theravada Buddhist nations of Southeast Asia and the religious pantheon of Vietnam have long been recognised. Even among Theravada Buddhist Myanmar, Thailand, Cambodia and Laos, it is actually unclear to what degree one can claim they share a similar religious pantheon, either substantively, structurally or in terms of its classificatory logic. It is even unclear whether there is in fact a shared national religious pantheon within each country, which might more accurately be described as containing a collection of regional or even local pantheons. In many ways, this seemingly deep-seated diversity of religious pantheons at the regional, national and sub-national levels mirrors the diverse landscapes of religious virtuosos and religious expertise on display across mainland Southeast Asia. All of this makes it challenging to compare non-sectarian religious beliefs and activities concerned with worldly well-being and auspiciousness, since the religious virtuosos, ritual practices, forms of knowledge and religious pantheons involved are not easily analogous or comparable.

Moreover, in addition to the need to re-examine the similarities, differences and comparability of pantheons across the religious landscapes of mainland Southeast Asia, future studies also need to rethink the structural logics and dynamics underlying religious pantheons and their pantheon politics. Many past scholarly approaches seem to have presumed that religious pantheons in mainland Southeast Asia were relatively cohesive, singular, enduring and bounded orders of moral hierarchy within which historically new waves of sacred personas are deposited and sorted like civilisational sedimentary layers. As Sorrentino's chapter suggests, however, the messiness arising from the combination of a generic and combinatory logic of classification with an excess of substantively rich and variable hagiographies might be better appreciated through new analytic models of what a pantheon is and how it works. These new models conceptualise pantheons as historically shifting assemblages and cultural templates that prioritise and enable incoherence, contradiction, analogism and articulation between and across multiple spatial scales of cosmology, history and social authority. From this perspective, normative religious pantheons look instead like the formal end products of discrete historical projects of cultural hierarchy, social mobilisation and political domestication that are advanced by particular social interests in specific times and places. The presence of multiplicity and contestation between pantheons, therefore, should be taken for granted as axiomatic. In these models, moreover, questions of autonomy, autochthony, dominance and governance should be repositioned as central concerns in the everyday, apotropaic search for auspiciousness and well-being through ritual communication and transactions with a diverse field of nonhuman 'spirits' and those virtuosos with expertise in communicating and interacting with them. In their respective chapters both Sorrentino and Baumann explicitly highlight this perspective in different ways, but this analytic focus is indirectly suggested by many other contributors to this volume as well.

Spirit possession – Central, historically changing and plural

Spirit possession is a persistent topic of discussion in the volume's case studies, and frequently the primary object of study. The introduction advances a persuasive argument that spirit possession is a prominent, if consistently neglected, thread within the religious history and landscape of mainland Southeast Asia, as well as a uniquely prominent facilitator of the efflorescence of enchantment currently underway in the region. Jackson and Brac de la Perrière's genealogy of a long-standing, indigenous Southeast Asian spirit possession complex – one that is unique to the region yet also undergoing dramatic reformulation in light of postcolonial modern enchantment – offers a novel and illuminating reframing of contemporary Southeast Asian religious dynamics that productively displaces world historical religions from the centre of analysis.

The contributors to this volume document in detail the prominence of these religious dynamics since the colonial era and before, as well as the dramatic transformation of spirit possession in the postcolonial present. In the process, they foreground a series of dynamics across the region that are worthy of systematic exploration. How widespread is the growing status, prestige and authority of spirit mediums? How sustained is the growing appeal, meaning and value of experiences of trance and possession? How common are strategies to increase the ritual autonomy, formal organisation and social mobilisation of spirit mediums? How typical is it for spirit mediums to resist, and even deny, religious subordination vis-à-vis mainstream, normative religious authorities such as Buddhist monks, either publicly or privately? How frequently are possession-like oneiric experiences of trance, dreaming and visions hiding behind and within otherwise normative mainstream practices of Buddhist devotion and piety? To what degree have modernist drives to purify religion of the magical and the superstitious displaced the psychological needs and social functions served by an indigenous spirit possession complex, in the process relocating them within the new interstices of mainland Southeast Asia's changing religious landscape?

The chapters by Baumann, Fukuura, Visisya, Stengs, Christensen, Brac de la Perrière and Foxeus all make clear that the relationships between spirit mediums and Buddhist monks, the Sangha, devotional piety and merit-making is much more intimate, entangled and contested in mainland Southeast Asia than seminal analyses argued. They also make clear that these relations can exist in complicated, sometimes contradictory, configurations along a spectrum between subordination and domination, collaboration and opposition, dependence and autonomy. Documenting and mapping these various possibilities remain future challenges, as does analytically explaining which social and cultural factors facilitate certain possibilities rather than others. Reinterpreting the meaning, significance and value of spirit mediums and spirit possession within mainland Southeast Asian religion, especially Southeast Asian Buddhism, however, also demands that scholars rethink most seminal models of religious diversity and the religious field in Southeast Asia. Long-standing assumptions about religious syncretism, encompassment, domestication, hierarchy and dominance, which privilege the perspective, position and authority of world historical religions like Buddhism, are clearly tested by what contemporary spirit mediums are saying, doing and imagining. Whether these assumptions need to be revised only in the contemporary or post-colonial moment, or whether this rethinking should reach back into the colonial and pre-colonial eras of Southeast Asia, is a further question that needs to be explored. While the rhetoric of contemporary crisis and rupture is appealing, the editors astutely note that it may be a misleading consequence of our limited and fragmentary historical data on non-sectarian, vernacular forms of religiosity, including spirit possession, in earlier historical periods.

Another important issue raised by Baumann, Fukuura, Brac de la Perrière and Foxeus is that multiple forms or modalities of spirit possession are at play in mainland Southeast Asia. Each of these scholars explicitly makes the interactions and contestation between different modalities of spirit possession central to their argument. While Jackson and Brac de la Perrière foreground a distinction between exorcism and adorcism within spirit possession praxis, the case studies by Baumann, Fukuura, Brac de la Perrière, Foxeus and others point to plural forms of adorcism within the cultures of spirit possession in Buddhist mainland Southeast Asia. Elsewhere I have suggested the existence within contemporary Thailand of at least five discrete traditions or modalities of spirit possession: malevolent possession requiring exorcism; possession as playful entertainment; possession by guardian spirits; possession by empowered teachers; and possession by virtuous deities (White 2014).[3] The more important general point is that plural forms of spirit possession exist within the mainland Southeast Asian religious landscape, and, as the case studies in this volume suggest, this plurality may be expanding and diversifying even further. This raises the question of whether there exists a singular Southeast Asian possession complex, either in the past or the present. It also raises questions about the adequacy of seminal scholarly models of religious diversity and the religious field in Southeast Asia. Almost uniformly, early models of religious pluralism and syncretism posited the existence of a singular, generic 'spirit possession' located within the strata of 'animism', and against which world historical religious traditions like Buddhism were starkly counterpoised (White 2017). Rigorous empirical work like that presented in this volume implicitly questions the usefulness of this model in the present, and it is easy to suspect that it fails to capture the complexity of the past as well. Regardless, empirically documenting and comparatively analysing this diversity of spirit possessions and the various ways they interact with each other as well as with the wider field of religious actors, ideologies and practices – including but not limited to world historical religions like

---

[3] The first modality of spirit possession conforms with exorcism and the latter three with adorcism, while the second seems to fall outside either of these options. Possession by guardian spirits, empowered teachers and virtuous deities in Thailand can be further distinguished along other dimensions, such as whether they are treated as occasional or primary occupations, as well as whether they are primarily framed and organised according to Buddhist, Hindu or Chinese religious cosmological and symbolic schemas.

Buddhism – is another project worth pursuing if we are to better understand the character and dynamics of securing well-being and auspiciousness within non-sectarian, vernacular Southeast Asian religiosity.

And finally, the contributions to this volume ironically raise questions about just how central spirit possession is to the general social dynamics and processes of modern enchantment. Spirit mediums and spirit possession have an oversized presence in the various substantive case studies of this volume. In their introduction, moreover, Jackson and Brac de la Perrière prioritise and even privilege the significance of spirit possession in shaping and driving modern enchantment in contemporary Southeast Asia. While they also discuss divination, magic and ritual in general, spirit mediums and spirit possession consistently rise to the forefront of their discussion and analysis. This is true in terms of making sense of the past and the deep history of Southeast Asian religiosity vis-à-vis the recovery and reconstruction of an enduring indigenous Southeast Asia possession complex, and in terms of making sense of those recent religious transformations unleashed by neoliberal occult economies, technologically mediated spectacle and ritualised devotional excess. The importance and salience of spirit mediums and performances of spirit possession in these dynamics is undeniable. At the same time, the deeper structural processes Jackson and Brac de la Perrière identify as unleashed within non-sectarian, vernacular religiosity by urbanism, capitalism and new media – ritual specialisation, professionalisation, heritagisation, de/relocalisation and religious upgrading – arguably are not uniquely characteristic of spirit mediums and spirit possession. These processes are remaking not only spirit mediums and spirit possession. They are also remaking the lives of other non-monastic religious virtuosos as well as the Sangha, new Buddhist movements, non-sectarian devotional cults and a wide assortment of religious groups, institutions and activities. The roiling power of modern enchantment, from this perspective, is sweeping across the whole Southeast Asian religious field, from its centres to its margins, from its dominant voices to its subordinate counterclaims. Documenting and analysing its uneven consequences and idiosyncratic trajectories, consequently, is also an important task of future research.

Reimagining mainstream Buddhism

It is very easy for official, ecclesiastical authorities and voices, particularly those influenced by modernist reform ideologies, to treat spirit cults and spirit mediums, astrologers and fortune-tellers, esoteric masters and brahmins as marginal and irrelevant to normative Buddhist piety. This common stance has been repeated over and over during the Southeast Asian colonial and postcolonial eras. As the various chapters here make clear, however, these excluded groups and religious virtuosos frequently tend not to perceive themselves as marginal to or outside of mainstream normative Buddhist belief and practice. They patronise and financially support Buddhist monks and the Sangha. They endorse and cultivate Buddhist values and ethics. They make merit and devote themselves to protecting the Buddhist dispensation. They are ordained as monks, worship Buddhist relics and go on pilgrimages to Buddhist sacred sites. They organise robe offerings, finance and participate in Buddhist ceremonies, renovate pagodas and offer daily alms. Even more dramatically, they often reach for conventional Buddhist ideologies and idioms as they explain the meaning and value of their acts of possession, divination, healing, blessing and sacralisation. They use a mainstream Buddhist language of karma, merit, moral perfections (*paramita / barami*) and piety to explain their entanglements with 'supernatural' figures within the religious pantheon as well as their potency, auspiciousness and efficacy. They employ Buddhist-inflected moral idioms of gratitude, indebtedness, care and protection in order to make sense of the reciprocal social relations they cultivate with both nonhuman sacred beings within the religious pantheon and their human clients and devotees.

All of this strongly suggests that the character and boundaries of mainstream Buddhism in mainland Southeast Asia are much more diverse and contested on the ground than official, ecclesiastical institutions and voices would lead one to believe. It suggests that the efflorescence of non-sectarian vernacular techniques and virtuosos centred on worldly well-being and auspiciousness that has arisen in the wake of modern enchantment is remaking the meaning and practice of Buddhist piety in mainland Southeast Asia. Given the dominance of Buddhist ideologies, symbolism and praxis within the religious fields of Buddhist-majority communities in mainland Southeast Asia, non-monastic religious actors often reach for Buddhist idioms and frames to legitimate their claims to status, prestige and authority. Similarly, new and 'more Buddicised' forms and hybrid articulations of spirit possession, divination, esotericism, blessing and sacralisation are distinguished from and counterpoised against more 'traditional' modalities, which practitioners of the newer forms posit as non-Buddhist. In the process, the horizons and complexity of what counts as mainstream Buddhism shift and expand.

These claims challenge the logics of inclusion and exclusion that inform not only official and ecclesiastical Buddhist authorities, but also the structural logics that underlie seminal scholarly models of religious diversity and syncretism in mainland Southeast Asia. Experiences, practices, cosmologies, ontologies and actors that previous scholars had situated outside Buddhism and within alternative religious 'traditions' – such as animism, spirit cults, Brahmanism, Hinduism or Chinese popular religion – are now repositioned inside the expansive, messy umbrella of mainstream (if not official) Buddhism. And while this inclusion is often resisted by established ecclesiastic authorities, it is driven by the actions of monks, non-monastic religious virtuosos and laypersons. Modern enchantment and its transformative effects upon the non-sectarian religious practices and techniques of worldly well-being and auspiciousness, therefore, has destabilised and thrown into contestation the character, boundaries and dynamics of what constitutes mainstream Buddhism across the region. At a minimum, they make it clear that our scholarly models of everyday vernacular Southeast Asian Buddhism need to recognise that Buddhism is deeply concerned with securing worldly well-being and auspiciousness, as more and more scholars demand we recognise (McDaniel 2011).

Given the demographic, cultural and institutional pre-eminence of Buddhism in mainland Southeast Asia, most religious virtuosos or authorities – whether monastic or non-monastic – want to claim that they represent and endorse in some fashion mainstream Buddhist values, beliefs or goals. As the case studies in this volume reveal, the salient question instead for many Southeast Asian religious practitioners is how idiosyncratically they situate themselves within mainstream Buddhist discourses and idioms, since novel and innovative reworkings of conventional Buddhist values, techniques and goals can serve as an occupational advantage within a robust field of religious competitors. From this perspective, neoliberal occult economies, mass-mediated technologies of spectacle and the embodied rituals of devotion underlying modern enchantment are fuelling the production of multiple subcultural visions of mainstream Buddhist piety and practice within Southeast Asia. And as the case studies of this volume suggest, in order to accurately map the structure, dynamics and character of this ferment within mainstream Buddhism, we need to expand our scholarly horizons beyond such stereotypically conventional objects of study as monks, monasteries and meditation.

Plurality and periphery

Two final insights offered up by this volume are the analytic importance of diversity and the margins if we are to adequately understand the religious worlds of mainland Southeast Asia, both in the past and in the present. These are long-standing scholarly tropes in the study of Southeast Asia, but a renewed commitment to them yields additional, unexpected interpretive gains. In order to better understand modern enchantment and religious efflorescence in mainland Southeast Asia, we need to account more comprehensively for the plurality of religious actors, practices, ideologies and experiences at play across the religious landscape. This is especially true when dealing with the non-sectarian domain of religious expertise and techniques focused on securing worldly well-being and auspiciousness. In combination, the contributions to this volume foreground the plurality of non-monastic religious virtuosos claiming such expertise and knowledge. They highlight the plural pantheons of sacred beings communicated with in the pursuit of well-being and auspiciousness. They document the diverse range of ritual techniques deployed to secure assistance from those sacred entities and potencies. They point suggestively to the plural forms of spirit possession, as well as divination and esotericism, circulating beyond the formal reach of ecclesiastical institutions and authorities. In all of these ways, the rich tapestry and interpretive complexity of everyday, vernacular, contemporary Southeast Asian religiosity is more clearly revealed. As are the multiple ways that this diversity and complexity is a product of the underlying social and cultural processes fueling modern enchantment in Southeast Asia.

In their introduction, Jackson and Brac de la Perrière argue that reconsidering the religious field from the perspective of spirit possession yields numerous interpretive benefits, especially when placed in a comparative regional perspective. This is a position I fully agree with and have endorsed (White 2014). The view from the stigmatised, 'subaltern' margins is illuminating not only for how it reorients and reconceptualises our approach to the total religious field of Southeast Asian societies and cultures, but also for its reimagining of the world-historical religions that typically dominate and define national religious fields. In much of mainland Southeast Asia, that means rethinking the character, boundaries and dynamics of Theravada Buddhism as a localised, vernacular religious reality.

I would push Jackson and Brac de la Perrière's argument even further. We should take the plural reality of the margins very seriously and reconsider the religious fields and Buddhisms of mainland Southeast Asia from the perspective of the various stigmatised, 'subaltern' margins. Thus, in addition to that of spirit mediums, we should add the perspectives of astrologers and fortune-tellers, brahmins and esoteric masters, magicians and sorcerers. To the degree that each of these types of non-monastic virtuoso has come to constitute a relatively distinct, autonomous and self-organised occupational subculture of religious authority, status and identity around itself, the contemporary landscape of Southeast Asian religion offers up a multitude of differing marginal perspectives on both the total religious field and those establishment religious hegemonies which centrally define and shape it. In fact, careful investigation actually reveals multiple subcultures of possession, divination, esotericism and 'magic' at play within Southeast Asian religious landscapes, subtly in contested conversation not only with each other but also with the dominant institutional religions and ecclesiastical authorities that shape Southeast Asian religious fields.

The various case studies in this volume have opened up windows into this dialogue between centre and margin, this struggle between hegemonic and subaltern voices, this rhetorical play between similarity and difference in and through which religious prestige, status and legitimacy are asserted. More sustained and expansive comparative explorations of these frequently overlooked perspectives from the peripheries will help to better reveal exactly just how central and dominant the hegemonic frames of Buddhism and other world religions are in defining and structuring the religious fields of contemporary Southeast Asia. These studies will also allow us to document and analyse more precisely the rich fabric of collaboration and contestation, agreement and contradiction that characterises contemporary Southeast Asian religiosity. We can hope, therefore, that this volume will inspire others to carry out detailed social histories and ethnographic cases studies of those spirit mediums, astrologers, esoteric masters and other religious virtuosos in mainland Southeast Asia flourishing both beyond the formal reach of establishment ecclesiastical institutions and in an ever more enchanted world.

References

Brac de la Perrière, Bénédicte. 1989. *Les rituels des possession en Birmanie: Du culte d'Etat aux cérémonies privées*. Paris: ADPF (Recherches sur les civilisations).

Brac de la Perrière, Bénédicte, Guillaume Rozenberg, and Alicia Turner (eds). 2014. *Champions of Buddhism: Weikza Cults in Contemporary Burma*. Honolulu: University of Hawai'i Press.

Cohen, Erik. 2001. *The Chinese Vegetarian Festival in Phuket: Religion, Ethnicity and Tourism on a Southern Thai Island*. Bangkok: White Lotus Press.

Cook, Nerida. 1989. 'Astrology in Thailand: The Future and Recollection of the Past', PhD dissertation, Australian National University.

Endres, Kristen. 2011. *Performing the Divine: Mediums, Markets and Modernity in Urban Vietnam*. Copenhagen: NIAS Press.

Ferguson, John P. and E. Michael Mendelson. 1981. 'Masters of the Buddhist Occult: The Burmese Weikzas', in John P. Ferguson (ed.), *Essays on Burma: Contributions to Asian Studies 16*. Leiden: E. J. Brill: 62–80.

Fjelstad, Karen and Nguyen Thi Hien (eds). 2006. *Possessed by the Spirit: Mediumship in Contemporary Vietnamese Communities*. Ithaca: Cornell Southeast Asia Program.

Gandour, Mary Jane and Jackson T. Gandour. 1976. 'A Glance at Shamanism in Southern Thailand', *Journal of the Siam Society*, 64(1): 97–103.

Guelden, Marlane. 2018a. *Dancing for the Gods: The Nora Bird Dance of Southern Thailand*. Bangkok: White Lotus Press.

———. 2018b. *Dancing for the Gods: The Endangered Spirit Lineage of Nora Dance in Southern Thailand*. Bangkok: White Lotus Press.

Heinze, Ruth-Inge. 1988. *Trance and Healing in Southeast Asia*. Bangkok: White Lotus Press.

Irvine, Walter. 1982. 'The Thai-Yuan "Madman" and the "Modernising, Developing Thai Nation" as Bounded Entities Under Threat: A Study in the Replication of a Single Image', PhD dissertation, School of Oriental and African Studies, University of London.

———. 1984. 'Decline of Village Spirit Cults and Growth of Urban Spirit Mediumship: The Persistence of Spirit Beliefs, the Position of Women, and Modernization', *Mankind*, 14(4): 315–324.

Jackson, Peter A. 1988. 'The Hupphaasawan Movement: Millenarian Buddhism among the Thai Political Elite', *Sojourn*, 3(2): 134–170.

Kirsch, A. Thomas. 1967. 'Phu Thai Religious Syncretism: A Case Study of Thai Religion and Society', PhD dissertation, Harvard University.

———. 1977. 'Complexity in the Thai Religious System: An Interpretation', *Journal of Asian Studies*, 36(2): 241–266.

McDaniel, Justin. 2011. *The Lovelorn Ghost and the Magical Monk: Practicing Buddhism in Modern Thailand*. New York: Columbia University Press.

Morris, Rosalind. 2000. *In the Place of Origins: Modernity and its Mediums in Northern Thailand*. Durham and London: Duke University Press.

Nash, June. 1966. 'Living with *Nats*: An Analysis of Animism in Burman Village Social Relations', in Manning Nash (ed.), *Anthropological Studies in Theravada Buddhism*. New Haven: Yale University Press: 117–136.

Norton, Barley. 2009. *Songs for the Spirit: Music and Mediums in Vietnam*. Champaign: University of Illinois Press.

Pattana Kitiarsa. 2012. *Mediums, Monks and Amulets: Thai Popular Buddhism Today*. Chiang Mai: Silkworm Books.

Patton, Thomas. 2018. *The Buddha's Wizards: Magic, Protection, and Healing in Burmese Buddhism*. New York: Columbia University Press.

Phuong, Pham Quynh. 2009. *Hero and Deity: Tran Hung Dao and the Resurgence of Popular Religion in Vietnam*. Chiang Mai: Mekong Press.

Rozenberg, Guillaume. 2015. *The Immortals: Faces of the Incredible in Buddhist Burma*. Honolulu: University of Hawai'i Press.

Schober, Juliane. 1980. 'On Burmese Horoscopes', *South East Asian Review*, 5(1): 43–56.

———. 1989. 'Paths to Enlightenment: Theravada Buddhism in Upper Burma', PhD dissertation, University of Illinois at Urbana-Champaign.

Spiro, Melford E. 1967. *Burmese Supernaturalism: A Study in the Explanation and Reduction of Suffering*. Englewood Cliffs: Prentice-Hall.

———. 1970. *Buddhism and Society: A Great Tradition and its Burmese Vicissitudes*. Berkeley: University of California Press.

Tambiah, Stanley J. 1970. *Buddhism and the Spirit Cults in North-east Thailand*. Cambridge: Cambridge University Press.

Taylor, Philip. 2004. *Goddess on the Rise: Pilgrimage and Popular Religion in Vietnam*. Honolulu: University of Hawai'i Press.

Terwiel, B.J. 1979. *Monks and Magic: An Analysis of Religious Ceremonies in Central Thailand*. London: Curzon Press.

Textor, Robert. 1962. 'A Statistical Method for the Study of Shamanism: A Case Study from Field Work in Thailand', *Human Organization*, 21(1): 56–60.

Wales, H.G. Quaritch. 1983. *Divination in Thailand: The Hopes and Fears of a Southeast Asian People*. London: Curzon Press.

White, Erick D. 2014. 'Possession, Professional Spirit Mediums, and the Religious Fields of Late-Twentieth Century Thailand', PhD dissertation, Cornell University.

———. 2017. 'Rethinking Anthropological Models of Spirit Possession and Theravada Buddhism', *Religion and Society: Advances in Research*, 8: 189–202.

Wijeyewardene, Gehan. 1981. 'Scrubbing Surf: Medium and Deity in Chiang Mai', *Mankind*, 13(1): 1–14.

Yagi, Shusuke. 1988. 'Samnak Puu Sawan: Rise and Oppression of a New Religious Movement in Thailand', PhD dissertation, University of Washington.

COLOUR ILLUSTRATIONS

Figure 0.1. Central section of a spirit medium's domestic shrine in Yangon picturing part of the Burmese spirit possession pantheon in the hierarchical Buddhist cosmogony. Text p. 29.

Figure 0.2. Bangkok shrine displaying images of a Thai spirit medium's personal pantheon of Indian and Chinese deities. Top row left to right: Ganesh, Guan Yin with many arms, Guan Yin, Durga, Durga. Bottom row left to right: Shiva, Krishna, Ardhanarishvara (hermaphroditic deity of Shiva with Parvati), Durga and two Chinese deities. Text p. 29

311

Figure 1.1. A spirit medium embodying the Third Great Mandarin of the Palace of Water performing an offering of incense to the altar of the Four Palaces. Text p. 49.

Figure 1.2. Extract from a video featuring special effects when the spirit medium embodies the Third Prince of the Palace of Water. Text p. 50.

Figure 1.3. A woodprint featuring spirits of the Four Palaces. Text p. 54

Figure 1.4. The Seventh Prince in the 2013 calendar based on Trịnh Yên's portrait series. Text p. 55.

SPIRIT POSSESSION IN BUDDHIST SOUTHEAST ASIA

Figure 2.1. Devotees presenting a glass of milk to Mya Nan Nwe in her green attire. November 2010. Text p. 72.

Photo: Bénédicte Brac de la Perrière.

Figure 2.2. The original tiny image of Mya Nan Nwe holding *naga* heads and with a *naga* headdress, in a *naga*-decorated glass box full of donated banknotes. Text p. 77.

Photo: Bénédicte Brac de la Perrière.

COLOUR ILLUSTRATIONS

Figure 2.3. Mya Nan Nwe palanquins departing on the Yangon River. January 2016. Text p. 87.

Figure 2.4. Performing the arch in the *thaik-naga* dance in front of the palanquin and with a *shan Osi* orchestra. A group of devotees helps to control the possessed woman. January 2020. Text p. 89.

SPIRIT POSSESSION IN BUDDHIST SOUTHEAST ASIA

Figure 3.1. The Third Lunar Month Festival at *Ajan* Tho's *wat*. Monks and laypeople are performing a clockwise procession around the offerings before the spirit possession trance begins. Text p. 101.

Figure 3.2. *Ong* Tue stone Buddha image at Wat Sila-at. Text p. 109.

COLOUR ILLUSTRATIONS

Figure 4.1. The Three Kings Ritual in April 2004: the statues became an altar for spirit mediumship rituals. Text p. 128.

Figure 4.2. Three Kings ritual in April 2004: all the participants joined together to dance at the final stage of the ritual. Text p. 129.

Figure 4.3. Medium A possessed by Shiva at his annual ritual in March 2018. Text p. 135.

COLOUR ILLUSTRATIONS

Figure 4.4. Khuang Sing ritual in June 2018. Text p. 139.

Figure 6.1. The seven children from the treasure trove, Nagayon Pagoda, 2017. Text p. 174.

SPIRIT POSSESSION IN BUDDHIST SOUTHEAST ASIA

Figure 7.1. Cover of the Thai divination book *Patithin Nueng Roi Pi* (100-year calendar). Text p. 200.

Figure 7.2. Cover of the astrological book *Tamra Phrommachat*, published in Thai. Text p. 200.

COLOUR ILLUSTRATIONS

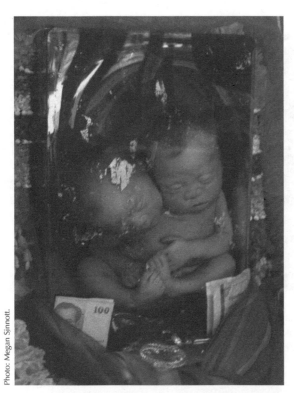

Figure 8.1. *Kuman thorng* Shrine at Wat Pradu, Samut Songkhram Province, July 2011. Text p. 220.

Figure 8.2:. Sign advertising special *kuman thorng* figurines available for adoption at Wat Phai Ngoen, Bangkok, June 2012. Text p. 226.

Figure 10.1. Villagers' mutual sharing of mystic potency during a *sador khror* ritual performed by Buddhist monks in rural Buriram, with all participants connected by the *sai sin* cotton thread wrapped around their heads. Text p. 269.

Figure 10.4. The village medium presiding over a *len mae mot* ritual in my fieldwork area. Text p. 279.

COLOUR ILLUSTRATIONS

Figure 10.5. Collective possession dance of active devotees of the Hindu goddess Mahakali during a *khrorp khru* ritual in urban Buriram. Text p. 280.

Figure 10.6. An older female semi-professional and a younger professional medium, classified as *kathoey* by the audience, both channeling *Ya* Mo (*Thao* Suranari), an early nineteenth century heroine from Khorat, during a *yok khru* ritual in urban Buriram. Text p. 283.

Index

f=figure; n=footnote; **bold**=extended discussion or key reference

abbots **107–108**, 112, 114, 116, 234, 248n
abortion 222, 225
active devotees 274, 275f, **279–281**, 323f; *see also mi ong, nat shi*
adorcism 9, 272, 279, **301**
ahlu (Burma: religious donation, meritorious deed) **81–82**, 90; *see also dāna; hlu dan*
ajan (Thailand: teacher) 275f, 282; *see also khru, khruba-ajan, khu, khuba*
ALA-LC Cambodian transliteration system xii, 114n
Amarapura 171, 183
Amay Shway Nabay **88**, **89**, 92, 93
Amazonian ontologies **15–16**; *see also* animism
aṃboe (Cambodia: black magic) 153
amnāca (Cambodia: worldly power) 158
amnat (Thailand: power) 201f, 263-264
amulets 9, 23, 31, 82, **82n**, 216, 218, 224-225, 228, 233
anak dhaṃ (Cambodia: 'big people') 154, 157
anak tā (Cambodia: spirits) 145n3, 147, 147n7, 148, 149, 150, 152, 157, 297; *see also neak ta, nia ta*
analogism 15, 16, 259, 260; *see also* animism
ancestral spirits 125, 215, 270, 271, **271n25**, 275f, 277n32, 282, 297; abandonment 283; ~ versus 'spirits that belonged for ancestors' **275n**; *see also phi*
Anderson, Benedict R. 263
aneikaza (Burma: Buddha's sermon) 89-90

Ang, Chouléan 153
animism 11, 73, 103, 111, 294, 301, 304; hierarchical ~ 15, 16, 254, 260; *see also* analogism, Descola, new animism
Animism in Southeast Asia (Århem and Sprenger eds 2016) 15
animist collectives 74, 255, **256–257**, 259, 264, 267–273 *passim*, 279, 280n
anthropology: material turn 233-234; ontological turn 255
Apinya Feungfusakul 242
apiya jaṃnya (Cambodia: superstition) 197n4
arahan (Thailand: enlightened Buddhist saints) 241
arak (phi arak) (Thailand: undomesticated nonhumans) 278, 278n36; *see also phi*
Århem, Kaj 9, 15, 27, 254, **259–260**, **265**, 270; model of Southeast Asian possession complex **271–273**, 281
Arimetteyya (or Metteyya) 170
Aristotelian logic 266, 267
Ashin Nyāna (monk) 181n22
Assembly of Spirit Mediums in Lan Na 120, **130–131**; driving force (Medium A) **130–131**, **134–137**; full title 130; Medium B **132**, 134, **137–141**; opponents and proponents **131**; significance **133–134**; stagnation **131–132**, 136
astro-numerology 194, 198; *see also* numerology
Astrological Association of Thailand 198
astrology 34, 36, 193, 194, **197**, **199**, 238, 306; Hindu teachings 197n3; Thai ~ 206

325

ateit kan (Burmese: karma from previous lives) 181
Aulino, Felicity 270n21; 'competing Buddhist practices' concept 261n
Aung Hsu Shin (Uncle Hsu) 76n11, **79–81, 85–86n23**, 95
Aung San Suu Kyi 70n3, 166
Austin, J.L. 24n
autochthony of Southeast Asian spirit cults 31, 42, 43, 52, 53, **57–63**, 65
Ayutthaya period (1351–1767) 199n6

Bà Chúa Xứ (Vietnam: Southern Lady of Realm) 64
Ba Mười Sau Gia (Vietnam: Thirty-Six Chariots) **58**, 60
Bà Vũ (Vietnam: Lady Vũ) 62
Baby Ae shrine (Bangkok) **219–220**; *see also* child spirit practices
bai si (Thailand: ritual banana-leaf structure decorated with flowers) 127, 249 245, 278; *see also pāy sī*
Baird, Ian G. 233n2
Bakhtin, Mikhail 249
bản địa (Vietnam: indigenous religion) 42; *see also* autochthony
bản sắc dân tộc (Vietnam: cultural identity) 65
Bangkok 26, 27n, 100, 120, 121, 124, 134, 135, 136, 166, 167, 198, 225, 232, 240, 248n, 260; spirit medium's personal pantheon 29f, 311f
barami (Thailand: charisma) 99, 108, 245, 263, 303; *see also* charisma
Baumann, Benjamin ix, 5, 9, 16, **25–26**, 35, 73, **253–291**, 299, 300, 301; active devotees 26–27; fieldwork 253n1; new language game **253–258**; publications **284–285**, 287
ben Phật (Vietnam: Buddha's side) 42
ben thanh (Vietnam: spirits' side) 42
Bennett, Caroline 147
Bertrand, Didier 150, 151, 201

bhāsā khmoc (Cambodia: language of spirits) 152, 153; *see also phasa thep*
bhjum pinda (Cambodia: ceremony of dead) 148n8
Bilmes, Jack 241n13
bilu (Burma: voracious ogres) 69, 84, 170, 297
black magic 153, 188, 189n, 201, 212n, 220, 228; *see also len khorng*, magic
bleng purāṇa (Cambodia: ancient music) 156
Bo Min Gaung (Bho Min Khaung) 164, 166, 170–178 *passim*, 183; *see also* Bomingaung
bobogyi (Burma: respected grandfathers) 31, 69, **75–76**, 82, 82n, 83, 84, 297; *see also* Botataung Bobogyi
bodaw (Burma: cult leader) 84, 85, 86, 93, 94, 178
body elements theory (Thailand) **267–268**
boek bai si ritual (Thailand) 245
Bokenkamp, Stephen R. **59**
Bomingaung 73, 85n22, 91; *see also* Bo Min Gaung (Bho Min Khaung)
Boran (Cambodia: old, antique, historical authenticity) 235, 237
boriphut (Thailand: soul concept) 268, 270
Botataung Bobogyi (grandfatherly spiritual figure) 31; *see also bobogyi*
Botataung dockyard community 89, 91, 92
Botataung *medaw* (Botataung Lady) *see* Mya Nan Nwe
Botataung Pagoda (Yangon): forum-like ritual event **32**, 74, **85–90**, 94; hair reliquary 76, 79; place in Buddhist city landscape **74–76**; reconstruction of stupa 76; transformation of local economy **77–78**; World War II 76
boun ho khao padap din ritual complex (Laos) 257n9

INDEX

Bourdieu, Pierre 72n7; field theory 262; *see also* habitus

Brac de la Perrière, Bénédicte ix, **1–41**, 64-65, **69–97**, 159, 164n1, **294–295**, 300, 301, **302**, **305–306**; fieldwork **74n**; genealogy of Southeast Asian spirit possession complex **299**

braḥ buddha sāsanā khmaer (Cambodian Buddhism) 144, 145, 150

braḥ Eysor (Cambodia: Shiva) 154n

braḥ sangḍh ceḥ sro ḋyk (Cambodia: monks who perform *sro ḋyk* ritual) **152n13**

Brahma 134, 135n, 136; *see also* Hindu deities

Brahmanism 18-19, **29**, 30, 104, 304; advantage **152n14**; Cambodian understanding **145n2**; 'category of negotiation and context' 151; contemporary practice **154–157**; 'prosperity religion' 33, 146, 153, 158; rise (Cambodia) **33**, **144–163**

Brahmaṇya sāsanā (Cambodia: Brahmanism, *q.v.*) 144

brahrājabidhī puṇyacratbrahnanggāl (Cambodia: Royal Ploughing Ceremony) 193

Bua Khiaw, *Mae* **241–242**

Buddha 18, 71, 73, 80, 85, 89-90, 101, 110, 215, 260; hair relics **75**

Buddha images 109, 110, **112**, 113, 114, 216, 280

Buddha *Phanit* (Thailand: Buddha-business, Pattana Kitiarsa) 221; *see also* commodification

Buddha's dispensation 168n8, 169, 170, 170n11, 185; promoting and saving ~ **176–179**; *see also* thathana pyu

Buddhism 12, 13, 14, 20, 43; ari ~ 73; construction as 'religion' 72; 'hard prosperity' ~ **169**; institutional ~ 17; kammatic ~ 34; modernist purification 300; popular ~ 23-24; purified imaginations 283; rationalisation 103; reimaging mainstream ~ **302–305**; 'unorthodox' forms of practice 9-10; urban contexts 146, **146n6**; *see also* Buddha *Phanit*, Cambodian Buddhism, *Dhammayut* order, Mahānikāy order, Mahayana Buddhism, monks, prosperity Buddhism, Thammayut Order

Buddhism and spirit mediumship: changing relations to possession rituals **28–30**, **101–104**; medium-sponsored ~ **104–108**; mutual incorporation **108–110**; transposable inversion of hierarchy **110–116**

Buddhist-mediumistic pantheon (Isan) **32–33**, **98–118**, 316f

Bun, *Grū* 34, **196**, 207; fortune-telling **200–202**; improvising divinatory traditions after Khmer Rouge **196–199**, 200f, 208, 320f; communication with clients **202–205**, 208; numerological technique **200–202**, 205-206

Bun Ly (spirit medium) 153, **154–157**

Bun Rany 152

Bunnag, Erb 240

bureaucracy 48, 49, 50, 52

Buriram Province 253n1, 254, 263, 266; mediumship rituals **275**; dividual person in folk etiology **267–269**; possession complex 256, 260, 263, 268, **269–284**; professionalisation of mediumship **274–283**

Burma 2, 3, 9, 12, 15, 20, 26, 27, 28, **64–65**, 151, 165, 170, 297, 298; colonial legacy 17, 180-181; general elections 70n3; illegal lotteries **166–168**, 175; lottery mania 31, **33–34**, **164–187**, 319f; new cults since 1990s **168–171**; rapid change (2011-2021) 185; state lottery 166

Burmese transliteration **xii**

câkgambīra (Cambodia: scriptures) 193

Camadewi, *Chao Mae* 246

Cambodia 2, 3, 12, 15, 17, 20, 26, 29, 297, 298; differentiation of religions

327

146–148; enchantment of divination, magic and spirit rituals **34, 188–210,** 320f religious revitalisation (1979-) 33, **148–153;** rise of Brahmanism 33, **144–163;** spirit mediums 144

Cambodia: Ministry of Cults and Religion 144, **197,** 197n4

Cambodian Buddhism 144, 145, 150; Buddhist monkhood (two orders) 149, 149n10; re-established or invented rituals 149, 149n8-9; *see also* Buddhism

Cambodian People's Party (CPP) 149

Cambodian transliteration xii

căn (Vietnam: spirit root) 46

Cao Bằng 60, 61

Cao Tiên 61, 62

capitalism 5, 12, **24–25,** 103, 121, 133, 142, 165, 168, 182, 183, 214, 215, 216, 262, 302; cultural basis **224–229;** neoliberal ~ 4, 16, **20–22,** 23, 265; *see also* commodification, market

card-reading 195, 197; *see also* divination

Chaeng Si Phum (Chiang Mai city pillar spirit) 33, 138n; *see also* Chiang Mai

Chaiyaphum Province and city: 98, 100-108, 110-116

Chang Phueak 140; White Elephants monument 138n, 139, 141; *see also* Chiang Mai

charap (*phi charap*) (Thai: undomesticated nonhumans) 278, 278n36; *see also phi*

charisma 6, 99, 107, 116, 122, 128, 227, 263; *see also barami*

Châu Bát (Vietnam: Eighth Lady) 62

Châu Bé (Vietnam: Small Lady) 62-63

Châu đệ Nhị (Vietnam: Second Lady) 62

Châu Lục (Vietnam: Sixth Lady) 62

Chiang Mai: 28, 114, 115, 138, 138n, 140; city origins 126; guardian spirit 139; matrilineal ancestor spirit cults **123–124;** merging genres among religious traditions of spirituality **125–126;** pillar of Indra and group of spirit mediums **124–125;** professional mediums and their spirits **122–123;** spirit mediumship 33-34, **119–143, 232–252;** 317-319f; spirit worship and mediumship (historical perspective) **120–121;** tutelary spirits 128; visited by King Chulalongkorn **241–244;** *see also chomrom anurak khumsing,* Lan Na

child spirit practices (Thailand) **34–35, 211–231,** 298, 321f; figurines **220;** *see also kuman thorng, luk krok, luk thep*

child spirit shrines 216, 219

China: geomancy 136; popular religion 304; religious traditions (Vietnamese opposition to) **47;** Vietnamese nationalist narrative 43; *see also* Confucianism, Kuan Im

China-Vietnam border war (1979) 47

chomrom anurak khumsing (Community of Lions Conservation Club, Chiang Mai) **140–141**

Christensen, Paul **ix, 29, 33, 144–163,** 278n35, 300

Christianity 10, 12, 43, 72n5

chronotype (Bakhtin) 249

Chúa Sơn Trang (Vietnam: Princess of Mountain Estates) 51

Chulalongkorn, King (Rama V, r. 1868-1910) 22, 34, 122, 133, 138n, **232, 245, 246, 248n, 261;** teakwood statue **235–237;** cult of **234, 242–243;** *phor piya* (beloved father) **249;** second coronation (1873) **235–236;** statue **235–237;** Vimanmek Palace 237; visit to Chiang Mai **241–244**

Chulalongkorn Day 248

Chulalongkorn University 239

Cô Bé (Vietnam: Small Damsel) 63

Cohen, Eric 235

INDEX

Cold War and aftermath 12, 14, 17, 19, 20, 21, 165
collectivity 255, 258n10, 266, 284; definition **255**
colonial era 165, 193, 299, 300, 303
colonial knowledge **11–12**
Comaroff, Jean 14, 16, **24**, 182; 'occult economies' 21
Comaroff, John L. 14, 182
commission-sa (Burma: eater of commission) 167
commodification 82, 221, 226, 264; *see also* Buddha *Phanit*, marketisation
Communist Party of Vietnam 46, 47
comparative perspectives 2, **13–16**, 305
Condominas, Georges 9, **13–14**, 15, 27
Confucianism 19, 65; *see also* China
corruption 166, 192
cosmology 36, 59, 77n, 112, 113, 223, 260
cosmopolitanism 66, 77, 83, 189
court music (Vietnam *lưu thủy* theme) 49
Crosson, J. Brent 11
cūl rūpa (Cambodia: mediumistic divination) 193
cultural capital (Bourdieu) 261, 262
cultural identity 19, 65, 120, 126, 133, 141, 294
cung văn (Vietnam: musicians) 44, **45**

daing gyi (Burma: lottery founder) 167, 168
dāna (Pāli: Buddhist religious donation) 82, **156**; *see also* ahlu, hlu dan
dance, in possession ritual 32, 33, **45**, **84–85**, 92, 99, 105, 107, 115, 123, 126, 137, 280f, 323f; not allowed for monks 107n, 111; *see also* music, possession ritual, *ram*
Đạo Mẫu (Vietnam: Mother Goddess Religion, *q.v.*) 42, 46
Dara Rasami, *Chao* (1873-1933) 232, 232n, 234, **238–240**, 241, 242; residence near Chiang Mai (1910-1933) **239**
Dara Rasami Commemoration Day 239, 244
dark powers 217, 218; *see also* black magic
dat (Burma: energy) 93
Davis, Eric 9
Davis, Richard B. 240n11
Day of Tying Anger (Cambodia) 148n9
de Heusch, Luc 13
death: localised possession complex **269–273**
Deities and Divas (Jackson and Baumann 2022) 5
Descola, Philippe **15–16**, 255, 260n; 'analogism' **59**; ontological multiplicity model **259**; *see also* animism
Dhammayut Order 149n10; *see also* Buddhism, Thammayut Order
dharma 147, 151
dhvoe punya (Cambodia: merit-making) 145
dhvoe vedamant (Cambodia: magic rituals) 150
Diguet, Édouard: *Annamites: Société, coutumes, religions* (1895) **60–61**
disenchantment 1, 1n2, **5–6**, 8, 103, 208, 213; differentiated from 'secularisation' 6n
dividuality (dividual personhood) **258**, 258n10, 258n12, **265–269**, 270, 284; Thai dividuality **265–267**; *see also* individualism, personhood
divination 8, 10, 16, 24, 25, 27n, **30–31**, 36, 188, 189, 190; definition **193–194**; definitions **194n2**; Phnom Penh **193–195**; reformulations **1–41**; *see also* mediumistic divination
Đổi mới (Vietnam: Renovation) 19, 46, 65, 91; *see also* economic liberalisation
đồng (Vietnam: spirit medium) 44, **45**

Dongting Lake (China, Hunan Province) 48, 54
dreams **30–31**, 255; *see also nimitta*, oneiric spaces, visions
Dror, Olga 54, 60n, **65**
du duang (Thailand: divination) 280
du lịch tâm linh (Vietnam: spiritual tourism) 66n
Dumézil, Georges 57, 59
Dumont, Louis 253
Durand, Maurice: *Imagerie populaire vietnamienne* (1960) 64n; *Technique et panthéon* (1959) **56–57**
Durkheim, Émile 215, 255, 279

École Française d'Extrême-Orient 56
École Pratique des Hautes Études (Paris) 56, 57
economic capital 281, 283; *see also* capitalism
economic development 20, 150, 153, 158, 184
economic liberalisation 33, 150, **150n12**, 153, 158, 180, 184; see also *Đổi mới*
Eipper, Chris 60n
Eisenstadt, Shmuel Noah 14
elephant hunters **275**, 277
Eliade, Mircea 57
elites 21, 103, 150, 151-152, 196, 240
enchantment 2, 5-8, 294, 296–297, 302, 303; current efflorescence 299, **305–306**; performative generation **23–24**; produced by modernity 3; technologies of ~ **22–23**; *see also* disenchantment
Endres, Kirsten W. 2
Enlightenment (European) 10, 72n5
esoteric masters **168–171**, 178n, 306
esoterism (Buddhist) 18, 28; *see also weikza* path
everyday life 98n2, 99n4, 100, 101, 184, 190, 193, 213, 234, 239, 250, 254, 261-268 *passim*, 282

everyday lifeworlds 255, 258
everyday rituals in Thailand (listed) **257**
everyday village life 255, 256, 260, 276, 283, 284
exorcism 9, 257, 270, 272, 301
Eysey, Lok Tā (Cambodia, spirit) **154-155**, 157
Eysor *see brah Eysor*

feng shui rituals 136; *see also* China
fetishisation **207–208**
field-specific: ~ forms of capital 262, 264; ~ forms of power 264; ~ language games 262, 266; ~ logics 261
Fifth Great Mandarin (Vietnam) 50, 53, 54
Fifth Lady (Vietnam) 55, 62
Fjelstad, Karen 2, 15
floral decorations in spirit ritual 86, 86n24; *see also bai si*
fetal ghosts 222, 222n
Formoso, Bernard **263**
fortune-tellers 34, 151, 188, 189, 193, 195, 198, **206–207**, 306; definitions **194n2**; communication with clients **202–205**, 208; *see also* divination
fortune-telling 146n6, 190, 194, **200–202**, 280; *see also* divination
Foucault, Michel 256n5
Four Palaces cult (Vietnam) 26, 27, 31, 53, 297; 'could be called Four Prefectures' 51; abstract totality principle 58; aesthetics, imagery, poetics 49; articulation of autochthony and state 57–63; further research 65-66n; genealogies of a Vietnamese pantheon **31–32**, **42–68**, 312-313f; imaginary [n] **49–53**; invention of indigenous religion **46–48**, 49f, 312f; less about 'nature' than about politics 49; listed 45; *longue durée* dynamics 63-64; as 'pantheon' 30, **53–57**; reasons for in-

volvement **46**; scholars as promoters **63–66**; spirit possession **44–46**, 48; **63–66**; statuary **53**, 61, 61n10, 64; woodprints **53–54**, 54f, 64, 313f; *see also* Mother Goddess Religion
Fourth Prince (Vietnam) 55, 62
Foxeus, Niklas **ix**, xii, 27, **30**, 31, **33–34**, **164–187**, 300, 301; publications **186**
Frankfurter, David 274; 'peripheral ritual experts' 281
Frazer, James G.: *Golden Bough* 264
Fukuura, Kazuo **ix–x**, 26, 28, 71, **119–143**, 300, 301; fieldwork 121

Gauchet, Marcel: *Disenchantment of World* (1997) 1
gawpaka ahpwe (Burma: lay authorities) 169
gender **5**, 93, 122, 282, 283
Ghana: Hauka *maîtres fous* 48
ghosts 148, 180, 189, 212-213, 222, 226-227, 258n10; *see also* phi
giá (Vietnam: manifestation of particular spirit; lit. celestial chariot) **44–45**
Giran, Paul: *Magie et religion annamites* (1912) **58**, 58n8
globalisation 2, 4, 6, 14, 20, 119, 121, 133, 142, 190, 294; *see also* capitalism
gold leaf, use in ritual 216, 219, 235
Goody, Jack 59-60
Gottowik, Volker: *Dynamics of Religion in Southeast Asia* (ed. 2014) 2-3
Great Mandarins (Vietnam) 45, 48, 49f, 49, 52, 312f
grū cūl rūpa (Cambodia, mediums possessed by spirits) 146n6; *see also grū pāramī*
grū dāy: (Cambodia) astrologers 146n6; fortune-tellers, diviners 193
grū meol (Cambodia: traditional healer) **194**
grū pāramī (Cambodia: spirit mediums) 153

guardians of treasure trove (Burma) 34, **168–171**, 175, 176, 178, 178n, 179; *see also* pagoda guardians
Guillou, Anne Yvonne 145, 145n3, 259; 'religionisation' 146

habitus 262, 266; *see also* Bourdieu
hae bokfai (NT: fire rocket procession) 128
Hamayon, Roberte N. **233**, 233n3
Hanks, Lucien M. 266
Hanoi 26, 43, 56, 61; 'thirty-six streets' 58
hap khan (NT: ritual trays) 137; *see also khan ha*
Harris, Ian 18, 193
hầu bóng (Vietnam: serving the shadows) 44
hầu dâng (Vietnam: assistants to spirit medium) 44, **45**
Hefner, Robert F. 19, 208
heritagisation 31, 43
hermits 28, 200, 246, 275f, 279, 292
hierarchical animism (notion) **15–16**; *see also* animism
hierarchy 36, 45, 49, 61, 102, 215-216, 224; transgression and inversion 100; transposable inversion (Buddhism and spirit mediumship) **110–116**
highlanders 52, 52n
Hindu deities 33, 120, 121, 123, 130, 131, 134, 135, 135n, 147n7, 275f, 280, 282; *see also* Brahma, Indra, Mahakali, Shiva
Hinduism 59, 92n, 199n6, 304
hlu dan (Burma: religious donating) 177; *see also ahlu, dāna*
hóa thán (Vietnam: reincarnations or avatars) 62
Holt, John 110
horā (Cambodia: royal astrologers) **193**
horng phra (Thailand: religious space for prayer or meditation) 238

Horton, Robin 208
hpaya (Burma: pagoda) **69n1**
hpongyi kyaung (Burma: monasteries) 69n1
hsaing waing (Burma: classical music orchestra) 87
hsayama (Burma: semi-professional female mediums) 172, **172n16–17**
hto tha (Burma: gambler) 167
htwek yap pauk (Burma: exit from life cycle) 85n22; 'mystical transformation' 170n11; *see also* weikza, weizzā
Hue 26, 44n
Hun Sen **149**; destiny **149–150n11**
hương hành (Vietnam: pilgrimage) 66n
hybridisation (Brahmanism and Buddhism) **150**; *see also* syncretism
hymns 49, **50**, 52; *see also* văn chầu

identity politics 16, 33, 121, 133, 141
In, *Pu* 249
individualism 181, 185, 215, 216, 218, 257, 258; *see also* dividuality, personhood
Indonesia 3, 152
Indra **124–125**; see also Hindu deities
Internet 183, 183n24
Inthakhin, Chiang Mai city pillar 33, 124, 126
invented tradition 66, 141
involuntary possession 272
Irvine, Walter 271n24, 274, 276n30

Jackson, Peter A. **x**, **1–41**, 69n2, 159, 164n1, 180, 246n21, 256n6, 280, **294–295**, 301, **302**, **305–306**; genealogy of Southeast Asian spirit possession complex **299**; publications **38**, **287**; Thai 'power' (multiple forms) **263**
Jade Emperor 43, 48, 57, 58n7
jaṃnya chven (Cambodia: superstition) 146

jao: (Thailand) honoured figures 279; lords 29; noble tutelary spirits 246, 250, 297
jao phor (Thailand: spirits) 106
Jao Phor Lak Mueang (Lord Father of Pillar of Mueang Chiang Mai) 124
Jao Phor Sing Dan (Lord Father of Lion Protecting Checkpoint) 137, 139
jao thi: (Thailand: guardian spirit) 101; masters of land 278, 278n35; masters of place 267
Japan 3, 25
Jayavarman VII, King 149n11
Jenkins, Richard 1n4, **6**
jettaphut (Thailand, from Pāli: *catubhūta*; soul-like concept) 267
jit (Thailand: soul-like concept) 267, 268
jit orn (Thailand: soft-souled) 272
Johnson, Andrew 2
Johnson, Paul C. **10–11**

kadaw bwe (Burma: basin with coconuts, bananas, leaves; ritual offerings) 77n, 83, 87, 173, 176; 81n
kae bon (Thai: ritual votive offering) 257, **264–265**; *see also* votive offerings
kalok (Mon dance) 124n7
kamma (Pāli): same as karma (*q.v.*) **164n2**
Kapferer, Bruce: magical practices 'thoroughly modern' **7–8**
karma 168, 211, 213, 224, 263; *see also* kamma
Kataoka, Tatsuki 17
kathoey (Thailand: trans women) 281, **282–283**
Kawila, King (Lan Na) 129, 138, 138n, 140
Kawila Army Barracks 236
keji ajan (Thailand: magic monks) 23, 28, 201, 233, 233n2, 248n, 279, 297
Kendall, L. 15
Keyes, Charles F. 22, 25

INDEX

khaen (Thailand: bamboo mouth organ) 99n3, 109

kham mueang (Northern Thai language) 242

khamen (Khmer socio-cultural category in lower NE Thailand) 254

khan ha (Thailand: ritual offering bowl) 98, 98n2, 113; *see also hap khan, khan khu*

khan khu (NT: teacher's tray) 122; *see also khan ha*

khantoke (NT: wooden table) 238, **238n**

khatha or *khathaa* (Thailand: magical or Buddhist mantras) 115, 115n11, 269

Khelang Nakhon (Lampang's traditional name) 244

Khmer Empire 145, 146

Khmer Rouge era (1975–1979) 14, 18, 31, 33, 34, 144, 146, **147–148**, 158, 190, 197, 199, 199n5

khon mueang (Thailand: 'people of city-state') 120; *see also* Chiang Mai

khon song (Thailand: spirit medium) 27n; *see also khon song jao, mor song*

khon song jao (Thailand: spirit medium) 233; *see also khon song, mor song*

Khorat Plateau 110, 113, 115

khrorp khru rituals (Thailand) 272, 280; *see also wai khru, wai khu, yok khru, yok khu*

khru (Thai: multiple meanings) 280n; human and nonhuman patrons 280n; potent nonhumans 280; principal nonhuman familiar 279; teacher 245, 282; tutelary spirit 278; mentioned 275f; *see also ajan, khruba-ajan, khu, khuba*

khru khorng banphaburut (Thailand: teacher spirits of ancestors) 275n

khru mot (Thailand: spirit medium) 282

khruba-ajan (Thailand: teacher as nonhuman being) 274; *see also khru*

khsae (Cambodia: social networks, patron-client relationships) 155, 157

Kinh Xuyên 54

khu (NT: teacher) 122; *see also ajan, khru, khruba-ajan, khuba*

Khuang Sing: statues of two lions and ritual **138–140**, 319f; *see also* Chiang Mai

khuba (Thailand: spiritual master) 99n4, 105, 105n, 107; *see also ajan, khru, khruba-ajan, khu*

Khun, *Luang Phor* 115, 233n2

Khun Chang, Khun Phaen **216–217**, 218

khwam-jaroen (Thailand: progress, prosperity) 243

khwam-khlang (Thailand: magical power) **263**

khwam-pen-thai (Thailand: Thainess) xiii

khwan (Thailand: life essence or soul) 122; lost soul 108; soul-like concept 267, 268; soul-like potencies **257n8**

khwan hai (Thailand: absence of soul-like component) 272

khye (Burma: three-digit lottery) 166, 167, 168, 171, 179; *see also* lottery mania

kinship 266, 271

Ko Nyunt Win, Naga Ni 86n24

kpuan (Cambodia: formal knowledge) 198

Kruṅ Bālī ritual for Earth Goddess 151

Kuan Im (Goddess of Mercy) 122, 246; *see also* China

Kui (ethnic group) 274, 274n28

kuman thorng (Thailand: 'golden child', child spirit) 123, **123n4**, 211, 212n, **216**, 218, 220f, 221, 224, 226f, 228, 279, 321f; *see also* child spirit practices

kumaradeba (Thailand: child spirits) 200; *see also* child spirit practices

La, *Chao* (Thailand) 241, 241n13, 242

Lacan, Jacques: 'dignity of thing' 228

Lady of Kingdom festival (Burma) **91–92**

333

Lae, *Phaya* (Thailand) **103**, 106, 113
lai phi (Thai: exorcism) 257, 270, 272
lak mueang (Thailand: traditional city-state pillar) 124
lam (Isan dialect: sing and dance) 109n
Lambek, Michael **249–250**
Lan Na (Northern Thailand) 129, **130–131**; arts and crafts **235–237**; guardian spirits of city-state 120; identity 234, 237, 240; integration into Siam 124, 139; *see also* Chiang Mai, *khon mueang*
Lan Na era 124n5, 128, 138, 232, 234
language games **253–271**, 276, 278, 284; *see also* Wittgenstein
Lào Cai province (Vietnam) 51, 55
Lao people 240, 240n11
Laos 3, 17, 110, 198, 298
lap (Northern Thai minced-pork salad) **238–239**
Latour, Bruno 255, 266
Lauser, Andrea 2
Le Bon, Gustave 58n8
Lê dynasty (Vietnam, 1428–1788) 19, 52, 54, 60, 65; restoration era (1533–1788) 51, 54
Lê Khôi 54
Lê Lợi, King 50, 52
Lê Thánh Tông, Emperor 62
Lebensgeister (*spiritus animales*) 257n8
Lee, Raymond L.M. 20
lek atta or *lek prumpi tua* (Cambodia: numerological formulas) 194; *see also* numerology
lekha prāṃbīrtua (Cambodia: numerology) 193; *see also* numerology
lên đồng (Vietnam: spirit possession, lit. 'riding the medium') ritual 44–46, 48, 52, 56, 60, 62
len khorng (Thailand: malevolent magic) 282; *see also* black magic
len mae mot (Thailand: mediumship ritual) **275–276**, 277, 278, 279f, 322f

Lent, Buddhist 103, 107, 108, 114, 123, 134
Lévy-Bruhl, Lucien: law of participation **256, 266**
Lewis, I.M. 178
Library of Congress (USA) xii
Liễu Hạnh, Princess (Vietnam) 13n, 19, 48, 54, 60n, 65; also called Duc Thanh Mâu (Great Mother Goddess) 61
lineage ancestors, Thai 278–279; *see also* ancestral spirits
lineage mediums, Thai **274–277**, 279, 281, 282, 284
Little Lady of High Regions (Vietnam) 45
lộc (Vietnam: spirit blessings) 45
loeng anak tā (Cambodia: spirit ritual) **155–156**, 157, 158; see also *anak tā*
lok tā (Cambodia: honourable grandfather) **154n**
Lom Pengkaeo 212n, 217n
lottery mania (Burma) 33–34, **164–187**, 319f; predictions of winning numbers (mediums and devotees) **171–176**
Lower Northeast Thailand 27, **253–291**; *see also* Buriram
Luang Phor (Thailand: reverend father) definition 115n13
luk krok (Thailand: preserved fetal remains) 211, **212n**; *see also* child spirit practices
luk sit (Thailand: devotees, disciples, followers) 122, 241, 248n, 266, 280, 283
luk thep (Thailand: angel child dolls) 34–35, 214, 216, 218, **220–222**, 223–227, 298; purchase of airline tickets for ~ 228, 228n14; *see also* child spirit practices
luk thung folk songs (Thailand) 109
lunar calendar 98, 108, 112, 127, 139, 316f

Mạc Kính Vụ 60

Mạc Thị Cao Tiên's cult (Vietnam) 61
mae (Thailand: mother) 102n, 276n31
mae mot (Thailand: female adept of mystic knowledge) 276
mae pakam (Thailand: leaders of *pakam* cult) 275f, **275–277**, 278
magic 3, 5-6, **8**, 10, 24, 188, 189, 296, 306; 'problematic analytical category' 7; *see also* black magic, *len khorng*
magic monks (Thailand) 23, 28, 201, 233, 233n2, 248n, 279, 297; *see also keji ajan*
'magical' capitalism 21; *see also* Buddha Phanit
Magritte, René 250
Mahakali 280f, 323f; *see also* Hindu deities
Mahāmyaing (Burma: mystical forest) 170n11
Mahānikāy order 149n10; *see also* Buddhism
Mahayana Buddhism 10, 19, 246; *see also* Buddhism
mainland Southeast Asia 119, 124, 259, 271, 282n40; efflorescence of spirit possession **16–25**; rethinking vernacular religions **292–309**; spirit mediumship and divination (reformulations) **1–41**, 311f
makkhanayok (Thailand: liaison between monks and laity) 247
Mala, Mae **102–103**, **106**, **114**
malevolent spirits 217, 275f; *see also phi*
mamot and *mamuat* (Khmer in Thailand: female adept) 276n30
Mananya Boonmi (*Mae* Ning) 220
Mandalay 26, 33, 165, 166, 179; lottery monastery 167, 167n5
Mangrai, King 126, 128, 138n
market: rise of (Southeast Asian religious field) **16–20**, 70, 70n3, 165, 208; *see also* capitalism, commodification, marketisation

marketisation 2, 4, **20–22**; *see also* capitalism, commodification
Marston, John A. 18
mass media; *see* media
master mediums 52, 106, 114, 126, 277
Masuzawa, Tomoko 72n5
matrilineal ancestors **123–124**, 126n6, 271n24, 275f, 278; *see also* ancestral spirits
matrilineal cults 33, **123–124**, 125, 126n6, **127–129**, 274
Mẫu Cao Tiên (Vietnam: Mother Goddess Cao Tiên) **60**
Mẫu Thượng Ngàn (Vietnam: Mother Goddess of High Regions) 51, 62
Mẫu Tiên La (Vietnam: Mother Goddess of Tiên La) 61
Mauss, Marcel: 'spirit of gift' 265
McDaniel, J. 215-216
medaw (Burma: cult female leader) 84, 84n, 85, **86**, 93, 94
media, and spirit possession **22–23**, **24–25**; *see also* new media
Medium A: devotees **136**; driving force behind Assembly of Spirit Mediums in Lan Na **130–131**; life story and calling of spirits **134–135**; possessed by Shiva (2018) 135f, 318f; realignment of mediumship with translocal values 131, **134–137**, 141-142
Medium B **132**, 134; Khuang Sing ritual 139f, **139–140**, 319f; life story and calling of spirits **137–138**; ordination as monk 137-138; possessing spirit (Sing Dan) 138; realignment of Northern Thai mediumship with local values **137–141**, 142; relationship with local community **140–141**; relationship with local government **139–140**; statues of two lions at Khuang Sing 138
medium-abbot 105-106
mediumistic divination 193, **194**; *see also* divination

mediums: *see* spirit mediums
mediumship: *see* spirit mediumship
Mendeleev's periodic table of elements 63
meol bhea (Cambodia: card-reading) 193, 195; *see also* divination
merit-making 33, 34, 134, 138, 139, 152, 153, 157, 158, 168, 169, 176-181, 189, 211, 217, 225, 296, 300, 303
mi ong; (Thailand: having a possessing spirit) 26, 32, 112, 116, 272; 'propensity for or susceptibility for possession' **247–248**, 250, 275f; *see also* active devotees, *nat shi, ong*
middle class 103, 122, 136, 137, 183, 214-215, 217, 223, 224, 226, 228
Min Aung Hlaing 70n3
mở phủ (Vietnam: opening of palaces) ritual **52**
modernisation 3, 70, 119, 121, 172, 181, 182, 184, 208, 262
modernity 2, 4-8, 19, 21, 182, 208
monasteries (in Burma, *hpongyi kyaung*) 32, 69n1, 90, 99, 104-110 *passim*, 126, 150, 294
Mondaw (village) 172n18
Mongkut, King (Rama IV, r. 1851-1868) 199n6, 261
monks 7, 9, 31, 70n3, 79-80, 86, 87, 89, 91, 98n1, 100, 148, 149, 152, 164, 303; blessing of spirit medium shrine **156**; *see also* Buddhism
mor (Thailand: doctor) 99n3
mor bun (Thailand: village seer) 276
mor du (Thailand: fortune-teller) 27n
mor khaen (Thailand: ritual musician) 99, **99n3**, 106, 112; *see also khaen*
mor lam (Thailand) 109; two meanings **109n**; *see also lam*
mor song (Thailand: master medium) 275f, 277; *see also khon song, khon song jao*
moradok (Thailand: heritage) 235

Morris, Rosalind C. 2, 13, 16, **22–23**
mot (Thailand: ant) 124n5, 276n30; *see also mae mot*
Mother Goddess Religion 19, 22, 30, 31, 42–43, 47, 49, 66; Sinicised elements 43, **48**; websites **55–56**, 64
Mt Popa 73, 85n22, 91, 166, 170n11, 171
Muecke, Marjorie A. 28, **114–115**, 126
Mukhopadhyay, Bhaskar 22
music and musicians 44-46, 49, 53, 55, 85-91 *passim*, 99, 109n, 112, 113, 122n, 123, 126, 139, 151, 155-156, 257n8; *see also* dance, *lam, luk thung, mor khaen, mor lam*, possession rituals, singing
Mya Nan Nwe (Botataung Lady) 22, 31, 71, 84, 169; ability to flourish despite banishment 78; ambiguity 73-74; 'Creeper of Emerald Palace' 71; day-to-day devotional rituals **83–85**; displacement (pluralistic history) **79–83**; green attire 72f, 314f; image **76–77**, 77f, 80, 314f; *naga*-like guardian spirit 32, 69, 73, 74-75; new shrine (1999-) **78**, 81, 85, 91, 94; popularity 84; research setting **76–78**; spiritual presence without embodiment **83–85**; *thaik nan shin* ('in charge of treasure palace') 69; 'Whispering Lady' 71, 82
Mya Nan Nwe (birthday celebration) 32, 74, **85–91**, 315-316f; forum-like aspect 32, 74, **85–91**, 94; further research 91; main devotee leaders **86n24**; palanquins 87f, **87–92**, 93, 315-316f; ritual innovations **92**
Myittu festival 88n27, 92
mystic bonds (Sahlins) **267**
mystic capital (Baumann) 261, 262, 266, 281, 283
mystic participation (Lévy-Bruhl) 266

INDEX

mystic potency 263-266, 269f, 269, 280-283, 322f

naammon or *nam mon* (Thailand: sacralised water) 115, 115n12
naga (serpent spirit) 18, 81, 169, 297; linked to water realm 81; take on human appearance for short time 81; foods (fruits, milk) specific to worship of ~ 83; see also *thaik naga*
naga king 88
naga medaw (Burma: *naga* mother) 169, **179**
nagani (red *naga*) 86
Nagayon Pagoda 166, 170-171n13, 172, **172–173n18**, 175; seven children from treasure trove 174f, **174**, 319f
Nak, Mae 227; shrine (Bangkok) 215, 219, 220
nak cūl rūpa (Cambodia: mediumistic fortune-teller) 194, **195**
Nan Way Aung, Hsaya U 86n24
Nang Rua Lom ('lady of capsized boat') 246, **246n20–21**
nang samathi (Thailand: meditating) 237
Nantiya Sukontapatipark 211n
Naresuan, King (r. 1590–1605) 232, 236, 237, 238, 244, 245, 248n, 249
nat (Burma: tutelary spirits) 72, 74, 297
nat cults 168, 168n8, 185
nat kadaw (Burma: spirit medium) 91, 94, 171n15; spirit mediums (professional) 84-85; wife of spirit 93, 172, 172n16
nat kana bwe (Burma: spirit possession ceremonies) 87, 88, 93
nat shi (Burma: having a spirit) 27; see also active devotees, *mi ong*
nation-state 3, 119, 124, 262; nation-building 64; state-building 294
National Day of Remembrance (Cambodia) 148n9
national identity 57, 66, 235, 261

National League for Democracy 70n3, 166
National Office of Buddhism 105
nationalism 14n11, 19, 34, 43, 237, 294
naturalism 15, 259, 260, 261
Ne Win, General 18, 70n3, 165; *sangha* reform (1980) **17**
neak ta (Cambodia: tutelary spirits) 18, 29, 197; see also *anak tā*, *nia ta*
necromancy 34, 218, 223, 227
Neeranoch Malangoo 82n
neo-functionalism **264**, 265, 266
neoliberalism 4: cultural logic **20–22**; see also capitalism
new animism 35, 73, **255**, **258–260**; see also animism
new media 4, 5, 16, **20–21**, 302; see also media
Ngammueang, King (Phayao) 126, 128
Nghệ An 54, 62
Ngô Đức Thịnh **46–47**, **64**
Nguyễn Duy Lạc 54
Nguyen Thi Hien 2, 15
Nguyễn Xí 54
Nhạc Phủ (Vietnam: Palace of Mountains) 51
nia ta (Khmer in Thailand: masters of land) 278, **278n35**; see also *anak tā*, *neak ta*
nimitta 30, 34; see also oneiric spaces, visions
non-monastic religious virtuosos **292–295**, 298; see also religious virtuosos
Northeast Thailand (Isan) xiii, 26, 28, 35, 132, **253–291**; Buddhist-mediumistic pantheon **32–33**, **98–118**, 316f; see also Buriram, Chaiyaphum
Northeastern terms (NE) (Thailand) xiii
Northern Khmer language 254
Northern Thailand xiii, 26, 28, 33, 35, 116, **119–143**, 271n24-25; see also Chiang Mai, Lan Na

Norton, Barley 53
Northern terms (NT) (Thailand) xiii
Num, *Mor* **103**, **107–108**
numerological divination 193, **194**, **196–199**, 200f, 320f; *see also* astro-numerology
numerological method (elements) **200–202**
nuns 71, 80, 83; *see also* Buddhism

O'Connor, Richard 267
O'Lemmon, Matthew 18, 147
occult economies (Comaroff and Comaroff) 21, 165, 168, **179–184**; neoliberal ~ 297, 302, 304; *see also* capitalism, commodification, Buddha Phanit
Okell, John: *Guide to Romanization of Burmese* (1971) xii
Okkalapa, King **75–76**
oneiric spaces **30–31**, 34, 84, 85n23, **232–252**; *see also* dreams, *nimitta*, visions
ong (Thai: supramundane beings) 27n, **247–248**; *see also* mi ong
ong tham (Dhammic entity) 248n
ontological turn (anthropology) 15, 255
ontology 73, 254-255, **259**, 261
orientalism 2, 10, 11

Pagan: Ananda Pagoda 80, 81
pagoda clusters (Burma) 34, 166, **170–171**, 172, 175
pagoda guardians (Burma) 27, 69-71, 78, 89, **92–93**, 94; *see also* guardians of treasure trove
pagodas (Burma) 18, 61; **69n1**, 168n8, 169, 170, 176, 181, 185, 303; *see also* stupas
pakam (Khmer: ancestral spirits) 274, 275
Palace of Mountains (Vietnam) **51–52**
Palace of Water (Vietnam) 62

Pāli Canon 147, 158
pan zaydi (Burma: flower *cetiya*) prayer 86
pantheonisation process **57–63**
pantheons 30, 31-32, 121, 223, 227; comparability issue **297–298**; dynamic and expanding ~ **27–28**, 29f, 311f; Four Palaces **53–57**; politics **297–299**; structural logics and dynamics **298–299**
pāramī (Cambodia: spiritual power) 18, 29, 33, 145, 145n3, 149, 155, 156, 157, 158, 201, 297
Patithin Nueng Roi Pi (Thailand: 100-year calendar) 199, 200f, 202, 206, 320f
patronage 17, 106, 107, 150, 263, 266, 280n
Pattana Kitiarsa 2, 9, 28, 94, 113, 114, **115**, 221, 232, 233n2, 237, 248n, 260, 274, 281; postmodern mediums 23
pāy sī (Cambodia: shrine) 145, **145n4**, 153; *see also* bai si
pchum ben ritual complex (Cambodia) 257n9
People's Republic of Kampuchea **148**
People's Revolutionary Party of Kampuchea 149
personhood **257–258**, 265, 266, 284; *see also* dividuality, individualism
Phạm Quỳnh Phương 60n
phasa klang (Standard Thai language) 242
phasa tham (Thailand: dhammic language) 248n
phasa thep (Thailand: language of deities) 134, 248n, 249; *see also bhāsā khmoc*
phi (Thailand: spirits, ghosts) 29, 213n, **217–218**, **226–227**, 297; ambiguous ontological position **222–223**; Thai meanings **212**; witch-like ~ 273n; *see also* ghosts

INDEX

phi arak (Thailand: guardian spirits) 297
phi banphaburut (Thailand: ancestor spirits) 267, 275n, 287
phi dek (Thailand: child spirit) 212, 218; *see also* child spirit practices
phi jao nai (Thailand: tutelary spirits of high rank) 122
phi khru (Thailand: lineage teacher spirits) 297; *see also khru, khu*
phi khu (Thailand: spirit of teacher) 122; *see also khru, khu*
phi krasue (Thailand: witch-like being) 272
phi meng (Thailand: Mon spirits) 123–124, 124n7; matrilineal descent group 127, 128
phi mot (Thailand: ant spirits) **123–124**, 124n5; 276n30; 'matrilineal descent group' 127, 128; *see also mae mot, mot*
phi pakam (Thailand: matrilineal ancestral spirits) 275n, 276, 283; *see also pakam*
phi porp (Thailand: witch-like being) 272
phi pu ta of Lao-speaking villages 278n35
phi pu ya (Thailand: matrilineal ancestor spirits) 122
phi rai (Thailand: wrathful spirits) 297
phi rai, phi na (Thailand: spirits in fields) 101
phi re-rorn (Thailand: roaming spirits) 211
phi sing (Thailand: malevolent entity's forceful penetration of collective's ritual frontiers) 272
phi suea ban (Thailand: guardian spirits of villages) 122
phi suea mueang (Thailand: tutelary spirits of traditional city-state) 122
phithi sador khror (Thailand: mending of luck ritual) 257, 268-269, 269f, 322f
phithi yok khru (Thailand: honouring of khru ritual) 283; *see also wai khru, yok khru*

Phnom Penh 34, 188, 189, 190; conflicting dreams **190–193**; divination **193–195**; numerology fortune-tellers **196–199**, 200f, 320f
Phnom Penh: Nak Kawann monastery 198, 199n5
phor (Thailand: father) 243n17
phor pu piya (Thailand: beloved father and grandfather) 245; *see also* Chulalongkorn
phra ong 248n; *see also mi ong, ong*
phra phum (Thailand: tutelary gods) 101
phủ (Vietnam: palace, realm) 42, 51
Phuket 120, 130, 134, 135, **136**
phuttha phanit (Thailand: Buddha-business) 221; see also Buddha *Phanit*
Picard, Michel **20n**, 35, 72n5
pilgrimages and pilgrimage sites 66n, 75, 104, 166, 170, 281, 303
pilgrims 82, 87, **108–110**, 169, 171, 173
plueng (*braling*) (Khmer: soul-like entity) 268, 268n19
pluk sek (Thailand: sacralisation) ceremony 248
police officers 106, 155, 157, 166, 196, 219
Poonnatree Jiaviriyaboonya **x**, 31, **34**, **188–210**; fieldwork 190; numerological table and chart 201f
Possessed by Spirits (Fjelstad and Nguyen 2006) 15
possession: *see* spirit possession
possession complex in Southeast Asia: *see* spirit possession complex
postcolonialism 294, 299
postmodern mediums (Pattana) 28
power **263**, 263n
pret (Thailand: ghost) definition 212; *see also phi*
Princess of High Regions (Vietnam) 58
professional mediums (Baumann) 274, 275f, **281–283**, 283f, 284, 323f
prosperity Buddhism **33–34**, **164–187**, 319f; promoting Buddha's

339

dispensation **176–179**; *see also* commodification, Buddha *Phanit*, *purāṇa* Buddhism
prosperity cults 15, 30, 69, 221, 296
prosperity religions (Jackson) 29, 33, 153, 161, 165, 168, 180, 262
pu (Thailand: grandfather) 243, 243n17
Pu, *Chao* (spirit) 244
pu ruesi (Thailand: grandfather hermit) 246
Pumpuang Duangjan 227, 227n
purāṇa (Cambodia: ancient, unreformed) Buddhism 146, **146n5, 147**, 149, 151, 152, 158; *see also samǎya* Buddhism
puzaw bwe (Burma: devotional offerings) 81

Qin Chinese 54; *see also* China
Quan Lớn Tuần Tranh (Vietnam: Great Mandarin Warden of Tranh) 50
queer ritual specialists **5**; *see also* gender
quyền hành núi non (Vietnam: wield power on mountains and hills) 50

rak yom (Thailand: child spirit amulet) 211, 212n; *see also* child spirit practices
ram (Thailand) inexplicable urge to dance 276-277; possession dance 280f, 280, 323f; *see also* dance
Rama I, King (r. 1782-1809) 246, 247, 247n, **249**
Ramkhamhaeng, King 126, 128, 232
rang song (Thailand: spirit medium) 27n, 233, 248n, 275f, 277, 282
rationalisation 3, 6, 8, 12
Red River 43, 61, 62
Reid, Anthony 208
reincarnation 62-63, 211
religion 13; delineation 71-72, **72n5–6**; restrictive understandings 13
religionification (Picard) 20, **20n**, 35

religionisation dynamic 18
religious capital (Bourdieu) 261
religious field: reconsidered from perspective of spirit possession **8–9**
religious studies: material turn 233-234
religious virtuosos 73, 74, 292-304 *passim*; plurality **305–306**; *see also* non-monastic religious virtuosos
riak khwan (Thailand: calling of lost soul-like components) 257, 270
ritual 3, 10, 16, 22, **23–24**, 256-257; 'defies disenchantment' (Jean Comaroff) 24; embodied (enchanting intensities) **24–25**; performative influence **24–25**; *see also* spirit possession rituals
ritual arts of efficacy (White) 7
ritual specialists: professionalisation **25–27**
Rouch, Jean 48
Royle, Nicholas 224n
Rozenberg, Guillaume 166, 168n7, 171, 171n15, 184
rūpa (Pāli: body) 150, 154
rural areas 148, 150, 152, 193, 281
rural lifeworlds 254, **254n3**, 255, 281, 283
rural traditionalists 146n6, 147
rural-urban migration 190, 206, 207, 208, 262

Sadan, Mandy 79n
saen don ta ritual complex 257n9
Sahlins, Marshall 256, 260, 266, 267
sai sin (Thailand: ritual thread of white cotton) 269
Sakalava possession performances 249
saksit (Thailand: form of power) **263**
Saler, Michael 1n4, **5–6**
samǎya (modern) Buddhism in Cambodia 146, 158; *see also purāṇa* Buddhism
sane ya faet (Thailand: love magic) 273

INDEX

sangha 17, 110, 111, 147, 169, 292, 294, 296, 300, 303; disbanded (by Khmer Rouge) 18
Sangha Maha Nayaka Ahpwe (Burma) 17
Saṅgharājas (Supreme Patriarchs, Cambodia) 149, 149n10
Sanguan Chotisukharat 276n30
sāsana (Pāli: Buddha's dispensation) 69, 72n6, 73, 164, **164n2**, 176; *sāsanā* (Cambodia) 144, 147; *see also* religion, *thathana*
Sat Haeng Hon (Thailand: *Astrologer's Teachings* 2000) 196n3
Saw, Shwe Naga Daw 79, 86n24
Saw Mun Hla 78, 78n, 85, 93, **169n10**, 173, 176
Schober, Juliane 17, 70n4
Schroeder, J.E. 207
Sdech Khan, King 149n11
séances 44–45, 46, 50, 52, 56, 58, 62, 63, 88n26, 89, 92, 93, 121, 123; *see also* mediumship, possession
Second Lady of Palace of Mountains (Vietnam) **51–53**
Second Lady's Hymn (Vietnam) 50
secularisation 1, 6n
Seventh Prince (Vietnam) 53, 55f, **55**, 62, 313f
shamanising individuals (Hamayon) 233
shamanism 11n, 13, 15, 57
shamans 11, 270, 233, 281
shan Osi orchestra (Burma) **87–88**, 89f, 90, 91, 316f
Shiva 120, 130, 134, 135f, 135, 318f; *see also* Hindu deities
shrines **154–155, 264–265**
Shwedagon Pagoda 75, 76; *see also* pagodas
Shwezayan (Shwe Sa Ya) Pagoda 85, 93, 172n18; *see also* pagodas
Siani, Edoardo 27n
Siem Reap 193, 199
Sihanouk, King 149-150n11

Simon, Pierre-Jean 56
Simon-Barouh, Ida 56
sin ha (Thailand: Buddhist ethical precepts) 281
Sing Dan 139
Sing Du 139
singing 107n, 111, **112–113**; *see also* dance, music
Sinnott, Megan x, 29-30, **34–35**, **211–231**, 298; fieldwork **211n**
sirimongkhon (Thailand: auspiciousness) 104
sneh° (Cambodia: rituals) 153
social media 191, 281
social ontology 256, **256n7**, 257, 262, 268; animist ~ 260, 266, 284
socio-economic issues 167, 169, 183, 184, 196, 207, 254, 283
Som Korn (monk) 198, 199n5
Somsak, *Ajan* 248n
Sơn Trang (Vietnam: Mountain Estates) 51
songkran (Thai New Year) 108, 242
sorcery and sorcerers 188, 306; *see also* black magic, magic
Sorrentino, Paul x, 13, 19, **26**, 27, 28, 30, **31–32, 42–68, 298–299**
Southeast Asia: spirit cults 5; spirit possession complex **8–16, 35–36**
Sovanna (student) **194–195, 206–207**; conflicting dreams **190–193**; consulting numerology fortune-tellers 196; fortune-telling session **200–202**; communication with fortune-teller **202–205**, 208; plan to open coffee shop 192, 195, 204, 205
spirit cults 4, 5, 10, 13, 15, 16, 29, **32–33**, **98–118, 295–296**
spirit dances 127, 128; *see also* dance
spirit mediums 33, 43, 98n2, 194, 213; Burma **171–176**; Cambodia 144-153 *passim*, **154–157**; gay ~ 281, 282, 282n40; Northern Thai terms 122;

professional ~ 25; religious practice
123; status **299–300**; *see also* village
mediums
spirit mediumship 72, 72n7; Chiang Mai
34, **120–126, 232–252**; realignment
33, **119–143**, 317-319f; reorganisation **126–134**; reformulations
(worlds ever more enchanted) **1–41**,
311f; relatedness to Buddhism
re-examined **101–104**; *rites de
passage* **277–278**; *see also* possession,
séances, village mediumship
spirit mediumship and Buddhism:
mutual incorporation **108–110**;
transposable inversion of hierarchy
110–116
spirit possession 13, 32; anthropological category **10**; as 'continuum of
possibilities' **233**; distinguished from
'shamanism' 11n; efflorescence in
Buddhist Southeast Asia **16–25**; Four
Palaces **44–46**; historically changing
and plural **299–302**; literature review
292–294; multiple forms **301**;
reconsideration of religious field from
perspective of ~ **8–9**; 'refers to wide
range of phenomena' **9**; reorganiza-
tion and realignment (Chiang Mai)
33, **119–143**, 317-319f; *see also*
dance, music, séances, trance
*Spirit Possession in Buddhist Southeast
Asia* (this book): explores processes
of globalising neoliberal modernity 16; further research **35–36,
295–309**; perspectives (international
and multidisciplinary) 3-4; plurality
and periphery **305–306**; presents
novel perspectives 1-2; taking
forward previous studies **12**
spirit possession complex **8–16, 27–28**,
124, 254, 295; comparative regional
perspectives **13–16**; independent
genealogy **9–13**

spirit possession rituals 13, **28–30**, 33,
121, 123, 126, 145, 152, 173, 185,
276n30, 279, 296; *meihsa* (heresy)
90; offering of incense to Four
Palaces 45, 48, 50, 63; *see also* rituals
spirit shrines 98, 152, 215, 219n5
spirit world 35, 213, 214, 227, 229, 233,
237, 240, 250, 271
spirit worship: historical perspective
(Chiang Mai) **120–121**
spirits: differentiation between
malevolent and good ~ 34, **217–218**;
multiplying ~ **297–299**
spirituality: merging genres among
religious traditions **125–126**
Spiro, Melford 7, 28, 30, 292
Sprenger, Guido 15
Sri Lanka 24; Ceylon 73
Sri Wichai, *Khru Ba* (1878–1939) 241,
246
sro dyk ritual (Cambodia) **152n13**
Stadner, Donald M. 76, 79n
state **57–63**, 65; retreat of **16–20**
State Law and Order Restoration
Council (SLORC) 17, 18, 70n3, 165,
170
State Peace and Development Council
(SPDC) 70n3, 165, 170
statuary 98, 103, 114, 126, 138, 138n,
145, 170, 173, 244, 250, 280;
Chulalongkorn **235–237**; Dara
Rasami 239; *see also* Buddha images
stem houses 271, **271n24**
Stengs, Irene **xi**, 9, 26, **30–31**, 34, 71, 84,
232–252, 300
stereotyping 188-189n, 292
Stolow, Jeremy 22-23
Stonington, Scott 258n12
structure versus anti-structure (Turner)
99n4
stupas 71, 75; *see also* pagodas
subaltern groups 48, 296, **305–306**
subcultures 26, 30, 296

superagency (Pattana) 9; *see also mi ong, ong*
superstition 10, 13, 14, 19, 30, 184n, 220, 228, 262, 300
Surin province 254, 282
Suwan, *Khun* (pseudonym) 234, **237–240**
syncretism 111, 115, 120, 125, 300, 301, 304; *see also* hybridisation

taboo 267, 273, 276
tai di (Thailand: good death) 270
Taiwan **180**, 219
takhian (Thailand: sacred tree trunk) 110
Taksin, King (r. 1767–1781) 232, 236, 237, 246, **247**, **247n**, 248n; old age **249**
Tam Phủ (Vietnam: Three Palaces) 58, **58n7**
Tambiah, Stanley J. 16, 24, **24n**, 25
tambon (Thailand: sub-district) 276, 278
tamnak (Thailand: royal abode) 241, 242, 243-244
Tamra Phlu Luang 199, 206
Tamra Phrommachat 34, **199**, **199n6–7**, 200f, 206, 320f
Taoism 19, 43; Daoism 59; *see also* China, Confucianism
Tarabout, Gilles 11
tattooing 233, 245n19
Taylor, Philip 2, 91, 184, 208
teakwood houses **237–240**, 283
Tenth Lady of Palace of Earth (Vietnam) 51
Tenth Prince (Vietnam) 54, 62
Terwiel, Baas J. 245n19
Thai names and titles xiii
Thai religion: functional-structural viewpoint **102**
Thai religious ecumenism 116
Thai transliteration **xii-xiii**
thaik (Burma: treasure trove) 169

thaik hsek (Burma: connection to treasure trove) 172, 176, 179
thaik ladies (Burma) 84, 85, 93; green scarves 83
thaik medaw (Burma: treasure-guarding ladies) 77
thaik naga (Burma: *thaik* of *naga*) 77, 77n, 80, 81, 83; *see also naga*
thaik-naga possession dance 32, **88**, 89-94; *see also* dance
thaik nan shin (Burma: in charge of treasure palace) 69, 71, 78, 80, 89
Thailand 2, 3, 7, 9, 12, 15-26 *passim*, 82, 151, 180, 183n25, 188, 192, 297, 298; social changes 133, 142; Buddhist-mediumistic pantheon 32–33, **98–118**, 316f; child spirit practices **34–35**, **211–231**, 321f; lotteries 166, 166n3; mystic field **260–265**; mystic field (rules) 262; new animism **258–260**; oneiric encounters **34**, **232–252**; social and economic change 213; spirit cults 178
Thailand: Department of Religious Affairs 17
Thaksin administration (2001-2006) 132
tham bun (Thailand: merit-making, *q.v.*) 263
tham bun ban (Thailand: merit-making for village) 257, 278n35
Thammakai temple 242n14
Thammayut Order 98; see also Buddhism, *Dhammayut* Order
That Panom Chronicle 110
thathana (Burma, from Pāli *sāsana q.v.*) 69, 72n6, 73, 92
thathana pyu (Burma: promoting Buddha's dispensation) 169, 173, 176, 177, 180, 181
thawai bangkhom (Thailand: royal salute) 244

thầy cung (Vietnam: master of ritual) 43
Thein Sein, President 165
thep (Thailand, from Pāli *deva*, deities) 29, **226–227**, 233n2, 279, 297, 298; 'angel' 217, 223; 'good, higher order spirits' **217–218**
Thep Than-jai (Thailand: deity who grants boons expeditiously) 31, 82n
Theravada Buddhism 9, 10, 19, 24, 36, 82, 101, 111, 119, 120, 125, **136**, 197, 233n2, **261–262, 265–266**, 298; rethinking ~ 306; *see also* Buddhism
Theravadin countries 69
Theravadin kingship 17
Thidja/Sakka (Burma: guardian of Buddhism) 75
Thiên Y A Na 64
Third Damsel of Palace of Water (Vietnam) 45
Third Great Mandarin (Vietnam) 50
Third Lady (Vietnam) 54
Third Lunar Month Festival 98, 101f, 112, 316f
Third Mother Goddess (Vietnam) 54
Third Prince of Palace of Water (Vietnam) 50f, 312f
Thirty-Seven Lords (Burma) 27, 28, 32, 34, 64-65, 72, 78, 85, 88, 89, 92, 168, 169n10, 172, 172n16, 181n22, 185
Tho, *Ajan* 32, 98, 99, **104–105**, 107, **112–113**, 116; on Buddhism and local supernaturalism **101**; definition of *Ajan* 98n1
thờ Chu Vị (Vietnam: Cult of Many Honourable Beings) 42
thờ thiên nhiên (Vietnam: worship of nature) 49
thờ Tứ Phủ (Vietnam: cult of Four Palaces) 42
Thongsamrit, *Luang Pu* 105
Three Kings Ritual (Chiang Mai, 1996-2014) 33, 120, **126–127**; 1996 original 127, **129**; 2001 version 129; 2002 onwards **129–130**; 2004 celebration **127–129**, 128-129f, 317-318f; crisis (2010 onwards) **130–132**; organisers **129–130**; significance **133–134**
thuat (Thailand: ancestors) 278; classificatory great-grandparent 271
Thuat, *Luang Pu* (c. 1582–1682) 200, 241
Tin Myint, Daw 86n24
To, *Somdet* (*Somdet Phra* Phutthajan, 1788–1872) 200, 241, 244, 245, 246-247, 249
Tokarev, Sergei 57
totemism 15, 16, 259, 260
tourism 17, 31, **82–83**, 132n, 235
traditional healers 122n, **194**
trance 31, 34, 109n, 121, 233, **250**, 300; *see also* spirit possession
transgender people 5, 93, 93n31, 109, 281, **282–283**
Trịnh Yên 55f, 55, 313f
Tứ Phủ Cong Đồng văn (Vietnam: Hymn for Community of Four Palaces) 57
Tue, *Ong* **108–110**; stone Buddha image at Wat Sila-at 109f, 316f
Turner, Victor 99n4
tutelary spirits 30, 121, 215, 244, 249n, 278; *Chao* La, *Chao* Noi and *Chao* Pi 241; *see also* nat
Tylor, Edward B. 255, 258, 259

Ubon Ratchathani Province 114
uncanny [n] (Freud) 224n, 278n36
UNESCO (intangible cultural heritage list) 2, 19, 31, 42, 47, 51, 64, 66
Union for Solidarity and Development Party (USDP) 70n3
United States 192, 204, 221
Upagot (Upagutta) 74, **89–91**, 92
upper class 136, 137
urban areas 70, 147, 152, 169, 184, 248n, 264, 281

INDEX

urban culture (Cambodia): enchantment of divination, magic and spirit rituals **34**, **188–210**, 320f
urbanisation 4, 91-92, 121, 172, 262, 294

văn chầu (Vietnam: hymns) 44, 51, 53-54, 55, 57, 61, 63, 66n
vedamant (Cambodia: magic) 151
vernacular religion **292–309**; amorphous object of study **295–297**; structural processes **302**
Vernant, Jean-Pierre 59
Verter, Bradford 261
videos 50f, 50, 219n7, 312f
Vietnam 2, 3, 9, 12, 15, 17, 19-20, **91–92**, 152, 180, 182n, 184, 293n, 297, 298; Communist government 14; professional spirit mediumship **26**; revolution (1945) 42; socialist period (1945-1985) 19; spirits of dead 148; 'Three Teachings' 19
Vietnam: Ministry of Culture 47
Vietnam Academy of Social Sciences 46
Vietnamese Studies (journal) 47
village mediums (Baumann) 274, 275f, **277–279**, 279f, 281, 282, 284, 322f; *see also* spirit mediumship
village mediumship: professionalisation **35**, **274–283**; active devotees 274, 275f, **279–281**, 323f; lineage mediums **274–277**; professional mediums 274, 275f, **281–283**, 284, 323f; village mediums 274, 275f, **277–279**, 279f, 322f; *see also* spirit possession
Vimanmek mansion **237–240**; *see also* Chulalongkorn
vinaya 111
viññāṇa (moral consciousness) 268; *see also winyan*
visions 30–31, 233, 250; *see also* dreams, *nimitta*, oneiric spaces
Visisya Pinthongvijayakul **xi**, 5, 12, 26, 27, 28, **32–33**, 71, **98–118**, 300

Viveiros de Castro, Eduardo 253
votive offerings 257, **264–265**; *see also kae bon*
Vũ Nương *Công Chía* (Vietnam: Princess Vũ Nương) 62
Vũ Thị Thục Nương 62
vũ trụ luận (Vietnam: cosmological aspects) 49

Wa Wa Tan, Daw 86n25
wai (Thailand: show respect, pay homage) 114; definition 114n
wai khru or *wai khu* (Thai: paying homage to teacher ceremony) 25, 26, 35, 123, 123n3, 139, **245n19**; *see also khrorp khru, yok khu, yok khru*
Walker, Andrew 271n25
Wan, *Mae* (pseudonym) (spirit medium) 234, 239, **241–244**, 246
wan phra (Thailand: Buddhist holy day) 241, 242, 242n14
wan sat duean sip ritual (Thailand) 257n9
wan sia (Thailand: inauspicious days) 241n13
wat (Thailand: monastery) 98, 99, 100, 104, 105
Wat Pradu: *Kuman Thorng* Shrine 220f, 321f
Wat Sila-at (pilgrimage site) **108–110**, 316f
wealth acquisition: moralisation **179–184**; *see also* prosperity Buddhism
Weber, Max 21, 208, 213; *Protestant Ethic* (1905) 41, 103; sociology of religion 1, **5–6**, 119
Weberianism 8, 12, 294
websites 220, 221
Wednesdays: inauspiciousness 241, 241n13
weikza (Burma: from Pāli *vijjā*) xii, 85n22-23, 88, 93, 94, 297; definition 73; *see also weizzā*

weikza path (Burma: esoteric Buddhist practices) 70, 79, 84, 85, 89, 91; *see also* esoterism
weizzā xii, 164, 170, **170n11**, 181; *see also weikza*
Weller, Robert P. 17, 180
West Africa **10–11**
White, Erick **xi**, **6–7**, 8, **21–22**, 26, 29, 35–36, 92n, 247, 248, 248n, **292–309**; 'Buddhist regimes' 261n; 'modalities of possession' 233, 233n2, **301**
wihan (Thailand: temple building) 235, 236
Willerslev, Rane **255**
Wilson, Constance M. 110
Win Hlaing, U 88, 89, 90
Winch, Peter 256
winyan 270; life force 268; soul-like concept 267; spirit or soul 245, 263; *see also viññāṇa*
witchcraft 7, **272–273**; *see also* black magic, magic
Witoon Buadaeng 119n
Wittgenstein, Ludwig **255–256**; *see also* language game
women 5, 52, 84, 93, 98, 109, 111, 122, 150, 156, 166, 172, 174, 175, 181n22, 183, 240, 254, 275, 276; out-migration from Thai rural areas 283
Woodhouse, Leslie 240, 240n10-11
worldly well-being 295, 296, 297, 298, 303, 304, 305

Ya, Chao (spirit) 244
Yai, *Mae* (pseudonym) (spirit medium) 234; *tamnak* 244, 245; *yok khru* ceremony **244–250**
yakkha 170
yan 248n; insight; sixth sense 247; spiritual connection 234, **234n4**
Yangon xii, 26, 31; Buddhist urban landscape 76, 76n12; spirit medium's domestic shrine 29f, 311f; *see also* Botataung Pagoda
yantra (magical designs) 153, 199
Yāy Mao (Hindu deity) 147n7
Ye Myint, U 90
yok khru or *yok khu* (Thailand: paying homage to teacher ceremony) 26, 33, 123, 123n3, **244–250**, 244n, 280; *see also khrorp khru, wai khru, wai khu*
yoya (Burma: traditional) 91

Zamaṇi Thaik (pagoda) 170-171n13

Critical Acclaim

Spirit Possession in Buddhist Southeast Asia emphatically puts to rest any lingering notion that capitalist modernity has disenchanted religious life in the region. With ten well-informed and thoughtful contributions, the volume offers a powerful argument that the retreat of state control of religious practice and the rise of prosperity aspirations and market anxieties is engendering a flowering of spirit possession rituals in a multiplicity of forms. At the same time, the several authors challenge longstanding distinctions between a pure Buddhism and the messier stuff of popular practice as the wishful thinking of modern apologists, policymakers, and academics. Ethnography offers a more complicated and interesting picture in this compelling read, a volume that is likely to provoke similar discussions well beyond mainland Southeast Asia.

– Laurel Kendall, author of *Mediums and Magical Things:
Statues, Paintings, and Masks in Asian Places*

Spirit possession is flourishing in mainland Southeast Asia and anthropologists are keeping pace. Anyone interested in questions of enchantment and modernity, ontological pluralism, or the boundaries of Buddhism in practice will find much of benefit in these substantive, engaging essays offered by a truly global array of scholars.

– Michael Lambek, University of Toronto

This superbly edited, theoretically progressive volume of ten meticulously re-searched case studies is focused on spirit possession within SE Asian Buddhist cultures illustrating how modernity, through globalizing neoliberal capitalism, increasing urbanization, digital media platforms, and the politics of ethnic identities, is producing, through ritual articulation, new forms of enchantment concerned with worldly well-being. Book-ended by a masterful introduction and an incisive afterward by Erick White, upending Weber's secularization thesis and indexing how the 'marginal' and 'magical' are becoming mainstream, this is a landmark contribution inviting serious attention by anthropologists, historians of religions, and especially Buddhist Studies scholars.

– John Clifford Holt, author of *Spirits of the Place:
Buddhism and Lao Religious Culture*

More critical acclaim

This is an important collection that significantly furthers our understanding of the role of spirit cults in modern Southeast Asia. These cults continue to play a crucial role in political life and in the understanding of history and agency at all levels of society. A must-read for anyone interested in the social life of the spirits in today's world.

– *Peter van der Veer, author of The Modern Spirit of Asia*

Brac de la Perrière and Jackson's edited book brings for the first time Buddhist Southeast Asia as a land of spirit possession into dedicated studies. The authors, coming from various academic backgrounds, show altogether that spirit possession has characterised practices of contact with the supernatural in these societies, not only historically but also through the societal changes that they have undergone since the end of Cold War. Most chapters are about new enchantments produced by growing urbanisation, diversification of social worlds and globalising neo-liberal modernity rather than drying up of ritual creativity. They draw an overall picture of rich and diversified practices of interactions with the spiritual worlds, with common patterns of pantheonisation, professionalisation of spirit mediums and mediatisation of their practices, according to regimes of presentification deeply rooted in local cultures.

– *Roberte Hamayon, author of La chasse à l'âme: Esquisse d'une théorie du chamanisme sibérien*

Further appreciation for this study will be posted on its book page on the NIAS Press website, www.niaspress.dk/book/spirit-possession-in-buddhist-southeast-asia/